RV Vacations

7th Edition

by Christopher Hodapp and Alice Von Kannon

RV Vacations For Dummies®, 7th Edition

Published by: **John Wiley & Sons, Inc.,** 111 River Street, Hoboken, NJ 07030-5774, www.wiley.com

Copyright © 2023 by John Wiley & Sons, Inc., Hoboken, New Jersey

Media and software compilation copyright © 2023 by John Wiley & Sons, Inc. All rights reserved.

Published simultaneously in Canada

For general information on our other products and services, please contact our Customer Care Department within the U.S. at 877-762-2974, outside the U.S. at 317-572-3993, or fax 317-572-4002. For technical support, please visit https://hub.wiley.com/community/support/dummies.

Wiley publishes in a variety of print and electronic formats and by print-on-demand. Some material included with standard print versions of this book may not be included in e-books or in print-on-demand. If this book refers to media such as a CD or DVD that is not included in the version you purchased, you may download this material at http://booksupport.wiley.com. For more information about Wiley products, visit www.wiley.com.

Library of Congress Control Number: 2023937593

ISBN 978-1-394-16498-1 (pbk); ISBN 978-1-394-16499-8 (ePDF); ISBN 978-1-394-16500-1 (epub)

Contents at a Glance

Table of Contents

Introduction

Congratulations! After seeing all those motorhomes and travel trailers rolling down the highway and wondering what driving one would be like, you've decided to find out for yourself. Maybe you've had the road trip of a lifetime percolating in the back of your mind for decades and just never got around to actually taking it. Maybe it's a bucket list of "100 Places to See Before I Turn 30." Or 50. Or 70. Or maybe it's just a random itch to discover some new places over a long weekend. Whether you want to get away for the weekend, vacation for a few weeks, host the world's greatest tailgating parties, or hit the road full-time to fulfill a lifelong dream, it's easy to do in an RV.

About This Book

RV Vacations For Dummies, 7th Edition, is the book you need after you've already picked out, bought, or rented a trailer or motorhome. Now it's finally time to contemplate some of the many routes and destinations you can discover by traveling in your RV.

REMEMBER

Our companion book, *RVs and Campers For Dummies* (Wiley), tells you all about choosing, buying, owning, and operating a trailer or motorhome. If you're hunting for that kind of detailed information, we humbly suggest you procure a copy.

In this book, we tell you about places with no airports — places off the interstate exits you won't, or can't, see by traveling any other way than by land vehicle. You find the book organized this way:

>> **Parts 1:** If you're inexperienced, you should be armed with some specialized information that only RVers need. So, the first part of this book helps you figure out when (and where) to go, strategies for managing your money, and how to find and stock the right stuff for eating well on the road. You also get practical advice about discovering the perfect stopping spots for you and your rig — informed by our own experiences after living with various types of RVs for travel, work, and play.

>> **Parts 2 through 5:** The meat and potatoes of this volume are the chapters you find in these parts. Throughout our suggested travel itineraries — 12 in all — you get a look at some all-time favorite routes that you might hear about around the campfire: Route 66, the Blue Ridge Parkway, and the Pacific Coast Highway. We believe these treks through the U.S. explore the most diverse,

beautiful, and exciting travel venue in the world. (We stick with the Lower 48 in this book. With more than 3 million square miles, that should keep you occupied until we come up with an Alaskan, Hawaiian, and Canadian sequel.)

For each RV itinerary, we suggest the roads to take and point out the best sights, fun spots, interesting museums, local shops, and more. We highlight some of our favorite campgrounds, and because you've got your own kitchen on board, we also try to steer you to places where you can pick up local produce, regional farm-to-table foods, or one-
of-a-kind carryout meals. Each chapter also has a "Fast Facts" quick reference section where you find info ranging from fuel taxes to speed limits, as well as numbers to call if you get in trouble on the road.

>> **Part 6:** Check out this part when you're looking for more places to go. The Part of Tens highlights attractions (museums and factory tours) beyond the itineraries in this book.

All travel information is subject to change at any time. This state of flux is always true for prices and operating dates and times, and it's *especially* true in this post–COVID–shutdown world. While we really did contact every business mentioned in this book before press time, we strongly urge you to e-mail or call ahead to confirm details when making your travel plans. And *never* just trust a website, particularly if you're planning your whole day around getting to a single, special attraction or restaurant.

To keep this book from being longer and less understandable than the unabridged version of *War and Peace* (in the original Russian), we use these abbreviations for road names in the driving chapters:

>> **I-#:** Denotes an interstate highway, which is usually a high-speed divided roadway with no traffic lights or stop signs, no driveways or side roads, and a limited number of exits and on-ramps.

>> **U.S. #:** Refers to roads in the U.S. Numbered Highway System. These are often considered secondary to interstates, but some are built to interstate highway standards. U.S. roads comprise an older federal highway system that predates the Eisenhower administration's interstate system. They can be 2- or 4-lane roads, divided or not divided. And they may have side roads, driveways, traffic lights, and stop signs.

>> **SR #:** Indicates a state road or state route. In most states, a state road is actually designated by the state's abbreviation (for example, NY 30 is New York state road 30; IA 25 is Iowa state road 25, and so on). Other states just use SR, particularly on their maps. Once you get to state roads, all bets are off on uniformity.

>> **CR #:** Signifies a county road.

In our campground lists, we include general pricing information to help you decide where to camp. The following system of dollar signs is a guideline only and denotes the range of prices for one night in a campground:

Designation	What it means in dollars
$	$25 or less
$$	$26 to $50
$$$	$51 to $75
$$$$	$76 to $100
$$$$$	$101 or more

Foolish Assumptions

As we wrote this book, we made some assumptions about you and your needs as an RVer. Here's what we think might be true about you. You may be:

>> A brand-new RVer hunting for some inspiration about places to visit in your new vacation cabin on wheels. Whether you buy your own rig, or just rent one for a single trip, your next step is to decide where to go.

>> An inexperienced RVer looking for ideas to help you plan your future adventures.

>> A veteran RVer looking for new experiences, new attractions, or new roads to travel.

>> Someone hunting for a book that clues you in on trip itineraries to places you may not have known or thought about before.

And you're *not* looking for a full-blown directory that provides detailed lists of every single campground, attraction, photo op, or restaurant on the route. If you fit any of these criteria, *RV Vacations For Dummies* gives you the information you're seeking!

Icons Used in This Book

In the margins of this book are helpful icons intended to focus attention on certain kinds of information. Here's what the icons mean:

BARGAIN ALERT

This icon points out bargains and money-saving tips for your RV vacation, so you don't quickly blow through your hard-earned simoleons.

KID FRIENDLY

This icon lets you know when something special is available for the younger set. It helps cut down on "Are we there yet?" syndrome.

REMEMBER

This icon highlights information worth taking note of.

TECHNICAL STUFF

This icon points out interesting details or information that's not necessarily essential to understanding the subject at hand. If you're in a hurry, you can skim over anything marked this way.

TIP

For hints, tips, or insider advice to make your trip run smoother, look for this icon. The real point of any travel guide is to serve as one gigantic tip from cover to cover, but this icon singles out nuggets of information that may be new to you.

WARNING

Accompanying this icon are special alerts for RVers, whether you face a low bridge ahead or a difficult parking situation. We probably learned it the hard way, so do as we say, not as we did.

Beyond the Book

There's never enough room to cover everything in a book like this. To help fill in the whole picture, we've rendered up some more tips for readying your RV for travel. To access the Cheat Sheet for this book, visit www.dummies.com, enter **RV Vacations For Dummies Cheat Sheet** in the Search box, and click the link that appears in the search results. There we pass along a little more background on some of our tour locations or favorite sites, offer questions to ask yourself when choosing to purchase an RV, and more.

Where to Go from Here

There are a couple ways to use *RV Vacations For Dummies* as a reference guide. You can start at the first page and read our dazzling prose all the way through to the end — we always recommend buying a copy for every bathroom. Or, if you're a more experienced RVer, you can flip straight to a travel route that intrigues you and check out our recommended destinations and campgrounds. This way, you can move from chapter to chapter, picking and choosing information that interests you, sort of like the book version of an all-you-can-eat sushi bar. *Remember:* The table of contents and index will always help you find that particular piece of information you're looking for.

If you want to interact with us, that's great! We love hearing about readers' own RV experiences, your trips, your escapades (good and bad), and best of all, your special discoveries on the road. Visit our Facebook page at www.facebook.com/rvsfordummies for updates, videos, tips, tricks, and anything else we can think of.

Ready? It's time to bask in the freedom of the open road! With an RV, home will always be where you park it.

1

Getting Started on RV Vacations

IN THIS PART . . .

Get to know the many benefits of vacationing by RV and why it's perfect for *you*.

Choose the perfect time of year to visit the best places in America in your RV.

Create a realistic travel budget for your RV adventures.

Equip your personal chuckwagon so you can chow down on the move.

Select the perfect campgrounds along the road, from national chains to national parks and chain store parking lots.

IN THIS CHAPTER

» Meeting the RV crowd

» Realizing the travel advantages

» Living and working your way

» Making your travels an adventure for everyone

» Looking beyond the daily pleasures of RVing

» Taking romance on the road

Chapter **1**

All the Best Reasons to Take an RV Vacation

You can find all kinds of reasons to support the idea that traveling and vacationing in recreational vehicles (RVs) is more convenient and pleasant than other methods. Perhaps, as you read this book, you can come up with some of your own ideas to add to our list of the best reasons to go by RV when you travel.

In reality, there are just as many different RV lifestyles as there are RVers. We often take RV vacations just to spend time alone with each other; that's important for every couple. But the world is also filled with single people who crave solitude and families who crave togetherness; they're all hunting for a new vacation experience or challenge.

In this chapter, we offer an overview of RVing as a wonderful transportation option, including its benefits (cost, convenience, control, and so on) and its unique adaptability for living and discovering the world around you. There's a special romantic attraction for the open road that comes with vacationing in an RV, and we'll give you lots of ways you may discover that remarkable kind of romance for yourself.

Who's RVing These Days?

When we discovered RVing, we loved how perfectly it fit our personalities and desire to live a slower, downsized lifestyle. We were surprised by how comfortable, convenient, and liberating this type of travel is. And we soon began to savor the rewards of having new adventures and meeting new people around every turn.

Ignoring RVer stereotypes

REMEMBER

Sadly, clichés about RVers turn off some people who've never experienced this kind of travel. If your only image is of Cousin Eddie in *National Lampoon's Christmas Vacation*, dressed in a bathrobe with a beer in his hand, emptying his Winnebago's sewer tank into the neighborhood storm drain, try to set aside that impression.

You may think that RVers are mostly aging, melancholy retirees who sit around smoldering campfires sipping twice-baked Folger's coffee or Bud Lights while swapping tedious tales of their latest mechanical breakdowns and comparing regional prescription drug prices. Or that RVers routinely caravan to group-gawk at the local cultural hot spot — say, the Museum of Frontier Spleen Pills — and then rush off to the closest all-you-can-eat buffet. Although plenty of people enjoy doing the kitschy stuff (which can have its merits), they make up a tiny sliver of the whole RVing pie.

According to the RV Industry Association (http://www.rvia.org), which keeps track of these things, 67 million American travelers planned on taking an RV trip in 2023. That's a sizable platoon of folks — almost 40 percent of all Americans. The top reasons given include a chance to explore the outdoors and the ability to work or attend school remotely from almost anywhere in the world.

Noting the interest from various groups

The biggest interest in RVing these days comes from younger travelers. Forty-nine percent of Generation Z and 48 percent of millennials planned to take an RV trip in 2023. Their buying intentions were also higher, with 41 percent of Generation Z and 35 percent of millennials planning to buy an RV during the following year.

RVing isn't just a passing whim, either. Among people who already own an RV, half planned to buy a different rig in the next year. That was up 14 percent over the previous year, in what was already a massive increase in RV ownership in the U.S. after the COVID pandemic lockdowns.

OUR OWN JOURNEY TO THE JOYS OF RVing

We've always loved to travel: Our life together began with a 10-day driving and sightseeing trip as we moved all our worldly possessions to California for school. We started vacationing overseas in our late 20s, just as soon as our paychecks made it possible. Our first truly major trip together was a 10-day guided tour of Egypt and its most stunning antiquities, taken aboard planes, buses, boats, taxis, and trains. We convinced ourselves we'd never get the chance to take such a trip again, so we had to see *everything*. Every single day began before sunup and ended at midnight, leaving us as wrung out as the dishcloth at a Chinese *smörgåsbørd*. Instead of loving our trip of a lifetime, we took hundreds of photos just so we could enjoy the trip *after* we got home. That was typical of our trips then — no matter where we went for vacation, we were almost always guilty of trying to see and do too much.

A few years later, during a grueling three-week vacation, we were exhausted the whole time, and it didn't help that we both caught the flu, while several crew members on a ship we'd been on had come down with hepatitis and had to be quarantined. Two weeks into the trip, going home looked very attractive. Late one particularly miserable evening, Alice put into words what we both were thinking: "I wish we could just go home for a day or two, just to recharge our batteries!"

Years later, that seems like the ideal praise for RVing: You can always go home for a while, because you've always got a bit of home with you. Every night you're wrapped up in its comforts, and if things come unglued for any reason, you have the freedom to take a couple days, park somewhere nice, and just chill out. You can indeed recharge your batteries, just as you would at home. And *then* it's on to Glacier National Park!

As RV rental options become more common, it's easier than ever to discover the RV lifestyle without jumping in and investing in an expensive trailer or motorhome (see Chapter 3). Something we've noticed on the road in the last ten years is the dramatic increase in the number of international travelers who rent an RV and hit the road to discover "the real America." It's not unusual anymore to walk past campfires in RV parks at night and hear conversations in Spanish, German, Arabic, Russian, Chinese, or Japanese.

Counting the Benefits of RV Travel

Freedom. If you want to sum up RV travel in one word, that's it: *freedom*. Anyone who's ever been barked at by a flight attendant for running to the bathroom knows why that word has meaning, because when you're flying, you're giving up a great deal of personal autonomy, not to mention personal space. To an airline, you're often treated like troublesome cargo, whereas in an RV, no TSA agent is going to paw through your luggage and demand you throw away your shampoo bottle, along with the nail clippers and contact lens solution you packed.

And if you bought this book, you've probably at least toyed with the dream of RV ownership, so the fun of the lifestyle is something you've already thought about. But a few obvious — and some not so obvious — benefits of traveling by RV may not have occurred to you.

Containing costs

Saving money comes down to control, the control RVing gives you over food and lodging costs, and yes, even over fuel costs. It's the kind of control that just isn't possible when you're flying to a destination and then staying in hotels and eating in restaurants for every meal. RV vacations won't strain your travel budget to the screaming point. An RV trip costs half of what a typical hotel-and-plane trip will set you back, and a third less than driving your car and staying at hotels.

Have you ever been on vacation at an all-inclusive hotel or on a cruise ship, or bought some other "package" vacation, and realized you're paying for all sorts of things that don't particularly interest you? You don't care about the 18-hole championship golf course; you don't want a full English breakfast with baked beans, kippers, and black pudding at 7:00 in the morning; you get nauseated by the heat in a Scandinavian sauna; the "entertainment" in the lounge is anything but entertaining; and you don't want any of the "complimentary" snacks in your room. But you're paying for all these things, and many more besides.

REMEMBER

On an RV trip, you're paying for what matters to *you*, period. You're in complete control of the campgrounds you stay at, the food you eat, the places you see, and the things you do. You can *boondock* (camp without external water, power, or sewer hookups) for free on a piece of federal wilderness land, or you can pony up for a luxury RV resort with its own Scandinavian sauna, and to hell with that nausea. You can take in the entertainment you enjoy anywhere along the route. Without even thinking about it, really, an RV trip ends up being completely tailored to what you want to pay for and experience.

TIP

Check out Chapter 3, where we talk in depth about managing your vacation money. In that chapter, you discover the many ways to save money on an RV trip, and why RVing is the best vacation choice for families on tight budgets.

Enjoying maximum convenience

The little things really do matter; where travel is concerned, they create either a placid experience or an anxious one.

When you're traveling and you or the kids need to use the restroom, it can be a real hassle, and a thoroughly unpleasant ordeal, in airplanes and trains, in gas stations and fast-food places, or, worse, in a Porta Potty. That one alone can make you long for the nearest shrubbery. You may love street fairs and wine festivals and historical reenactments, but as the hours pass, you can start to dread having to "go." The relief of being able to slip into your own home on wheels and use your own bathroom, as well as grab a drink or change your shoes, is hard to overstate.

You may contend that RVing puts you at the mercy of traffic jams, but that's a tough argument to make with a straight face to anyone who's been parked on a runway in an Airbus 330 for five hours with no air-conditioning in the cabin. At any rate, on the rare occasions when jams and roadblocks occur, you can deal. We were once trapped on the highway in Arizona in a 14-hour traffic stoppage caused by a chemical spill. We began to feel downright guilty over our comfort level with an onboard kitchen and bathroom, compared to everyone else scrounging for stale crackers in the glove compartment or running for the bushes.

Controlling the destination

Freedom translates to being in control of your own direction and destiny. If you like to go with the crowd on a trip, do it. Go ahead and join the throngs for July 4 at Mount Rushmore, the Albuquerque balloon festival, or the Bonnaroo music festival. In a crowded situation — when it's difficult to get simple things like a seat in a restaurant or a bed for the night — you can never be more comfortable than in an RV, where you've got both at your disposal. (No seat is better for a NASCAR event than one of the infield RV parking spaces in the middle of the track!)

On the other hand, if you like out-of-the-way places — if you want to go into the backcountry and see Promontory Summit, where the last golden spike in the transcontinental railroad was driven — getting there in an RV ensures that you're far more comfortable than you'd be in a car. You can even choose to boondock nearby, staying the night and watching the stars come out in the Utah sky. If out-of-the-way exploring is your thing, RVing should be your ticket there and back again.

Not every getaway has to be a two-week expedition. The U.S. is loaded with national, state, and county parks, historical preservation sites, conservation areas, famous landmarks, festivals, shows, sporting events, and lots more. Consider the aspect of vacation flexibility. Loads of people dream of faraway destinations while ignoring the wonder and excitement of what's in their own backyard. Your state doubtless has a tourism board that publishes annual guides to give you vacation ideas. An RV lets you visit places you've never seen just an hour or two away, and it becomes your own private hotel room and refuge.

Finding your rhythm on the road

RV travel can help you leave the rush-rush of the everyday world behind the minute you turn the key in the ignition. But it's a good idea to *know thyself*, as the saying goes, when making your travel plans. Some people who travel in RVs consider driving 250 miles a day to be enough; you're on your own schedule, and it's time to mellow out. Others take 600 miles or more in stride. Your route, days allotted for travel, and temperament all come into play when you get on the road.

It's also good to know your traveling companion's taste or tolerance for road miles before you hit the asphalt. For example, after two major knee surgeries, Alice can no longer handle endless hours of riding in our SUV, where the legroom isn't much better than a car. So, we began breaking up long trips, taking a few more days on the road and a few more breaks during the day.

Of course, if it's just a question of staying fresh, you can break a long trip into legs that vary in distance and time. Think in terms of short, long, and medium stretches of travel for each day on the road. You usually have so much to do the night before the journey and the morning of departure that making the first day's ride a short one makes sense. Go long the next day. Again, RVing expands and contracts to fit your temperament and your needs. Planning your travel tempo can eliminate the urge to rush — *you're* in control, not anybody else.

When you're making your travel plans, pay attention to speed limits. California has a 55 mph speed limit statewide for all trucks and other vehicles towing trailers or cars. Speed limits do impact the number of hours it takes to finish your miles for the day. For example, following historic U.S. 41 to Florida is going to take more time than traveling I-75, but it's very pleasant additional time.

You'd be surprised at how quickly you can still get to your destination when you choose state roads or vintage "through the towns" federal roads like old Highway

40 (U.S. 40). After you shrug off the mindset that you're not getting anywhere if you're not going 75, you begin to realize that driving faster may not get you to your destination as quickly as you thought it would. The illusion of speed may not be worth it.

Having room for extras

Choose your must-have items wisely, and you should have room for the little extras that can enhance your vacation and are difficult (or impossible) to take when you're flying. It's up to you to decide what rolls down the road with you. The only baggage handler involved is you, and no tipping's required. If you want to take along anything from an extra little black dress to a set of golf clubs, you can probably find places to put them in your RV or tow vehicle.

Being close to events

Airplanes and trains get you to the city where your event is, but the right-size RV gets you to the team's tailgate party. Whether you're going to a NASCAR race, a professional football game, a college sporting event, or a family reunion at the beach, an RV is a great way to get there and get up close while being "at home" in your own space. And when the event is over, you don't have to be the first vehicle out of the parking lot anymore: Make a sandwich, flip on the TV, sit back, and let everybody else fume in the traffic jams at the exits.

Easing mobility issues

If you or a companion is physically challenged, the ability to get an RV close to whatever's happening is one of the many benefits of traveling in one. In an RV, you're setting up everything around you to accommodate your state of mobility. It creates a reassuring feeling of comfort and confidence while you take back your life, and go on seeing the world regardless of the physical issues that are thrown at you. You can travel at your own pace, adjusting to your own level of physicality.

Bringing your pets for free

More than half of all campers travel with some sort of pet (most commonly dogs). Our miniature poodle started traveling with us in the RV at the age of 10 weeks. When we say to Sophie, "Wanna go on an adventure?" she launches herself joyously at the door, lunging into her dog bed in the SUV, goofy grin on her face. No more misery and guilt over the drop-off at the kennel — she's enjoying the trip even more than we are.

REMEMBER

We've never been turned away from a campground for having a dog, and most of them have fenced-in dog runs where you can let your pet pals run free. We've encountered many campgrounds that even have canine obstacle course/agility training areas.

Even though cats can arguably be left home alone, at least for a few days, far preferring it in many cases to being moved, we've been amazed by the ability of so many cats to adjust to RVing. And in case you wondered, parakeets and parrots (yep, we've seen them), and other caged pets are almost always welcome at campgrounds.

Keeping a clean living space

We almost hate to talk about this one, but the fact is, not all hotels are five-star. Even the best hotels occasionally slip up on maintaining cleanliness to acceptable standards. But you're the housekeeping department when you're vacationing in your RV, and you set the standard for cleanliness. Also, if you have certain sensitivities — for example, respiratory issues or allergies — you can control your environment much more easily in an RV than in a hotel room.

The flip side — being your own maid — isn't as miserable as you may think. Normal housekeeping tasks such as bed making, floor sweeping, mopping, and shaking out the rugs may take an average of 15 minutes a day in an RV. Of course, it takes longer if you do things like cooking an elaborate meal that dirties all the dishes in your cabinets. In the end, a 30-foot-long rig is far easier to care for than a house. And maintaining your space can make all the difference in your quality of life on the road.

Embracing the RV Lifestyle

The COVID pandemic lockdown forced millions of Americans to rethink their living and working environments, maybe for the first time in their lives. And hundreds of thousands of them went out and bought their first RV when air travel became too problematic, foreign destinations shut down, schools were shuttered, and businesses closed.

Trading traditional living space for an RV

Some people are so taken with the road that nomadic living becomes a happy and affordable option, especially during times of hyper-inflated housing prices. For decades, full-time RV life has been a big hit with retirees who no longer want to deal with a big house, loads of unneeded possessions, or cold winter climates.

But the record-setting sales of RVs since 2019 have shifted to younger people, as we mentioned earlier in this chapter. Average family size has shrunk dramatically since the end of the 20th century, and you find more single-parent households than ever before. Even the most gargantuan rigs can get claustrophobic with two parents and four or five children on board. But families with just one or two kids — often with a single parent — are quite comfortable in smaller motorhomes or trailers.

Working and staying connected on the road

COVID forced millions of employees to work strictly via computer and phone, and technology now permits that to happen almost anywhere. So why not wake up with a totally different view outside your office window every morning? There are lots of ways to make your living on the road, and though we've met high-powered executives who use computers, iPads, and smartphones to run businesses from their folding chairs by the campfire, the fact is, you don't need a special skill set to make a living in your RV.

RV manufacturers and remodelers have been swamped with requests from owners to modify their rigs to create dedicated office space and install the latest in cellular and Wi-Fi technology. Some owners just don't want to give up their Netflix binge-watching habits or online gaming sessions. But loads more want the latest equipment to handle their business requirements. The recent entry of Elon Musk's Starlink service into the satellite-based broadband internet provider market is the latest development that makes RV communication systems and internet connections more dependable, no matter where you happen to be. And even before 5G cellular networks have been completely rolled out nationwide, even faster 10G networks are already being installed in some areas.

Adding variety to your RV stops

Similarly, once you reduce your truly necessary possessions enough to fit into your RV, there's no reason to stay in the same place day after day. An RV gives you the ability to move your vacation home on wheels from the beach to the mountains, chase the warmest weather or the most ideal skiing conditions, hunt antiques in the Midwest, savor the best barbecue in Texas, or watch the sun rise over the Catskills.

And for pesky considerations like establishing a legal domicile with a permanent mailing address (something the government tax people really want you to do), the RV community has come up with creative solutions. **Escapees RV Club** (www.escapees.com) offers a mail forwarding service that provides a post office box address, collects your mail, boxes it up, and sends it to you wherever you happen to be on the road.

RVing as an eco-friendly alternative

If climate change is your big concern, you can't even begin to calculate the differences between the carbon footprint of a plane flight, an Über to and from the airport, and a week in a hotel room eating every meal in a restaurant, versus the same week in an RV.

Solar panels and large rechargeable batteries are becoming commonplace on the newest RVs, as are more efficient appliances and smart-use plumbing fixtures. Decades ago, RVers began keeping water use to a minimum, and RVing off the grid has always been the Holy Grail of boondocking. Boondockers, in particular, are inspired by the motto "leave no trace" when it comes to camping.

Manufacturers offer trailers made of lightweight material so that smaller, more fuel-efficient vehicles (instead of pickup trucks or giant SUVs powered by gas or diesel fuel) can tow them. At the time of this writing, electric trucks (and hybrids) as well as experimental trailers that use axle-mounted generators and spinning tires to charge onboard batteries have entered the marketplace.

Taking an RV vacation is the most eco-friendly way to travel, apart from maybe riding your bike to a park, sleeping in a tent, and eating beans straight from the can. RVs are a *lot* more comfortable.

RVing as a kid-friendly way to travel

One of the best things about RVing is the fun children have, and the learning experiences they enjoy. You can often sense a special closeness in families that go RVing. We've watched many parents share teaching moments with their kids in national parks and historical monuments. Many of these children are home-schooled on the road, but most are kids on vacation, having fun but learning at the same time.

So much of what's in this book is a great beginning for those enriching experiences. The drives in our itinerary chapters include a wealth of show-and-tell and how-I-spent-my-summer-vacation material, from discovering how baseball was invented at the National Baseball Hall of Fame in New York (Chapter 7), to seeing spectacular underground rock formations at Carlsbad Caverns National Park in New Mexico (Chapter 14) and finding out at the McKinley Presidential Library and Museum in Ohio (Chapter 11) why President William McKinley always wore a red carnation. Kids remember the McKinley story because they hear it from the animatronic version of the man himself.

Finding Temptations for Everybody

Whether you're jonesing after the trek, exploring attractions along the route, looking for a good workout in the Great Outdoors, or enjoying what's on offer at food, music, or sports venues, you can satisfy all your heart's desires from an RV. Best of all, after a day of driving, breaking a sweat, sightseeing, or whatever, you can return to a hot shower and a comfortable RV bed instead of a communal bathhouse and a leaking air mattress on the hard, unforgiving ground. Consider your options:

» **Tantalizing trails:** Hikers and bikers can get their endorphin fix at state and national parks with great walking and bicycle trails. Oregon Dunes National Recreation Area (Chapter 17) is just one of many parks in that state with hiking trails that skirt the coast. Cyclists can take advantage of 45 miles of carriage roads in Maine's Acadia National Park (Chapter 6) or wooded roads that are regularly closed to traffic in Great Smoky Mountains National Park (Chapter 8) on the Tennessee/North Carolina border.

» **Disarming drives:** Do you want to settle into the driver's seat and just cruise? We've got the roads for you. Scenic highways like Blue Ridge Parkway and Skyline Drive (Chapter 8), Natchez Trace (Chapter 10), and California's Pacific Coast Highway (Chapter 15) were built for slow, easy driving and frequent stops to admire the view or set out a picnic. For a slice of Americana and the wide-open spaces of the American West, drive what remains of old Route 66 between Oklahoma and California (Chapter 16).

For more of what makes America unique, look no farther than the country's colorful icons. New Mexico brings William H. Bonney to life again along the Billy the Kid National Scenic Byway (Chapter 14), while the Buffalo Bill Center of the West in Cody, Wyoming, celebrates many of the legendary figures of the American West (Chapter 13).

» **Tasty treats:** For a delicious taste of America, sample fresh-from-the-sea Maine lobster with melted butter right on the dock (Chapter 6), Santa Maria barbecue along California's Central Coast (Chapter 15), succulent shrimp and oysters across the Gulf Coast (Chapter 9), Virginia country ham on a fresh-baked biscuit (Chapter 8), and New Mexico's spicy chile dishes (Chapter 14).

» **Vibrating venues:** Music lovers can tap their toes to the rich sounds of America. Enjoy authentic mountain music at Ozark Folk Center State Park or pop/country music productions in Branson, Missouri (Chapter 12); hear funky blues and soul at the Alabama Music Hall of Fame, or visit the birthplaces of W. C. Handy and Elvis Presley (Chapter 10); and listen to rock in all its forms at Cleveland's Rock and Roll Hall of Fame and Museum (Chapter 11).

» **Sporting spots:** Sports fans find great entertainment in the National Baseball Hall of Fame in Cooperstown, New York (Chapter 7), which has the gloves, bats, and uniforms of famous players from the past; and the Mississippi Sports Hall of Fame and Museum (Chapter 10), where you can make like a sports announcer and tape your own play-by-play commentary.

Reaping the Essential Rewards of RVing

Seeing the U.S. when you break free of the expressways and take the historical routes across the country brings to life history, geography, archeology, architecture, and feats of engineering and monument building, as well as the natural beauty of whatever area you're traveling through. And that's a key phrase: *traveling through*. You're not *flying over*.

It's true that the roar of Niagara Falls and the drama of the Grand Canyon are unforgettable for everyone. But in an RV, you see and hear and experience even more. You get to know the country at ground level, and meet the people who live there. You never forget stepping out of your rig and experiencing the eerie silence of the deepest valleys along the Appalachians, which aren't really silent at all (Chapter 8). Or stopping for lunch near Petrified Forest National Park and seeing the prairie dogs, yapping at you with their funky little barks, on your way to the Grand Canyon (Chapter 16).

You'll always remember the time you saw a total eclipse in Montana on the way to Yellowstone (Chapter 13), or the first time you really experienced the millions of stars in the Milky Way unfolding into infinity. You can see the latter only when you're in total darkness, far from civilization (check out http://www.darksky.org). Little things, like a quiet sunrise over New Mexico at a distant boondocking site, or a July 4 party around a communal campfire in Michigan, stay with you.

REMEMBER

These experiences become treasured memories in a journey that seems longer and fuller somehow, particularly with the unexpected pleasures that are a big part of getting there. Often, you find unlikely beauty on the road. Driving from the east on U.S. 10 toward Tucson, Arizona, gives you a glimpse of Earth's violent past when you encounter row after row of magnificent boulders precariously perched alongside the freeway near Texas Canyon. It looks like a scene from a John Ford Western. Even better, in an RV, you can just as easily detour and head for Northern Arizona and visit Monument Valley itself along the Utah border, where Ford actually made those Westerns.

Understanding the Romance of the Road

Romances often begin in mystery and grow with discovery. In this chapter's earlier sidebar, we said our first really elaborate vacation took us to Egypt. Forty years after that trip, we sold a Class B motorhome and bought an Airstream trailer. It's funny the way people fall for romantic ideas. We'd never really considered one of these iconic aluminum trailers until we attended an Ohio RV show with several on display.

Company founder Wally Byam designed Airstreams in the 1930s, and he fully understood the romance of the road. In the 1950s, he began organizing RV caravans and rallies for Airstreamers. And we're talking international gatherings. The trips began as driving tours, first in the U.S. and then in Canada and Mexico. Eventually, the adventurers decided to cover longer distances by chartering their own trains and loading their distinctive silver bullet–shaped RVs onto flatcars. When they ran out of places they could easily reach over land, they loaded their rigs into chartered ships and went overseas.

The ultimate Airstream romance rally

In 1959, Byam audaciously took a caravan of 41 families and their trailers to South Africa; they spent the next few months driving northward, up the length of the African continent, winding up in Egypt, 221 days and 14,000 miles after they left America.

When we climbed into that first Airstream trailer at the show in Columbus, Ohio, a video was showing a famous photo from that legendary rally: an aerial shot of a ring of 40 silver trailers and Byam's special gold one, all glinting in the Cairo sunlight, parked at the base of the 4,500-year-old Great Pyramid of Giza. For us, it was our moment of instant RV romance. That very first trip of ours to Egypt had come full circle, and we couldn't plunk down a deposit fast enough.

Byam understood romance, in spades. And for so many people, including us, once you've traveled by RV, you're in love.

Romancing the Badlands

In the June 2022 issue of the Airstream Club International's magazine *The Blue Beret*, author and RVer Kristy Halvorsen wrote about visiting the isolated location of President Theodore Roosevelt's ranch in the Badlands of North Dakota, which became a national park in 1947.

REMEMBER

Teddy Roosevelt was a determined crusader for the preservation of America's wilderness areas, natural wonders and beauties. As president (from 1901 to 1909), he created five new national parks and enacted the Antiquities Act, which gives presidents the authority to proclaim historic or national landmarks and national monuments. Roosevelt went first, and designated the Grand Canyon, Petrified Forest, Devil's Tower, and other prominent locations as national landmarks. He was a tireless conservationist; his work helped lead to the establishment of the National Park Service in 1916. His mission to protect America's natural wonders and wildlife is the reason his face is on Mount Rushmore with George Washington, Thomas Jefferson, and Abraham Lincoln.

Roosevelt's ranch is hard to get to (about 3½ hours west of the state capital at Bismarck), far from any civilization, and those who do visit rarely find anyone else nearby to disturb the quiet. When describing his ranch, Roosevelt once wrote, "It was here that the romance of my life began."

Halvorsen, describing her visit, put into words what so many RVers feel about the RV lifestyle:

I am grateful I landed in this dusty sanctuary nestled between the Little Missouri River and the tall orange and saffron striped bluffs that were once Roosevelt's front and back yards. And I am grateful that, at last, I realize the significance his legacy has had on my life:

It was here that the romance of my life began.

These words lie beneath every road I've driven and every path I've walked or will walk again. In this space, this place . . . it is here that the romance of my life begins.

Chapter **2**

Deciding Where and When to Go

This is less of a "Here's how to" chapter, and more of a "You know, gang, we can do THIS!" chapter.

The 12 RV vacation drives we present in Parts 2 through 5 of this book explore different regions of the United States with its diverse four-season weather, so certain drives are best during certain seasons. In each chapter, we suggest the best times for the trip. But in this chapter, we offer some general advice about the seasons and about planning any RV vacation — including the special trip you can create for yourself.

An RV vacation lets you dispense with the nightmares of air travel, overpriced hotel rooms, and the expense and frequent disappointments of restaurant dining, since you're traveling in your own vacation home on wheels. You don't even have to pay extra luggage fees if you take enough clothes to last a month and dress for weather extremes. With all those headaches gone, you're free to create the trip of a lifetime. In this chapter, we throw some inspiration your way.

Revealing the Secrets of the Seasons

When planning your RV vacation, give a thought to the season you're going, and which part of the country you're in, to get the most out of your trip.

REMEMBER

Always check thoroughly for the most recent information for any park, museum, or event that's central to your vacation. Off-season means smaller crowds and lower prices, but it can also mean that some campgrounds, restaurants, and shops are closed. Campgrounds in the northern states are especially likely to shut down from late fall until spring. In each driving chapter, we list opening and closing dates for seasonal campgrounds and attractions, so pay close attention if you schedule your trip during the transitional months of April and October. Since the COVID pandemic, closing times often come sooner, and seasons have been shortened.

Selecting summer for your RV jaunt

Summer is the most popular vacation time for families because the kids are usually out of school for an extended summer break, daylight hours are longest, rain is infrequent, and campgrounds and attractions are all open for business (unless you're hunting for a ski slope, and even then, some resorts offer ski-lift rides for viewing the countryside). Summer is prime time almost everywhere in the North, but it's often too hot for optimum comfort in the snowbird winter retreats of the South. For example:

>> Summertime temperatures in parts of Texas, New Mexico, and the California deserts are regularly well above 100 degrees F. Don't let anyone fool you with that "Yeah, but it's a DRY heat!" balderdash — that's hot enough for your shoes to sink into the asphalt.

>> In the Southeast, upper 90 degrees F temps combine with soggy humidity to create something that's definitely *not* a dry heat. Of course, the heat of summer doesn't stop anybody from doing Disney World in Orlando. But for RVers who are looking for fewer crowds and milder weather, spring and fall may be preferable.

Watching out for winter

In the southernmost parts of the United States, winter is the best time to visit for mild, sunny weather, but in the resort areas, prices climb with popularity, peaking between Christmastime and the weekend of Presidents' Day.

SNOWBIRDS

In RV-speak, retirees from northern regions fleeing winter weather are known as *snow-birds,* and they're warmly welcomed in the sunny South — from Georgia to Florida, the Gulf Coast to Louisiana and Texas, New Mexico, Nevada, and Arizona, on in to Southern California. Snowbirds begin hotfooting it south from Canada, the Northeast, and the Midwest when the first cold weather hits. They spend the winter months basking in the sun, and then head back north in the spring. RV-owning snowbirds have it all over second-home buyers, for the freedom to move as often as they like without long-term commitments. You'll find lots of RV resorts with outstanding facilities and activities in these Sunbelt states.

WARNING

Wintertime RV camping in areas with subfreezing temperatures requires special equipment to prevent your water supply and wastewater from freezing, including heated hoses and tanks, extra insulation, and reliable, continuous heat. Many campgrounds shut down entirely before cold weather hits, just to keep their exposed water pipes from freezing. However, always call and ask. Often an on-site manager is still renting spaces, without water hookups, to us poor souls out on the road.

Opting for RV trips in spring and fall

One more word on seasons and RVing: Summertime trips may be a necessity, especially if you have kids involved in a traditional September-to-June school year, but spring and fall are a lot more than just the off-season. Many of the trips in this book are better when you don't take them in the crowded heat of the dead of summer, but wait for the times when scenic areas are at their best. Exploring the Sunbelt and western states is just more pleasant this time of year.

REMEMBER

Many of the national parks have annual events to welcome the profusion of wildflowers in spring — such as the *Wildflower Pilgrimage* in late April in the Great Smoky Mountains. The wildflowers bloom later in parks like Yellowstone; each park has its own wildflower calendar, so check their websites. Like cherry blossom time in the South, these eruptions of color are worth seeing.

As for the other end of summer, we grew up in the Midwest, and we're a pair of autumn leaf fanatics, sometimes known as *leaf peepers.* Many times we've taken RV fall foliage trips, just to watch the leaves turn in Vermont or Massachusetts or Minnesota, and we were surprised at how many other campers do the same thing. Fall festivals, harvest festivals, and *Oktoberfests* can be found all over the country, and autumn is by far our favorite time of year to go traveling. It's heavenly to camp out in the thick foliage of the state parks and just soak in the color as the sun sets over the campfire, and a leaf–peeping trip can easily be folded in with something else nearby you'd like to see.

All that is to say, from Labor Day in September through early October is a very desirable time for travel, and you can find fun seasonal activities all over. Consider these options:

» **Wine Festivals.** Fall is grape harvesting time in wine country regions. When the perfect day arrives for pulling the grapes off their vines, growers send out a distress call for anyone and everyone to pitch in and help. Many welcome RVers to camp on their property in return for volunteer grape-picking labor. You might even take part in traditional grape-stomping parties at some vineyards. Festivals always turn into parties, with lots of tasting of previous vintages. Check out: Napa Valley, Sonoma Valley, and Big Sur in California; the Niagara region in upstate New York; the Willamette Valley in Oregon; Newport in Rhode Island; and the Central Virginia region along the Blue Ridge Mountains.

» **Apple festivals** can be found in Delaware, Massachusetts, Michigan, New York, Washington state, California and Wisconsin. Pennsylvania even hosts an annual National Apple Harvest Festival.

» **Albuquerque International Hot-Air Balloon Fiesta.** Albuquerque, New Mexico has the best-known hot-air balloon festival in the country. More than 500 balloons take advantage of the perfect October climate, and the event draws more than 900,000 visitors each year. You'll also find terrific autumn balloon festivals in Colorado Springs, Colorado and Reno, Nevada.

» **Flying pumpkins!** The art of using innovative mechanical means to hurl pumpkins across great distances started as a fun and unique way to get rid of the excess, unsold orange gourds after Halloween, but it became an international fall phenomenon by the 2000s. The annual Punkin' Chunkin' Festival that goes on in early November at Clayton, New York, is probably the nation's biggest these days, but you'll find good ones all over the country wherever pumpkins are grown.

Most leafy states have small historic towns that come alive in autumn, in the Ohio River Valley, all of New England, much of the South, and the Midwest. Towns in heavily wooded regions become tourist magnets every fall. You can find great dining, shopping, and fun local festivals, while basking in the rich colors and the cool, sunny weather. Even in the Rocky Mountain states where leafless evergreens dominate the landscape, or the desert states with nary a leafy tree in sight, the celebration of autumn is universal.

REMEMBER

As we mention in the winter section of this chapter, many RV campgrounds in areas that experience freezing temperatures shut down as early as the week after Labor Day in September, and may stay closed until April or even Memorial Day in May. Business is almost nonexistent in the colder months, and campgrounds also try to prevent their exposed campsite water pipes from freezing. So, fall and winter RV trips may require more advanced planning if you need an overnight camping spot with water, electric and sewer hookups.

Scoping Out Your Perfect RV Vacation

We chose the 12 favorite RV vacation drives in Parts 2 through 5 carefully, and they have a wide appeal:

» **The Coast of Maine: Lobster Land** follows along Maine's dramatic seashore where you'll be eating more lobster at cheaper prices than you believed possible.

» **Western New York: Cooperstown to Niagara Falls** lets you see why we love Lucy, discover where Jell-O came from, see why baseball is a uniquely American sport, and find out why millions of honeymooners weren't wrong when they went to Niagara Falls.

» **The Blue Ridge Mountains: Skyline Drive and Blue Ridge Parkway** brings together two great American roadways and the Great Smoky Mountains National Park, where dogwood blooms and autumn leaves turn vivid crimson and gold — all without the hassle of any commercial traffic.

» **The Gulf Coast: Tallahassee to New Orleans** explains how you can you dig your toes into the sugary sands of the Gulf of Mexico, maybe catch sight of a Blue Angel or two, walk the deck of a WWII battleship, and soak in the sights and sounds of Bourbon Street.

» **The Natchez Trace: Natchez to Nashville** leads you through both the old and new South, with historic sights from the Civil War, and takes you to the birthplaces of such icons as Elvis, W. C. Handy, and Oprah Winfrey.

» **The Heart of Ohio: A Circle around Circleville** helps you discover the authentic Wright stuff and rub shoulders with rock 'n' roll greats. And you get a trip through the Ohio River Valley and a pause in the world's largest Amish community.

- **Northern Minnesota: Paul Bunyan Country** chases the very big footsteps of an American legend in the Land O' Lakes, takes you to the trickling source of the mighty Mississippi River and past a man-made Grand Canyon, and leads you to North America's largest shopping mall.

- **The Ozarks and Branson: Hot Springs to Springfield** directs you though the mountains and valleys of America's oldest mountain range, introduces you to some of the country's oldest and most hidden resorts, lets you discover the wildest sporting goods shop anywhere on Earth, and brings you to one of the most popular travel destinations for music lovers from all over the world.

- **Montana and Wyoming: Tracking Buffalo Bill** is a route where you can savor a buffalo burger, follow showman Buffalo Bill across Yellowstone and through the Bighorn Mountains, and see where Custer made his big mistake.

- **New Mexico: Billy the Kid Meets E.T.** helps you peruse real X-files (after space aliens may have dropped in near Roswell), discover the wide world of chile peppers and great chile chili, and walk the streets where Billy the Kid made his last escape.

- **California's Central Coast: Malibu to Monterey** hugs the Pacific Ocean, takes you past America's most famous castle, directs you to camp among migrating monarch butterflies, and cruises the classic Southern California surfer beaches.

- **Route 66: OK to L.A.** follows the remnants of (arguably) the world's most famous highway and kicks up both little-known and big-name landmarks all along the famed Mother Road.

- **The Oregon Coast: California to Washington** combines rugged scenery with seafood, beachcombing, dune buggying, oyster catching, kite flying, and brew pubbing.

We tried to fashion each drive so that you don't have to follow it start to finish — you can jump in anywhere and stay as long as you please. They're all great trips that are popular for a reason. But in the end, once you get the hang of it, the best thing about RVing is the freedom to build your own itinerary, based on what *you* want to see. And the possibilities are endless.

TIP

Obviously, some geographic areas you want to see are closer to you than others. Always remember that if you plan to rent an RV for your vacation, you don't have to rent one close to home. With nationwide RV rental companies and online RV rental services, you can fly to another part of the country and rent your rig there.

Taking the road less traveled

In his 1996 bestseller *Undaunted Courage,* historian Stephen Ambrose shared the story of his Bicentennial trip in 1976, with family, friends, and students, following the path of the Lewis and Clark expedition, camping and canoeing from Illinois to Montana, up the long Missouri River. The journey of Lewis and Clark to explore the Louisiana Purchase moved technology forward and captured the public's imagination in much the same way as the Mercury, Gemini, and Apollo space missions a century and a half later.

Ambrose is lyrical when he describes sitting around the campfire each night, reading aloud from Meriwether Lewis's journal entry about their location. On July 1 Ambrose and his companions canoed through the Gates of the Mountains, and by the 4th they were at Lemhi Pass on the Continental Divide, which Ambrose describes as the most glorious night of his life.

Yes, it's an astonishing trip, but you don't have to be rich, or a famous historian, to undertake it; lots of RVers have traveled the route of Lewis and Clark, or at least some part of it. Others have done similar historic routes, from the Oregon Trail to the Donner Pass. (Pack a lunch!) The sources of information are many; not only are lots of these routes marked by the government, through state and national parks, but the bloggers who've gone before have left terrific itineraries for others to follow. When we were RVing across the Dakotas, even the local Kampgrounds of America (KOAs) had all sorts of info about nearby Lewis and Clark sites.

So, what's your passion? You can make almost anything into an RV camping trip. We met a fellow Airstreamer who did, arguably, a camping trip too far — he had his restored vintage Bambi trailer shipped across the Atlantic, and then he RVed across Europe, particularly exploring Norway, his ancestral home. That *is* a bit much, but it illuminates a point: An RV trip is your own baby. You don't have to follow anyone else's vacation itinerary if you don't want to. There's always the road less traveled. You can devise your own journey, based on your interests and whatever it is you've dreamed of seeing. And you'll be surprised how often that "road less traveled" is still loaded with people who share your interest and leave behind lots of bread crumbs of useful information to follow.

Creating an RV itinerary all your own

What follows are just a few examples of itineraries you can build, some suggestions to get your brain going, and a few of the possible attractions accessible from an RV in every part of the country.

OH, CANADA!

If you plan to cross the border into Canada — for example, to visit the Canadian side at Niagara Falls — be prepared. To cross the border by road into Canada and back into the U.S. again, everyone over 16 must have a current passport, passport card, or enhanced driver's license (EDL, sometimes called *Real ID*). Children under 16 — even newborn infants — must have a birth certificate. If any minor kids are traveling with your family without their birth parents, each one must have their own birth certificate, plus a written and notarized affidavit from their parents granting permission for their child to travel in your custody. Be sure your pets have up-to-date written proof of vaccinations from your vet, and be aware your smartphone may not work in Canada unless you've added international service to your wireless plan.

If you plan to cross with your RV refrigerator full, check food rules on both sides of the border. They're different in each country, and often change. We had our rig searched once because we admitted to buying apples in Ohio, and the inspector nearly had apoplexy over it.

TIP

We've left off the website addresses for the many attractions we mention in the following examples, but it's easy to find these on your own. Just type the name of the museum, center, memorial, historical site, and so on into your favorite browser, click the link to that attraction, and go from there.

Calling all space explorers

For a lot of grown-up kids born in the 1960s and '70s, there may be nothing more exciting than a **NASA/space museum RV trip.** You can build your itinerary around one or two of the greats; picture a trip that starts at the **Smithsonian Air and Space Museum** in Washington, D.C., and goes the 869 miles to NASA's most famous home, the **Kennedy Space Center** at Cape Canaveral on the Space Coast in Florida. With luck, you may be able to catch a launch while you're in the area.

If the East Coast is too far off track for you, there are space experiences all over America. In the South, there's **Space Camp** at the **U.S. Space and Rocket Center** in Huntsville, Alabama, and we can attest that it's a fantastic, fun experience for both kids and adults. Among its artifacts, you find the biggest collection of rockets and spacecraft in the world, including the Apollo 6 Command Module capsule, the Space Shuttle *Pathfinder,* and the world's only complete remaining Saturn V moon rocket. While there, you can also take a bus tour of the **Marshall Space Flight Center,** where NASA designs and builds its rockets.

In Texas, there's **Mission Control** at the **Johnson Space Center** in Houston, and though there are no tours of Elon Musk's **SpaceX,** you can see their frequent rocket launches from South Padre Island. In Pasadena, California, you've got the famed **Jet Propulsion Lab,** where NASA develops Mars landers and other interplanetary spacecraft. And while it's not really related to space exploration per se, you can tour a decommissioned **Minuteman II nuclear missile silo** and the **Delta-01 Launch Control Facility** just off I-90 in western South Dakota.

Tracking the North and South

The American Civil War was the deadliest war in U.S. history, with more than 650,000 perishing in the battle to end slavery. Between 1861 and 1865, there were nearly 400 major battles fought between forces of the North and South, in 19 states stretching from Vermont to New Mexico. A trip to visit **American Civil War battlefields** is incredibly popular among RVers. Because the major sites are in the eastern portion of the country, you can see an awful lot in a comparatively brief time. For example, we came across an itinerary for a 20-day trip of roughly 1,200 miles that hit an incredible number of key sites, running from **Fort Sumter,** where the first shot was fired, to **Gettysburg,** where the tide turned and the end to the conflict began, and finally to **Appomattox,** where Robert E. Lee officially surrendered to Ulysses S. Grant.

You can do a planned trip, with help from historians and professionals, like this one from **Fantasy RV Tours** (www.fantasyrvtours.net/civilwar), or save money and follow advice from one of the many bloggers who've set out on their own. We found **Our Wander-Filled Life,** a site by a pair of schoolteachers, to be particularly good (www.wanderfilledlife.com/civil-war-road-trip-national-parks). Their list of Civil War battlefields makes a special effort to tie in to the national parks, as well as some cities to visit. It's a great place to start your planning.

Discovering Black history

An inspiring **Black heritage** RV trip may be a great choice for your family this summer. There are so many sites to visit, and an excellent place to start looking for a list of suggested heritage sites is on the **National Park Service** website (www.nps.gov/subjects/africanamericanheritage/index.htm).

Point Comfort on the coast of Virginia marks the spot of the first arrival of African slaves in America in 1619. **Freedom House** in nearby Alexandria (just across the Potomac from Washington, D.C.) preserves the location of a busy slave market from the 1830s, as does Charleston, South Carolina's imposing **Old Slave Mart** museum.

Sites connected with the civil rights movement in the 1960s can be found throughout the Southern states: Downtown areas in Atlanta, Georgia, and Birmingham, Alabama, feature locations of the founding of the Southern Christian Leadership Conference (SCLC) and the National Association for the Advancement of Colored People (NAACP), along with places connected with Martin Luther King, Jr. There are many websites dedicated to tracing the route of the **Freedom Riders** throughout the South in the early 1960s. Check out the **U.S. Civil Rights Trail** website (https://civilrightstrail.com) which has a very detailed list of landmark sites, museums, districts, tours, and much more.

Living history museums are another resource. One of the best is the **National Underground Railroad Freedom Center** in Cincinnati, Ohio, while nearby central Indiana has **Freetown Village.** And the **Whitney Plantation** museum in Louisiana is an unsparing look at what slavery was really like. There are several **Buffalo Soldiers** museums around the South and West that tell the story of Black soldiers since the mid-1800s. One of the best is the **Buffalo Soldiers National Museum** in Houston, Texas. And Detroit, Michigan, has the outstanding **Tuskegee Airmen National Historical Museum,** which tells the historic exploits of Black military pilots, along with offering plane rides and a "flight school" for teenagers.

Of course, Washington, D.C.'s **Martin Luther King, Jr. Memorial** and the Smithsonian's **National Museum of African American History and Culture** would be the highlight of any trip.

Rockin' and rollin'

For a rock music junkie, it's pretty easy to plan a **rock and roll RV vacation.** You can shape it to your brand of rock, to heavy metal, acid rock or classic, or to any area of the country — even go so far south as New Orleans if you love rhythm and blues. Start at **Sun Music Studios** in Memphis, Tennessee, the acknowledged "birthplace of rock 'n' roll." B.B. King, Elvis Presley, Johnny Cash, and Jerry Lee Lewis all recorded here. Then hit nearby **Graceland** mansion, the home of Elvis, the King. Once there, you're only 200 miles from Nashville, where you can see the famed **Music Row.**

Or you can hit a couple of the summer music festivals, like **Lollapalooza** in Chicago or **Summerfest** in Milwaukee. Hunt down **Yasgur's farm,** the original site of the 1969 Woodstock festival outside Bethel, New York, and stay overnight at the nearby Happy Days campground. Eat at all of the Hard Rock Cafés in America. Tour **Paisley Park**, Prince's home and studio, which is now a museum.

And don't forget the **Rock and Roll Hall of Fame** in Cleveland, Ohio. If you're up for it, go all the way to California, to **Haight-Ashbury** in San Francisco or the **Whiskey a Go Go** in Hollywood, the most famous dive on the West Coast, where Jim Morrison and the Doors were the house band and the heart-stopping list of regular performers ran the gamut from Janis Joplin to Mötley Crüe. These are all very popular trips; do an internet search for "Rock and Roll Road Trip" and stand back.

Riding the rails

Chris was engineer on a steam locomotive by the age of 14, so we've done lots of **steam train museums;** they make for a great experience. Pennsylvania has two of the very best railroad museums in the world: **Steamtown National Historic Site** in Scranton and the **Railroad Museum of Pennsylvania** in Strasburg (kids will love them both). While in Pennsylvania, don't miss the spectacular **Horseshoe Curve** outside Altoona — dozens of trains pass through each day, and it's possible to see as many as three trains side by side snaking around the valley and crawling up the steep grade.

Almost every state has at least one railroad museum: The **Illinois Railway Museum** is the largest in the U.S., and the **California State Railroad Museum** is also outstanding. Visit **Promontory Point, Utah,** where the Union Pacific and Central Pacific railroads met and connected the first transcontinental railroad in America with a golden spike in 1869.

Some of the most picturesque steam train operations are narrow gauge railroads, which feature smaller, lighter steel rails laid closer together. These were commonly used in rugged mountain areas by the logging and mining industries. They include the **Cass Scenic Railroad** in West Virginia and the **Durango and Silverton Narrow Gauge Railroad** in Colorado. Though the Durango ride takes a full day, typically these trips aren't long — one or two hours at most. Some of them dress up the experience, with dinners, "great train robberies," or even "murder trains," where you'll get to play detective on an old-fashioned onboard murder trip.

These historic trains are running in some of the most gorgeous areas of the country, which means there are generally an abundance of RV parks nearby. Even if you can get away for only a weekend, it's an RV trip you'll remember.

Sailing the seas

It's one if by land and two if by sea, for a **maritime museums RV trip.** America is loaded with them, not just on the two coasts, but also in the Great Lakes area. There are many sailing museums along the East Coast, and more than a few individually docked sailing ships to visit. **Mystic Seaport Museum** in Mystic, Connecticut, is the best maritime museum in the country, with a living history village, a planetarium, a shipyard, and the biggest collection of historic vessels in the U.S. From here, you can drive about 400 miles to the east to reach the Great Lakes and all the maritime experiences that dot the shores of Lake Erie from Buffalo, New York, to Sandusky, Ohio, including the **National Museum of the Great Lakes** and Oliver Hazard Perry's brig, *Niagara*, which has a home in Erie, Pennsylvania.

The **Maritime Museum of San Diego** is home to another outstanding fleet of restored ships that includes the *Star of Indiana*, the world's oldest active sailing ship. Stationary 20th century naval ships can be found all over the coastal U.S. For instance, if you venture into New York City, the **Intrepid Sea, Air and Space Museum** is located on the **USS Intrepid**, a retired WWII-era aircraft carrier. And don't forget that the **National Museum of the U.S. Navy** is in the Washington Navy Yard in D.C.

Exploring ghost towns

Western ghost towns are a great RV experience, and kids love them. The American West is loaded with ghost towns, and while many have been turned into amusement parks with events, train rides, and ghost story–telling sessions, others still sit in glorious isolation, which can send a shiver down your spine. Most ghost towns were mining towns, and they're deserted because the mine was played out. The easiest way to plan a ghost town trip is to go state by state; some areas, like Aspen, Colorado, seem to be magnets for ghost towns: **St. Elmo, Independence,** and **Ashcroft** are all nearby.

Montana is a blast, with at least 13 bona fide ghost towns — and almost all of them are packed into the southwestern portion of the state, where there are also lots of RV parks and campgrounds. While you can even ride the train between Montana's "twin" ghost towns of **Virginia City** and **Nevada City,** another site of particular interest is **Bannack,** one of the few ghost towns preserved as part of a state park.

Most of the Western states have ghost towns; google each state you want to visit and be sure to size up your prospective town for safety. Many are a "visit at your own risk" proposition — no one really owns or maintains them, and many are crumbling, deserted ruins. (Do we really need to tell you that spelunking through an abandoned mineshaft is a lousy idea?) Ghost towns can be an excellent chance to polish up your *boondocking* (camping without external hookups outside a designated campground, see Chapter 5) skills. Websites like **Campendium.com** help you find free camping areas (sometimes called *disbursed camping*) near the ghost town of your choice.

Peering into a galaxy far, far away

Consider a **stargazing RV trip** — it pairs incredibly well with a boondocking trip, because you want to be as far from city lights as possible. A few years ago, Alice confessed that she'd never seen the Milky Way except in pictures. We became more aware of the issue of light pollution and began looking for places where the constellations can still be seen with binoculars and the naked eye. We discovered a thriving RV subculture of stargazers, and even some RV parks with telescopes and organized star parties, particularly in Arizona.

If you're a newbie, a book may help; our favorite is *Nightwatch: A Practical Guide to Viewing the Universe,* by Terence Dickinson. But if you don't like to read, there's a gang of websites out there that will get you started, including a great one from the International Dark-Sky Association (www.darksky.org) with tons of information on light pollution and where to go to find your first dark zone, as well as what to look for when you find it.

Also consider stopping at an observatory to look through their massive telescopes and peer deeper into the vast universe: **McDonald Observatory** in Fort David, Texas, **Lowell Observatory** (where the first sighting of Pluto occurred) in Flagstaff, Arizona, **Adirondack Sky Center** in Tupper Lake, New York, and **Lick Observatory** in San Jose, California, are some of the best. As for other stops on the road to the stars, take a look at one list of America's best planetariums, at www.vacationidea. com/ideas/best-planetariums-usa.html, and you'll find excellent locations to fold into your itinerary.

Living history

You don't have to like history to get a big charge out of a **living history museum RV trip**. Kids in particular adore these places, where history isn't a lecture, but comes alive with reenactors dressed as pioneers, British military officers, Native Americans, Wild West gunslingers, and more. You can cross the country in every direction to find these sites — one trip might start with the queen mother, Virginia's **Colonial Williamsburg,** and **George Washington's Mount Vernon** estate, and then move to nearby locations to the east or south.

Northwest Ohio is home to **Heritage Village** in Sharonville; **Greenfield Village** is in Dearborn, Michigan; and **Stone Mountain's Historic Square** is just outside Atlanta, Georgia. One of the nation's best, **Conner Prairie** in Fishers, Indiana, recreates life across several different decades of the 19th century in a fictional prairie village. We mentioned both **Mystic Seaport Museum** and the **Maritime Museum of San Diego** in other trip ideas — both are excellent living history museums as well.

There are lots of living history museums in the West: **Oglala Lakota Living History Village** in South Dakota, the **Museum of the Rockies** in Bozeman, Montana, **O.K. Corral** in Tombstone, Arizona, all the way to **Old Town San Diego State Historic Park** in California. These stationary museums make your journey easier to plan, but remember that there are also tons of reenactor events throughout the year, particularly in summer and fall, and these are worth googling; look for them in any state you may be passing through.

Following America's most famous roads

If you spend any time at all sitting around the communal campfires in RV parks, you're going to hear about someone doing a **Route 66 RV trip** (see Chapter 16). In 1926, it took two hard-driving months to cross the U.S. east to west by car. After 1956, when America went on a road-building binge, that had dropped to two weeks. Today's federal Interstate Highway System makes it possible to drive cross-country in just 40 hours (if you don't sleep), but you miss so much of the passing country. Interstate travelers tend to stick to the truck stops and fast food joints off the exits, and almost never explore nearby towns just down the road.

Many of the grand old roads — the **King's Highway** and the **Dixie Highway**, the **Lincoln Highway** (America's first transcontinental highway), and **U.S. 40**, the **National Road** — constitute what we call the scenic routes, and they still go right through the heart of America. The **Great River Road** follows the length of the Mississippi River. The 1,671-mile long **Pacific Coast Highway** (also called **PCH**, made up of **U.S. 101,**and **California Highway 1**) is a breathtaking trip that starts at San Diego, follows California's Pacific coastline northward, with its many beach-front communities, on up through dramatic coastal Oregon (where it's called the Oregon Coast Highway), and the shoreline of Washington state, ending at Olympia, on the Canadian border. A 107-mile-long stretch at the southernmost end of U.S. 1, known affectionately as the **Overseas Highway,** is a modern miracle of engineering that connects the Florida Keys as though you're driving on water. The 450-mile **Blue Ridge Parkway** (see Chapter 8) offers magnificent views of the Shenandoah and Great Smoky mountain ranges.

And then, of course, there's the **Mother Road, Route 66** (see Chapter 16), from Chicago, Illinois, running south and west to Santa Monica, California. Route 66 went through rural towns all across the Midwest and the West, becoming their life's blood. But because it's been officially decommissioned as a highway and superseded by interstates, following it all the way to the end is a badge of honor; in some sections, just *finding* it can be a challenge. We talk a lot more about finding the old roads in our companion book, *RVs and Campers For Dummies,* and a ton of books and blogs offer advice for doing Route 66 and all the other old U.S. Routes, as well as the lore of roadside kitsch from the days of courtyard motels, neon-lit cafes, Indian jewelry shops, and "Come See the Thing!" billboards. These trips meld very well with others, such as ghost town or autumn leaf-peeping trips.

Ultimate tailgating for sports fans

Fans of team sports have endless possibilities for RVing. With your own rig, you can have a **tailgating party** and crack open a cold one in a different city every weekend. We've encountered plenty of folks who have toured every Major League Baseball park, all the National Football League stadiums, or all the Big Ten college basketball fieldhouses. Racing fans (of both horses and cars) tour the best tracks in the nation.

Gamblers tour casinos. More of a golfer? Play a round at the most famous courses in the country without paying resort hotel prices by staying in your RV. Check out your favorite sports shrines, like the **Baseball Hall of Fame** in Cooperstown, New York, the **Football Hall of Fame** in Canton, Ohio, or the **Basketball Hall of Fame** in Springfield, Massachusetts.

Show Us Yours

In the previous section, you can get ideas for building your own special RV route and sightseeing trip. So, what's your favorite thing on Earth? How about the finest craft beer breweries, or the fastest roller coasters, or the best antique shopping, or the prettiest seaside campgrounds, or the scariest haunted houses? Follow Kentucky's famous Bourbon Trail. Hunt down the best air shows or car shows in the country. Maybe military museums, aircraft museums, or automobile museums are your passion. There's even an RV museum in Elkhart, Indiana.

There won't be a test later, but we'll be looking for your day-by-day blogs, Facebook posts, or YouTube videos on the exciting road trip you invented! The only limits are money and time, but not imagination.

IN THIS CHAPTER

» **Being good to your budget with an RV vacation**

» **Saving on the price of essentials**

» **Staying frugal with your camping supplies**

» **Spending wisely for attractions and activities**

» **Getting the lowest RV rental rate**

Chapter **3**

Managing Your Money

B udgeting for a trip in an RV has a few different wrinkles to it than planning for a typical vacation, where you're not driving around in your accommodations. In this chapter, we provide you with basic information, tips, and how-to instructions for planning the budget for your upcoming RV trip.

We start this chapter with some hard numbers and a brief discussion of the reasons that — even in bad economic times — an RV vacation can save you lots of money over any other kind of getaway. We look at the principal costs of fuel, campgrounds, and food, and other expenses you may not have thought about. We also touch on tried-and-true methods to save money on everything from local attractions to RV rentals.

Add Up the Savings When You Go by RV

As of this writing, Americans are facing unprecedented economic hardships, and the high price of gas and diesel is at the top of the agony list, followed closely by the price of food. Many families are giving up vacations as a luxury they can no longer afford. We would argue that, enduring the stresses of hard times, families need the relaxing togetherness of a vacation more than ever. And we contend that you can take an RV/camping vacation at a lower cost than just about any other vacation type (with the exception of a *staycation*, of course, where you just stay home and paint the garage).

Looking at it from a money standpoint, compare and contrast two popular vacations, which we plucked out of the number-one and number-two positions on a typical online list of *Most Popular Family Vacations*.

» **Disneyland (in Anaheim, CA) or Disney World (in Orlando, FL):** Of course, this destination (no surprise) is the number-one family vacation choice. The sad thing is this: The cost of a Disney vacation is now outside the reach of most of the families the parks were built for in the first place.

  If you're planning a vacation of less than a week — five days in a Disney park for a typical family of four in 2022–2023 — you're facing a cost (with variants accounted for) somewhere between $4,000 and $7,500. This is a staggering amount of money for such a brief fling. Many families also include a trip to a nearby park such as Universal to round out the week, which adds to the total cost. We guarantee you can do the South of France for less.

» **Yellowstone National Park:** A week in this park comes in as the gold-standard RV trip, but we contend that you're just not going to be in the crippling zone of expense you face with a Disney vacation. We saw an article claiming an average cost of well over $5,000 for a family of four for one week at Yellowstone ($3,000 for a couple). That included airline tickets, staying in the park hotels (which are magnificent but pricey), and dining out for every meal. Consider the savings you get with RVing for just one of these costs:

  • The article assumes a per-night lodging cost for a family of four to be $176–$234, just for 2- to 3-star accommodations.

  • In the 12 campgrounds of Yellowstone, nightly costs are much lower. You pay more for the famed Fishing Bridge campground, where sites cost around $80 a night, because it's the only campground within Yellowstone that has full hookups. But you can find spots for *dry camping* (camping without hookups) for as little as $25 a night or a tent site for $15. **Note:** Some of these parks have RV length restrictions that may affect you. But if you choose for that reason to camp in the larger private RV parks outside the West Gate, you can still find bargains.

TIP

You don't have to fight the crowds and go to Yellowstone. The great thing about RVing is the level of *control* it gives you over destination and costs. Yellowstone is just one destination, and every one of the 50 states is loaded with fun places to go camping, so your possibilities are endless. For one thing, you can choose to give the big-name national parks the cold shoulder. State parks are a bargain hunter's dream, with gorgeous RV campsites to be had for $20 to $30 per night.

If you're really adventurous (or have a generator or solar panels), you can *boondock* (camp without hookups) and find free camping all over the U.S. For more about boondocking, see Chapter 5.

TALES OF THE UNEXPECTED

So what *is* the worst-case scenario for unexpected RV vacation expenses? Opinions may differ, but we can tell you from bitter experience that most RVers are haunted by the possibility of a transmission failure, either in the tow vehicle or the motorhome. It's a nightmare expense, and it happened to us during a major heat wave in the height of the COVID pandemic. (Yes, we had to be on the road at the time.)

Our factory warranty refused to cover a new transmission, for a typical reason. (Lack of all verifiable receipts for the maintenance schedule in the owner's manual. Miss one oil change by a thousand miles, or fail to produce receipts for every one, and you won't be covered.) GM dealerships couldn't even look at it for an estimated three months, which didn't matter since shipments of factory replacement GM transmissions had been delayed by more than six months. Cost of the disaster? $6,700 for the transmission, plus five days stranded in an expensive KOA in Omaha, Nebraska, where the price of rental cars had quadrupled and there were none to be had anyway, due to the pandemic. An additional expense: the cost of the rental truck we eventually found to tow the Airstream home, because we were still waiting for service. In total, the unexpected expense was nearly $10,000.

Our takeaway advice? Don't depend on factory warranties; they can let you down. Get a comprehensive RV service plan that covers not only your motorhome or trailer but also your tow vehicle.

Calculating the Cost of Essentials

For the purposes of this chapter, we assume that you're a newbie who's planning your first RV vacation. However, even an old hand may find some helpful budgeting tips. We hope so.

Note: The costs we present in this chapter don't include the price of a new or used RV. Regarding the price of renting an RV, we offer related information in the section "Testing the Waters: RV Rentals" later in this chapter.

So, sit down at the kitchen table and run a few numbers. On a typical RV trip (and most of them are), the primary costs are fuel, campsites, and food. It's easy to go through these essentials one at a time, to see what you can afford.

Figuring the cost of gasoline or diesel fuel

There's no question whatsoever that the budget-buster expense these days with an RV vacation is fuel. But one of the advantages of RVing is that it's filled with options. Look at some real-world numbers and follow these steps to estimate your fuel costs:

1. **Evaluate your rig's miles per gallon (mpg) and travel distance covered per full tank.**

   We tow a 30-foot Airstream trailer with a Chevy Suburban. Towing a full load, our Suburban's gasoline engine gets 9–11 mpg — depending on speed and topography — so typically, we can cover an average of 300 miles on a tank of gas. This can be an airy-fairy figure, but it gives you a starting point.

2. **Figure out the length of your round-trip route.**

   To plan your budget, divide the daily mileage or the total trip mileage by the estimated miles per gallon that your RV gets, and you can get an idea of how many gallons you'll use per day or for the entire drive. For instance, the drive to Yellowstone from our home base is roughly 1,500 miles one way, or 3,000 miles round trip.

   3,000 miles ÷ 10 mpg = 300 gallons for the trip

3. Determine an average fuel cost per tank of gas.

At the moment of this writing, we're paying $3.99 per gallon to fill our 30-gallon tank. So, $3.99 × 30 = $119.70, which we round up to $120 for a tank of gas.

TIP

No one can predict the global and local swings in fuel prices, but the free phone app **GasBuddy** (www.gasbuddy.com) gives you current retail fuel prices wherever you are throughout the country and indicates the lowest prices at specific stations in any particular area.

4. Estimate your total fuel cost based on the length of your route and the average cost per tank.

With a route length of 3,000 miles, and a full-tank range of 300 miles, we figure we need 10 (3,000 ÷ 300 = 10) full tanks to cover the route (not counting any side trips). So the total fuel cost becomes the average cost per tank multiplied by the number of tanks required.

$120 × 10 = $1,200

Start saving on fuel by considering destinations that offer more advantages related to miles covered, as follows:

>> **Choose a destination closer to your home base.** Perhaps your financial year has been rough, and you think you can probably enjoy Gatlinburg and Great Smoky Mountains National Park just as much as Yellowstone. Using the example from the step list, that puts the destination at only 400 miles from home. That change does major surgery on the total gas price. The 800-mile round trip divided by the miles per tank (300) brings the number of tanks required down to 2.67 (instead of 10 for the Yellowstone trip). Your total fuel expense becomes

$120 × 2.67 = $320.40 (which you can round to $320)

>> **Choose a campground where you can anchor your RV near an area with lots to see and do.** That way, you're not trying to move your RV from place to place — you're parking it and using your tow vehicle (a.k.a. your *toad*) or even an Uber or rental — to do things nearby. Pick a town, any town, and type into Google search "things to do near Salem, Massachusetts," or "attractions near Savannah, Georgia," for example. All sorts of vacation possibilities that may be near your RV campground appear.

WARNING

RV gas or diesel engines are thirsty fuel hogs, and filling up the tank the first time is likely to scare you out of five years' growth, especially with a Class A or C rig. Fuel tank sizes can range anywhere from 25–35 gallons for a pickup truck or a Class B van-type motorhome, to about 50 gallons for a Class C motorhome, all the way up to 100–150 gallons for a big Class A unit. These rigs can weigh in anywhere from 25,000 to 40,000 pounds, not counting a towed car, and the heavier the rig, the bigger the fuel tank needs to be. With diesel fuel currently at $5.50/gallon, that's $550 just to fill up a 100-gallon tank. And a fully loaded Class A unit towing a car behind it is likely to get no better than 5–8 mpg on a flat road.

Charging electric vehicles costs money, too

Many people feel that EVs are their key to escape runaway fuel costs. Here's a reality check when it comes to the topic of using an EV for towing your RV and what it will cost you on the road.

SLOW DOWN: YOUR PASSENGERS AND YOUR WALLET WILL THANK YOU

We don't care what the Sammy Hagar song says, you CAN drive 55, and it's more than just a good idea. Out West in the wide-open spaces, several states have raised their inter-state highway speed limits to 75 — or even 80 — mph. Texans get to drive 85 in some areas! That's fine if you're out where the buffalo roam and skies are not cloudy all day in a typical car, when you can see everything ahead of you for the next ten miles. But avoid trying for those top speeds in your rig. Most seasoned RV owners agree that anything over 65 mph is reckless, no matter what kind of rig you've got, what the signs say, or what the road conditions are. Also, many states have slower speed limits for RVs or trucks by law. In California, for example, state law restricts you to 55 mph in an RV or truck.

Over time, experiment with your driving speed and you'll discover that dropping from 65 mph down to 55 makes your rig much easier to handle in all situations. It also makes a dramatic improvement to your gas mileage. For every 5 miles per hour you *increase* above 55, your mileage *decreases* by as much as a whopping 8 percent. When you see the cost savings to your overall fuel budget, the reduction in your anxiety, and the vast improvement in your mood, you'll soon get over being passed by everyone else on the road. Besides, you're on vacation. What's your hurry?

The good news is, if you're heading for a campground with 30/50-amp hook-ups, you can use their power pole to recharge your EV without having to pay the price of a public charging station. (We anticipate that this situation will probably change in the future.) Be sure you've got the correct plug adapters to fit the 120-volt/30-amp outlet, or the 240-volt/50-amp outlet. The question is whether you can deal with the shortened towing range and recharging on the road in order to get to your destination in the first place.

Electrify America (www.electrifyamerica.com) is presently the biggest national chain operating more than 3,500 chargers at almost 800 public charging stations, and their chargers are equipped with the three most common EV power plug connections. They provide a phone app for finding stations and buying sessions. Electrify America's current prices are $0.43/kilowatt-hour (kWh) for non-subscribing members and $0.31/kWh for Pass+ members.

Currently, there are about 20,000 EV charging stations nationwide. Congress passed funding in 2022 for the beginning of a $5 billion network of 500,000 chargers close to the interstate highway system in all 50 states, and another $2.5 billion for community charging units. And Tesla is expected to open up its proprietary chargers to non-Tesla owners. But one major hurdle is how to charge uniform electricity rates nationwide when utility companies everywhere are facing severe strains on the electrical grid as it is.

Just be aware that less populated states such as Maine, Minnesota, Montana, the Dakotas, and Wyoming — extremely popular RV tourism states — have very few chargers, often *hundreds* of miles apart, and almost none appear on desolate sections of the most common roads leading to the major national parks and other sites.

In 2021, *Motor Trend* magazine road tested a new all-electric Rivian R1T pickup towing a 9,000 pound trailer, a fairly realistic 80 percent of its 11,000-pound capacity (www.motortrend.com/features/how-far-can-you-tow-with-electric-truck-range/). There were some surprising positives: On an uphill acceleration, torque was excellent and was unaffected by the lack of oxygen in the high altitudes. But this is still technology in its infancy, subsisting on billions in federal largesse, and unfortunately, all the usual EV issues were there. For example, the vehicle's Environmental Protection Agency–estimated range of battery life was cut in half by towing, with an ability in this instance to go only 150 miles before needing a charge. Considering the distances RVers routinely travel, the main question being asked now isn't "How much will a charge cost in the future?" but "How far can I get without a charge?" It's still a little way off for towing with an EV to be routine. Whether it will be any cheaper than gas or diesel is open to strong debate.

Planning out your campsites

Saving money on campsites is definitely key to staying on a budget, though it's gotten tougher to do. Apart from post-pandemic inflation hurting everyone, whatever you have a shortage of gets more expensive. But how bad are the shortages anyway? Consider these points:

>> RV purchases are at an all-time high and have been since before the pandemic. Purchases are rising each year until many a dealer is short on stock to sell, because manufacturers can't keep up with demand. That has, in turn, led to a shortage of RV campground spaces in some parts of the country. That means full campgrounds in some, but not all, areas and not all the time.

>> Along with soaring prices, the biggest problem may be finding a campsite at all, according to some online sources. But that may be overstated. We're not hearing or seeing that on the ground. We talk to lots of campground owners and managers. Most of them, especially the ones who aren't in the super-high-traffic zones, are telling us that yes, they're more crowded, but typically only in the high summer months of July and August. And obviously, the weekends are busier.

REMEMBER

We know that when you're planning a family vacation, summer is prime vacation time, because the kids are out of school. But take a look at your own schedule. If it's at all possible, try for a vacation at a less busy time. Look at April and May, perhaps over Spring Break, or go for the glories of September and October, popular months for old hands. Tons of people are homeschooling now, which makes vacation time with children more flexible. Whatever you can do to avoid epic crowds, such as the ones on holidays like Memorial Day, Independence Day, and Labor Day, pays off, both in money and in hassle.

Dealing with rising campground fees

Starting about a decade ago, the regular campground we used to stop at that cost $25 a night suddenly doubled to $50; now, it may be nearer $75. The "luxury resort" campgrounds are well over $100 a night — it's not unusual for one of these, with a lake or ocean view, to charge $200–$300 a night!

REMEMBER

The $25-a-night campgrounds are still out there; they're just a bit harder to find. You've got plenty of small family-owned campgrounds as well as low-priced state and local parks to choose from. Various apps — for example, AllStays RV or Campendium — are powerful tools to help you find these sites.

HIGHER PRICES HAVE CAUSES

It's a little like a life-saving autopsy, but it may help steer you toward the bargains to know why campgrounds have gotten so expensive.

- It can be very difficult and expensive to build new campgrounds. Local, state, and federal regulations, along with more vocal NIMBY ("not in my back yard") neighbors objecting to new campgrounds, have had a chilling effect on new facilities for RVers.

- The rise of full-timers who live in their RVs year-round has caused many owners to set aside a percentage of spaces for them, guaranteeing a steady income, which means fewer spaces for vacationing campers.

- Hedge fund managers and Super Big Conglomerate Companies always want land that generates income. And so the real estate investment trust, or REIT, was born. REITs run around buying up things like income-producing apartments, hotels, and now, of course, RV campgrounds for incredibly bloated amounts of money, driving out many family owners of the past (and even some chains). Then they jack up the prices for the fastest maximum return on their investment.

Campgrounds in state and national parks generally have a much better price than private campgrounds. They can also be more crowded, particularly in season. Other downsides include:

>> **Smaller range of hookups:** Unlike the pricier private campgrounds, publicly owned parks don't commonly offer full hookups — usually it's water and electric, or even just electric, with a central dump station. Many don't offer 50-amp electrical service for larger units.

>> **Self-service for water needs:** If there's no water hookup at the site, you may have to fill your freshwater tank before parking and limit your water use so it will last longer. But for most of us, it's not that hard to live out of our own water tanks, pulling up stakes every two or three days to dump the grey/black tanks and refill the water tank.

As long as you can handle a short stay, rationed water use, or pulling up the campsite periodically, you can save substantially when you choose public campgrounds over almost all private campgrounds. For a gorgeous $20-a-night site, it's worth it.

Saving by boondocking

Crowded campgrounds, high prices, and limited full-hookup spaces have all contributed to the rise in *boondocking*, also called *dry camping*. Boondocking means camping in your RV without any external hookups whatsoever, relying solely on whatever battery power, propane, and water supply you have on board. Nothing excites RVers more than the notion of free campsites. It's especially attractive when you're just stopping for the night while headed for an ultimate destination; this is where sleeping in a Walmart parking lot was born (jokingly referred to as *Wallydocking*). Every night you can boondock comfortably enough to not be miserable is one more night you can save the price of a campground. That's a big savings on a long trip.

Getting clubby

Are campground clubs another answer to high costs? Yes, clubs can help, but their value really does depend on many factors, including how often you camp, and where and when you go camping. How often is a big issue, since a single one-week camping trip per year may not give you the chance to amortize the cost of membership in the savings you get.

The most popular RV club by far is also the oldest, Good Sam Club. Its features — a low cost of $29 a year for membership, discounts on campgrounds and supplies bought at Camping World stores, dependability, and popularity, with more than 2,000 member campgrounds — represent the best ways a club can help you save.

All these issues — boondocking, camping clubs, and both finding and saving on campgrounds — are discussed in more detail in Chapter 5, where you find a list of the major camping clubs and an explanation of their benefits. Check it out. Any one of them may be a good fit for your budget and travel style.

TIP

Take advantage of the rewards cards you can get at your favorite restaurant and use on the road. Most of the national chains offer these, with either a card you carry in your wallet or an app you download on your phone. When we were young and dumb, we thought it was a bit of a pain, and not worth it, just a way for them to know too much about you. Now, we always take advantage of rewards cards; we've found the savings to be considerable.

Saving on supplies and souvenirs

You can find all sorts of ways to save money on general camping supplies. If you're just getting started, the best advice we can give you is — and carve this in stone — *don't overbuy*. You may be tempted to buy too much, because it's great fun and some of the things available to campers and RVers nowadays are adorable as well as practical. A slick YouTube video can have you believing you can't hike without an upscale backpack, you can't fish without a deluxe vest, and so on. But buy with caution. Buy secondhand equipment as often as you can. Even better, consider renting it.

Most campgrounds, especially in season, rent you the supplies you need to take advantage of area activities. These items range from kayaks to canoes, bikes to skis, fishing gear to hiking shoes, and so on. You can even join a club, such as **REI** (www.rei.com), which has a $30 lifetime membership plan that enables you to rent just about anything you need through your local store.

TIP

If you'd rather own than rent, shop for the best price and look beyond Walmart. eBay used to be a gold mine for camping supplies, but now many items are more expensive there than on Amazon.

Check out these sources for your camping supply needs:

» **Camping World:** Lots of people grouse about Camping World (www.camping world.com) for a variety of reasons, but we've always liked their large, clean, and reasonably priced camping stores. They're the world's largest supplier of RV parts, and they've got 180 retail/service locations in 46 states. We regularly stop there for our RV-specific needs. Take a look at the one nearest you. They are affiliated with the Good Sam family of companies and services, and a membership card saves you 10 percent at the stores.

» **Army-Navy surplus stores:** Don't overlook your local army-navy surplus store. A surplus store may not be the best place for RV supplies, but if you're a hiker or a hunter who enjoys these activities on your RV vacation, you can find solid stuff at a great price. If you've never been in an army-navy surplus store in your life, check out "The Rise and Fall of the Army Surplus Store" on the Art of Manliness website (www.artofmanliness.com/character/military/rise-fall-army-surplus-store/).

As for the shopping you'll inevitably do on the road and when you arrive at your destination, it's part of the fun of a trip, and budgeting for something that personal is difficult. Of course, it helps if you're honest about your own weaknesses. We like to buy local things the area is known for, and we love finding factory outlet stores for popular companies. It may be a weak argument, but we think we're actually saving money by buying stuff. You'll figure it out based on your own idea of what's a bargain and what makes a great souvenir. The good thing about a large RV — that it can accommodate large souvenirs — also can be a bad thing. That antique flea market bureau may be too big to haul comfortably.

Saving on Attractions and Activities

We list attractions and activities that have admission fees throughout this book. We also recommend free attractions that you can visit without adding to the bottom line. But we can't cover everywhere you may go — just know there are lots of ways to save in the places you choose to visit.

Finding city passes

Most cities have money-saving passes that give you discounts to area museums, landmarks, guided tours, amusement parks, and lots more. **CityPASS** (www.citypass.com) offers different passes for 15 major North American cities; Go City (https://gocity.com/en-us) is a more international company with passes for cities all over the world, at least a dozen of which are in the U.S.

Check tourism sites for any major or medium-size cities you pass through (or close to) and find out whether they offer their own passes. Our hometown of Indianapolis has something called the Indy Attraction Pass, which saves you about 50 percent on some great kid-friendly places, including Conner Prairie living history museum and the famed Indianapolis Children's Museum. You can get a City-PASS for nearby Chicago, and St. Louis has the Family Attractions Card. These passes are usually set up through the local tourist board, and they are very much worth checking out.

Picking up passes for parks

For the national parks and federal recreation sites, the America the Beautiful Pass program offers several money-saving options: an Annual Pass, an Annual or Lifetime Senior Pass, a Military Pass, and an Access Pass for people with disabilities. You can purchase these passes at national parks and recreation sites or on the **USGS Store** website (https://store.usgs.gov/recreational-passes). A special pass specifically for 4th grade students must be purchased in person at a park entrance. Passes are valid at more than 2,000 federal recreation sites operated by the following agencies:

Agency	Its Website
Bureau of Land Management	www.blm.gov
Bureau of Reclamation	www.usbr.gov
U.S. Fish and Wildlife Service	www.fws.gov

Agency	Its Website
USDA Forest Service	www.fs.usda.gov
National Park Service	www.nps.gov
U.S. Army Corps of Engineers	www.usace.army.mil

Loving the local entertainment

Because we like to do our sightseeing during the day and spend evenings in the campground, our entertainment costs are minimal. Many campgrounds offer free movies or live music during summer. But there may be terrific entertainment opportunities such as nearby theaters, music venues, and local fairs that you won't want to miss.

If you're taking the Ozarks and Branson drive covered in Chapter 12, for example, factor in the cost of buying tickets to one or more shows — the highlight of that itinerary. Matinees usually are less expensive than evening shows, although ticket prices in Branson generally aren't as high as those for other major venues nationally. The same money-saving rules apply for a pricey restaurant you may want to eat at — lunch is usually less expensive than dinner.

Testing the Waters: RV Rentals

The biggest expense we haven't addressed in this chapter is the cost of the RV itself. If you know you love the life and want to buy your own rig, you're probably investigating how to select an RV setup that uses your money wisely. But if you don't want to buy yet, and you don't have a cousin willing to loan you their Winnebago, another option is renting.

Interest in RV renting has exploded in the last five years, for everyone from vacationers to tailgaters. When we talk to renters in the RV parks, we meet a whole lot of foreign tourists who've decided to taste a bit of the American dream by renting an RV and seeing the country. But this chapter is about budgeting, so, of course, your question is, what does renting an RV cost?

REMEMBER

The answer to the cost-of-renting question isn't that easy because you find so many variables. Do you want a single-axle Outback trailer for one, or a 42-foot luxury Class A? Industry sites say that $150 a day is about *average* for an RV rental, and that's not a bad figure. We've seen small towable RVs advertised for as little as $99 a day, while a big Class A can go for $500.

Though it's not popular in the newer person-to-person model of RV renting, older companies often charge a mileage fee as well. If the budget is tight, you have to decide what you want and what you're willing to spend, and then cruise the sites looking for the best price you can get at the moment.

Traditional rental companies

A growing number of RV rental companies are scattered across the U.S., but the largest and best-known ones are the following:

>> **Cruise America** rents several sizes of Class C motorhomes and small travel trailers (as long as you own a suitable tow vehicle that's registered in your name). They have 120+ pickup locations in the U.S. and Canada, which makes them sort of the U-Haul of RVs.

  800-671-8042; *www.cruiseamerica.com/.* **Beware:** *Not every type of unit they offer is available nationwide, so read their website carefully or call to talk to an agent directly to get the most up-to-date info on which rigs can be had across the country.*

>> **El Monte RV** rents Class A and C motorhomes. Their Class As are mostly 33-footers with gasoline engines, making them easier to drive, park, and refuel than giant rigs, and their Class Cs are 21–32 feet long.

  888-337-2214; *www.elmonterv.com/.* **Beware:** *Outside of multiple locations throughout California, El Monte has pickup sites only in Reno and Las Vegas, NV; Seattle and Ferndale, WA; Salt Lake City, UT; Denver, CO; Dallas, TX; Chicago, IL; Orlando and Miami, FL; and New York City.*

  Both companies offer one-way trip rates, which are popular with international tourists exploring the U.S. A one-way rental lets you fly into a city, pick up the RV, drive it across the country, and then turn it in at your final destination before flying home. Class Cs predominate, because they're great for newbies, being self-contained, with no need for a tow vehicle, and easier to drive than a bloated Class A.

TIP

If you can be flexible in your route planning and vacation times, you can often get a better deal. Because so many RV renters want to explore the American West or the sunny South, there tends to be a pileup of rental rigs at the most popular destinations. Both companies offer vehicle relocation deals if vacationers are willing to move a unit from those popular vacation spots back east or north. They also offer lower rates if you're willing to deliver a new RV from the factory to their primary locations around the country.

Private RV-sharing rentals

Airbnb changed the face of the hotel and travel business forever by connecting property owners with tourists. It was inevitable that a similar concept would take root in the RV world, especially with the massive number of new RVs hitting the market in recent years. Owners have come to the realization that the worst thing an RV can do is sit unused. And with prices on new RVs being what they are, it makes sense to try to recoup some of their investment by renting out their rigs.

Some of the best-known RV-sharing rental websites include the following:

>> **Outdoorsy** (www.outdoorsy.com) and **RVshare** (https://rvshare.com/): The two largest *peer-to-peer* (person-to-person) RV rental services connect owners with renters. Unlike the traditional RV rental companies that have a limited selection of vehicles, these sites offer every size, type, and shape of trailer or motorhome available. Both companies provide insurance protection, roadside assistance, and online marketing for their rental listings, and they supply all application forms and other paperwork. Because of their similarities, many RV owners list their rigs with both companies.

>> **RVnGO** (www.rvngo.com): This is the newest entry in the online person-to-person RV rental business. While they have a smaller selection than Outdoorsy and RVshare, RVnGO is unusual in that their services are free: Owners aren't charged for listing their RV for rent, and they receive 100 percent of the rental rate charged. Renters aren't charged an extra fee, apart from a 3 percent credit card service charge. The company provides insurance coverage. Owners may also list RVs for sale on the site.

>> **RV Trader** (www.rvtrader.com): Technically, this is a used RV sales website, but they also connect people with RV owners who want to rent out their units.

A great aspect of these services is that you find a much bigger choice of RVs to rent, compared to the traditional rental companies. They don't just offer Class C motorhomes — you find everything from the tiniest teardrop trailers and the snuggest van campers, right up to the biggest motorhomes and fifth-wheels. There are as many packages available as there are types of RVs, with perks like airport pickup of the rig and discount vacation bundling. If you want a trailer, but don't have a beefy enough truck or SUV to tow it with, many owners will also rent you their own tow vehicle.

TIP

Wherever you pick up your rental RV, make sure all the systems and components are functioning *before you leave*. Take as much time as you need and *don't* feel like a fool for taking notes — or better yet making smartphone videos — on how everything functions. If you can't remember how to drain the blackwater tank, you'll be incredibly grateful that you took the time to ask for guidance up front, especially if you're a newbie. As is true with rental cars, check for dents and damage from previous use before leaving the lot, and photograph it with your phone.

Be sure you're given a full set of instruction booklets and emergency phone numbers in case of a breakdown. Having a 24-hour emergency toll-free number to call in case of a problem is best, but in a person-to-person rental situation, have *somebody's* number.

REMEMBER

If you fall in love with your rental vehicle, you may be able to negotiate a purchase price that subtracts your rental fee from the total. Give it a shot. Particularly at the larger companies, rental turnover is high, and they may be motivated to sell. Once you develop a relationship with a particular RV, it's hard to let go. That's why we all have special pet names for our RVs.

Chapter **4**

Eating on the Road

In the itinerary sections of this book, we talk about regional restaurants that would be a shame to miss along the various routes. But one of the biggest appeals of RVing is the freedom it gives you to control what you eat. Whether you love to cook or hate to cook, or you're somewhere in between, you're going to face many of the same issues. After all, eating well when you travel is always a problem. But with RVing, you have a big advantage — your kitchen is always with you. There's no haughty hotel manager to tell you room service ended at 8:00 p.m., especially when you didn't really want an overcooked $40 hamburger and a $7 bottle of water to help choke it down anyway.

In our book *RVs and Campers For Dummies* (Wiley), you can find a chapter with loads of RV packing advice. It contains some hard-won wisdom on RV kitchen organization, and we offer a few highlights here, and then go more in depth on issues of cooking and eating while RVing.

In this chapter, we talk about what you probably want to have available in your RV's kitchen and how to save time and hassles — for example, with disposable dishware for boondocking. We also tell you about strategies for coping with special problems (such as the dearth of RV storage space) as well as having fun with campground cooking.

Setting Up Your Rolling Kitchen

For some people, cooking is fun, but for others, it's one of the chores they're vacationing to get away from. The fact is, lots of people love to cook, and being on the road is just another challenge — a unique place to make white wine salmon and shallots with the fresh herbs they found at the farmers market. But there are lots of RVers who have to cook for a family of five on the road, and s'mores by the campfire is as gourmet as they want to go. So, when you set up your RV kitchen, make it responsive to your needs.

Working in an RV kitchen is a game of utilizing small spaces efficiently — only the biggest, most bloated Class A or fifth-wheel is going to have a kitchen the size of a home kitchen, with residential appliances and vast acreage of counter-tops. Our first RV was a Class B van with a *really* tiny kitchen and a single kitchen drawer. When we moved up to a full-size travel trailer, we thought, "Boy! We'll *really* be spreading out now!" And sure enough, our brand-new 30-foot rig came with *one* kitchen drawer. So, RV kitchens require strategy.

REMEMBER

The trick for effective RV cooking is to allocate your limited space to fit the style of cooking that's right for you. After several years of using our Airstream's built-in oven as a storage cabinet, we finally had the oven taken out; it was fussy and not dependable on temperature (with a tendency to burn stuff). Now, we do great with a built-in convection microwave plus a toaster oven we've attached to our tiny countertop with museum putty.

So, what did we install in the space where our old oven was? Drawers. It's a good thing.

TIP

One of the cleverest cooking-on-the-road hacks we've ever seen came from a couple we met who loved to cook and didn't much care for restaurant food. They wanted to eat their own creations. But, on a camping weekend, they wanted to camp, not cook. Solution? Through the week they made a bit extra every time they cooked, then divided it up into meals in sealed, reusable plastic trays, and froze them. When they camped, they tucked these trays in the RV freezer, and all they had to do after a long day of hiking or fishing was pop them in the microwave, and *voilà!* They're like the Swanson TV Dinners of the 1950s, only delicious. Segmented meal containers with covers are available online or at cooking and home stores, or of course, you can salvage them from TV dinners. They offer a way to help you eat well, and easily, on the road.

COOKING ON THE GO?

RVers with motorhomes have an advantage over those who haul trailers: Their kitchen can always be open. It's never safe to get up and wander around in a moving motorhome — that's why manufacturers put seat belts on their couches and easy chairs. You don't want to become a hurtling, high-speed projectile if the driver has to jam on the brakes! But the truth is, all sorts of little things can be done in a motorhome on the move. And they're great for a quick pit stop to make a bowl of SpaghettiOs, with your ability to fire up the onboard generator and have power.

Still, terrific as motorhomes are, there can be a major fly in the proverbial ointment that makes a rest-stop kitchen raid in a motorhome tougher; slideouts. Too many designers fail to consider access to RV kitchens and bathrooms in relation to slides. In many large RVs, the dinette smashes right up to the kitchen counters when the slides are closed. If an evil designer arranged it so the refrigerator door or the bathroom is blocked by a closed slide, it can be more than a little annoying — who wants to open five slides for a quick stop?

Obviously, you can pull off the road for a pit stop with a trailer and do most of the same things, but it's just not quite as convenient as a motorhome that gets power at the flip of a switch. For example, remember that unless you have a 2,000-watt generator, you're running on your batteries, and you won't be able to power up the microwave. Even a toaster or an electric teakettle can be problematic; anything that heats things up draws lots of power.

Warning: *Never turn on a propane range-top burner or oven while driving!* Don't try cooking on the move. We witnessed a spectacular motorhome fire on a trip through Billings, Montana, started by a passenger using an oven at 70 mph.

Getting Ready to Roll

The first consideration you need to keep in mind is that the interior of an RV rocks — literally. The world in the back of a moving RV can be like a rolling earthquake hitting about an 8 on the Richter scale. That means cute little decorative crockery pots with dried flower arrangements are going to go sailing off the countertop, along with anything else you haven't taken steps to permanently or temporarily mount.

TIP

One of the very first items to order from Amazon is a miracle substance known as *museum putty*, which was developed to gently anchor small antiques and protect them from the murderous brush of a stray sleeve. It's sold under names such as *Quakehold!*, *Fun-Tak*, or *Sticky Putty*. You can do all the countertop and tabletop decorating you like, as long as you hold everything down with a wad or two of this removable, reusable putty.

Keeping it simple

You probably don't need five spatulas, eight mixing spoons, or a full set of carving knives in an RV. Ditto for colanders, mixing bowls, cookie sheets, or roasting pans. Or even an electric can opener. Take only what you need.

Robbing your home kitchen and plopping the stuff in your RV isn't a great idea, especially if you store your rig somewhere besides your home driveway. If the kitchen tools get left in the RV, they're not at home when you need them. And lots of kitchen items are just too big and clunky for an RV. When we tried to take a selection of our own saucepans from home, it just didn't work — we piled them into an empty space under the bed out of exasperation.

Here are the kitchen basics you should consider taking along with you:

>> **Dishes:** After falling out of public favor for several decades, *Melmac* (also called *Plaskon* or *melamine*) dishes have made a roaring comeback, and they're great in an RV. You may have encountered these dishes back in your elementary school cafeteria or in a military mess line. Cast from a special kind of dense plastic, they're durable and almost unbreakable (almost), and they come in a variety of colors, styles, and designs — including a growing number of fun RV-themed patterns.

WARNING

Melamine dishes *cannot* be used for cooking in a microwave oven: They will shatter! Check the underside of all plates or dishes and be sure they say they're microwave safe before hitting the start button. Or stick with glass, paper plates, or plastic that's safe for cooking.

>> **Disposable dinnerware:** This may rankle if you're concerned about sustainability of natural resources, but if you're boondocking, paper plates, bowls, and cups are a real necessity in an RV. Boondocking requires serious stinginess when it comes to water usage, and the job of doing the dishes is a lot simpler when you can just burn most of them in the campfire. We stick with the heavier-duty types made by Chinet, or Kroger's Simple Truth cellulose fiber/bamboo versions, because they are uncoated and will completely burn up. They're more expensive but strong enough for almost anything you serve.

» **Pots and pans:** If you're going to do any stovetop cooking at all, get a set of nesting pots and pans from Magma (`https://magmaproducts.com/`). They stack inside each other like a set of Russian nesting dolls. A one-square-foot section of precious cabinet space holds three saucepans, a frying pan, and a decent Dutch oven. One lid fits them all, as do the two removable handles you can stow in a drawer, which eliminates a great deal of cabinet clutter and aggravation. The Magma pans come in several finishes, with either nonstick or stainless steel interiors.

When you pack your nesting pans, be sure to place two full-size paper towel sheets or a cushioned shelf pan liner between each pan to prevent road jiggling from scratching them.

» **Storage containers:** Pack some plastic microwave-safe food storage containers of varying sizes (look for the kind that nest inside each other to help save cabinet space). With both cooking and storage functions, they do double duty. Because RV refrigerators are usually smaller than your home fridge, you may find yourself relying on plastic zipper-lock bags. They lie much flatter and can be stuffed into odd spaces.

To avoid chaos, we keep some plastic storage tubs at home to store RV things — it makes life easier when you can just haul out the bins and put them on board the RV, instead of confusing them with your home kitchen things and trying to reinvent the wheel on every trip.

» **Washtubs:** Bring one or two collapsible silicone tubs for washing or rinsing dishes and pans, handwashing dirty clothes, or soaking the mud off the dog's feet. Try to find one that will accommodate a small dish rack laid on top so you can wash dishes in the sink and dry them over the washtub. A collapsible silicone 1- or 2-gallon bucket is also helpful, in case you need to carry water by hand.

» **Knives, tools, and kitchen fiddlyboos:** Keep these kitchen items to a minimum. (**Note:** Our RV, like many, has a single kitchen drawer.) Try to stick to items you really use; a can opener, a meat thermometer, a couple good carving knives, one plastic and one metal spatula, a pair of tongs, and kitchen scissors. Some bag clips are helpful, but large rubber bands are also useful for keeping snack bags closed. Pick up a set of cheap plastic-handled steak knives for steak dinner nights. Also grab a silicone bottle-and-jar-lid-twister-opener (we call it our *cap snaffler,* but you may have a different pet name).

» **Outdoor cooking tools:** If you're going to barbecue on a grill or cook over a campfire, be sure to have a set of long metal tongs, a metal spatula, plus a heavy iron fire poker to rearrange burning logs. For Dutch oven baking, you need an inexpensive charcoal chimney starter to heat your coals quickly and efficiently. If hot dogs are your thing, grab a couple of toasting forks for the fire;

they also come in handy for marshmallows and such. A pair of heavy-duty oven mitts or fireproof leather gloves are a necessity.

>> **Paper towel holder:** It seems so trivial to mention this one dumb item, but most of us use paper towels on the road more than at home, and they've become too expensive to waste. Yet, RV manufacturers almost never install a holder in their rigs at the factory. Hunt down a horizontal one that screws to the underside of a cabinet to save precious counter space. As you drive, road jiggling will unspool a dozen feet of paper towels on a freewheeling rack, so either put a rubber band around the roll, or buy a spring-loaded holder like Kamenstein's Perfect Tear models from Walmart or Amazon.

Taking only the appliances you use

Most RVs these days come with at least a microwave oven and a 2- or 3-burner propane cooktop. But many RVers just can't do without various countertop appliances — popular ones are toaster ovens, coffee makers, air fryers, and Instant Pots. Take what you know you will *really* use on the road, as long as you have the room. But remember, an appliance needs to be securely stowed in a cabinet or under-seat compartment each time you move the RV — unless you anchor it to your countertop. Otherwise, you may find it in the middle of the floor when you stop for the night.

Other popular appliance choices include

>> **Electric water kettle (or hot pot):** For boiling water, we're never without our electric water kettle, which is great for coffee, tea, and hot chocolate. A hot pot boils five times faster than an open pot on your propane cooktop, and it uses the campground's electricity instead of your limited (and expensive) propane supply.

>> **Countertop ice maker:** When we started RVing, we couldn't believe how many people travel with these. No self-respecting margarita lover should be without one, and they're cheaper than you'd imagine. Pour a quart of water in the top, and a few minutes later you've got ice. RV fridges almost never have an ice maker built in, and refillable ice trays are slow to freeze, leaving you to run out for bagged ice.

>> **Countertop oven:** Multiuse appliances help you make the best use of your space. Toaster ovens can toast, bake, and broil, and may come with a convection or air fryer option that usually works better and more efficiently than the propane ranges installed in many RVs.

PUTTING ON THE COFFEE

Even if they can't squeeze through the drive-thru at Starbucks or Dunkin' in their RV, coffee lovers want their favorite coffee, and we get it. Fortunately, gone are the days when coffee on a camping trip meant a fistful of grounds dumped into a rusty steel pot and stewed over the campfire all day long for that authentic, twice-baked-coffee flavor.

Single-serve K-Cup brewers have conquered the at-home coffee-making market in recent years, with loads of name-brand coffee shop varieties, and the size and convenience of a Keurig K-Mini unit is tough to beat. If you're in a campground with electricity, it's the perfect solution, and the size and weight makes it easy to mount on the countertop or stow away until needed.

Even if you're boondocking, you still have options:

- If you can boil water, you can make decent coffee. Many RV websites recommend using a French press to make coffee with your boiled water, and they work well, though they've gotten a bit pricier than in days gone by.

- We love single-serve coffee bags, like tea bags, but with a smaller variety of exotic flavors. Stalwart legacy brands such as Maxwell House and Folgers are most commonly found in supermarkets, but Mondo, Steeped Coffee, Lardera, Bean & Bean and a few other companies are available on Amazon. You also find brands such as Copper Cow and Ippuku that are Asian-style pour over bags (a bit more complex bag that drapes over the sides of your cup). The appeal is that they *don't* taste like the old freeze-dried instant coffee crystals the Army used to pack in K-rations. You get brewed flavor that's incredibly convenient and takes up a fraction of the space a couple dozen K-Cups do. (And believe it or not, we vote for old school Maxwell House as having the best fresh-roasted taste.)

RV doodads and helpers

Shopping for your RV is like shopping for your home — it never really stops. You never know when you'll stumble across the perfect-sized trash can for your RV's tiny bathroom, and you don't want to get it home only to find it's a mere ½ inch too wide to fit.

TIP

Pick up a small, inexpensive notebook or leatherette diary, and record every possible measurement in your RV you can think of. Take the time to jot down all the oddball measurements, including the height and depth of various drawers, closets, cabinets, and wall spaces. Then, tuck the little book in your purse or glove compartment, someplace where it's always with you. And remember to congratulate yourself on your own cleverness.

We recommend that you gather these items for help with organized storage:

>> **Command® strips:** RVers love wall hooks for the convenience and added storage, but you don't usually have to go drilling on your walls. After you start building your RV spaces, you may become an evangelist for easily removable stick-up products such as the 3M Command products. We love them so much in the RV that we use them all over our house, too. And the products aren't just hooks — you can use Command strips to anchor almost anything to an RV wall. We found an adorable turquoise thingamabob for office organization and used sticky strips to mount it on the wall near our stove. We use it to store big and tall cooking tools such as spatulas and mixing spoons that don't easily fit in RV drawers.

>> **Drawer and cabinet organizers:** Hunting for and collecting the right organizers for your cabinets takes time. At The Container Store, IKEA, or a variety of home stores, these little containers go by all sorts of names: office or kitchen drawer organizers, silverware trays or caddies, but almost never RV accessories. These organizers are open rectangular trays, with sides from one to four inches tall, that anchor your bottles (everything from dish soap to bug spray) when you hit the road. They also provide a bit of a safety factor when a bottle springs a seam leak from temperature fluctuations, age, or just being jostled around. Even stuff made for an office can be great in an RV kitchen, so check the office supply stores. For example, we use magazine holders from Staples (see Figure 4-1) to handily store aluminum foil, boxes of zipper-lock bags, and trash bag rolls.

Photograph courtesy of Christopher Hodapp

FIGURE 4-1: Tray caddies stabilize your bottles and help prevent messes from leaks.

Shopping for Food

Weekenders may be able to escape this chore to a great degree, but the fact is, sooner or later you must go to the grocery during your trip. And shopping for food on the road can be annoying. First, you need to park your RV in the farthest reaches of the lot. Second, you must make certain that you don't buy a bunch of stuff you don't have room for. (We promise, this skill will come.) But third, you need to find a grocery store in a strange town where you don't know the chains.

Where did my grocery store go?

People get comfortable with their local grocery store and tend to look for it on the road, which can be tough once you leave your own state. If you live in an area with a quality regional supermarket chain and you haven't traveled much, you may not have ever realized that your favorite grocery doesn't exist everywhere. And every day brings news that another regional chain has been swallowed up in a merger or takeover.

As you cross the U.S., it's not always easy to recognize the names of the bigger, better supermarkets in a given area. Here's a partial list of independent regional store chains (keep reading, because this gets more complicated):

U.S. Region	Regional Store Chains
Northeast	Market Basket; Price Chopper; Price Rite; ShopRite; Tops; Weis Markets; Wegmans
South	Brookshire's and H-E-B (Texas); Food City; Harps Food Stores; Harvey's; Ingles; Piggly Wiggly; Publix; Winn-Dixie
Midwest	Fareway; Hy-Vee; Meijer; Schnucks; Giant Eagle; Family Fare; Family Fresh Market; Martin's; No Frills Supermarkets
West	Bel-Air Markets; Gelson's; Lucky; Raley's; Save Mart; Smart & Final; WinCo

With runaway inflation and persistent post–pandemic shortages, more and more shoppers turned to their store's private brands, and now depend on them, often preferring them. Our local grocery is a Kroger, and we've come to rely on many of their Private Selection products. When we began to see those same items, in the same packaging, at strange, faraway grocery stores on the road, we figured out that Kroger has a much longer reach than we thought.

NAVIGATING THROUGH FOOD DESERTS

Rural America is undergoing a serious economic crisis on many fronts, and one result is what's known as *food deserts,* huge areas of the country that no longer have nearby grocery stores. For many small-towners, a Walmart 30 or more miles away is their regular grocery, and monthly trips are a big deal. It's the 21st-century version of hitching up the wagon and heading for the trading post on the other side of the mountain. Apart from that, the closest they may get to fresh fruit is a banana and a fruit cup at a truck stop out on the interstate.

Bad economic times pull little groceries under, and the giant chains don't relish the expense of opening big, shiny new stores in rural areas. It's absurd that Google will claim an area has a grocery store when what it really has is a dollar store, which is most certainly not the same thing. Dollar stores (principally Dollar General and Dollar Tree) prey on poverty — that's their business model. In most of them you won't find any fresh produce, meat, poultry, dairy, or other healthy food options. They offer cheap, easily stored cereals and snack foods, Ramen noodle packs, canned goods, pop, and miscellaneous junk food items.

Quite often, in a rural area, a Walmart came in, and the independent mom-and-pop markets folded. Then, starting in 2016, the Walmarts began to close — 269 that year alone, including a hundred smaller "express" groceries that served rural towns. Walmart continues to close "underperforming" locations. At that point, the dollar stores arrived, often in a bundle, leaving absolutely no incentive for another independent or regional chain grocery store to open.

In the 1980s, we had to travel every year between L.A. and the Midwest. Thirty years later, when we began RVing over the same territory, one of the biggest changes we noticed was the proliferation of huge yellow Dollar General signs everywhere, and the death of other grocery options.

Understanding all this can make grocery shopping a bit easier to prepare for. Forewarned is forearmed. For one thing, if you see a grocery store in Tucumcari and there's no other town for miles, stop and buy any staples you need right then and there. Don't wait and hope for better — you may not find it.

Recognizing national chains and their aliases

Kroger is the biggest of all the national supermarket companies, but like other major grocery conglomerates, they continue to operate under the names of regional chains they bought. So, here's a helpful list (by no means exhaustive) of the names that Kroger and a few other giant chains masquerade under when they're playing out of town:

» **Kroger** has more than 2,800 supermarkets nationwide. In addition to their own branded stores, Kroger operates the following regional supermarkets: In the Western states, Smith's and City Market are owned by Kroger, as is Ralphs in California. In the Midwest, Kroger is Dillons, Roundy's, Ruler Foods, Baker's, and JayC. In the Northwest, they own the Fred Meyer chain of superstores (not to be confused with the Meijer superstore chain in the Midwest), as well as Quality Food Centers. Kroger also owns Food 4 Less, Fry's Food and Drug, Harris Teeter, King Soopers, and Pay Less.

» **Albertsons** and **Safeway** merged in 2015 and now operate more than 2,200 supermarkets across the U.S. Safeway and Albertsons stores are principally west of the Mississippi, in the far Northeast, as well as in Virginia. The many Signature products made for Safeway are also available at Albertsons. Stores also include Acme, Carrs, Haggen, Market Street, Jewel-Osco, Pavilions, Randalls, Shaw's, Star Market, Tom Thumb, United, and Vons. *Note:* At the time of this writing, Kroger announced merger plans with Albertsons. If approved by federal regulators, this will become a 5,000-store giant, which has brought strong criticism of the monopoly it will create.

» **Ahold Delhaize** is a huge international retailing corporation based in Holland with stores all over the world, including more than 2,000 in the U.S. Their American stores include Food Lion, Giant Supermarkets, Giant Food, Hannaford, and Stop & Shop. They also own the Peapod online grocery delivery service.

Here are some large national chains that never change their identity:

» More than 2,000 **Aldi** discount grocery stores are in 36 states currently, and the German parent company wants to expand to 2,500 by 2023.

» Aldi also owns the 557 **Trader Joe's** markets, and neither one of these brands hide as anything else.

» **Walmart Neighborhood Market** is that corporation's smaller standalone grocery store (as opposed to their giant superstores — see the next section), and there are 682 of these around the country.

Big-box hypermarket stores

Following in the footsteps of Meijer in the Midwest and the Carrefour chain in France, Walmart embraced the *hypermarket* concept of a huge, one-stop department store containing an equally huge grocery store. By the 1980s, Walmart was the big guy on the block in the big box business, the most profitable retailer in America. Convenience is a big draw — you can buy a hammer and a package of underwear along with milk and bananas if you need them. Plenty of shoppers love the hypermarket concept (or at least, they love the prices), and the three major operators today are:

>> **Walmart:** Worldwide, Walmart operates more than 10,000 stores and clubs, and the world relies on them for cheap prices on every kind of household item imaginable, plus groceries and pharmaceuticals. We're putting Wally World at the top of the list, out of alphabetical order, because everybody knows about these stores, and RVers often seek them out across the country.

Besides groceries and household items, Walmart has an aisle dedicated to RV products like hoses, chemicals, trailer hitch parts, and lots more. Plus, they often permit free overnight parking for RVers needing a spot in which to boondock overnight (fondly called *Wallydocking*).

>> **Meijer:** This Michigan-based chain of 276 stores in the Midwest was the first to open a hypermarket-type store in the U.S. (in 1962), and they don't operate under any other names. However, they've recently expanded with a smaller store called Fresh Thyme Market, which is becoming increasingly popular for bulk foods, specialty items, and organic choices.

>> **Target:** It's tough to generalize about Target. Initially, Target was a chic alternative to Walmart, with suburban stores getting ever-larger, including the Super Targets of the 1990s. Corporate problems brought changes along with the new millennium. Now, Target has diversified its store sizes, moving into urban markets with small-format stores such as CityTarget and TargetExpress. If you shop Target regularly, you get to know the store sizes.

Out of 1,900 stores, only 239 are Super Targets, which try to compete with Walmart in the hypermarket world and include a full grocery and pharmacy. Standard Target stores typically don't sell perishable foods. The company also has a store format called PFresh, which is a smaller grocery within a general merchandise store, but not as huge as the Super Targets. Most CityTargets — usually less than half the size of a Super Target — are small and lie in crowded downtown locations. Smallest of all, TargetExpress locations (often around college campuses and dense urban areas) are designed for customers who rely on public transportation and only buy food and merchandise an armload at a time. Target got out of the prescription medicine business in 2015 and turned their in-store pharmacies over to CVS.

REMEMBER

You find different Target stores for different customers. And you could wish for better signage; when RVers see that red bullseye (and nothing else), they may find themselves fighting to find a parking space in a strange town while making their way to a Target that doesn't at all meet their needs.

Membership warehouse chains

Loads of RVers swear by the giant membership warehouses that charge customers an annual fee to shop their stores. In addition to groceries and other home supplies, they often offer discounted gasoline, vacation packages, car rentals, and special discount-ordering programs on new automobiles and appliances. Most specialize in big, family-size packages of groceries, meat, and frozen foods, which aren't always ideal for the tight limitations of an RV kitchen or refrigerator. But if you're stocking up for a long road trip and have enough storage room, it's tough to beat their prices. The main players are

» **BJ's Wholesale Club,** which operates 216 warehouses in 17 states, mainly in the Northeast.

» **Costco,** the third-largest retail chain in the world. It's an American-owned company. (Don't confuse it with Cosco, a Chinese merchandise shipping company.) Costco operates 578 warehouses in the U.S., 107 in Canada, and 40 in Mexico.

» **Sam's Club** (owned by Walmart) has the most membership warehouses in the U.S., with 600 locations nationwide. The only states *without* a Sam's are Alaska, Massachusetts, Oregon, Rhode Island, Vermont, and Washington. The District of Columbia doesn't have one either.

Farmers markets

Farmers markets are a great resource for RVers. They're not something you can count on, like a grocery store, but the serendipity of what you find is fun. It's not just corn and tomatoes and potatoes. You may find locally grown herbs, eggs, honey, baked goods, cheese, jams and jellies, flowers and plants, organic beauty products, fresh-cut meats and fowl — just about anything you can think of that's been locally grown or made.

Most towns of any size have a regular farmers market — just google for the time and place. In warm states, you can find farmers markets all year round. In the Midwest and Northeast, it's a summer and early autumn tradition. Some regular farmers markets have gotten so big that they're nearly like a fair, but you must keep a sharp eye while you're on the road. In rural areas during harvest times, you can find farmers, or a small group of them, at roadside tables selling produce picked that morning. Nothing's better.

MANAGING YOUR PRESCRIPTION MEDICATIONS

So many people do their grocery and pharmacy shopping in one location, we decided to mention drugstores in this chapter. Half of all Americans take at least one prescription medicine every 30 days. If that means you, talk to your doctor and pharmacist about them *before you leave town,* because the road is a lousy place to try to handle Rx problems.

Medicine refills on the road are a persistent problem for RVers, especially since new and increasingly oppressive prescription laws have made it tougher to get a refill at an out-of-state pharmacy. Giant chains like CVS, Rite Aid, Walgreens, and Walmart blanket the country, but they may be hundreds of miles away in many areas. Even if one is close by, they may not be able to help you. Most of the time, a druggist or pharmacy tech only sees the computer's approval or refusal of your prescription; they have no way of knowing whether you've been denied by local, state, or federal regulations, your doctor's orders, Medicare, or your insurance company.

Take note of these important considerations for your prescriptions:

- **Take care with controlled substances.** U.S. doctors can usually write a 90-day prescription for most common drugs, and Canadian docs can often prescribe a 6-month supply (which is great for Canadian snowbirds wintering in Arizona and Florida). However, anything labeled a *Schedule 2 drug* or *controlled substance* (and lots of things are) is especially problematic. Such drugs are not just opiates, tranquilizers, or other painkillers — even blood thinners (such as Warfarin), erectile dysfunction meds (for example, Viagra), and some antibiotics fall into this category. These are usually restricted to 30-day supplies, and believe it or not, you may have to return home once a month just to get them — national pharmacy chains can't refill them across state lines.

- **Keep medical information accessible.** If you're in a serious accident with no way to communicate for yourself and no one to be your responsible advocate, EMS teams are trained to go to your smartphone first when trying to properly care for you. Enter your medical details in the built-in Health app (on iPhones) or download a medical ID app (on Androids). Be sure you list all your meds, allergies, and conditions like diabetes or high blood pressure, along with all doctors' names and contact information.

Cooking Adventurously

The image of kids roasting hot dogs or making gooey s'mores on sticks over an open fire is common shorthand for "outdoor fun." Lots of rigs, especially fifth-wheels, have a secondary outdoor kitchen that makes campout cooking easy. But on an RV trip, you may want to give some old-style campfire cooking a try. The simplest food that's been cooked over your own campfire has a special taste, and that's a joy not to be missed.

A firepit at your campsite often has a flip-down grate attached, but you can't really count on that. You can buy a portable metal grate to set over the top of any campfire. We recommend the sort that straddles the fire on stable metal legs. We've had trouble with the model that extends from a single steel stake pounded into the ground beside the fire because they can wilt under the weight of an iron skillet. In addition to the grate, get an inexpensive Lodge fry pan at Cabela's or Walmart or Camping World, and you're in business. Fry some bacon or hamburgers for grease; then scramble some eggs. Our first-time recipe that turned out best was sausage gravy. It's incredibly easy — just stir a little flour and milk into the sausage grease. You can find campfire recipes all over YouTube.

Cast-iron cooking

Cast-iron pots and pans are almost indestructible, and they're the most durable vessels for cooking over a campfire — that cheap set of copper-painted nonstick As Seen On TV pans just wasn't designed for it. You can get a fairly inexpensive cast-iron frying pan and a metal spatula at Cabela's, Bass Pro Shops, Walmart, or Camping World. The best iron cookware is made in Tennessee by Lodge, but even though it's not that expensive, you can find lots of even cheaper alternatives. True lovers of cast-iron cooking gather around the campfire and tell wistful tales of heirloom pans passed down from their 19th-century pioneer relatives.

Another type of campfire cooking uses a cast-iron *Dutch oven* (a heavy-duty pot with a tight-fitting lid), hanging on a tripod over your fire, or literally set down into the campfire coals. We use a Lodge camp Dutch oven with short tripod legs and a rimmed lid. You can even bake inside it, using heated charcoal briquettes.

Baking inside the Dutch oven is a method that was taught to rangers and scouts for a century. Heat up some charcoal, place your food inside the Dutch oven, and cover it with the lid. Then use tongs to place a set number of hot briquettes beneath and on top of the Dutch oven. The number on your lid (which indicates the width of your Dutch oven in inches) is your guide for how many briquettes to use, and doubling that number is the classic formula. For example, use 24 briquettes for a 12-inch Dutch oven by placing two-thirds of them (16 briquettes) on the lid and one-third (8 briquettes) under the bottom. Figure 4-2 illustrates this cooking method.

Hussman/Shutterstock.com

FIGURE 4-2: Cooking with briquettes in a Dutch oven.

You can cook everything from biscuits and dump cake to chili, stew, or whatever you please. This cooking method is a lot of fun, and kids in particular will come away with a sense of accomplishment. If you've never done this, drop into YouTube; you may be overwhelmed by the volume of Dutch oven camp recipes, with great videos. Also, there's a solid informational website, www.campfiresand castiron.com, that has recipes, and tips on cast-iron care when RVing.

TIP

For the sheer fun of it, we highly recommend a book called *Camp Cooking: 100 Years*, published by the National Museum of Forest Service History. It's an inexpensive spiral-bound time machine, going back to the century from 1905 to 2005, with recipes and cooking methods developed by the U.S. Forest Service. In the book, you find great photos and stories of the forest rangers and fire lookouts, all the dedicated men and women of the service. But apart from nostalgia, the book contains simple how-to instructions for setting up your camp kitchen, and a lot of fantastic recipes, from the more exotic elk stew and fried rattlesnake, to the bedrocks of camp cooking such as chili, jalapeño scrambled eggs, and hearty Dutch oven fried potatoes.

Grilling and chilling

Cooking over a campfire is lots of fun, but without question, the method of camp cooking you see in RV parks more than any other is outdoor grilling. Barbecue grilling is family- and group-oriented fun, and it keeps the cook outside, at the center of the socializing. Seven out of ten American households have an "outdoor cooking device," so most people already know how to grill — most, but not all. People who don't grill at home are often reluctant to take their learning curve on the road. We respectfully disagree with this position. When RVing, you're in a new situation, you're relaxed and having fun, so it's a great time to master something new.

Using a portable grill

It's easy to haul a portable grill along with you — your only limitation is size. If you've got a toy hauler trailer and want to grill up dinner for 12, you can roll your giant gourmet backyard grill on board and you're in business. But the rest of us with limited storage space look for one of the many small portable grills on the market that we can tuck away until needed.

You don't need to jump off the high dive and spend hundreds of dollars on a mini Big Green Egg or a Weber travel grill. If you've never grilled on the road and don't know whether you'd like doing so, pick up an inexpensive portable grill at Walmart — they come in charcoal (under $20) and propane gas (under $35) models — and practice with a pound of hamburger or a pack of hot dogs.

Grills use different types of cooking fuels, with different pros and cons:

>> **Charcoal:** Charcoal briquettes are ubiquitous — you can find them in supermarkets, truck stops, big-box stores, and hardware stores. Some come mixed with wood chips like hickory or mesquite to add more flavor to the smoke. Self-lighting briquettes (like Kingsford's Match Light) infused with lighter fluid are handy and easier to fully ignite, but be aware that charcoal has a very narrow window of perfect cooking time, after the coals turn ashen and dull red.

>> **Propane gas:** Gas grills come in a wide range of sizes and propane delivery systems. Truly portable tabletop grills usually use little green disposable 1-pound propane tanks, while larger residential backyard grills usually use refillable 20-pound tanks. You can find the small tanks at truck stops, camping stores, and hardware stores. You can refill the bigger tanks at a propane dealer (such as U-Haul) or exchange your empty tank for a refurbished, refilled one. You can find propane tank exchange racks at truck stops, hardware stores, and

convenience stores. Another option is to use a long extension hose run from your RV's propane tank to the grill. (**Note:** Some RVs come with an external propane port for this kind of application.)

>> **Electricity:** Purists scream that it's heresy to barbecue over an electric heating coil, but loads of apartment dwellers who aren't allowed to have smoky outdoor charcoal grills have done this for years. Outdoor electric grills are especially popular in California, where environmental regulations have mostly forbidden outdoor charcoal cooking statewide. As long as you have full hookups at your campsite or a generator, go for it.

>> **Wood pellets:** Special grills burn hardwood pellets, which provide a slower cooking method and much smokier flavor than a standard gas or charcoal grill. These grills aren't well-suited to cooking in the wild because they can be quite large, and many require both gas and electricity to work properly. You dump the pellets into a barrel-shaped hopper on the side, and an electric motor feeds them into the flame at a controlled rate while a fan circulates the heat. This operation is essentially an outdoor convection oven.

After the grill reaches the right temperature, plop on the meat, close the cover, and wait patiently as your food slowly roasts. Grills like the singular-looking Big Green Egg fall into this category, and they do make a small portable version that's great for camping, though it's a bit heavy. But this is also a very expensive option that's probably reserved for smoking and grilling fanatics.

Practicing safe grilling

WARNING

Always, *always* be aware that campgrounds forbid using a grill on top of their wooden or plastic picnic tables because of the possibility of setting them ablaze. Use a *fire pad* (fire-resistant mat) underneath the grill (buy them on Amazon or at a camp store), use your own portable metal camp table, place the grill on the ground, or consider using the community grill you find in many parks and campgrounds.

Most modern RVs come from the factory with at least a small *A+B+C fire extinguisher* (suitable for wood, cloth and paper, liquid and gas, and electrical fires) on board. Anytime you're cooking in or around your rig, be sure your fire extinguisher is close by. Also, keep a cup of water handy for dousing flare-ups.

Grilling isn't difficult, but it does take practice to avoid undercooking your $18 steak or burning it up in an uncontrolled grease fire. If you're nervous about getting your steaks or burgers right when cooking on the grill for the first time, the solution is simple and cheap: We're never without our pocket-size, flip-out Taylor digital meat thermometer, which has performed like a trouper for years and cost less than $15.

TIP

Use an inexpensive digital meat thermometer instead of your instincts, so you can easily check the temperature on a piece of cooked meat and know it's fine. Before you start grilling your dinner, check Google to find out the sweet spot of doneness for what you're grilling — probably between 145 degrees F and 165 degrees F — and keep testing for that spot. Checking for doneness with the thermometer takes mere seconds — we even use ours on meat as small as stir-fry pieces. Always slightly undercook meat, because it continues cooking slowly for another 10 minutes after you remove it from the grill.

On the road again, and again, and again

A word now about the RVers who spend all day, every day, on the road, eating up the miles and desperately trying to reach a location by a certain date. Even if you're planning on two weeks in the ritziest campsite in a Palm Beach RV resort, the fact is, you may be working hard to get there faster. You may find yourself in a place where it's difficult to locate a restaurant, a grocery store, or anything apart from a convenience store filled with junk food. And you'll probably arrive at your campsite on plenty of evenings tired, hungry, and perhaps with limited options.

Some people (us included) love nothing more than RV trips that wander, going where you please, without definite plans, letting the road decide. But even the most carefully planned RV trip has little hurdles that make you deal with the unexpected. For years we've made it a point to always have five meals in the cabinets of our RV, and it's a good idea. So, when supplies run low or you're camping far from a grocery, replenishing your food stock is important.

Staying stocked for five meals really isn't difficult. Based on your own tastes, make sure you have a supply of canned goods on hand (probably not enough for the coming zombie apocalypse, but a reasonable supply). Even if you don't whip up a gourmet meal every night, you can still feed yourself with canned soup or stew. And when you're exhausted, hungry, and miles from nowhere, that's what counts.

Table 4-1 outlines how we stock our RV pantry for easy meals and convenient storage.

TABLE 4-1   Must-Have Food Stock

Category	What to Stock	Its Ease and Convenience
Canned goods	Chili, soups, baked beans, tuna, beef stew, or roast beef hash	Just heat and eat, or open the can and dig in.
Nonperishable perishables	Canned or powdered milk	For use in your coffee or a recipe, keep easy-to-store milk on board instead of dealing with space-hogging milk jugs.
Side dishes	Chicken or turkey gravy, instant mashed potatoes, rice, and a box of instant stuffing	These give you a full meal in case you find a place along the road selling rotisserie chickens.
Packaged pantry staples	Pasta and your favorite pasta sauce	Boil the pasta, warm the sauce in the microwave, and you've got dinner in ten minutes.
Refrigerator items	Eggs, microwave bacon, cheese, and lunchmeat	After a long day of white-line fever, breakfast food for dinner is a welcome change of pace. Or just make a simple sandwich. A microwave poached egg on toasted English muffin is great.

We highly recommend a vacuum food storage system like the FoodSaver lineup of products. A few weeks before we leave home, we hunt down coupon deals and specials on beef, pork, and chicken parts, cut them into individual serving sizes, vacuum seal each portion, and freeze the packets. They take up remarkably little room in the RV's freezer when packed this way, and one major meat purchase often lasts long enough to get us from coast to coast.

TIP

If you love to cook, we hate to sentence you to canned chili. We've found several imaginative online cooking sites that have yielded easy and delicious recipes, including "49 Recipes with Canned Goods" (www.bestrecipes.com. au/entertaining/galleries/best-canned-food-camping-recipes/fycqs5kt). They're downright elegant.

TIP

If we know we're going to arrive near sunset in an RV park far from a town, we often stop a little early for dinner and eat before we get to the campground. Especially when moving through the western states, RVers are quick to discover that casinos may be their best bet for services, especially far from a major town. Many casinos have overnight campgrounds to serve their customers. But for tired RVers who are on the move, a casino can be a great place to get a quick meal, even late into the evening. Many casinos have elaborate all-you-can-eat buffets at fairly reasonable prices. It's almost a tradition. And we've never heard of anyone being turned away from the buffet because they were too smart to play the slots. Just pay them and eat; they don't care.

Food spoilage and contamination

Food spoilage may become an issue when you're camping. Your RV refrigerator can let you down by experiencing a rise in temperature while you're driving; it's a situation you need to stay on top of. Hang an appliance thermometer inside both the refrigerator and the freezer, and check them after two or three hours of driving.

REMEMBER

The FDA recommends 40 degrees F or below for proper perishable food storage, but that can push the limits of your fridge's abilities on a hot day on the road, especially in a trailer without the air-conditioning running.

Campers have a tendency to keep food past its use-by date because getting to a store can be problematic. You need to routinely check your food's expiration dates — even canned goods and dried fruit won't store till the crack of doom. So stay date-aware: After three days, you need to throw out leftovers. We like to mark the storage bag with a Sharpie, noting the original date of the meal's preparation.

WARNING

Is it safe? All experts agree that you can let your eyes and your nose be the judge whenever you're in doubt about whether food is still edible. If food is discolored or has picked up a dicey smell, toss it out. People on the road who think they've caught the flu have quite often, in reality, got a case of mild food poisoning.

And remember, you aren't the only one who likes your food. Pests attracted by food can appear in any home, but you're more susceptible to them in an RV. Gnats and fruit flies often hitch a ride in your RV and quickly make a new home on and around your fruits and vegetables. Stink bugs are now all over the U.S. after being imported from Asia in cargo containers two decades ago.

Consider using these practices to help keep food fresh and safe from pests:

>> **Watch for food on the loose.** Keep a lookout for stray potatoes or onions that roll under furniture or into the back of a cabinet, and corral them immediately.

>> **Keep a bare minimum of spices and condiments on board.** Seasonings such as salt and ground pepper, sugar, garlic powder, curry powder, ground cinnamon, and chili powder don't do well for very long when traveling through even

mildly humid climates. They absorb moisture from the air, and when they dry out again, they can become clumpy or turn into solid pillars. So take the seasonings into your house when the trip is over. As for jarred or bottled sauces and condiments, check the labels to determine what has to be refrigerated after opening. The inside of a parked RV on a hot day can easily climb to over 100 degrees F, which can ruin open sauces and condiments.

» **Use an airtight plastic bread box on the road.** You can find one online for around $20, and you'll be amazed how much longer your loaf of bread will last, without the hassle of using up limited freezer space.

» **Make the most of protective containers.** Put your sugar and flour, instant hot chocolate, crackers, and cereal — all your pantry staples — in protective containers. A zipper-lock food storage bag is good, but even better are plastic jars with twist-on lids and food storage bins with pop-up airtight lids.

Dealing with pests (the flying and crawling kind)

Your RV lives its life in the Great Outdoors, and that's where the gangs of bugs, rodents, and other vandalizing vermin hang out. If you crawl under your rig and look at the underside, you'll see all kinds of potential entry points where wires, pipes, and hoses are fished through the floor. What looks like a tiny crevice to you looks like the Jersey City entrance of the Holland Tunnel to a thuggish army of ants or a homeless field mouse hunting for new digs.

You're least susceptible to a pest invasion when you're driving each day, spending one night at a campsite, and moving on. You're at your most vulnerable when your RV is in long-term storage or while you're boondocking off the beaten path, especially if you're close to a grassy field or some deep woods. You don't need to panic, but do keep your eyes peeled.

It's a good idea to have these items on board to help deal with invaders:

» **Flyswatters:** Buy one for every area of your rig — there's nothing more maddening than spotting an annoying fly and then losing it while you hunt for something with which to pulverize it. Nobody reads newspapers anymore, and the last time we tried rolling up our Kindle and whacking a wasp, it didn't go well.

» **Glue traps:** Have some of these on hand for trapping crawling insects and mice.

» **Insecticide:** Outdoor flying insect spray is for the morning you open the door and find 5,000 stink bugs warming themselves on the sunrise side of your rig's exterior walls; crawling insect spray is for use on door transoms, in hard-to-reach corners, under cabinets, and inside exterior storage compartments. For long-term RV storage, just a bit of spray every week on the doormat and tires can be incredibly effective to keep out ants and spiders.

>> **Insect repellent:** This doesn't do much for your rig, but it's handy for you to have. Remember that the chemical DEET found in Deep Woods OFF! and other "extra-strength" insect repellents can cause truly alarming allergic reactions in some people, so be cautious. But mosquitoes can be thick when you're fishing at dusk in summer. Swarms are infamous in places such as Yellowstone. Protect yourself.

REMEMBER

And finally, when your RV is in storage, make certain you don't leave a crumb in it. Seriously. We once had a mouse infestation in our Class B while it was sitting right in our driveway, unused for three winter months. And what were they eating? Kleenex and the stuffing out of the arm of one of our captain's chairs. Even an old used Lipton tea bag will look appetizing to rodents by mid-January.

IN THIS CHAPTER

» **Recognizing campground types**

» **Evaluating public versus private camping**

» **Outlining your desired camping experience**

» **Getting the scoop on boondocking**

» **Exploring government land for camping**

Chapter **5**

Finding Campgrounds and Boondocking

O kay, it's time to pick a campsite; you may even be planning your first night on the road!

The flexibility of an RV is one of the biggest attractions of owning one. From the simplest, most inexpensive pop-up camper, right up to the million-dollar Class A motorhome, all RVs are designed to operate in two modes: either on full hookups in a campground (with water, electrical power, and sewer, just like home) or on battery power, self-contained. When you're choosing a campground, one of the key questions is, which mode do you plan to use?

This chapter gives you the basic tools you need to find the right campground at the right price, with the right amenities you want or need. And we tell you about the basics on roughing it out in the sticks without any hookups at all, which is colorfully known as *boondocking.*

Knowing the Big Names in Campgrounds

Picking a campground is a lot like picking a hotel. Different things are important to different people, and your decision depends on whether you're looking for a place just off the highway for a single night or a resort campground that will suit your family for a week-long stay.

A good place to start is to know the players and what they tend to offer. This section introduces the major players in the United States. Almost all the chain campgrounds have amenities like a camp store for basic supplies, showers and bathrooms on-site, as well as laundry facilities and a central wastewater dump station. From these basics they go up the price scale, with full hookups and pull-through sites, and additional frills like fenced dog-walking areas, patios, grills, Wi-Fi, putting greens, playgrounds and petting zoos for the kids, as well as organized activities, a pool, and even food service of various kinds.

BARGAIN ALERT

Whenever you reserve a campsite or check in at a campground, be sure to ask whether they offer discounts for veterans, active military or first responders, seniors, or AARP, AAA, or Good Sam members. Almost all facilities will give you 10 percent off for any one of these groups.

Recognizing national campground chains

The names in this section are the nationally recognized chains of privately owned or franchised campgrounds. You can generally count on the chains for a uniform level of cleanliness, amenities, and services at all their locations.

Kampgrounds of America

Kampgrounds of America (KOA) (http://www.koa.com) is the big kid on the block, a chain of more than 500 campgrounds in the U.S. and Canada. We like KOA, and like many newbies, we used them often when we were starting out. We do agree with the biggest gripe about KOA; their prices have gotten out of hand. On the most popular cross-country routes, KOA has attempted to place campgrounds at 200- to 300-mile intervals so travelers can make logical overnight stops; they also have a strong presence in traditionally popular camping venues such as Mt. Rushmore and Niagara Falls.

KOA campgrounds are privately owned and certified by the company. They have strict standards and a quality level you can generally rely on. KOAs use a classification system for properties with rising levels of cost and amenities. These classifications are

>> **Journey:** A basic campground designed primarily for an overnight stop. They're great for a quick in and out, with locations near the highway.

>> **Holiday:** Campgrounds with a good selection of features, such as pools, playgrounds, sites with concrete pads and picnic tables, and plenty of basic grass sites for tent camping. Holiday campgrounds also offer rental cabins, which can be great if you're meeting up with friends and family who don't have their own RV, especially if your rig can't accommodate a lot of houseguests.

>> **Resort:** Campgrounds designed for a full-on family vacation, with lots more amenities, activities, and plenty of kid-friendly facilities. Cabins are a bit more upscale, and you'll find locations with little village designs, petting zoos, pedal cart rentals, and even the occasional small-scale amusement rides. Resorts also have lots of organized activities.

KOA publishes a free annual directory, available in all their campground offices. You don't have to be a member to stay at KOA, but $33 a year gets you an easy check-in "Value Kard" membership number and lets you rack up reward points for discounts and free nights. If you go RVing a lot, membership may be worth it to you.

Yogi Bear's Jellystone Park Camp-Resorts

KID FRIENDLY

If you're traveling with young children, Jellystone Parks (www.campjellystone. com) are a great kid-friendly option. Jellystone has 79 campgrounds, designed around the classic 1960s Hanna-Barbera cartoon characters Yogi Bear, Boo-Boo Bear, and Ranger Smith. Yogi and his friends make an appearance (in full costume) daily in the high season, and the parks provide loads of activities too. For the non-RVers, the campgrounds also have *yurts* (circular domed tents), cabins, and even tree houses.

Sun Outdoors

Sun Outdoors (www.sunoutdoors.com) is a chain of 175 RV campgrounds and resorts that promotes glamping (a more luxurious and high-end style of camping than your average KOA offers). They're top-end resorts, with beautifully manicured full-hookup sites, plenty of recreational and social activities, and lots of amenities on-site, including upscale shops, bars, and restaurants. Many offer vacation rental cabins and vintage trailers decked out in delightfully retro splendor. The Sun Outdoors goal is to make the experience feel more like a full-fledged vacation and less like camping out. Some are more kid-friendly than others, so check their listings. No membership fees are required, but count on campsites costing more than $100 per night.

Thousand Trails

The Thousand Trails network (www.thousandtrails.com) owns over 80 resort properties in the U.S. and Canada, and they cling to the coasts and borders: California and the Northwest, the Great Lakes and the Northeast, Florida, and South Texas. Think of this network as a time-share scheme for RV resort campgrounds instead of condos, with all the pluses and minuses of that. You buy a membership that gives you access to all the campgrounds in the chain, though it's not that simple.

Thousand Trails has a partnership with Encore RV Resorts, which has RV parks in California, Arizona, Texas, and Florida; they are owned by the same parent company. There are more than 200 locations between them, in many U.S. states and in British Columbia. But Thousand Trails is not KOA, and there's not one in every state. Also, there are all sorts of restrictions to park access, based on general rules and on your type of membership, and it's vital that you research park locations before you even think of a membership, to determine if they have campgrounds in areas you wish to travel. There's money to be saved here, if you're clear on what you're getting; many of the people we've heard singing their praises are full-timers who live on the move.

WARNING

Do your homework before purchasing a membership with Thousand Trails. Different levels of membership offer different perks and restrictions. We've been told even by fans that the various contracts are confusing, and loaded with company-specific terminology. Membership can be expensive, particularly if you buy what's called an Elite pass. (We're talking thousands of dollars here.) Though you can't transfer it, companies that trade in reselling Thousand Trails memberships have sprung up, much like time-share condos. For lots of people, buying a "resale membership" is a great way to save money.

Camping associations and networks

With independent campgrounds, amenities are harder to predict. They run the gamut, from pricey "resort" RV parks, to isolated wilderness campgrounds, to small no-frills parks catering mostly to overnighters. It's also common to run across a standard residential mobile home park that offers a few open spaces for RVs in need of a place to stop for the night.

So, how to choose one? You can find many tools for discovery, but one of the best, for both you and the campground, is the association (club or network) directories listed in this section. These directories offer ratings of campgrounds and discounts or special privileges for their members.

Good Sam Club

Good Sam (www.goodsam.com), with an info-packed website and phone app, is the granddaddy of RV clubs, going back to the 1930s. It's the largest organization of mutual aid for campers, with more than two million members. Think of them as AAA motor club for RVers. Consider these aspects of the Good Sam organization:

>> The campgrounds aren't owned by the club, and the club doesn't dictate standards and quality level to campground owners.

>> Good Sam isn't a franchise either, but more like a seal of approval.

>> The organization rates their listed campgrounds based solely on number of amenities, so it's possible for a two-star campground to be much newer, cleaner, and nicer than a four-star one just because it lacks a pool, laundry, or putting green.

When you are planning a trip and determine that the independent Zeke'n Lester's RV Park you never heard of is the one with the best location, their listing in the Good Sam guide gives you an edge for finding credible info about a campground that's not part of a chain.

TIP

You have a better chance of finding independent campgrounds in the *Good Sam Campground & Coupon Guide*, which offers an incredible amount of information for RVers. This massive annual guide lists more than 12,000 RV parks and campgrounds (that's not a misprint!) with info such as price, type of sites, phone and address, and so on. Some 2,300 of these campgrounds are Good Sam–approved, meaning they are also rated and offer a 10 percent discount to Good Sam members. The guide is available at all Camping World locations, Gander Outdoors, and Overton's, which are owned by the Good Sam parent company. For Good Sam members, the price for this whopping tome is $10, and you should be able to recoup the cost pretty quickly with all the discounts and coupons inside.

As of this writing, a Good Sam membership costs $29 a year. They publish a monthly magazine and offer loads of services, such as roadside assistance, RV insurance, and extended warranties. Your membership card also gets you 5¢ off gasoline and 8¢ off diesel at Pilot and Flying J truck stops.

Escapees

Like Good Sam, Escapees (www.escapees.com) is an RVer membership organization and campground discount club with more than 800 participating campgrounds.

Dues are $40 annually, and the club offers many benefits and services to members, including an efficient mail-forwarding service for full-time RVers who live on the road. They also have a wide variety of special-interest clubs-within-the-club, for young members, retirees, full-timers, and everyone down the line, from pet lovers and boondockers to ham radio operators. Escapees offers outreach, education, and all sorts of sponsored events. Their magazine for members is excellent.

Harvest Hosts

Harvest Hosts (https://harvesthosts.com) occupies an unusual niche. It's a membership organization linking property owners with RVers who want to boondock (see the later section "Embracing Boondocking" for more about this type of camping). Often these sites are on working farms, ranches, museum grounds, golf courses, wineries, or breweries, and they offer a truly unique camping experience. The $99 annual membership gives you free access to nearly 4,000 sites with no further camping fees. Properties do request a $20 minimum purchase of their products to help support the system; this is the only money they make, and the reason they open their property — to find new buyers. Some hosts go out of their way to give you a truly one-of-a-kind experience.

There are a few restrictions. You can't just show up — you need to request a stay at a location beforehand, and you may stay for only 24 hours. You'll be boondocking without hookups. No outdoor cooking and no tents are allowed.

If there's a problem at all with Harvest Hosts, it's a problem that accompanies their biggest plus: This is "event" boondocking, often a memorable experience. You may have driven quite a bit off your track in order to reach the next Harvest Host. You also may be made to feel that you should take the factory tour, or meet the owners, or fulfill some other obligation. It's great fun if you're on vacation. But if you're tired and trying to simply eat up the miles, it may be a hassle.

Boondockers Welcome

Boondockers Welcome (www.exsplore.com/blog/boondockers-welcome) is an online platform, à la Airbnb, where owners of RVs willing to host for the night welcome boondockers looking for a place to overnight, hopefully creating a social club and mutual aid society of RV owners. There are more than 3,000 host locations. The cost is $79 a year.

 A great general site for helpful boondocking information is Boondocker's Bible, www.boondockersbible.com.

TIP

Using campground apps and directories

Like everything else these days, the RV world seems intent on getting you to use your smartphone apps for finding a campsite, and to tell you the truth, these apps are great. We find campgrounds in all sorts of ways, including old-fashioned word of mouth, but apps such as the following can make life easier:

Allstays Camp & RV	Campendium
The Dyrt	FreeRoam
iOverlander	MobileRVing
RV Life	

In fact, the number of RV apps can seem a bit overwhelming, and new ones continually appear.

TIP

Download three or four RV apps — most are either free or relatively inexpensive — and get comfortable with at least one. These apps help you find campgrounds anywhere, provide pictures and reviews at a tap, and you can navigate your way to dispersed campsites, outside of designated campgrounds. They can also filter search results to locate things like dump stations, RV-friendly fuel stops, RV dealerships and repair shops, propane dealers, and even Walmarts and Cracker Barrels that offer overnight RV parking. Also, if you don't use tons of apps all the time, you might try using these on a laptop or other device. It's how we often use them, and for us, it's easier to find important links, and just plain see various features.

Smartphones are a godsend, but we also find the dead-tree edition of some campground directories to be invaluable, especially Good Sam's campground guide and KOA's free annual directory (see the previous section). It's tough to get a wide overview of a state or region on a 6-inch smartphone screen when it's a scrolling map with very faint state lines. So being able to study a comprehensive statewide map helps, particularly in the planning stage of a trip.

Comparing Public and Private Campgrounds

There are many essential differences between public and private campgrounds, including ease of making reservations, availability in busy seasons, and likelihood of certain amenities. But increasingly, the biggest difference between public and private campgrounds is price.

More than half the campgrounds in America are privately owned. At one time, these private campgrounds were overwhelmingly family businesses — often generational. But economic forces beyond the families' control are changing both ownership status and prices charged for an overnight stay (they're going up). On the other hand, the various public agencies that have campgrounds deliberately keep prices low, so most campers can afford a space, which is great but creates its own problems. Consider these situations for campground owners, private or public:

>> **The private campground bubble:** Like overinflated house and car prices during and after the COVID pandemic, the market value of campgrounds has been skyrocketing out of control. Suppose a couple owns a campground that was worth a million bucks when they bought it, and now it's worth $10 or $15 million (according to the overinflated market). The couple can't possibly leave the campground to their kids because they'd never be able to afford the resulting estate taxes. Also, the kids would find it difficult to raise a million smackers to buy the campground from the couple during estate planning. And so, sooner or later, the family sells out, and another faceless Real Estate Investment Trust gobbles up another campground, driving the price of an overnight stay much higher.

>> **Government funding:** Of course, the government agencies don't have the economic bubble problem, but they have problems nonetheless. Government campgrounds aren't driven (or funded) to make improvements in order to attract new business — they can't handle the number of campers they attract now. Being on the government payroll means that these public facilities rarely bother to upgrade to accommodate modern rigs; many state and national park campgrounds look much as they did in the 1960s. Federal parks and national forest campgrounds tend to be cheapest for campers. In the last decade, some states have attempted to upgrade their campgrounds, but prices have risen at many accordingly.

You should note that in at least 19 states, all of them popular for RVers, there's an upcharge for out-of-state campers, running from as little as $5 to $30 or more. In an expensive state, like Idaho, this can drive a full hookup campsite to the price you'd pay at a private campground, if not more. But still, on the whole, public campgrounds are almost always the least expensive spaces you'll find, if you can find them. Once again, in the busiest times of year, these bargain campgrounds can be tough to get into, especially the most famous or popular ones.

You often find the prettiest scenery in public campgrounds run by state and national parks, the forest service, or even county parks. Again, what you won't usually find are full hookups, as well as up-to-date facilities or sites long enough for a Class A towing a jeep. Don't expect a laundromat and a bathhouse with squeaky clean modern restrooms; blockhouse bathrooms, if not outhouses or even portable toilets, are commonly the only facilities you'll find. Bring your own toilet paper. And wasp repellent.

REMEMBER

In general, older campgrounds laid out in the 1950s and '60s have smaller spaces because huge motorhomes with slides were nonexistent. Canned ham trailers reigned supreme, and parks often have extremely narrow back-in sites. Pull-through sites are rare, so be prepared to back in to most public park sites.

Lack of good amenities is a common complaint in private campgrounds, too. So many campgrounds need upgrades and aren't getting them. All experienced campers have war stories. Here's one: We saw a lineup of Class A motorhomes in an aged KOA in Billings, Montana (the first KOA opened in the U.S.), all with slides deployed. The slides were nearly touching, with certainly no more than 3 inches of space between them.

TIP

If having more space that readily accommodates your RV matters to you — and it should for a long stay — be sure to ask the adequate-space question and look for reviews of the campground on sites such as Allstays and Google.

Assessing the amenities

Table 5-1 shows some basic comparisons of the facilities and amenities between public and private RV parks; you may find these helpful at the trip-planning stage. No, these differences are not hard-and-fast rules, but count on them more often than not.

TABLE 5-1   Amenities in Public Versus Private RV Parks

Amenity	In a Public Campground	In a Private Campground
Hookups	Of 59 national parks with campgrounds, a dozen have full or partial hookups available. In most national park campsites, you're not going to have either electrical or water. *Note:* Yellowstone is fairly typical; out of the dozen RV campgrounds within the park run by the park service, only one has full RV hookups available.	It's a rare thing to find a private RV campground that doesn't have full hookups available, though smaller independent ones may have full hookups in only a limited number of spots.
Electricity	In state or federal campgrounds that have an electrical connection, it probably won't be 50 amps. It will most likely be a 30-amp hookup, and may go as low as 15 or 20 amps.	Offering 50 amps is a relatively recent development, arriving with bloated luxury RV amenities like dual air conditioners, washers and dryers, and residential refrigerators. Still, most private campgrounds can accommodate you if it's a must-have.

(continued)

TABLE 5-1 *(continued)*

Amenity	In a Public Campground	In a Private Campground
Water and sewer	Freshwater supply and sewer dumps are often located near the park entrance, forcing you to pull up stakes to empty and repark whenever your freshwater tank runs low or your wastewater tank gets full. A few campgrounds may offer a mobile wastewater tank pump-out service that comes to your site for an extra fee, but don't count on it.	These services are commonplace in private campgrounds. In some small, independent campgrounds, you'll still find a percentage of sites that have only water/electric, as individual sewer hookups are expensive to install and maintain.
Scenery	Because public parks and forests are usually older installations, their campgrounds may have very mature trees deep in the woods or sites along lakes, rivers, or creeks. Bear in mind that most are back-in sites, and heavily wooded ones can present a tricky, obstacle-filled parking task. Because so much prime land in America belongs to the national park system, public parks tend to have some of the most gorgeous scenery. Ditto with state parks.	Without question, a typical KOA can feel like a parking lot. Many people consider the hassle of the limitations with hookups to be well worth it for the chance to camp in the splendors of a public park. However, if scenery is what counts for you, it's certainly out there in private campgrounds, as well, particularly in areas famed for it; states like Wyoming and Montana, Colorado and Utah have breathtaking scenery in most campgrounds.

It's much harder to gauge the overall amenity situation in state parks, with each state having different levels of money invested, different ages of facilities, and so on. At the state level, you commonly find campsites with power only, no water, and certainly no sewer, but it's a shifting target. For example, in our home state of Indiana, almost all campsites in state parks have electrical; sometimes you can get full hookups. But traveling to Vermont, we found there were *no* hookups in *any* state campground. So, when planning a trip, choose a state and just google the question "Do state park campgrounds in Georgia have electrical hookups?" You'll get the answer that in Georgia, all of them do.

REMEMBER

You **cannot** run an air conditioner, even if it's a single unit, on a 20-amp hookup. Microwaves in combination with blow dryers are bad enough, and you may trip a circuit breaker or blow a fuse.

WARNING

Resist the urge to dump wastewater outside the designated areas. Another convenience you may see in a public campground is a small freestanding *greywater disposal*, or dump site for shower and dish water only. As a rule, your greywater tank will fill up much faster than your *blackwater tank* (the one that holds toilet water), which tempts people to drain their greywater tanks surreptitiously into the woods, *which you aren't supposed to do.* But if you have a rolling cassette cart for wastewater disposal, or even a bucket, you can drain off some of it and haul it by hand over to the communal dumpsite to keep from having to break camp so soon.

Some coastal campgrounds (and they're tough to get into) permit you to camp right by the water: Doheny State Beach in Dana Point, California, and Camping on the Gulf, an RV park on Miramar Beach near Destin, Florida, are just two examples. But some states don't permit water, electric, or sewer hookups in RV campgrounds on the beach or by a lake or river — campgrounds on the Texas Gulf Coast are one example. The fear is that blackwater sewage may leach through underground pipes or soak into the ground from accidental spills and contaminate the adjacent ocean water.

Scoring a season-sensitive campsite

We talked in several places in this book about dealing with the campground crush, but it bears repeating here: Some of the most crowded campgrounds in the U.S. are in what we think of as the big-name national parks like Yellowstone, Yosemite, the Grand Canyon, or Utah's string of natural monument parks. If your heart is set on Arches National Park, and it's full clear back to the ranger station, try the nearby private campgrounds. But remember, they'll be playing host to the spillover, particularly in season, and their prices will reflect this. If that's not a problem, be sure to make reservations.

TIP

When you're camping in popular national parks, try to reserve a site months in advance, or you'll be disappointed. And we'll say it again: If your rig is large (over 30 feet in length), you'll probably want to look into RV sites outside the parks. Check with the individual park's website. Call them if you're at all confused.

Making reservations and paying

While most campground chains offer online reservations or an 800 number, if you don't know the campground, and especially if you have any odd problems — like a particularly big rig that needs a pull-through site — it's always a good idea to talk to a human being. Any halfway-decent owner or manager in a private campground will pick up the phone or return your call, and they'll answer all your questions. Let them know if you're arriving after the office closes, and they'll tell you how to check in, where to find your site map, and other important info. Usually they just tack it up with your name on it in a designated area by the door.

Most state parks now use centralized reservation systems that require you to call a toll-free number or make your reservation online or through a phone app. (Reserve America, www.reserveamerica.com, is an app that handles numerous state camping sites. California has its own dedicated online site and phone app, and their state parks must be reserved on the Reserve California site, https:// reservecalifornia.com/Web/.)

Unless it's the July 4th weekend, or some sort of important local event is going on, private campgrounds are generally not full, and easier on the whole to get into; just pick up the phone, give them a credit card number, and you're in. It's one of the overall advantages of going private, though it may be more expensive than the nearest public or state park.

TIP

Be aware that some campgrounds still do things the old-fashioned way. In many public parks, and even a surprising number of low-priced, family-run private ones, you'll be asked to pay in cash, particularly for late arrival. Even though you've left civilization behind for the joys of the wilderness, always try to keep a bit of cash with you at all times — $100 or $200 at least. If you're slipping into a first-come, first-served space in a county park, the cost may only be $20, but you may be asked to pop the cash into a provided envelope and drop it into an honor box. And in some areas, a bear can often be easier to find than an ATM. Some parks (but not all!) will even take personal checks. Remember those?

Choosing the Right Site

For a newbie, figuring out what you really need in a campsite takes time. Find out what's important enough to make an issue of when deciding on the campsite that's right for you. Most people can put up with just about anything for a single night. But if peace and quiet is really important to you, and your campground backs up to a major highway, with a busy set of railroad tracks on the other side, you're not going to be happy, particularly in an extended stay.

So first, scope out the campground itself. Campground maps are notoriously *unhelpful*. Probably the most important thing you can do is read the reviews, which are available for even the most distant Bureau of Land Management (BLM) primitive campground by looking on Google, TripAdvisor, or one of the camping apps. Reviews will give you a good idea of campground amenities, level of security, and other things you care about, or the ones that would drive you crazy.

In both public and private campgrounds, you may sometimes have to use a back-in site, so know how to do it with confidence. Remember, on the whole, back-in sites are far more common.

As for figuring out what matters most to you when making a reservation, the first thing you have to look at is your rig. A person in an Explorer towing a Little Guy Max teardrop trailer isn't going to have the same problems as someone in a 42-foot Tiffin motorhome with four slides. And if the Tiffin is towing a car behind, the owner may not be able to back up at all and may consider a pull-through site a necessity, not a luxury. This is one of the things that makes KOA-type campgrounds so popular, because it's easier to find a pull-through.

Here are some odds and ends to consider when you evaluate and choose a spot for your RV camping:

» **Size is everything.** Before you talk to the campground, know the length of your rig, including your tow vehicle; be able to reel that number off in your sleep. Or write your RV's dimensions out and tape them to the back of your sun visor.

- *If you're pulling a travel trailer,* know the height, width, and length of your complete rig, from the street surface to the top of the tallest air conditioner, and from the front bumper of your tow vehicle to the back bumper of the trailer.

- *If you're in a motorhome,* know its length from nose to tail, plus the length of any car or trailer you're towing behind it.

- *And very important, for any rig,* know how much room you need in width to be able to function happily with your slides and awnings fully opened.

» **The available extras vary.** A picnic table is the most common campsite amenity you'll find. You may get a fire ring or a grill (usually charcoal), although you'll often find a communal grill (or several of them) nearby instead. For tent campers or RVers who need to wash dishes after a big meal (and not use up all their fresh water or fill up their wastewater tanks), many campgrounds also offer a communal sink outside, usually on the side of the office building or a bathhouse.

Amenities go up from here. It's getting popular for private campgrounds to offer, for an upcharge, an enlarged concrete patio with a table and chairs, and that's nice for a longer stay.

COUNTING ON CAMPGROUND INTERNET SERVICE

In a word, *DON'T*.

Loads of RVers work on the road these days, and the Great Resignation during the COVID pandemic resulted in more people than ever attempting to work via the internet. But never count on any campground to have high-speed Wi-Fi service — you're more likely to encounter "No-Fi" service.

Federal, state, and local public camping areas don't generally have any Wi-Fi or cell service available at all — they figure you came to enjoy the wilderness, so "Get yer nose outta the phone and quit yer bellyaching, Poindexter."

Private campgrounds can run the gamut from no Wi-Fi service to decent internet speeds, depending on the area and their budget for keeping their routers and amplifiers up to date. Wiring up a large campground with more than a dozen sites for the web is costly. If they have just 15 to 20 campers simultaneously trying to stream the Super Bowl or binge-watch *Game of Thrones* at full resolution, that can slow the whole campground's system to a dead crawl. It's the electronic version of everybody flushing their toilets at the same time.

Embracing Boondocking

In our book *RVs and Campers For Dummies*, we go into much more detail on boondocking, with in-depth info on everything you need to know about roughing it, including ways to save water (for example, we suggest options to replace your daily shower). It's a lost art. But in this section we give you the essential info about boondocking.

Once upon a time, all camping was boondocking. That's why they called it "camping out." Nowadays, you can't even begin shopping for an RV without hearing the word. But why should you care about it? Well, the main reason is that, when you're planning an RV holiday, the potential for boondocking is an issue you'll probably have to face, sooner or later.

The terms *boondocking* and *dry camping* are pretty much interchangeable, though the older term *dry camping* sometimes refers to the old-style campgrounds that have been laid out and leveled but have no hookups; if these campgrounds have water or dump facilities, those are *communal*. You have to move your rig to use them.

TECHNICAL STUFF

Actually, let's settle a few terms here that get thrown around a lot. Boondocking just means camping without hookups, but it often describes people who are doing what's called *dispersed camping,* or camping out in the hinterlands, without even the outline of a campground. In many state or national forest campgrounds, you're allowed, like a backpacking hiker, to drive your RV off the road (or down a really lousy path) and pull off to camp anywhere you please. There are *developed* campgrounds out in the hinterlands, in places like BLM government land, or deep in national forests. But these are often *primitive* campgrounds. These usually have campsites laid out, perhaps even blacktopped, with a picnic table and fire-pit, but that's about it; primitive campsites have no hookups.

Sometimes, camping for a night in an urban area, particularly without permission, is called *stealth camping,* and you'll even hear the term *lot docking* for overnighting in a store parking lot. (Just to round out the nomenclature, overnighting in a Walmart parking lot is called *Wallydocking,* and parking in your grandma's driveway and plugging into her garage is *moochdocking.*)

Whatever you call it, *boondocking* means camping free of external hookups, and it's taken the RV world by storm, as people search for the freedom that was originally a big part of the attraction of camping. Considering that the price of an ordinary KOA campsite has soared to $60 or more per night, you can save a *lot* of money doing it. But boondocking isn't just for RVers trying to economize. Nobody who forks over $2,000 for lithium trailer batteries and $9,000 for rooftop solar panels is entirely motivated by cost. Here are other reasons for embracing boondocking:

» For some, boondocking is beyond a hobby and more of a passion — these campers love trying to extend the number of days they can camp with water and power they generate themselves.

» Many boondockers love camping for free on government land, which we talk about a bit more in the later section "Ah wilderness! Looking into dispersed camping" When you set up camp in complete isolation, you find a pioneer sort of feeling that you will never get in a paved parking space at a KOA.

» Other boondockers are only looking to slip the bonds of the trailer park for a single night, saving money and hassle when they're on the move. It can be annoying to pull into a campground at dark, hook up, eat and sleep, then leave early in the morning, and pay 50 or 60 bucks for the privilege.

Understanding a 12-volt kind of life

TIP

The best place to determine your system's limitations is at home, where you can't get in too much trouble. Just unplug your rig from all external connections and spend an evening in your RV while it runs on 12 volts, propane, and a tank full of fresh water. Better yet, spend the whole night. Cook in it, wash the dishes, take a shower, and keep cool just by opening the windows and running the ventilation fans. You'll quickly understand your system, discover the few appliances that work, and find out how long you can run them. What's more, you'll see how your batteries are doing after a full night of use and how fast they drained.

Powering an RV for boondocking

You don't necessarily need a big smelly gas-powered generator to boondock; it depends on what you're willing to do without. But here and now, we thought a very simple explanation of camper tech would be a good idea for anyone who's confused. And camper tech is 12- volt. It's all about batteries.

Almost all RVs can run some things without being plugged in to a power pole. Our Airstream makes a great example, because it uses the classic system RV builders have used for years. We have two deep-cycle batteries, like car batteries, that sit on our trailer's frame and supply it with 12 volts DC (direct current) power. We also have two propane tanks near the batteries for things that run on propane gas, such as our heater and cooktop. This is the 12-volt power system that's always with us.

All sorts of things in your RV can run just fine on this system: the lighting, the roof fans, and the water heater. But normal power that comes out of the wall in your house is 110 volts of AC, (alternating current). Microwaves, air conditioners, toasters and toaster ovens, and most TVs and DVD players are things that won't run on 12 volts. They're hungrier, and they want 110 volts.

When a converter or inverter come in to play

Now, your RV has something called a *converter*. It takes the 110 volts of AC coming out of the campground pole you're plugged into and converts it into the 12-volt power so many basic things in your trailer run on. Handily, it also recharges your batteries. When you unplug that external 110-volt line, everything that still runs is running on your batteries.

Alongside the converter, some trailers have something called an *inverter*, which does the exact opposite (of the *converter*); it can boost 12 volts DC up into a limited amount of 110 volts AC. (Needless to say, the two terms are constantly confused.)

An inverter is a nice convenience for boondocking. When you're sitting in the Walmart parking lot and aren't plugged into an external power supply, you can flip on your inverter, and it converts the 12-volt power from your batteries into 110 volts. This power goes through at least a couple of clearly marked outlets in your rig. Suddenly, you can watch TV if you want or plug in simple 110-volt devices.

But, an inverter won't power a microwave or air conditioner. In fact, our moderately-powerful inverter won't do things like operate high-wattage hair dryers or electric tea kettles. (Anything that heats up is usually a power hog.) You'd need a really high-capacity invertor to power these appliances. Installing a high-capacity inverter is usually an upgrade for a specialist to do, and it can be costly.

Foregoing some electricity drains

When you want to boondock, camping without hookups, it means you're doing without fresh water (which we address later in the section), an always-on waste-water connection, and a power pole providing 110 volts. The tough issue is power, and the question is always this: Do you need a big, heavy external generator, or a large set of solar panels, in order to function without the power pole? To a great degree, the answer hinges on how long you want to boondock, and on what it is you won't do without.

Anyone can boondock using just the 12-volt electrical system that comes built into your RV. The earlier section "Understanding a 12-volt kind of life" gives a simple, straightforward explanation of RV battery power. This 12-volt system is usually fine for a single night, depending on how high your expectations are. So get to know your own system *before* you boondock.

Choosing the power-hungry items that are must-haves

Many everyday kitchen appliances, such as toasters or electric water kettles, and of course microwaves, need 110 volts of electricity to run. Unless you have a generator or oodles of solar power and a sunny day, you won't be able to use these things. But face it, when you're boondocking, you can do without most of them. (Forgoing your morning latte for some camp coffee from time to time builds character.) It's when you contemplate boondocking for an entire one-week vacation in a dispersed campsite in Wyoming that the character of dry camping changes a great deal.

We understand why being able to run the air conditioner has become the holy grail of boondocking. RVs can get very hot, and so much camping is done in the dead of summer. When you're camping in Louisiana in August, even swimming or being on the beach may provide little relief from the relentless heat. Our most successful boondocking has been done either in the mountains (open all the windows for the luscious mountain air) or in spring or fall, when excessive heat isn't an issue. If the weather turns cold, your camper's propane heating system is incredibly efficient.

Cheating the system with a generator

If you want total freedom, with the ability to run all your 110-volt appliances, including your air conditioner, you're going to need additional power, usually a gas- or propane-powered 110-volt AC portable generator. Motorhomes have an advantage over trailers when boondocking because most have their own built-in generator. (You'll also find onboard generators in some high-end fifth-wheel trailers, too.)

REMEMBER

Onboard generators are still loud and smelly, and a large motorhome can have issues of its own when doing dispersed camping. These motorhomes are rarely capable of off-road exploration, and driving one down a pothole-filled logging road out on primitive federal land can be tough. You don't want to worm your way into some rugged, isolated area, only to discover (to your horror) that you can't manage to drive back out again.

Here are some basic generator facts:

>> **Portable 110-volt generators are heavy, noisy, and expensive.** They need gasoline or propane to run and have severe limits as to how much power they can put out. In the generator world, the free-market system reigns supreme: The more power you want, the heavier the generator you'll need, and the higher the price you'll have to pay. A generator big enough to handle the 30-amp 110-volt AC power needed to run your appliances or an air conditioner weighs 100 pounds or more.

>> **Most RVers compromise on a 2,000-watt or smaller unit** because they're lightweight enough to carry and won't dramatically overload their tow vehicle. But even with some magical electrical modifications (like an EasyStart) to reduce the big power surge needed to turn on an air conditioner's compressor, a portable generator should really only be used sparingly.

>> **Motorhomes and some fifth-wheel trailers have a built-in generator** that makes boondocking a bit easier. But even in a motorhome, 12 volts is the heart of your basic electrical system, just as in a simple trailer.

A built-in generator presents its own hassles. Our first Class B Pleasure-Way motorhome came with an onboard Onan generator. We used to boondock quite a bit, and on a swelteringly hot night in a very loud Louisiana truck stop, we needed the air-conditioning so we could sleep. And its blower vent was directly over the bed. Between the sound of the generator rumbling below the floor under our heads and the racket of the air-conditioning unit over our heads, it was like trying to sleep in the cargo hold of a 747 during takeoff. Not restful. At all.

One other issue to remember is that a built-in motorhome generator uses the same gasoline or diesel fuel that runs your engine. Consequently, on a long boondocking adventure, the generator is draining your rig's fuel tank. Fortunately, most are designed to shut down the generator's engine when your fuel tank drops down below a quarter of a tank.

Water, water everywhere (or not)

From a technical standpoint, water issues may seem much simpler than power issues. How much water can you carry in your freshwater tank, and how long can it last you when you're dry camping? But answering this question can get a bit more complicated than it seems. Consider these scenarios that affect boondocking:

>> **The relative size of your greywater and freshwater tanks:** Our current Airstream has a fairly generous 54-gallon freshwater tank (with 6 more gallons in the water heater) and a 38-gallon greywater tank. Huh? Isn't it just basic logic that the tank for the water coming off your shower should be roughly the same size as the one pumping it in? So, 60 gallons of fresh water can last us three days if we're showering frugally (and *much* longer if we aren't showering at all). But in either case, we'll be looking for someplace to dump the grey water much sooner than we use up our supply of fresh water. This is a persistent RV problem, and another place where motorhomes and fifth-wheels — with their typically larger tanks — have an advantage.

>> **The lack of amenities when you're boondocking:** Filling up your freshwater tank isn't an amenity at a boondock campsite. If you're on the road, the best and easiest way to fill your freshwater tank (and empty the others) is to spend one night in a pay campground. But some hard-core boondockers are resistant to this solution. Of course, you can drag out the hose and take on fresh water in all sorts of places (truck stops, for example). Or you may ask to take on water from a business you've bought something from.

REMEMBER

The water costs for residents and businesses in places like California are not insignificant. You must always *ask permission before* hooking up to a private water source. Most government campgrounds, even if they have no hookups, will have a source of fresh water on the grounds. But it may be a bit rusty and rocky; use a filter.

WARNING

If you're at a wastewater dump station and see a water spigot, look out for "Non-Potable Water" signs. Hoses around dump sites are there so you can clean out your blackwater tanks. *Don't use them for drinking water!*

TIP

To conserve your onboard water supply and avoid filling up your wastewater tanks too quickly, seasoned RV boondockers frequently suggest paying for a shower at a truck stop or travel centers. Love's, Pilot/Flying J, Travel America and Petro all have reward cards that can build up purchase points to earn a free shower.

Finding a safe place to stop

If you're going to attempt to boondock and you're not actually *in* the boondocks, you need to be aware of some issues that affect how and where you find places to stop. RVers (like you) are not the only group looking for a safe stop along the highways and byways, and you're going to be encountering truckers — and, to a lesser degree, *vanlifers* (people living full-time in their vehicle, often a van) — who are trying to do the same thing. Think about these points that affect RVers as well as the other groups you share the road with:

>> **Vanlifers** are a crossover breed — depicted in the 2021 film *Nomadland* — who have much in common with RVers who live full-time in their rigs. Vanlifers have an advantage over RVers in that not all of them live in an easily spotted white cargo van; many live in a vehicle like an SUV that can fly under the radar. They often sleep parked on city streets, and no one notices. The bigger your rig, the more noticeable you are. Vanlifers, like RVers, may be on the go frequently and need just an overnight stop before heading on to the next multinight stay.

>> **Truckers** with big rigs serve many industries and make up much of the traffic on major interstate highways and state roads. Truck drivers' rest and work times are regulated to a degree that's probably inconceivable to the rest of us, and they don't have oodles of unstructured time. Because they spend a good bit of their non-driving time in rest areas and truck stops, truckers are quite likely to frequently cross paths with RVers. The battle for a spot in the dwindling number of rest areas, truck stops, and other natural stopping places is becoming an issue, and a major headache, for truckers and RVers.

Looking for traditional (and unusual) stopovers

All the groups who share the road need a place to get off the highway, sometimes for a brief rest and sometimes to spend the night. Even if you're headed for a campground, time can get away from you, and night creeps up before you reach your destination. Here are the main options for an overnight stay on the road when you need it:

» **Rest areas have always been the officially sanctioned place to pull off.** These days, it's not a good idea to plan on just stumbling across one, though. Due to COVID and unrelated budgetary constraints, states have begun shutting down rest areas over the past several years. The last time we crossed the country, in January 2021, almost half the rest areas we came upon were closed.

» **Truck stops are another traditional place to pull off for rest and recuperation.** But the spiraling numbers of RVers, vanlifers, and truckers can make it tough to find a spot at a truck stop. Some truck stops have introduced parking reservation systems, which adds a layer of annoyance for truckers, who may spend nearly an hour a day looking for somewhere to pull off. But RVers drop a lot of money in truck stops — they're great places for us, too.

REMEMBER

Truck stops haven't been particularly responsive to RVers, but this is a situation that's changing fast. Flying J was the first to respond by installing dedicated fuel pumps for RVs, as well as paid sewer dumps and propane refill stations. Recently, they were the first chain to install RV-specific parking spaces that are incredibly convenient, and RVers are welcome to spend the night there if necessary. As announced in March 2023, the competing Love's truck stop chain has opened 23 travel centers with sites dedicated to RVs, and at these locations, you find 357 full-hookup sites where tired RVers can stop. This convenience is much like an overnight express RV park, which has been a crying need for some time. (Why didn't anyone think of this before?) These changes at Love's are welcome and ongoing, with more developments to be added.

» **Businesses' parking lots can offer an overnight stop option too.** A common situation for both RVers and long-haul truckers is this: It's coming on to dark, and the weather has turned on you, badly. You're 60 miles away from the place you'd planned on stopping for the night, and as the rain turns to ice, you've got a sinking feeling you'd be better off not trying to finish the planned journey. When you're in that situation, you're going to see places that look inviting — spots where you would bother nobody. For example, a big, empty, tree-shaded parking lot at a business that's open only through the week, and it's a Saturday. Why not just go for it?

Following the etiquette of overnight camping

It's hard to have a blanket set of rules for all overnighting situations and for all types of boondocking places. Some great spots can't even be categorized. For example, suppose you're rolling down the road and you see a really spacious scenic overlook or a pull-off or turnaround. You may wonder whether you can just spend the night there. It's a good question.

Keep these safe and mannerly practices in mind as you look for that perfect spot to boondock:

>> If you want to stay overnight in some business's parking lot, always attempt to ask permission first. Sometimes it's easier to just pull in and park because you may not find someone to ask. But remember, when you purchase goods from a business, they're more likely to be agreeable to your request for an overnight stay. Vanlifers are very good at making this bargain. Have a sandwich and a beer in someone's bar, and if the establishment has a fairly big parking lot, just ask if you can spend the night. You'd be surprised how often the answer is yes.

TIP

The more independent from the business you can be, the better. RVers have it over vanlifers in one aspect of the overnight stay: No one's going to get deeply annoyed when they find you doing your personal grooming in the business's bathroom the next morning. RVers have their own bathrooms, thank you very much.

>> **Look for businesses that give a nod to RVers, indicating that you can overnight in their parking lots.** Walmart has always been the most high-profile of these businesses. Founder Sam Walton made this nod to RVers as far back as the 1960s. But in the last decade, the bloom is off the rose. Walmart won't give an exact figure, but Jim O'Briant of the Overnight RV Parking website claims that only 58 percent of Walmarts allowed overnighting in 2022. Especially since the pandemic, and with the incredible rise in RV ownership, the traffic just became overwhelming in many locations. And too many RVers abused the privilege, treating the parking lot like a free campground.

REMEMBER

There's no such thing as a "blanket" okay: Corporations with multiple locations use escape clauses such as "RVers are welcome at *most* locations." Generally, this wording exists because some businesses have had problems and no longer allow overnight parking. Also, local ordinances can trump a business's willingness to accommodate RVers. If someone pounds on your door and asks you to leave, *don't argue with them*. Be courteous and go. You're on private property.

>> **Use commonsense security measures.** Lock all your doors, stay inside, and be at least a bit vigilant. Consider that you're in a truck stop or an unlit parking lot at 4:00 a.m., which is not like camping at a KOA in Yellowstone. Nobody is going to provide security for you.

WARNING

Anywhere that you're boondocking — whether you're alone in the backcountry or alone in an empty parking lot — can bring about security concerns. Be aware, be alert, and err on the side of caution.

So, above all, use your common sense when selecting an overnighting location. Check online reviews if possible, and for heaven's sake, try to keep a low profile. Most RVers aren't looking to pop out the awnings, string up the lights, fire up the grill, put out the chairs, and camp at Walmart. Most of them just want a place to spend the night, without searching out a campground that perhaps can't be found or may charge a great deal of money.

Locating specific parking-lot spots along your route

Table 5-2 in this section outlines some places that will usually allow you to spend the night in their parking lots. You can look for these businesses and public or private facilities along your route.

TABLE 5-2 **Places Friendly to Overnight RV Parking**

Name	Category	Specifics to Know
Walmart, Target, Costco, and Kmart	Big-box retail stores	Most still allow overnight RVers in their parking lot, but always ask the store manager.
Lowe's, Menards, and Home Depot	Retail home improvement stores	Most allow overnight parking.
Cracker Barrel	Chain restaurant and gift store	Welcomes RVers with incredible tolerance; some even have RV-specific parking areas. **Note:** Go in before closing and ask the manager for permission. It's an expected courtesy to have a meal in the restaurant or buy something in the Cracker Barrel store.
Casinos	Private gambling facilities	Most allow RVers to overnight.
Suburban movie theaters	Usually multiplex theaters with large lots	Most allow overnight RV parking.

(continued)

TABLE 5-2 *(continued)*

Name	Category	Specifics to Know
Cabela's and Bass Pro Shops	Outdoor superstores	Welcomes RVers for overnight parking. Cabela's stores usually have a pay dump station in their parking lots, which is very convenient. Also, if you shop there (and who doesn't love to shop at Cabela's?), they may give you a code to use the dump for free.
Camping World	RV sales and outfitter	Only some stores allow overnight RV parking. Others claim that their parking lot is too small. Call ahead and ask.
City-owned municipal parks	Parks with large parking areas	Some allow overnight RV parking.
Planet Fitness	Franchise fitness gym	Welcomes RVers for overnight stays.
Supermarkets	Retail food and supplies	Most allow overnight RV parking; be sure to stay in the distant areas of the lot. **Note:** Shopping there is both a convenience and a courtesy.
Moose Lodges and Elks Lodges	Fraternal orders	Allow members to overnight their RVs in the lot.

REMEMBER

RVers will often look for a place where they feel a comfortable connection; for example, veterans may look for a VFW Post. And many RVers overnight in church parking lots. Churches are generally very tolerant. But *don't* abuse the privilege, *don't* try to stay in a church parking lot on a weekend (when the lot is in peak use), and *do* try to ask permission.

Ah, wilderness! Looking into dispersed camping

In planning an RV trip, if you can boondock, it will broaden your access to campgrounds and other camping areas. Lots of RVers simply won't camp unless they have full hookups, and that's understandable, because of the comfort a rig offers when it runs just like home. But as noted earlier, if you want to access even the national and state park campsites, it will help if you're able to handle a little dry camping. And if you want to camp for free on federal land, going dry is pretty much a necessity.

REMEMBER

There are two kinds of camping on public lands: camping in developed campgrounds, which are either free or charge a small fee, and *dispersed camping*, where you simply go off the road and stake out your space like a pioneer on a wagon train. Needless to say, this is easier for a hiker with a tent, and it presents special problems for RVers.

Finding good sites for dispersed camping in an RV is more of a challenge, and we highly recommend that newbies stick to the campgrounds that have been laid out. Consider these factors when opting for a dispersed campsite:

» Just setting up your rig on land that hasn't been leveled can be a challenge.

» Always look for places where others have camped before you. Reusing an existing campsite is easier on the environment. The ranger station or agency field office can help with this, giving you rough maps to great dispersed camping sites.

» If you set up camp someplace you shouldn't, the kindly forest ranger will come and knock on your door to let you know that you need to move on. Don't resent the rangers: You'd be appalled at some of the dangers and abuses they have to deal with out there.

Making Good Use of Government Land

The federal government owns a staggering amount of land in the U.S. — 650 million acres of it, roughly one-third of the nation — and most of it is available for camping. Generally, you're allowed to stay for 14 days. Technically, federal land belongs to all of us. But the government has the final rights here. For example, the government may lease the land out to local ranchers or energy producers, and their rights will come before yours.

The vast tracts of government land are mostly a Western phenomenon. A mere 0.3 percent of Connecticut is federal land, while more than 80 percent of Nevada is. Still, most states have some sort of public-land camping. For example, there's no BLM land in Indiana, where we live, but you can still find opportunities to camp for free in the Hoosier National Forest, in the lush hills of southern Indiana.

TIP

If you're 62 or older, consider buying an *America the Beautiful Senior Pass*. The cost is $80 for a lifetime membership, or you can buy an annual pass for $20. Active military personnel can get their own free annual pass, and veterans and Gold Star families are entitled to free lifetime passes. All federal recreational lands and national parks honor these passes that give you either free access or a discount for campgrounds and other amenities, such as guided tours. Check it out at www.nps.gov/planyourvisit/passes.htm.

Federal agencies that offer camping opportunities

People often refer to all federal land as *BLM land*, but several agencies offer free and low-cost camping. You need to know a little about who they are in order to find these opportunities. These are the major federal agencies that administer public land:

>> **Bureau of Land Management (BLM)** (www.blm.gov): This is the big kid on the block, with 245 million acres, much of it *cast-off land* (land that's considered abandoned or discarded). Lots of BLM land is desert, but there are also conservation and wilderness areas, and even national monuments. Along with dispersed camping, you find free and low-cost campgrounds — but the BLM's idea of a campground and yours may be two different things. Some of these developed recreational areas may consist of merely a boat launch, a *vault toilet* (a waterless toilet that stores waste in an underground tank; a sophisticated term for *outhouse*), some fire rings, and a sign.

>> **U.S. Forest Service (USFS)** (www.fs.usda.gov): The USFS is the BLM's nearest competitor in size, with 193 million acres contained in 154 national forests located in 40 states. *Remember:* A national forest isn't a national park, and it's not a state forest, either. The beauty of our national forests makes them some of the best camping locations to be had. In a national forest, you find campgrounds run by the USFS, which oversees these lands; these campgrounds charge like any other, but the prices are kept reasonable. You can also do dispersed camping here.

TIP

You can get information online at the USFS website, including links to specialty maps like the Motor Vehicle Use Maps, which help RVers find camping space. Our friends at Boondocker's Bible have an excellent online article on the basics of these maps and how to use them (www.boondockersbible.com/knowledgebase/how-to-use-motor-vehicle-use-maps).

>> **Fish and Wildlife Service (FWS)** (www.fws.gov): The FWS has a big chunk of public land — 89 million acres (76 million of which is in Alaska) — but it doesn't really offer RV campgrounds. The FWS offers recreational opportunities, mostly related to hunting and fishing within the system of wildlife refuges it administers.

>> **National Park Service (NPS)** (www.nps.gov): Everyone wants access to the 85 million acres of national parks run by the NPS, but getting into their RV campsites can be difficult, especially during the high season. Plus, opportunities for boondocking in national parks are limited or nonexistent. These places are already so popular, they don't want to cope with a sea of boondockers pushing out the caribou.

» **U.S. Army Corps of Engineers (USACE)** (www.usace.army.mil): The USACE is the largest federal provider of outdoor recreational services and one of the best-kept secrets in camping. You find more than 450 Corps of Engineers (COE) campgrounds nationwide, and they have leases on many more. But they're not in every state — COE campgrounds tend to be where the USACE's projects have been and where they continue to manage bridges, harbors, and large-scale engineering projects. This situation means you're often in an area of historical interest as well (a nice plus).

COE parks aren't free, but they're cheap, clean, and well run. A site called Corps Lakes Gateway can help you find COE campgrounds in all 50 states; go to https://corpslakes.erdc.dren.mil/visitors/visitors.cfm to plan your trip. You need to make reservations at www.recreation.gov; type in your target state and then *Corps of Engineers*, and the campsites will appear. Our old friends at the YouTube network *Long Long Honeymoon* put together a terrific video about COE campgrounds and how to find them (https://youtu.be/kUTn67FCJuo).

Getting the campsite you want

National parks can be a great place to begin your search for places to boondock nearby. BLM and USFS land often borders a national park. So if you're just starting out adventure camping, begin in a national park, then find a promising piece of public land in the vicinity, and go for it. If you can detach your tow vehicle or you have a toad hooked behind your motorhome, consider leaving your rig in a nearby campground and searching out places to camp in the wild before you drive your whole rig out there.

TIP

COE campgrounds were shut down during the COVID-19 pandemic, whereas BLM campgrounds stayed open for the most part, highlighting the fact that you need an awareness of individual agencies and their policies. Sudden shutdowns are ongoing with the COE, often due to flooding and their common proximity to water projects. You should always check reservations on agency websites before departing for a trip.

WARNING

Give yourself plenty of daylight hours to find your campsite! It can be difficult enough after dark to find a well-marked private campground; it can be downright impossible to find a BLM campground with no lights, signs, or fixtures down an old dirt road in the middle of nowhere. In fact, considering the wilderness nature of so much of this land, if you get held up while searching out a particular place to do dispersed camping and the sun begins to set, you may be better off spending the night right where you are rather than attempting to go any farther in the dark.

LOSING AND FINDING YOUR WAY

Most roadies depend on two types of tech travel planners:

- **GPS standalone navigators:** The major companies are Garmin, Magellan, Rand McNally, and TomTom. They work well for many RVers, but in our experience, once you're in rural areas or places with unnamed, unmarked roads, the system can fail and give you wrong information. Some campgrounds will warn you to ignore GPS and take detailed directions from their website instead: Believe them if they say it.

- **Smartphone navigation systems:** Usually these apps employ Apple Maps, Google Maps, or Waze. In distant BLM land, and even in the national parks, cell phone service can be spotty or nonexistent, so if you're relying on your phone for navigation, you may be up a creek without a paddle or a map.

Both GPS units and cell phones can suffer signal loss. In a nutshell, so don't be entirely dependent on any electronic navigation system or app. Especially in the backcountry, have a good off-road paper map. Look online for anything called a "recreation map" or an "adventure map." Some apps and devices will let you use them offline by downloading a map for the area that doesn't require a signal from the internet gods or the cell phone angels to work. Depend as long as you can on your smartphone or GPS device, whichever one makes you most comfortable, but be ready to switch over to paper if it fails you.

A paper map is often your best way to find the road less traveled, particularly in the planning stage of your trip. For one thing, states are a natural point of reference when an RVer is planning a trip, and smartphone apps tend to see the world in small, difficult-to-discern chunks. It can be hard to see which state you're in as you search areas up close. We like paper Benchmark maps — their "recreation atlases" cover all relevant backcountry details, but they're large and cost around $25. A less-expensive alternative is the Benchmark recreation map (www.benchmarkmaps.com/atlas) for a particular state; at $7.95 it's a gold mine of information, with all public lands, as well as campgrounds and local points of interest, marked. Paper maps are easier for two people to look at together. Plus, you can tack them to the wall and use sticky notes or pins to mark out your potential route and plan other sights to see.

Exploring the East

IN THIS PART . . .

Count lighthouses and eat your fill of lobster along Maine's beautiful rugged coastline.

Explore Upstate New York, where baseball legends haunt Cooperstown's hallowed halls and romantics swoon at Niagara Falls.

Travel stunning Skyline Drive and Blue Ridge Parkway along the Appalachian Mountains.

Chapter 6

The Coast of Maine: Lobster Land

The rugged coast of Maine evolved through the centuries from a now-submerged mountain range. A sheet of glacial ice scoured the landscape, melted, and then flooded the mountains, leaving only the peaks visible. Somes Sound, which bisects the lower half of Mount Desert Island in Acadia National Park, is the only true *fjord* (narrow sea inlet bordered by steep cliffs) on the East Coast, so you don't have to go to Norway to find one.

For RVers, Maine is an exhilarating blend of incredible scenery, distinctive — and occasionally eccentric — historic architecture in picture-postcard towns. You'll find dramatic views, unique shopping opportunities and delectable dining that overcomes the sobering prospect of squeezing a big motorhome or fifth-wheel trailer into the state's typical older New England campsites. The Maine coast mystique includes the craggy shore and pounding waves, punctuated by the sharp screeches, squawks, caws, and mews of shorebirds mixed with the distant clanging of bell buoys. Stalwart lighthouses puncture the lingering fog, the crisp salt-water scent is pervasive, and vintage lobster pots lend their color, sound, taste, touch, and smell to the experience that is Maine.

In this chapter, find out how Maine offers the RV traveler a blend of scenic beauty, unique sights and sounds, and tempting culinary sensations — the vivid orange-red hue of a freshly boiled lobster; the creamy white-on-white blend of Maine potatoes, cream, clams, and fatty bacon in a bowl of chowder; the crisp golden tones of Maine's endless varieties of craft beer; and the naturally sweet taste of a handful of fresh-picked wild blueberries.

Planning Ahead for a Maine Stay

The best time to visit Maine is also the most crowded, because everyone enjoys the warm summer months and colorful fall season. Visiting in May, which is too early for the summer folk and the blackflies, can be a good alternative. Also consider planning your excursion for late August and September, which see fewer tourists and a slight reduction in insect annoyances. Unfortunately, after schools and colleges open in September, many small-town New England establishments close down for the long winter because the minimum-wage crowd goes back to their studies and only a few workers remain.

Reserving a campground and packing

TIP

You need to make campground reservations well in advance (think March or April if you're hoping to visit in summer) for the most popular RV parks, especially those in national or state parks. Reservations are particularly necessary if you're driving a larger motorhome (many New England campgrounds are short on long sites or 50-amp hookups) or planning a lengthy stay in any campground. Many campgrounds along this drive were built in the 1940s and '50s (the days of tents and tiny "canned ham" trailers), long before the advent of 40-foot Class A motorhomes towing cars behind them. Giant, wide-body RVs with two or more slideouts may fit with little to no room to spare in some of these older parks. Just make reservations as far ahead as possible — preferably by phone with an actual human so you can emphasize your rig's needs and guarantee a decent space.

When packing, take along an umbrella and raincoat, hiking boots, hot-weather gear (such as shorts and T-shirts), and cool-weather gear (such as slacks and sweaters or sweatshirts). Maine coastal weather changes fast and often, sometimes several times a day. Fortunately, with an RV, you're carrying your own closet and dressing room with you, so you can easily change outfits when the weather demands it. Also, packing some insect repellent, along with a can of fog-type spray, is a good idea in case a swarm of Maine's notorious blackflies decides to mob your campsite in May or June. Mosquitoes are almost nonexistent in Maine, but in early September, the bee and yellow jacket population can sometimes get aggressive.

Allotting sufficient time for your visit

Although the distance covered isn't great, you need to allow 10 to 14 days for a leisurely visit, with time to enjoy camping and to seek out *lobster pounds* (casual live-lobster markets with on-site cooking, takeout service, and/or picnic tables) and little antiques shops. If you want to spend more time in New England, you can add Massachusetts locations — for example, **Gloucester, Salem, Boston,** and **Cape Cod** — or venture north to the Canadian Maritime provinces of **New Brunswick, Nova Scotia,** and **Prince Edward Island**.

WARNING

If you intend to cross into Canada, make sure *everybody* in your party has a current passport and you have an up-to-date record of your pet's vaccinations from your vet, or you'll be turned away at the border crossing. See Chapter 2 for more information about restrictions for entering Canada.

Driving the Coast of Maine

The route we recommend starts in **Kittery,** located about an hour's drive north of **Boston,** Massachusetts. Kittery's the first town in Maine after you cross the border from New Hampshire. Sticking to U.S. 1 or its interstate parallel, I-95, should be no problem for even the most inexperienced RV driver. As an overview, the primary segments of the drive along Maine's coast include

>> **U.S. 1 (parallel to I-95),** which takes you 72 miles to **Brunswick** and turns east away from I-95 to follow the Maine coastline through **Bath**, **Rockland, Camden, Belfast, Bucksport,** and **Ellsworth**.

>> **SR 3,** which you follow for 10 miles to drop south toward **Bar Harbor** and **Mount Desert Island**. Take the bridge across Mount Desert Narrows to the junction with SR 102, turn east on SR 3, and continue for another 6 miles into Bar Harbor.

The total distance of this route is approximately 225 miles. Figure 6-1 maps out the route that leads you through the delightful Maine trek.

TIP

If you run into traffic snarls on U.S. 1, you can use the parallel I-95 for a much faster interstate route. Note, however, that between York Village at Exit 7 and Portland at Exit 48, I-95 is the Maine Turnpike, and a toll is charged. The turnpike still uses manual, cash-only toll lanes staffed by live human beings — no credit cards. They also accept E-ZPass (it's cheaper but requires preplanning). Tolls vary from $6–$12, depending on the number of axles on your vehicle and the occasional whims of the collector. You can pre-calculate your toll at the website for the Maine Turnpike Authority (www.maineturnpike.com/Traveler-Services/Tolls.aspx).

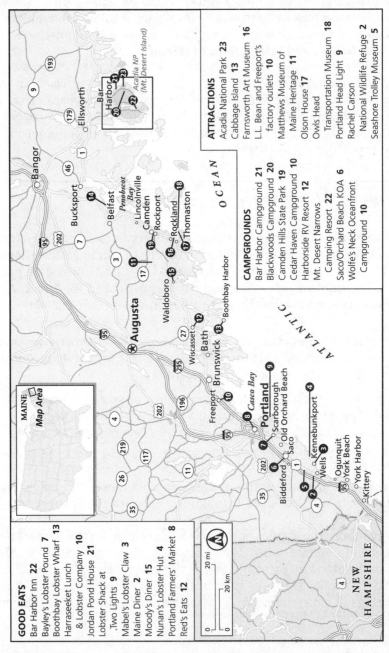

GOOD EATS
Bar Harbor Inn **22**
Bayley's Lobster Pound **7**
Boothbay Lobster Wharf **13**
Harraseeket Lunch
 & Lobster Company **10**
Jordan Pond House **21**
Lobster Shack at
 .Two Lights **9**
Mabel's Lobster Claw **3**
Maine Diner **2**
Moody's Diner **15**
Nunan's Lobster Hut **4**
Portland Farmers' Market **8**
Red's Eats **12**

CAMPGROUNDS
Bar Harbor Campground **21**
Blackwoods Campground **20**
Camden Hills State Park **19**
Cedar Haven Campground **10**
Harborside RV Resort **12**
Mt. Desert Narrows
 Camping Resort **22**
Saco/Orchard Beach KOA **6**
Wolfe's Neck Oceanfront
 Campground **10**

ATTRACTIONS
Acadia National Park **23**
Cabbage Island **13**
Farnsworth Art Museum **16**
L.L. Bean and Freeport's
 factory outlets **10**
Matthews Museum of
 Maine Heritage **11**
Olson House **17**
Owls Head
 Transportation Museum **18**
Portland Head Light **9**
Rachel Carson
 National Wildlife Refuge **2**
Seashore Trolley Museum **5**

FIGURE 6-1: Map of the RV route through Maine.

Great stops north of Kittery along U.S. 1

The three Yorks — **York Village, York Harbor,** and **York Beach** — often are crowded with summer visitors on a budget who gravitate to the small motels and rooming houses that give this area its old-fashioned aura. A bit more classic is **Ogunquit,** the next town north, with its well-trod **Marginal Way** seaside walk, art galleries, and lofty allusions to painters such as Edward Hopper.

REMEMBER

Take heart if you encounter slowdowns — even during the most crowded summer months, traffic jams and snarls get rarer and rarer as you head farther north on this route.

Environmentalists and birders will want to visit the **Rachel Carson National Wildlife Refuge** north of **Wells** to grow acquainted with the salt-marsh wilderness. You can also pick up and continue north on SR 9 past the wildlife refuge to **Kennebunkport,** the summer home to former president George H. W. Bush and his wife, Barbara. The lower village and dock square are almost too charming to be believed, and you also find these interesting spots:

Mabel's Lobster Claw	A charming, kitschy, and cluttered eatery formerly frequented by the senior Bushes (George H. W. and Barbara)
Nunan's Lobster Hut	A super-casual dining experience at Cape Porpoise that's a hit with almost everybody
Seashore Trolley Museum	A unique attraction that houses around 250 streetcars (the world's largest collection), including a New Orleans streetcar named *Desire*

Continuing north on U.S. 1, you come to **Saco, Biddeford,** and **Old Orchard Beach.** The last is a location where you're likely to hear more French than English spoken on the beaches and in the amusement parks. Ever since 1853, when the **Grand Trunk Railroad** ran between Montreal and Old Orchard Beach, thousands of French Canadians have flocked to the 7 miles of sandy beach lined with modestly priced lodgings and restaurants. This is the closest thing to Coney Island or the Jersey Shore that you'll find in Maine.

Around the Portland and Freeport areas

Traveling a few miles farther north on U.S. 1 brings you to **Portland,** one of America's great small cities; it's colorful, accessible, and fairly easy to navigate with an RV. One of our favorite detours from Portland is a drive around **Cape Elizabeth** to **Portland Head Light,** Maine's oldest lighthouse.

BARGAIN ALERT

But even the bright coastal light fades next to America's most appealing shopping mall, the town of **Freeport, a bit north of Portland.** In the center of town is the mail-order giant **L.L. Bean,** open 24/7, surrounded by some **200 factory outlet retailers** with every brand name you can think of, from Coach to Nike. Freeport is always full of shoppers, but don't let that deter you from stopping to snap up some bargains. The **L.L. Bean Factory Outlet** store, site of the best bargains in town, is next to the special free RV parking area, which, in turn, is just steps away from all the factory outlets. Although you aren't permitted to stay overnight in that lot or on the street, the town operates several campgrounds.

One of the great lobster pounds, **Harraseeket Lunch & Lobster Company,** is also in Freeport.

KID FRIENDLY

Camp inside the **Wolfe's Neck Center for Agriculture and the Environment**. Close to Freeport, it's a functioning, sustainable organic demonstration dairy farm where kids can gather eggs and help in the milking parlor.

North and east of Freeport

Wiscasset calls itself the prettiest village in Maine, and nobody yet has arm-wrestled it down on that claim. Many buildings in town are on the National Register of Historic Places. Be sure to check out the very unusual **Castle Tucker** mansion with its unique glass-front second story. The town was featured in the famous *Moosepath League* children's books by Van Reid. While you're there, grab a lobster roll at the world-famous **Red's Eats** roadside carryout diner.

Two miles east of Wiscasset, you can take a 12-mile detour south on SR 27 to **Boothbay Harbor,** a colorful fishing, lobstering, and boat-building town. From the harbor, you can take a day cruise on the *Argo* to **Cabbage Island** for the traditional **Cabbage Island Clambake**.

In **Waldoboro** on U.S. 1, **Moody's Diner** is the quintessential Maine diner. It opened in 1927 as a three-cabin campground and outhouse for hunters and fishermen. In 1935, the diner joined the scene and quickly built a lasting reputation for huge breakfasts at budget prices. We cheated on our midmorning repast here, politely forking up the rather bland corned beef hash and eggs, and then gobbling down a slice of fantastic chocolate cream pie for dessert.

Rockland and surroundings

For art buffs, **Rockland** is the equivalent of hitting the jackpot on a $1 Vegas slot. All available on one easy ticket, the **Farnsworth Art Museum** complex salutes three generations of the Wyeth family and other artists who lived or worked in this part of Maine, with its legendary light and mystique. Clustered in town you find the **Victorian Farnsworth Homestead;** the striking, contemporary, six-level art museum (most of it underground); and the Wyeth Center, austerely installed in a former church.

A few miles away, south of Rockland and outside the farm community of **Cushing,** is the evocative **Olson House**, the remote farm with its unpainted house and barn that's in the background of *Christina's World,* Andrew Wyeth's masterpiece. Wyeth spent more than 20 years painting in and around the Olson House, and today, visitors can match a room or view with a Wyeth print displayed on-site in the otherwise unfurnished house.

A short detour south from Rockland takes you to the **Owls Head Transportation Museum,** a dandy, if sometimes noisy, place on weekends, when aficionados crank up pre-1930s planes, steam farm vehicles, and antique automobiles in which you can take a ride. As you pass through **Thomaston** on U.S. 1, stop at the utterly unique **Maine Prison Showroom,** where much of what's for sale inside — furniture, toys, crafts, and other novelty items — has been hand-carved by (you guessed it) the more artistic guests of the Maine state prison system. The selection is surprisingly large, and it's a great place to find gifts.

Rockport, Camden, and on northward

TIP

Rockport and **Camden,** where the mountains meet the water, are picturesque enough to fill up your camera's memory card, but you need to find a parking spot big enough for your RV before you can settle down to shoot. Several public parking lots are adjacent to the **Rockland Harbor Trail,** a 4-mile footpath that winds through the historic waterfront. In Camden, look for street parking along Elm Street (U.S. 1) on the hill above the waterfront area.

KID
FRIENDLY

Off U.S. 1 between **Lincolnville** and **Belfast, Kelmscott Rare Breeds Foundation Farm**, a working farm featuring rare livestock breeds — sheep, Shire draft horses, and Gloucestershire Old Spots pigs — offers a diversion for pet lovers or families with children in tow. The shoppers among you can hurry to its shop to buy items made of wool shorn from the sheep on the premises.

Finally, to Bar Harbor

TIP

On your way into **Bar Harbor,** you may want to stop at the **Acadia Informa-tion Center (800-358-8550),** on SR 3 just after you cross the **Mount Desert Narrows** bridge, to pick up armloads of maps and brochures about the area and some information about **Acadia National Park.** The center is open daily mid-May through mid-October.

If you can, linger several days in **Bar Harbor** to check out the colorful and whimsi-cal town shops along **Main Street, Cottage Street,** and **Mount Desert Street** around the **Village Green,** and to spend some time exploring nearby Acadia National Park. If your time is short, spend most of the day in the park and hit the shops that evening after dinner; most shops are open late in summer. Seasonal shops open in early to mid-May and close down by the end of October.

WARNING

Don't count on being able to park a fifth-wheel, long trailer, or large motorhome anywhere in downtown Bar Harbor. A designated RV parking lot is on the edge of town at the south end of Main Street, but your wisest choice if you have a large RV or are towing an RV is to leave your rig at the camp-ground and use a car or the **free shuttle-bus service** offered in the summer months.

Must-See Maine Attractions

Acadia National Park
Mount Desert Island

Although you can cram the scenic wonders of Acadia National Park into one day's drive, you'll be rewarded if you allow some extra time. The park's main entrance is on SR 3 at **Hulls Cove**. The entrance fee is $30 per vehicle and is good for seven days. Like all U.S. National Parks, an *America the Beautiful* federal recreational lands pass is also accepted. Be sure to check the park's website (www.nps.gov/acad) for current RV restrictions, as several of these drives are accessible only by car. ***Note:*** The park offers ranger-led group tours as well as concessioner's bus and trolley tours.

Popular activities include:

>> **For a one-day visit, drive scenic Park Loop Road** (closed in winter), which makes a 27-mile circle out of Bar Harbor from SR 3 south of town, with all the attractions pointed out by signage. If you start by heading south on the loop

toward the **Wild Gardens** and **Sand Beach,** you can cover the sometimes traffic-clogged one-way stretch from **Otter Cliffs** to **Seal Harbor** earlier in the day, take a lunch or tea break at **Jordan Pond**, and top off the day with the drive up **Cadillac Mountain** (RVs forbidden). At 1,530 feet, it's the highest mountain on the Atlantic coast of North America.

» **For a two-day visit, consider taking a bike ride** along some of the 45 miles of carriage roads between **Hulls Cove Visitor Center** and **Jordan Pond**, where motor traffic is forbidden. John D. Rockefeller (who hated automobiles) commissioned these gravel roads for horse-drawn vehicles, walkers, and bicyclists.

» **For a fun option, hike up Acadia Mountain.** A moderate, 2-mile round-trip trail through pines and birch trees sets out from the Acadia Mountain parking area 3 miles south of **Somesville** on SR 102. (To get there from Bar Harbor, drive west on SR 233, which turns into SR 198 at Somesville.) After your hike, treat yourself to a lobster lunch at **Beal's Lobster House** in Southwest Harbor.

Find maps and information at Hull's Cove Visitor Center, 25 Visitor Center Rd. Bar Harbor; 207-288-3338; www.nps.gov/acad. *The center is open daily mid-April through the end of October.*

WARNING

Although Park Loop Road, one of the park's most popular attractions, is generally accessible for RVs, we suggest leaving your RV in the campground, especially if you're driving a large motor home or towing a trailer — parking space is limited in many park turnouts. RVs are prohibited on Cadillac Summit Road, and driving it in cars and pickups requires reservations. Likewise, if you have an unusually tall RV, note that the SR 3 bridge underpass on Park Loop Road near Blackwoods does not clear vehicles higher than 11 feet, 8 inches, and the Stanley Brook park entrance from the southeast does not permit vehicles higher than 10 feet, 4 inches.

TIP

You can avoid whacking your TV antenna or air conditioner off the roof by traveling the route in a car or by bicycle. Bike rentals are available from Acadia Bike and Coastal Kayak Tours, 48 Cottage St. (**800-526-8615** outside Maine, or **207-288-9605**; www.acadiabike.com) or from Bar Harbor Bicycle Shop, 141 Cottage St. (**207-288-3886**; www.barharborbike.com). You can also take the local shuttle bus (Island Explorer (**207-667-5796**; www.exploreacadia.com), which makes frequent circuits between campgrounds, town, and designated points in the national park during the summer. The shuttle buses are equipped with bicycle racks.

Farnsworth Art Museum
Rockland / Mount Desert Island

When the Farnsworth family's sole remaining member, an eccentric and reclusive woman, died in 1935 at the age of 96, executors were astonished to find that she left a sizable estate, along with directions to preserve the home and create an art museum. Today, the complex consists of the **Farnsworth Homestead**, the **Farnsworth Art Museum**, the **Wyeth Center**, a teaching center in Rockland, and the **Olson House** in Cushing. Open daily May 1 through October 31. Allow a half day for touring the complex.

>> **Farnsworth Homestead:** This well-preserved mid-19th-century home has many of its original furnishings. There are also informative displays about the Farnsworth family, and volunteer docents who tell you about the history of the house and the town.

>> **Farnsworth Art Museum:** The seven galleries of the museum (most of the floors in this contemporary building are underground) showcase not only the Wyeths — grandfather N. C., son Andrew, and grandson Jamie — but also American artists from Gilbert Stuart and Thomas Eakins to Winslow Homer, Childe Hassam, and Rockland-born sculptor Louise Nevelson.

>> **Wyeth Center:** Housed in a converted church, the center is stripped down to bare wood floors and movable sailcloth dividers framed in mahogany. The ground floor displays book illustrations from patriarch N. C. Wyeth, who lamented much of his life that his work wasn't appreciated as fine art; the upper gallery is dedicated to Jamie Wyeth, a strikingly original artist in his own right, best known for his portraits of John F. Kennedy and Andy Warhol.

16 Museum St. (U.S. 1); **207-596-6457**; *www.farnsworthmuseum.org.* ***RV parking:*** *Museum parking lots (some enclosed and too low for large vehicles) and street parking in the area. Admission varies by age.*

L.L. Bean and Freeport's Factory Outlets
Freeport

BARGAIN ALERT

The L.L. Bean dynasty has been around since 1911, when Leon Leonwood Bean sold 100 pairs of leather-and-rubber hunting boots, 90 of which were returned because the boot fell apart from faulty stitching. He refunded the buyers' money, corrected the problems in construction, and went into the mail-order sporting goods business backed by a retail store that was kept open 24 hours a day, 365 days a year. Today, the company he founded stocks more than 12,000 different items, and the main retail store at 95 Main St. (**800-441-5713**) is still open for business 24/7.

But L.L. Bean no longer is alone in the pretty little town of Freeport. Now, some 200 other name brands vie with Bean in an easy-to-stroll village atmosphere. Our favorite bargain spot is L.L. Bean's Freeport Factory Outlet store, across Main Street from the parent store and around the corner on Depot Street. Allow half a day to a full day for shopping, depending on your stamina and your pocketbook.

Outlet is at 1 Freeport Village Station; **800-341-4341** *or* **207-552-7772;** *Free visitor guide available by calling* **800-865-1994** *or* **207-865-1212**, *or by going to* www.visitfreeport.com. ***RV parking:*** *Free lot located 1 block south of Main Street at Depot Street; overnight parking not permitted.*

Portland Head Light
Cape Elizabeth

The historic Portland Head Light in Fort Williams Park is the oldest of the many lighthouses that line Maine's rocky coastline. It was commissioned by George Washington in 1790, built of "rubblestone set in lime," and officially lit in 1791. Still operated by the U.S. Coast Guard today and virtually unchanged from its beginning, the lighthouse is part of Fort Williams, a military outpost for coastal defense. On a clear day at the point where Portland Head Light stands, you can see four more operating lighthouse towers between Portland Harbor and Casco Bay.

The lighthouse interior is closed to the public at all times, except during the annual Maine Lighthouse Day in September, when about 20 of the state's lighthouses hold open houses (https://lighthousefoundation.org/maine-open-lighthouse-day). A small museum in the former lighthouse keeper's quarters next door chronicles the history of the lighthouse, along with anecdotal local details. Open early April through Labor Day. Allow one to two hours.

1000 Shore Rd., Fort Williams.; **207-799-2661;** https://portlandheadlight.com. ***RV parking:*** *Designated parking area in the overflow lot. Admission to Fort Williams Park is free, but the museum charges admission that varies by age.*

More Cool Maine Activities

The family-friendly coast of Maine offers lots to see and do. During your drive, you'll run across plenty of roadside attractions that may not be included in the list that follows:

» **Have a clambake.** The **Cabbage Island Clambake** on Cabbage Island is a traditional lobster-and-clam supper served in summer at lunch and dinner. You board the *Bennie Alice* at Pier 6 in Boothbay Harbor (12 miles south of Wiscasset on SR 27), cruise over to the island, and feast on local lobster, clams, corn on the cob, and boiled potatoes. Runs daily from late June through Labor Day. Reservations are required, and they don't take credit cards.

   *22 Commercial St., Boothbay Harbor; **207-633-7200**; www.cabbageislandclam bakes.com. **RV parking** is available on the street. Admission charged per person.*

» **Find your favorite brews on the Maine Beer Trail.** Lobsters taste better with beer, and if craft beer is your passion, Maine is the place to be. The national mania for craft beer brewing seriously caught fire in Maine, and despite its diminutive size as a state, you'll now find more than 100 different local breweries to visit along the Maine Beer Trail (https://mainebrewersguild.org). Visit the website first and sign up for an account to start filling up your Maine Beer Passport. You'll find links, locations, and a searchable map for all 100+ breweries on the site, so you're bound to discover one or more in almost every town along U.S. 1, from Kittery to Bangor. (We like Allagash Brewery at 50 Industrial Way in Portland, www.allagash.com.) Unfortunately, since the pandemic shutdowns, fewer breweries offer tours, but most still have tasting rooms or on-site pubs.

   Also, check out the beer festivals website (www.beerfests.com/us/maine-beer-festivals/) to find a beer fest that may be happening near you on your RV trip through Maine.

» **Drink a Moxie at the Matthews Museum of Maine Heritage.** You may never have heard of America's oldest soft drink, but Moxie was invented back in 1885 by Maine's own Dr. Augustin Thompson. Made from gentian root, it was first marketed as "nerve medicine" in 1884 ("It gives you spunk!") but gathered fame in the 1920s when its name began to appear in dictionaries as a synonym for "nerve, courage, and energy." Over the years, its makers claimed it cured ailments ranging from hangovers to "softening of the brain," and especially "loss of manhood." In 2005 Moxie was declared the official soft drink of Maine. Try it for yourself and see why millions have exclaimed after their first sip, "What the heck is THAT stuff!!!???"

There's a lot to see and do at the Matthews Museum while you try to get rid of your Moxie aftertaste. With more than 11,000 artifacts, it's one of the best little museums in New England in which to see what life in the pre- and post-Colonial era was like. Just beware of its unusual hours due to volunteer staffing — it's best to call ahead before visiting. Open daily.

1 Fairgrounds Ln, Union; **207-563-1544** *or* **802-476-2792;** *www.matthewsmuseum. org.* **RV parking** *is plentiful. (If you're overnighting, Mic Mac RV Campground is just east of Union on nearby Crawford Pond.) Admission varies by age.*

KID FRIENDLY

» **Ride a Stanley Steamer.** The **Owls Head Transportation Museum** isn't one of those boring places where you just walk past the exhibits. Here, you get to see machines in action, and maybe even ride on one if you visit on a summer weekend. From the Red Baron's World War I Fokker DR-1Triplane, to silent film actress Clara Bow's Rolls-Royce and a hissing Stanley Steamer steam automobile, the exhibits are still in working order. Call ahead to see what's going to be cranked up when you're in the vicinity. Open daily year-round; closed on major holidays. Allow one to two hours depending on your interest and available activities.

117 Museum St., Owls Head; **207-594-4418;** *https://owlshead.org.* **RV parking** *is available in a large lot. Admission varies by age.*

» **Take a walk on the wild side.** Environmentalists and birders need to visit the **Rachel Carson National Wildlife Refuge.** Pick up the map at the resident manager's office near the entrance and hike a self-guided, 1-mile nature trail through a pine forest and along the Little River, out to a salt marsh. You'll find the trailhead by the refuge headquarters north of Wells. Open daily, and it may be crowded in summer and fall. Allow one hour.

321 Port Rd., Wells; **207-646-9226;** *www.fws.gov/refuge/rachel-carson.* **RV parking** *is available in designated parking areas. Admission is free.*

» **Hop a trolley.** The **Seashore Trolley Museum** is the world's oldest and largest museum of electric railway equipment — classic electric streetcars (or trolleys) from the early 20th century that were powered by an overhead wire. Founded in 1939 with a single open-sided car from Maine's Biddeford-Saco interurban line, today's 350-acre museum houses some 250 railway cars displayed indoors and out. Visitors ride one of the trolleys to the large exhibit barn, where they can see a San Francisco cable car from 1910, an ornate 1906 Manchester and Nashua Street Railway car from New Hampshire, and even foreign streetcars from Glasgow, Rome, Montreal, and Budapest. Be sure to visit the restoration shop and see what goes into repairing and preserving these rare and unique railway cars. Open on various days, May through the second week in December. Allow one to two hours.

195 Log Cabin Rd., north of Kennebunkport; **207-967-2712**; `https://trolley museum.org`. **RV parking** *adjacent to the museum. Admission varies by age.*

Camping Along Maine's Roads

Along U.S. 1 between Kittery and Bar Harbor, you find no shortage of campgrounds — nearly three dozen — and loads of casual eating spots; Maine virtually invented the roadside diner. You can make reservations at most private campgrounds and some, but not all, public ones in state and national parks; having reservations June through August is usually a must. Between late September and early May, Maine's frigid weather compels many campgrounds to close down from lack of business and to shut off water to prevent frozen pipes from bursting. But if you're fearless and RVing in the cold anyway, call ahead and ask if you can camp there with electrical hookups, using a heated water hose, and firing up your propane furnace. On-site managers will generally allow it at a small price.

All campgrounds listed in Tables 6-1 and 6-2 have public flush toilets, showers, and sanitary dump stations, unless designated otherwise. Toll-free numbers, where listed, are for reservations only. (See Chapter 5 for how we choose our favorite campgrounds.) Be aware that Maine charges a 9 percent lodging tax on campground sites.

TABLE 6-1   **Our Favorite Maine Campgrounds**

Name and location	Contact Info	Cost	What to Know
Bar Harbor Campground; Bar Harbor	RFD 1, Box 1125; **207-288-5185;** www.thebarharbor campground.com	**$$–$$$**	Total of 300 sites; 175 with water and 20-, 30-, and 50-amp electric; 70 full hookups, 75 pull-throughs and back-ins. Laundry, pay showers, Wi-Fi, pool. This privately owned RV park on the north coast of Mount Desert Island accepts no reservations and lets campers select their own sites instead of assigning them. Procrastinators and fans of happenstance can chance to find a campsite in midsummer without planning ahead. No credit cards. Open: Late May–early October.

Name and location	Contact Info	Cost	What to Know
Blackwoods Campground; Acadia National Park	155 Blackwoods Dr., Otter Creek; **207-288-3338;** www. nps.gov/acad/ planyourvisit/ blackwoods– campground.htm	$$	Total of 60 RV sites with water only (seasonally); on-site dump, no sewer or electric hookups, no slideouts allowed, and a 35-foot maximum vehicle length restriction. Refrigerator, heater, and water heater must run off your propane supply. No cell or Wi-Fi reception. Sites are all back-ins only. Ten-minute walk to the ocean. Closed mid-October through early May. Reserve in advance; office begins accepting requests the first week of February for the summer months. Some credit cards accepted; 14-day maximum stay.
Harborside RV Resort, Stockton Springs	5 Harborside Way, (for GPS units, use 414 Cape Jellison Road); **207-567-8013;** www.harbor siderv.com	$$$	Total of 15 full-hookup sites with water, sewer, and 30-/50-amp electric, no pull-throughs. Big rigs welcome, but nothing over 45 feet long. Sites all back up to a deep forest. Pool, strong Wi-Fi. First opened in 2020 and near Fort Point State Park, lighthouse on Cape Jellison and other attractions. Boat launch and sailboat / kayak rentals are available. Open mid-May through mid-October.
Saco/Old Orchard Beach Campground, Saco	814 A Portland Rd.; **207-282-0502** or **888-886-2477;** www. sunoutdoors.com/ maine/sun– outdoors–saco– old–orchard–beach	$$$–$$$$	Total of 83 sites with water and 20- and 30-amp electric, 50 full hookups, 55 pull-throughs. Laundry, pool, Wi-Fi, CATV. A centrally located Sun Outdoors Resort campground (formerly KOA) offers big, wooded sites and a short drive to several excellent lobster pounds and other food opportunities. Seasonal snack bar serves hamburgers, hot dogs, and desserts, along with pancake and waffle breakfasts. Offers a lobster cruise. Good playground, pool, and kid-friendly activities. Some credit cards accepted; open late April through early October.
Wolfe's Neck Oceanfront Campground, Freeport	134 Burnett Rd; **207-865-9307;** www.freeport camping.com/	$$–$$$$	Total of 70 RV sites, May–October, 20 electric/ water hookups, 30-/50-amp electric, 30-foot maximum RV length; sits on the ocean, with many sites surrounded by forest. In the middle of a functioning, organic demonstration farm. Kids may participate in dairy farm activities, including animal encounters. Open: Year-round; May through October with full services; water turned off after November.

TABLE 6-2 **Runner-up Maine Campgrounds**

Name and Location	Contact Info	Cost	What to Know
Camden Hills State Park; Camden	280 Belfast Rd.; **207-236-3109;** www5. maine.gov/public/ index	$$	Total of 107 sites, 44 water/electric, 30-amp hookups. Handicap access, pay showers, public phone. Most sites are shaded, and all are back-ins. Part of a 5,500-acre park with 25 miles of hiking trails. Open mid-May to mid-October; some credit cards accepted; 14-day maximum stay. Park also charges day-use fee of $4 for adult Maine residents, $6 for adult non-residents, and $2 for out of state adult seniors.
Cedar Haven Family Campground; Freeport	39 Baker Rd; **800-454-3403** or **207-865-6254;** cedarhavenfamily campground.com/	$$–$$$	Total of 44 sites with water and 30-amp electric, some 50-amp sites, 22 full hookups, 40-foot maximum RV length permitted. CATV (some sites), laundry, mobile sewer service, pool. Close to town but inland, this Good Sam–member campground offers just three narrow pull-throughs — you're better off with one of the wide back-in sites. Some credit cards accepted. Open May through October.
Mount Desert Narrows Camping Resort, Bar Harbor	1219-T SR 3; **207-288-4782;** www. rvonthego.com/ maine/mt-desert-narrows-camping-resort	$$$–$$$$	Total of 258 sites, 120 with water and 30-amp electric, 61 50-amp electric, 75 wide pull-throughs. CATV, laundry, mobile sewer service, good cell reception, heated pool, Wi-Fi. An older Encore/Thousand Trails resort. Many sites overlook Somes Sound. Pricier waterfront sites are small and forbidden from having sewer hookups by environmental authorities. Live entertainment, two playgrounds, video arcade, canoe rentals, and Island Explorer shuttle-bus service into Bar Harbor. Some credit cards accepted; open mid-May to mid-October.

Finding Good Eats in Maine

Because we carry our own kitchen everywhere, we usually opt for casual eateries rather than fancy restaurants, and often order takeout, so we control the time and place we eat.

Lobster central

If you're near Rockland in early August, don't miss the annual **Maine Lobster Festival,** a five-day event with food, entertainment, music, local craftsmen, and more. Bring your bib!

Even if you skip the festival, the best reason to travel through Maine in an RV is that you can buy fresh lobster every day to eat in, take out, or cook later. Maine lobster is so beloved that you'll even find eateries selling lobster pie and lobster ice cream.

TIP

Look for places called *lobster pounds.* Almost every coastal town has at least one of these simple spots where the owner usually sends their own fishing boats to haul the lobsters home every day, and then dumps them in a huge vat of seawater. This isn't one of those wimpy little lobster tanks you see in fancy urban restaurants or grocery stores with a couple of pathetic, over-the-hill crustaceans lethargically waving what's left of a claw. A *real* lobster pound is a vat of spunky, fighting specimens that a lobster wrangler has to wrestle onto the scales and hurl into a vat of boiling water.

Just so you know, there's a difference between hard-shell and soft-shell lobster:

>> **Hard-shell lobster** is more plentiful, especially in the springtime fishing season, with more meat.

>> **Soft-shell lobster** is sweeter, more flavorful, and more tender, but slightly cheaper because these critters have less meat on them and don't arrive until summertime.

You pay by the pound to get your **whole lobster** cooked to order; a 1¼- or 1½-pounder makes a generous portion for one average eater and takes about 20 minutes to cook. (If you want to buy a live lobster and cook it later yourself, ask the lobster wrangler for their recipe.) An order usually includes a dish of hot melted butter and sometimes a package of crackers or potato chips. Everything else on the menu — fried potatoes, onion rings, chowder, steamed clams, and corn on the cob — is extra.

TIP

If an entire lobster seems too much to handle, order a *lobster roll,* made of hot or cold chunks of lobster mixed with melted butter (for the hot lobster meat) or mayonnaise and chopped celery (for the cold lobster meat), and heaped into a buttered, toasted hot dog bun sliced open across the top rather than the side.

THE LOWDOWN ON HIGH LOBSTER PRICES

If you think you're going to get deep-discount lobster in Maine, be aware that post-pandemic prices have . into the stratosphere. Maine's dockside lobster prices set record highs in 2022. Prices fluctuate daily according to the current market, and global demand for Maine lobsters is at an all-time high.

Lobster is always pricier in spring because of low supply, and it takes four to six of them to make a full pound of picked lobster meat. A basic four-ounce lobster roll can go as low as $16, but don't be shocked to pay as much as $30–$48 for a fully loaded one-pound jumbo roll during the season in popular Maine hot spots, even in a no-frills carryout lobster shack.

You can ship live lobsters home to a dear friend, but they'd *better* be dear, because those prices are high too — not just for the live critters themselves, but also for the air freight to keep them alive and kicking. They don't exactly fly in the first-class seats, but our last flight to California in the budget steerage section should have been as cushy. We suspect they hog all the peanuts and free drinks.

What follows are some of our favorite spots for whole lobster or lobster rolls. Most have no indoor seating (outdoor picnic tables are common) or no seating at all. So be prepared to occasionally fend off badly behaved seagulls who may swoop down and make a grab for your tasty lobster. Many of these locations open only seasonally (May–September) and may not follow a regular schedule, so definitely call ahead (if they have a listed phone number) before heading for one of them.

» **Bayley's Bait Shed,** Pine Point, Scarborough (**800-932-6456** from outside Maine or **207-883-4571;** www.baitshedrestaurant.com): Off U.S. 1 at the far northeast end of SR 9, the Bait Shed has all your favorite lobster and other seafood favorites, while the adjacent **Bayley's Lobster Pound** (https://bayleys.com) is the place to go if you want to ship live Maine lobsters home. The Bait Shed is open daily in summer and features all outdoor seating overlooking Pine Point Harbor.

» **Boothbay Lobster Wharf** (formerly Lobsterman's Co-op), 97 Atlantic Ave., near the aquarium in Boothbay Harbor; **207-633-4900;** www.boothbaylobsterwharf.com): Located on a working lobstermen's dock, so you can watch them unload their daily catch from the outdoor picnic tables, or eat inside in the dining room, with a bar that features live entertainment on weekends. Choose between hard-shell or soft-shell lobster, plus a full menu. Open for lunch and dinner from Memorial Day through Columbus Day.

» **Harraseeket Lunch & Lobster Company,** South Freeport Harbor (**207-865-3535**; `http://harraseeketlunchandlobster.com`): Swing by here for a quick picker-upper. Just don't try to go down the narrow road leading to the pier in a large RV; locals have passed an ordinance against it. Park up on South Freeport Road and walk the quarter mile down to the restaurant. If you don't want to pick your own lobster from their pound out back, line up at the lunch counter and order anything from lobster rolls to clamburgers and homemade *whoopie pies* (two patties of devil's food cake sandwiched with marshmallow cream and dipped in chocolate). If you want beer or wine, bring your own. Open Friday through Wednesday, April through October.

» **The Lobster Shack at Two Lights,** 225 Two Lights Rd., Cape Elizabeth (**207-799-1677;** `www.lobstershacktwolights.com`): Located at Two Lights lighthouse since the 1920s, the Lobster Shack sits atop a rocky plateau with plenty of picnic tables and a view of Portland Harbor. A rare lobster shack with indoor seating. The venerable family-run eatery serves homemade clam chowder, boiled lobster dinners, lobster rolls, fried clams, plus the usual burgers and hot dogs. Open daily April through mid-October.

» **Mabel's Lobster Claw,** 124 Ocean Ave., Kennebunkport (**207-967-2562;** `www.mabelslobster.com`): Established in 1953, Mabel's won the presidential endorsement of George H. W. and Barbara Bush. You can order a whole boiled lobster, a baked stuffed lobster, a lobster roll dressed with mayonnaise and garnished with lettuce, and (as if you needed a few more calories) peanut butter ice cream pie with hot fudge topping. Indoor and outdoor dining with a full bar. Open daily April through November.

BARGAIN ALERT

» **Maine Diner,** on U.S. 1 at 2265 Post Rd., Wells (**207-646-4441;** `https://mainediner.com`): The diner serves a wonderful hot lobster roll slathered in melted butter. Its famous lobster pie also is memorable. Or skip the seafood and go for the blueberry pancakes. Open year-round daily from 7:00 a.m. to 8:00 p.m. except major holidays.

» **Red's Eats,** on U.S. 1 at 41 Water Street (at the intersection with Main Street), Wiscasset (**207-882-6128;** `www.redseatsmaine.com`): First opened in 1938, Red's claims to be the "world's best lobster shack," and a shack it is — it's probable that your RV is bigger than Red's building. Everything is carryout only. The long lines in season can take an hour or more to get through, and it's been said to cause the biggest traffic jams in Maine at times. Serves humongous lobster rolls, clams, scallops, plus burgers, fries, onion rings, hot dogs, and blueberry desserts for the non-pescatarian seafood haters in your group. Ice cream too, for those warm summer days. Open daily May through October.

More than just lobster: Markets and meals

While Maine is mainly about lobster in our book, you can also track down regional goodies from chowders to popovers and all things blueberry.

» **Bar Harbor Inn,** Newport Drive, Bar Harbor (**207-288-3351;** https://barharborinn.com): At this classic inn adjacent to the municipal pier, you can get a great (albeit expensive) hamburger at lunchtime in the Reading Room, open for dinner, or outside on Gatsby's Terrace, which has a water-front view and is open daily.

» **Jordan Pond House,** Acadia National Park, Park Loop Road, north of Seal Harbor (**207-276-3316;** https://jordanpondhouse.com/): A park tradition since 1893. Despite the line during peak season, you'll want to queue up for a teatime feast of hot popovers and homemade jam, ice cream, cookies, and pastries. They also serve lunch and dinner, but teatime on the lawn, weather permitting, is tops. Open daily mid-May through late October.

» **Moody's Diner,** U.S. 1, Waldoboro (**207-832-7785;** https://moodysdiner.com): Opened in 1927, Moody's has a nationally famous diner, plus cabins, a motel, gift shop, and ice cream stand. When you tire of the lobster places, Moody's Diner has a big menu that's chock-full of great comfort food made from scratch ("Like Mother used to make!"). Their breakfasts, decent portions, and very reasonable prices are the biggest attractions. Open daily.

Maine supermarkets

The most common supermarket chains you find on this route are **Hannaford's Supermarket and Pharmacy** and **Shaw's** (which is part of the Albertson's/Safeway family of stores). Look for them in Bar Harbor, Belfast, Brunswick, Bucksport, Camden, Portland, Rockland, and other fair-sized towns. **Walmart Supercenters** are in Biddeford, Brunswick, Ellsworth north of Bar Harbor, south of Camden at Thomaston, and south of Portland in Scarborough.

Finding Maine's Farmers Markets

Farmers' markets are highly seasonal, and you can find a statewide directory of them at the **Maine Federation of Farmers Markets** website (https://mainefarmersmarkets.org/)

Portland Summer Farmers Market, in Deering Oaks Park on Park Avenue between State Street and Deering Avenue, Portland (**207-228-2016;** www.portlandmainefarmersmarket.org). Portland has had a farmers market here since 1786. At this great food-shopping stop, vendors offer the best of Maine foods, from farmhouse butter and cheeses to organic fruits and vegetables to local seafood and several different varieties of Maine potatoes. Visit on Saturday when plenty of street parking is available. Open Saturday and Wednesday from late April until late November. (*Note*: From December through April, the **Portland Winter Market** opens in the former Maine Girls Academy, 631 Stevens Avenue, on Saturdays.) Many vendors accept credit cards and even SNAP/EBT purchases, but not all do, so bring cash.

Fast Facts for Maine Travelers

Area Code
The area code in Maine is **207**.

Driving Laws
All RV passengers must wear seat belts. Passengers may not ride in trailers. Speed limits for cars, RVs, and trucks vary between 65 mph and 75 mph on rural interstates, and 50 mph to 70 mph on urban interstates. Speed limits in urban areas are lower.

Emergency
Call **911**.

Hospitals
Hospitals along the route include Penobscot Bay Medical Center, 4 Glen Cove Dr., Rockport (**207-596-8000**), and Mount Desert Island Hospital, 10 Wayman Lane, Bar Harbor (**207-288-5081**).

Information
Helpful sources include the Maine Office of Tourism, 59 Statehouse Station, Augusta (**888-624-6345**; https://visitmaine. com or https://maine.com), **and Acadia Information Center (207-667-8550**; www. acadiainfo.com**)**.

Pharmacies
Most towns have a Rite-Aid drugstore.

Post Office
The U.S. Post Office in Bar Harbor is located at 55 Cottage St. (207-288-3122).

Road and Weather Conditions
For weather and road construction information in Maine, New Hampshire, and Vermont, call **511** or visit the New England 511 website at www.newengland511.org/.

Taxes
Maine's general sales tax is 5.5 percent. Maine charges a 9 percent lodging tax on meals and lodging, which includes campgrounds. The state gasoline tax is 30¢ per gallon, including local taxes.

Time Zone
Maine is on Eastern time.

Chapter **7**

Western New York: Cooperstown to Niagara Falls

Y ou may find that the only image popping into your brain when you hear the words *New York* is a dense jungle of skyscrapers, a swarm of yellow taxicabs, Times Square on New Year's Eve, and old *CSI: New York* episodes. But once you get out of the sprawling megatropolis around the island of Manhattan in the far southeastern tip of New York, the rest of the state is a completely different place. This massive state has breathtaking natural beauty and friendly folks who don't seem a bit like the grizzled, neurotic New Yorkers you see in old Neil Simon plays.

History lovers rejoice over the heritage hot spots, while nature lovers find that Western New York has some of the most exciting natural wonders anywhere in the country. You can discover the area's innate beauty, ranging from the awe-inspiring roar of Niagara Falls (which was the most popular honeymoon destination for the first half of the 20th century), to the serene sights of the 9,000-square-mile Finger Lakes region (which is flanked by vineyard-covered slopes). Western

New York has plenty of awesome scenery lying around everywhere to lure any RVing vacationer.

In this chapter, you get acquainted with the plethora of natural wonders you find in Western New York — river gorges, waterfalls, caves, forests, lakes, and much more. You also find out about the truly original attractions of the area: the National Baseball Hall of Fame in Cooperstown, Erie Canal Village in Rome, the Lucille Ball Desi Arnaz Museum in Jamestown, the squeaky cheese curds for sale at the cheese factories around Cuba and Dewittville, and the Jell-O Gallery museum in LeRoy. And in case you always wondered how those scrawny chicken appendages got misidentified as *buffalo wings*, you can visit their birthplace in Buffalo at the Anchor Bar.

Planning Ahead for a Western New York Tour

Any time of year when it isn't snowing or freezing is a good time to visit Western New York, so cross out the winter months for a visit unless you want to ski or you have winter tires, four-wheel drive, an all-season RV, and nerves of steel. The very best times are spring and autumn, with summer a close second. The roads are decent; the campgrounds are spacious, appealing, and often unique; the food is tasty; and the locals are friendly. So plan a visit to Western New York for a unique journey through this beautiful, historic slice of Americana.

Meeting the campground and weather challenges

The biggest challenge with visiting this area is finding the sweet spot on the calendar when campgrounds are open, but the swarming hordes of vacationing Northeasterners aren't on the road. Whenever possible, make campground reservations for stays during the peak season from Memorial Day through Labor Day, and don't be shocked if you need to make them a year in advance.

REMEMBER

Niagara Falls-area campgrounds, in particular, are packed with visitors from both sides of the border. So are the most popular state park campgrounds, partially because state-run campsites are considerably cheaper than privately owned campgrounds. If you absolutely, positively need to visit once freezing weather sets in, open campgrounds with water and sewer hookups will be almost impossible to find.

TIP

When packing, take along a variety of clothing, because you may encounter warm, humid summer temperatures morphing quickly into cool, rainy days when you'll want a jacket or sweater.

Dealing with unique issues of the drive

Here are some driving tips to keep in mind while planning your Western New York trek:

>> Pretty, tree-shaded Cooperstown has limited parking even for cars, not to mention RVs and trailers, so we recommend parking in one of the free lots on the edge of town (signs are posted). Then use the trolley to shuttle among the attractions.

>> Ithaca, the home of Cornell University and Ithaca College, is one of many New York towns named for classical cities or places. (Among the others are Alexandria, Athens, Babylon, Damascus, Naples, Rome, Syracuse, Troy, and loads more.) Built on steep hills, Ithaca can present a challenge for drivers of large RVs. If you want to look around the town, park in one of the large lots downtown near the river around Buffalo Street and explore on foot.

REMEMBER

A part of your planned journey may include visiting Niagara Falls, and you may want to explore the Canadian as well as the U.S. side. Canada has some rules about documentation for RV drivers and passengers, as well as restrictions regarding the type of foodstuffs carried into the country. See Chapter 2 for a discussion of these rules and restrictions.

Engaging the New York phone apps

TIP

Take advantage of the smartphone apps the state of New York offers its visitors. These free apps are available to help visitors with vacation planning and sightseeing:

>> **NY State Parks Explorer:** This app from the New York State Office of Parks, Recreation and Historic Preservation provides visitors with tons of information about the variety of destinations, activities, and adventures available throughout the Empire State. It lists more than 250 parks, historic sites, trails, golf courses, boat launches, and (most important for us) campgrounds on interactive maps. Highly recommended.

>> **I Love NY:** This app from the New York State Office of Information Technology Services is a bit more ambitious in scope. It lists thousands of attractions, events, hotels, campgrounds, wineries, breweries, restaurants, and a lot more, but it seems to be skewed more toward sites in and around New York City. Still, the information is quite useful statewide, and the listings are updated regularly.

>> **511NY:** Like an increasing number of states, New York provides news about up-to-the-minute traffic and road conditions around the state, You can access this information by calling 511 or using this app.

Taking the Drive through New York

In Central New York, start your Western New York tour in **Cooperstown,** which is 225 miles northwest of New York City. Named for its founder, who was the father of author James Fenimore Cooper (author of *The Last of the Mohicans*), Cooperstown is a good all-American starting point for this drive. The town includes the **National Baseball Hall of Fame,** Cooper memorabilia and a fine art collection in the **Fenimore Art Museum,** and the **Farmers' Museum,** with costumed living history characters demonstrating crafts and farmwork in 1845.

Leaving Cooperstown and heading north

From Cooperstown, head north on SR 80 along the shores of **Otsego Lake** (which James Fenimore Cooper called *Glimmerglass* in his stories) and pass by **Hyde Hall** on the other side of the lake in Glimmerglass State Park, the ancestral home of the Coopers.

Turn west on U.S. 20 and then go north on SR 28 across the Mohawk River to **Herkimer.** If it's time to stop for the night, drive 7 miles north, continuing on SR 28, to the **Herkimer Diamond KOA** and the **Herkimer Diamond Mines.** Not really diamonds, the naturally faceted quartz crystals mined here are nice to display as mineral samples; prospecting season runs from April through mid-November.

From Herkimer, follow SR 5 north to **Rome** (it's nestled between I-90 and the Erie Canal) and then take SR 69 to SR 46 and SR 49, leading to the **Erie Canal Village,** a living history museum near the spot where the first shovelful of earth was turned for the original canal. The village is a reconstruction of a 19th-century canal village created by moving 15 historic buildings here from other places in the region. Costumed reenactors recreate the 1840s.

Moving on to Syracuse and Ithaca

Return to I-90 (it's south of Rome) and continue west to **Syracuse,** where, if you enjoyed the Erie Canal Village, you can visit the **Erie Canal Museum.** Then take SR 174 and SR 175 to **Skaneateles** (pronounced skin-ee-*at*-luhs and nicknamed *Skinny Atlas*), a pretty little town full of boutiques, flowers, and cafés. From Skaneateles, drive west on U.S. 20 through **Auburn** to the north end of **Cayuga Lake** and turn south on SR 89; follow the lakeside road, lined with wineries, south to **Ithaca.**

Ithaca, notable as the home of **Cornell University** and **Ithaca College,** is one of many New York towns named for classical cities. Built on steep hills, the city is a challenge for RV drivers; if you want to look around, park in one of the large lots downtown near the river around Buffalo Street (where the lake cruises take off) and explore on foot.

Heading toward Corning and back north

Head out of town on SR 13, driving southwest to **Elmira,** home of **Mark Twain's study,** now ensconced on the campus of **Elmira College**. From Elmira, continue west on I-86 to **Corning,** home of the famous **Corning Museum of Glass**. If it's snack time, try the 1880s ice cream parlor at **Ice Cream Works** on West Market Street for some imaginative flavors, including wine ice cream.

From Corning, take scenic SR 14 north to **Watkins Glen** and drive the western shore of **Seneca Lake** north to **Geneva** (to the west); then head east on US 20 to **Seneca Falls.**

From Seneca Falls, pick up I-90 West and take the short drive to **Rochester,** where shutterbugs may want to visit George Eastman's (founder of Kodak) former home, now the **George Eastman Museum**. Suffragist Susan B. Anthony and abolitionist Frederick Douglass also were born and buried in Rochester.

Turning south again and meandering

From here, head south again, first on I-490 to SR 19, and then on SR 19A south to **Belfast,** turning west on SR 305 to **Cuba,** home to the **Cuba Cheese Shop.**

The drive west along I-86 or SR 417 between **Olean** and **Salamanca** takes you past Allegany State Park, a 65,000-acre park with plenty of hiking trails and four different campgrounds with a total of 316 campsites. From Salamanca, take I-86 over to **Jamestown** at the east end of Lake Chautauqua. Native daughter Lucille Ball is remembered in the **Lucy Desi Museum** here.

Some of the Ohio Amish resettled in this part of New York in 1949 in and around the town of **Conewango Valley,** 5 miles farther north on U.S. 62. **Valley View Cheese Company** offers free samples of locally made cheese, along with other Amish cheeses from Ohio.

SENECA FALLS: FEMINIST TOUR STOP

In the same way that Memorial Day was first celebrated in nearby Waterloo, New York, as a holiday honoring soldiers who died in the Civil War, the town of Seneca Falls is noted for its role in highlighting the rights and achievements of women. Elizabeth Cady Stanton, a housewife and mother of seven, organized and led the first women's rights convention here in 1848.

Many powerful women are associated with this area. In addition to Stanton in Seneca Falls, there's Amelia Jenks Bloomer, a suffragist who spawned a fashion craze by parading around in the "pantaloon" underskirt drawers that were named for her. In Auburn, the remarkable former slave Harriet Tubman was a major force in the Underground Railroad. And in Rochester, serious feminists must pause to pay tribute at the Susan B. Anthony Museum & House, a National Historic Landmark.

Highlights in Seneca Falls include **Stanton's birthplace,** 32 Washington St. (**315-568-2991;** open daily except holidays.); the **National Women's Hall of Fame,** located in the historic Seneca Knitting Mill, 1 Canal St. (**315-568-8060;** https://www.womenofthehall.org/ — open daily except Wednesdays and major holidays; free admission, but donations encouraged), honoring outstanding women in the arts, athletics, sciences, government, and philanthropy; and **Women's Rights National Historical Park,** 136 Fall St. (**315-568-2991;** https://www.nps.gov/wori — open daily except holidays; free admission), where you can see the restored Stanton home and first women's rights convention site. Be aware that all three locations have limited parking areas and may not be able to accommodate your RV.

The cause of feminism may be the most common historical association with the Seneca Falls area, but it's not the only thing. Another significant historical landmark is the **Seneca Oil Spring,** located near the spillway end of Cuba Lake on the Seneca Nation's Oil Springs Reservation. At the base of the reservoir's spillway, Franciscan missionary Joseph de La Roche d'Allion discovered an unusual spring in 1627 where black tendrils of oil mixed with the water — the first recorded mention of oil on the North American continent.

Exploring west from Jamestown and back north

If you take SR 394 out of Jamestown, you come to **Mayville** at the west end of Lake Chautauqua. Here, **Webb's Candies** offers free factory tours and samples of goat milk fudge, a local delicacy. If you don't think you'd like it, don't worry — they also make several other types of candy.

SALAMANCA SECRETS

Salamanca is believed to be the largest U.S. city on an Indian reservation — in this case, the Allegany Indian Reservation. The town has two interesting museums. The fine **Seneca-Iroquois National Museum,** which you find at 82 West Hetzel; **716-945-1760;** www.senecamuseum.org, combines history with contemporary arts and crafts. It's open Monday through Friday. Admission price varies by age. The **Salamanca Rail Museum,** at 170 Main St.; **716-945-3133, is** open Tuesday, Thursday, and Saturday; a 1912 passenger depot (now used for exhibition space) marks the spot where three major railroad lines once converged.

From Mayville, SR 58 travels north to New York's Spiritualism centers, **Cassadaga** and **Lily Dale,** where Spiritualist assemblies delve into mysterious matters for ten weeks every summer. From Lily Dale, take SR 60 to **Fredonia,** home of a splendidly restored 1891 opera house that bears no sign of the Marx Brothers, who borrowed the town's name (spelling it *Freedonia*) for their film *Duck Soup.*

From Fredonia, take I-90 East to Exit 57A to **Eden,** the only place where metal kazoos are still made. And then, from Eden, drive north about 10 miles on U.S. 62 to the junction of Alternate U.S. 20, where you turn east to go to **East Aurora,** one of the most beguiling little towns in the state. Of interest to students of architecture and furnishings is the **Elbert Hubbard Roycroft Museum,** which celebrates the American arm of the early 20th-century Arts and Crafts movement.

Finally, turning toward Buffalo

SR 400 is the quickest way into **Buffalo** and the way to go if you want to taste what we consider the best roast beef sandwich in America — the **beef on weck** at **Schwabl's** in **West Seneca.**

Buffalo, of course, is the birthplace of the world-famous buffalo wing, a snack so popular, it has inspired its own humor ("What do you do with the rest of the buffalo?"). To taste the original, we visited the **Anchor Bar,** near downtown, where original owner Teressa Bellissimo is credited with inventing the spicy treat in 1964.

In **North Tonawanda,** north of Buffalo on SR 265/384, is the **Herschell Carrousel Factory Museum,** with its own historic carousel; a ride is included in the basic admission fee . On the way to or from the museum, plan a detour to Sheridan Drive (SR 324) in **Tonawanda** to visit **Ted's Hot Dogs,** one of America's great hot dog emporiums.

Buffalo is only 25 miles from **Niagara Falls** (see "Must-See Western New York Attractions"). We like to camp on **Grand Island,** a big island in the middle of the Niagara River near the falls. The KOA there can arrange rentals and tours to the falls, so you can leave your RV plugged in and strike out on your own.

The total drive, depicted in Figure 7-1, is 725 miles.

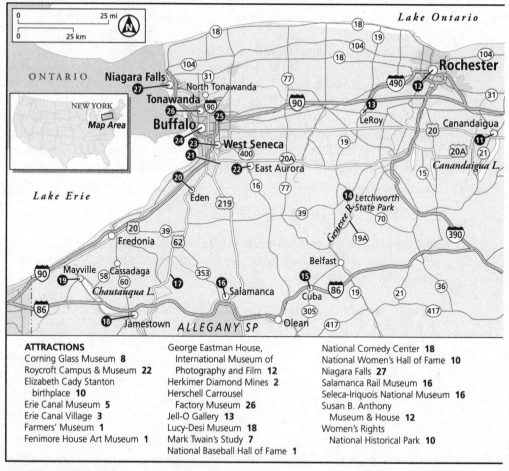

ATTRACTIONS

Corning Glass Museum **8**
Roycroft Campus & Museum **22**
Elizabeth Cady Stanton
   birthplace **10**
Erie Canal Museum **5**
Erie Canal Village **3**
Farmers' Museum **1**
Fenimore House Art Museum **1**

George Eastman House,
   International Museum of
   Photography and Film **12**
Herkimer Diamond Mines **2**
Herschell Carrousel
   Factory Museum **26**
Jell-O Gallery **13**
Lucy-Desi Museum **18**
Mark Twain's Study **7**
National Baseball Hall of Fame **1**

National Comedy Center **18**
National Women's Hall of Fame **10**
Niagara Falls **27**
Salamanca Rail Museum **16**
Seleca-Iriquois National Museum **16**
Susan B. Anthony
   Museum & House **12**
Women's Rights
   National Historical Park **10**

FIGURE 7-1: *continued*

Must-See Western New York Attractions

Corning Museum of Glass
Corning

The striking exhibit hall displays fine contemporary glass art, including several pieces by artist Dale Chihuly. The Glass Sculpture Gallery, the Hot Glass Show, the Corning Museum of Glass, the Studio, the Steuben Factory, the Windows Gallery, the Glass Innovation Center, and the Glass Shops offer a primer on everything you ever wanted to know about art glass, from simple glassblowing through the 3,500 years of glass history. Closed New Year's Day, Thanksgiving, Christmas Eve, and Christmas Day. Allow two hours or more if you want to browse the shops.

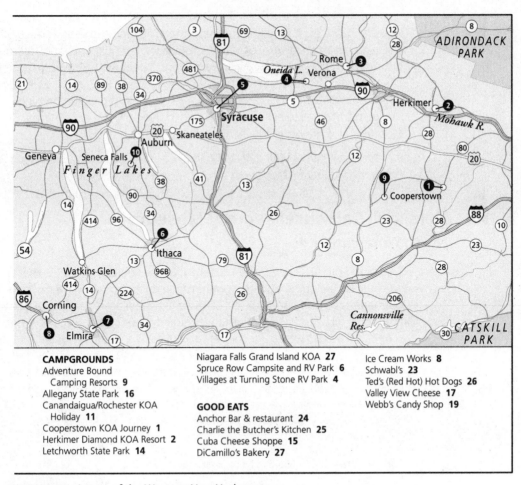

CAMPGROUNDS
Adventure Bound
  Camping Resorts **9**
Allegany State Park **16**
Canandaigua/Rochester KOA
  Holiday **11**
Cooperstown KOA Journey **1**
Herkimer Diamond KOA Resort **2**
Letchworth State Park **14**

Niagara Falls Grand Island KOA **27**
Spruce Row Campsite and RV Park **6**
Villages at Turning Stone RV Park **4**

GOOD EATS
Anchor Bar & restaurant **24**
Charlie the Butcher's Kitchen **25**
Cuba Cheese Shoppe **15**
DiCamillo's Bakery **27**

Ice Cream Works **8**
Schwabl's **23**
Ted's (Red Hot) Hot Dogs **26**
Valley View Cheese **17**
Webb's Candy Shop **19**

FIGURE 7-1: A map of the Western New York route.

1 Museum Way. **800-732-6845** *or* **607-937-5371;** https://home.cmog.org/. **RV parking:** *Designated lot. Admission varies by age.*

George Eastman Museum
Rochester

Bank clerk George Eastman worked for years to turn photography into a more portable, popular art, and by 1888 he had his first Kodak camera on the market. Soon afterward, he gained control of the celluloid-coating process that made film accessible to the average consumer. His elegant 1902 mansion — restored to how it looked in his day — is the largest and oldest photography museum in the world. The 50-room mansion features many original furnishings but also has modern galleries showcasing masterworks of photography and motion pictures.

Housing more than a million artifacts, the collection includes some 6,000 still cameras and a library of 42,000 books and manuscripts about film photography you can view by appointment. The on-site 500-seat Dryden Theatre presents more than 300 rare movies every year and is one of only a few theaters in the U.S. that can safely handle and project the highly flammable, nitrate-based celluloid film used in the early days of cinema. Closed Mondays and major holidays. Allow two to three hours.

900 East Ave. (SR 96). **585-271-3361;** https://www.eastman.org. **RV parking:** *Designated lot. Admission varies by age.*

Herschell Carrousel Factory Museum
North Tonawanda

This grand old factory-turned-museum focuses on carousels (or merry-go-rounds), including how they were made and who made them. It's been claimed that more hand-carved carousels came from Tonawanda, New York, than from all other U.S. cities that produced them combined. Allan Herschell's carousel factory was extremely successful in its day. A self-guiding brochure takes you through the various work areas in the factory and describes what went on in each area. A beautiful collection of carousel horses plus a working 1916 Allan Herschell carousel are on the premises. An additional exhibit area, the Kiddieland Testing Park, features motorized rides for younger children. Open Wednesday through Sunday. Allow two to three hours.

180 Thompson St. **716-693-1885;** www.carrouselmuseum.org/. **RV parking:** *Some parking in lot behind the museum; otherwise, street parking in a residential neighborhood. Admission includes ride tokens and is by age.*

Lucille Ball Desi Arnaz Museum
Jamestown

Lucille Ball, of *I Love Lucy* fame, was born in Jamestown in 1911, and this museum was dedicated to her and her first husband (and straight man), Desi Arnaz, in the summer of 1996. The museum features TV and movie clips, interactive displays, collections of artifacts and clothing, and even replicas of Lucy and Ricky's New York apartment and Hollywood hotel suite sets. A gift shop sells souvenirs. Allow two hours.

TIP

You can combine this museum tour with the nearby **National Comedy Center** (https://comedycenter.org), which features 50 immersive exhibits. Explore stand-up performances, movies, TV and radio shows, cartoons, comic strips, and viral internet memes to discover the great works and iconic performers — from Charlie Chaplin to Dave Chappelle — who elevated comedy to an art form. Open Thursday through Monday.

2 W. Third St. **716-484-0800;** *https://lucy-desi.com/.* **RV parking:** *Street parking. Admission varies by age.*

Mark Twain's Study
Elmira

A glass-windowed octagon built in 1874 to resemble a riverboat pilot house was created for Twain's use as a study when he visited his sister-in-law's Quarry Farm outside Elmira. Inside, he wrote some of his most famous works, including *The Adventures of Tom Sawyer* and *Adventures of Huckleberry Finn.* In 1952, the study was moved to the Elmira College campus. (Previously, the Langdon family resisted all efforts by Henry Ford to buy the study for his own Dearborn, Michigan, museum.) Memorabilia, period furniture, and photographs are on display. Open daily from Memorial Day to Labor Day. Allow one hour.

1 Park Place, Elmira College. **607-735-1941;** *https://marktwainstudies.com.* **RV parking:** *Street or designated lot. Free admission.*

National Baseball Hall of Fame
Cooperstown

This hall of fame is one of America's favorite family summer destinations. Many visitors stay in the area several days in order to cover everything. The legendary Doubleday baseball on display is believed to be the ball used in 1839 when Abner Doubleday invented baseball in Elihu Phinney's cow pasture one afternoon — if, in fact, that ever happened, which some experts doubt. Additional artifacts are on hand, ranging from Jackie Robinson's warm-up jacket to Joe DiMaggio's locker; Ty Cobb's sliding pads to Yogi Berra's glove; and bats used for record-breaking home runs by Babe Ruth, Roger Maris, Mickey Mantle, Hank Aaron, and Mark McGwire. The original game, called *town ball,* involved anywhere from 20 to 40 people and is reenacted occasionally at the **Farmers' Museum**. Allow three hours to three days.

25 Main St. **888-425-5633** *or* **607-547-7200;** https://baseballhall.org. **RV parking:** *Very limited in town; leave large RVs in designated parking areas on the edges of town and take shuttle transportation to the museum. Admission varies by age.*

Niagara Falls
Niagara Falls, New York and Canada

The majestic Niagara Falls, on the Niagara River connecting Lake Ontario and Lake Erie, have been the classic American honeymoon destination for more than 200 years. In 1801, future Vice President Aaron Burr's daughter Theodosia and her new husband traveled to Niagara Falls for their honeymoon. In 1804, Jérôme Bonaparte (Napoleon's brother) and his new wife took a stagecoach overland all the way from New Orleans just to honeymoon by the falls.

With all there is to see and do in the area around Niagara Falls, you can easily spend a week there without going anywhere else. You can view the awesome trio of waterfalls — **American Falls** and **Bridal Veil Falls** on the American side, and **Horseshoe Falls** on the Canadian side — on foot, in a boat, from an observation deck, and from vantage points in two countries. You also find zip lines, overhead cable rides, helicopter sightseeing tours, historic sites, shopping, arcades, casinos, and loads more.

The falls are spectacularly illuminated every evening from dusk until 1:00 or 2:00 a.m. year-round, and fireworks displays happen every evening at 10:30 from late May through early October. You can see the lighting and fireworks shows from both the U.S. and Canadian sides. And, of course, you hear the thundering roar of the falls at all times, from anywhere.

Destination Niagara USA, 10 Rainbow Boulevard. **877-FALLS-US (877-325-5787);** www.niagarafallsusa.com.

THE MANY ATTRACTIONS OF NIAGARA FALLS

A first-time visitor to the Niagara Falls area should take a guided tour and put up with being herded along instead of standing in long lines. This is especially true during peak season, when many of the 12 million annual visitors are milling about. You also need to consider just how wet you're willing to get in pursuit of a great photo op. Although virtually all the tours provide plastic raincoats, you're still going to get splashed. Here are some other suggestions for what to see and how to see it around Niagara Falls:

- If you're staying in one of the nearby campgrounds, such as the **Niagara Falls KOA,** you can book a bus sightseeing tour that picks you up at the campground. If you want to tour the area on your own, allow even more time, and try to leave your RV at the campground — motorhome RVers who aren't towing a car are at a serious disadvantage here.

- The **USA Prospect Point Observation Tower** has an open-air deck that extends to the very edge of the roaring gorge, and gives you a panoramic view of all three major falls. The most-praised vantage point (and one of the wettest) is the deck of one of the *Maid of the Mist* **boats** that cruise directly in front of all three falls. (*Maid of the Mist* has its own parking lot, accessed by Prospect Street.) If you're on foot, the **Cave of the Winds tour** begins with an elevator ride from Goat Island down to the base of Bridal Veil Falls and a stroll across a wooden walkway to within 25 feet of the falls. Total adrenaline junkies can experience Class 5 rapids on the Niagara River with **Whirlpool Jet Boat Tours** (www.whirlpooljet.com).

- **Niagara Falls State Park** (www.niagarafallsstatepark.com), south of town off Robert Moses Parkway, provides a close-up view of American Falls. **Goat Island,** with two big parking lots, is accessed from First Street, by the Niagara Rapids Bridge (also called Goat Island Bridge). On the northeastern point of town is the historic **Old Fort Niagara** (www.oldfortniagara.org), which played an important role during the colonial period in North America. There has been a fort on this strategic point since the French first built one in 1679 to guard the entrance to the Great Lakes. It was captured in 1759 by the British, turned over to the Americans after the revolution in 1796, and briefly fell back into British hands during the War of 1812.

- The **Niagara Falls Underground Railroad Heritage Center** (716-300-8477; www.niagarafallsundergroundrailroad.org), located downtown in West Niagara at 825 Depot Avenue, adjacent to the Amtrak station, explains the important role the area around the falls played for Black Americans escaping slavery before the Civil War. Crossing over the river to find sanctuary in British Canada by boat or over the former International Suspension Bridge was literally the last mile for fleeing slaves seeking their freedom and safety from pursuit by their former owners.

(continued)

(continued)

- The **Canadian side** of the falls offers its own fantastic views (`www.niagarafall stourism.com`). From **Table Rock House,** reached by Niagara Parkway, 1 mile south of Rainbow Bridge, three tunnels open to good vistas of the falls. The landmark 520-foot-tall **Skylon Tower** offers an incredible bird's-eye view of the whole area from its observation deck and rotating restaurant at the top. The **Clifton Hill** area has arcades and attractions, including the **Niagara SkyWheel** — a giant Ferris wheel adjacent to the river. And if you're able to leave the big RV behind, stop for breakfast, lunch, or dinner at the delightfully 1960s-style **Flying Saucer Restaurant** (`http://www.flyingsaucer restaurant.com`).

- Finally, if you're looking for the classic Niagara Falls honeymoon kitsch experience, park the RV and book a room in **Villager Lodge** (`http://www.villagerniagara.com`). Be sure to ask for a honeymoon suite with a red heart-shaped hot tub. Yes, really. And bring the bubble bath for taking that honeymoon souvenir bathtub photo.

More Cool Things to See and Do in Western New York

Deciding whether an attraction belongs in the *must-see* or *more-cool-things* category is often a toss-up. Following are some mainstream and offbeat places to go in Western New York. You may find that some of these qualify as must-sees on your trip:

>> **Live in style.** Fans of the **Arts and Crafts** (or Craftsman) movement of the early 20th century will want to stop and tour the **Roycroft Campus** in East Aurora, located south and west of Main and Grove Streets. The area, including the **Roycroft Campus Museum** in the visitor's center, is a National Historic Landmark district comprising nine homes and shops designed and built by one of the first proponents of the Arts and Crafts philosophy in America, Elbert Hubbard, and his fellow craftspeople known as the Roycroft guild.

At the height of the Roycroft movement, more than 500 artisans and craftspeople came here to work and study Hubbard's influential design philosophy. Gustaf Stickley was one of the most distinctive Roycroft designers, and his furniture (along with similar-looking knockoffs) remains in high demand today. Perhaps the most stunning display of this movement is the elegant **Roycroft Inn,** 40 S. Grove St. (**716-652-5552;** `https://roycroftinn.com/`), where you can stay overnight if you feel inclined to leave your RV behind. Docent-led tours of the museum and campus require reservations. You also find a separate museum in Hubbard's restored on-campus home.

31 S. Grove St.; **716-655-0261;** `https://roycroftcampuscorporation.com.`
RV parking on the street. Admission is free, or by donation.

» **Sing "Low bridge, everybody down! . . . Fifteen years on the Erie Canal."**
The 363-mile-long Erie Canal connecting the Atlantic Ocean to the Great Lakes
officially opened in 1825 and changed the exploration and immigration of
Midwestern and Western America forever. A National Historic Landmark, the
Erie Canal Museum is in the last of the *weighlock buildings* that once served
as weigh stations for barges along the famed canal. You can see crew quarters
inside a replica canal boat and find out about immigration along the canal
during the 19th century. Closed on holidays. Allow two hours, and you can
get a guided tour.

If cycling is your passion, check out the **Canalway Trail** (`https://www.canals.`
`ny.gov/trails/about.html`), a more-than-300-mile-long network of bicycle
trails that parallels much of New York's once-vast statewide canal system.

318 Erie Blvd., East Syracuse. **315-471-0593;** `https://eriecanalmuseum.org.`
*RV parking: Available in a designated lot or on the street. Admission is free, but
a $10 donation is accepted.*

» **See a real giant and get in touch with the riches of the land.** Most
Americans these days live in cities and suburbs and have no idea what rural
life was like before the end of World War I. The **Farmers' Museum** is a living
history museum with live interpreters and reenactors where it's eternally the
1840s. Visit the Lippitt Farmstead, an operating re-creation of a mid-1800s
Northeastern farm. Then explore the historic village with its blacksmith, print-
shop, general store, pharmacy, country church, and tavern. One odd highlight is
the Cardiff Giant, a famous mid-19th century sideshow hoax billed as a 10-and-
a-half-foot "petrified man," purportedly descended from an ancient race of
giants referred to in the Book of Genesis. "Mystifies scientists and theologians
alike!" One of showman P. T. Barnum's favorites.

Open from April through October, with hours changing seasonally. Also open
in March for sugaring off Sundays (featuring demonstrations of maple syrup
making), Thanksgiving weekend, and holiday lantern tours in December. You
can get combination tickets with the Fenimore Art Museum and/or the National
Baseball Hall of Fame at reduced rates.

5775 SR 80 (Lake Road), Cooperstown. **607-547-1450;** `www.farmersmuseum.org.`
RV parking: Available in a designated off-road lot. Admission varies by age.

» **Follow the Leatherstocking trails.** A large collection of American Indian art,
fine American art, and examples of folk art make up the permanent collection
of the **Fenimore Art Museum,** located in a house once belonging to *The Last*

of the Mohicans author James Fenimore Cooper. The historic house became home to the New York State Historical Society in 1899, and was converted to an art museum in 1990. Closed from January through March, and Thanksgiving and Christmas days. You can get combination tickets with the nearby Farmers' Museum and the Baseball Hall of Fame at reduced rates. Allow two hours.

5798 SR 80 (Lake Road), Cooperstown. **607-547-1400;** www.fenimoreartmuseum. org. **RV parking:** *Available in a designated lot. Admission varies by age and combined with nearby attractions.*

KID FRIENDLY

» **Dig your own glitter, New York style.** Gems unearthed at the **Herkimer Diamond Mines** are more likely to be double-terminated quartz crystals than diamonds, but would-be prospectors get to keep whatever they dig up. You can also buy samples from the gift shop if digging isn't your thing. If you know your gemstones and jewelry, you'll be excited that, in their raw state right out of the ground, these clear quartz crystals have 18 facets and 2 points, with a hardness rating of 7.5 (real diamonds are rated at 9, so these are close). The shop can even mount your new jewels in settings to make rings, pendants, necklaces, and bracelets. Digging equipment is available. ***Note:*** No sandals are permitted in the mining area — *closed-toe shoes only.* (Nobody wants to break a toe on a rock!) Admission includes the use of a rock hammer and zipper-lock bags. Open daily April through November 1, weather permitting. Allow two to three hours.

4601 SR 28, Herkimer. **800-562-0897** *or* **315-891-7355;** www.herkimerdiamond. com/. **RV parking:** *The mines are across the street from the* **Herkimer Diamond KOA Resort campground,** *so you find plenty of space for* **RV parking**. *Admission varies by age.*

KID FRIENDLY

» **Follow the Jell-O Brick Road.** A brick walkway leads to the **Jell-O Gallery** in LeRoy, where a carpenter named Pearle Wait invented this amazing dessert in 1897 while attempting to concoct cough remedies and laxatives. His wife, May, called it Jell-O, taking her inspiration from a coffee substitute named Grain-O. The pair couldn't market it successfully, so they sold the rights to Grain-O mogul Orator F. Woodward for $450. From these humble beginnings, the jiggly fruit-flavored gelatin went on to become "America's most famous dessert." This museum re-creates the product's history, including advertising art, Jell-O jokes, and interactive displays. Closed Thanksgiving and Christmas days; call to confirm open days and hours. Allow one to two hours.

23 E. Main St., LeRoy. **585-768-7433;** www.jellogallery.org/. *The parking lot in this residential area is small, but* **RV parking** *is available on the street. Admission varies by age.*

Our Favorite Western New York Campgrounds

Western New York has plenty of private and public campgrounds, plus New York's popular state parks, so no need to worry about where to sleep. Campground reservations are necessary in July and August around Cooperstown, Niagara Falls, and state parks that accept reservations. If you're traveling in spring or fall, you shouldn't have a problem finding a space without reservations except during major events, such as an auto race at Watkins Glen or the New York State Fair in Syracuse.

As mentioned previously, many Northeastern campgrounds shut down from October until April because business slows to a trickle, and because exposed water pipes at campsites and in bathhouses can freeze and burst. All campgrounds in this section are open year-round and have public flush toilets, showers, and sanitary dump stations unless designated otherwise. Toll-free numbers, where listed, are for reservations.

Tables 7-1 and 7-2 list our favorite and runner-up campgrounds.

TABLE 7-1 Favorite New York Campgrounds

Name and Location	Contact Info	Cost	What to Know
Allegany State Park; Salamanca, NY	2373 ASP, U.S. 1; **716-354-9101** or **800-456-2267;** www. reserveamerica. com/explore/ allegany-state-park/NY/31/ overview	$	Red House tent and trailer campground has 130 sites with 30- or 50-amp electric; no water. Quaker campground/Cain Hollow Loop has 134 sites with 30- or 50-amp electric; no water. Two pets allowed per campsite. Biggest state park in New York; fill water tanks before arriving; two dump stations. Most are back-in, not pull-through, sites. Hiking, boating, swimming, and mountain biking. Reservations recommended. Bargain rates; credit cards accepted. 14-day maximum stay. RV sites open mid-May–mid-October.

(continued)

TABLE 7-1 *(continued)*

Name and Location	Contact Info	Cost	What to Know
Herkimer Diamond KOA Resort; Herkimer, NY	4626 SR 28; **800-562-0897** or **315-891-7355;** `https://koa.com/campgrounds/herkimer`	$$$	Total of 95 sites with water and 30/50-amp electric; 50 full hookups; 23 pull-throughs. Amenities include CATV, data port, laundry, pool. Large grass campsites along West Canada Creek; close to Ferris Lake Wild Forest. Fishing and boating; magnificent views in fall. Kid-friendly diamond (really crystal) mine across the street, with dig sites containing sparkling quartz crystals. Nearby Miner's Table restaurant delivers to your campsite.
Letchworth State Park; Castile, NY	1 Letchworth State Park; **585-493-3600;** `https://parks.ny.gov/parks/letchworth/details.aspx.` For reservations, **800-456-2267;** `www.reserveamerica.com/explore/letchworth-state-park/NY/375/overview.`	$$	Total of 270 large sites with 30- or 50-amp electric; no water or sewer. Wheelchair access, laundry, 2 pools. Fill water tanks before arrival; on-site dump station. Reserve sites early for this popular park. The Grand Canyon of the East on the Genesee River features breathtaking waterfalls, lush forests, and magnificent views. Whitewater rafting, hiking, swimming, and hunting and fishing (licenses required). Can arrange horseback riding and hot-air balloon trips. Bargain rates; open mid-May–mid-October.
Niagara Falls/ Grand Island KOA Holiday; Grand Island, NY	2570 Grand Island Blvd.; **800-562-0787** or **716-773-7583;** `https://koa.com/campgrounds/niagara-falls-new-york`	$$$–$$$$	Total of 208 sites with water and 30/50-amp electric; 128 full hookups; 172 pull-throughs. Data port, laundry, pool. One of KOA's top campgrounds on an island in the Niagara River. Paved sites, grass, and kid-friendly activities: pool, playground, and fishing pond. Make reservations far in advance; book car rentals and tours at camp office. Also find nearby the Niagara Falls North/Lewiston KOA Journey in Youngtown and the excellent Niagara Falls KOA Holiday campground on the Canada side. Open April–October.

Name and Location	Contact Info	Cost	What to Know
Spruce Row Campground and RV Park; Ithaca, NY	2271 Kraft Rd.; **607-387-9225**; www.sprucerow.com	$$–$$$	Total of 213 sites with water and 20/30-amp electric; 99 full hookups; 30 pull-throughs. Data port, laundry, pool, Wi-Fi. Good-size sites; mature trees add privacy and shade. Amenities include a gym, fishing pond, and giant swimming pool with a sand/concrete beach on premises; many organized activities. Close to Watkins Glen racetrack, Taughannock Falls, Buttermilk Falls, Ithaca Falls, and the Cayuga Wine Trail. Open May 1–October 11.

TABLE 7-2   **Runner-up Campgrounds**

Name and Location	Contact Info	Cost	What to Know
Cooperstown KOA Journey; Richfield Springs, NY	565 Ostrander Road; **800-562-3402** or **315-858-0236**; https://koa.com/campgrounds/cooperstown	$$–$$$	Total of 100 sites with water and 30-amp electric; 27 full hookups; 52 pull-throughs. Laundry, pool. Grassy sites and spacious pull-throughs. A bit of a drive from Cooperstown, but a good overnight spot if your destination is the National Baseball Hall of Fame. Open mid-April–mid-October.
Canandaigua/ Rochester KOA Holiday; Farmington, NY	5374 Farmington Town Line Rd.; **800-562-0533** or **585-398-3582**; https://koa.com/campgrounds/canandaigua	$$$–$$$$	Total of 79 sites with 20/30/50-amp electric; 42 full hookups; 40 pull-throughs. Laundry, pool, zip line. Lies near the head of Canandaigua Lake and provides a kid-friendly environment with a pond and large swimming pool. Just 20 minutes from the George Eastman Museum in Rochester. Fairly wide sites with big-rig capability; many have side-by-side hookups. Convenient to Canandaigua and Seneca Wine Trails. Open April–October.

(continued)

TABLE 7-2 *(continued)*

Name and Location	Contact Info	Cost	What to Know
Adventure Bound Camping Resorts – Cooperstown; Garrattsville, NY	111 E. Turtle Lake Rd.; **800-231-1907** or **607-965-8265;** https://abcamping.com/cooperstown	$$$–$$$$	Total of 190 sites with water and 30-amp electric; 27 full hookups; 5 pull-throughs. Data port, laundry, pool. Older campground (formerly Yogi Bear's Jellystone Park) 30 minutes west of Cooperstown. Has 35-acre lake for fishing (no license required) and offers kid-friendly activities, including rowboats, paddleboats, miniature golf, and themed family activities. Many lakefront RV sites available, but they have no sewer hookups. Not as resort-like as the name implies, but still quite pleasant. Open May 1–mid-Oct.
Villages RV Park at Turning Stone; Verona, NY	5065 SR 365; **800-771-7711** or **315-361-7275;** www.turningstone.com/accommodations/the-villages-rv-park	$$$	Total of 175 full hookups with 30/50-amp electric; 50 pull-throughs. CATV, Wi-Fi, wheelchair access, laundry, pool, full spa. A highly rated Good Sam park with large paved sites that measure 50 feet by 60 feet, and free shuttle service to the nearby golf courses and the adjacent Turning Stone Casino. Kid-friendly video arcade and heated pool and spa for parents. Fishing and boating pond with rentals. Many dining and drinking options at the casino and hotel complex that are kept affordable to attract gamblers. Just don't lose the nest egg. Open mid-April–October.

Good Western New York Eats

Whether you're in the mood for dining or snacking, Western New York has a spot for you to quench your appetite.

TIP

If you're hunting food and supplies in this part of New York, the most common independent supermarket chain is **Tops.** To find up-to-date listings of farmers markets in this part of the state, check out the **New York Department of Agriculture's Farmers Markets** website at https://agriculture.ny.gov/farmersmarkets. But hauling around your own kitchen and dinner table in the RV doesn't mean you have to miss sampling the local favorites.

Around Western New York, just about anything can be breaded or batter-dipped and deep-fried as a meal or snack. Local favorites both in and out of the fryer include such treats as grape pie (you find it around Naples in the Finger Lakes); *white hots* (mild) and *red hots* (spicy) in the frankfurter category; Buffalo's beef on weck (served at Charlie the Butcher's and Schwabl's in the following list), buffalo wings, and *chicken lips* (breaded and fried cubes of chicken breast — see Anchor Bar in the following list).

REMEMBER

The area also produces plenty of cheese, mostly cheddar types, and does a lively business in fresh cheese curds, which around Salamanca may also be batter-dipped and deep-fried as snacks.

Try out these suggested food establishments:

>> **Anchor Bar,** 1047 Main St., Buffalo (**716-886-8920;** www.anchorbar.com): According to a duly notarized proclamation by the city's mayor in 1977, this restaurant is the birthplace of spicy buffalo wings. The late Teressa and Frank Bellissimo, proprietors, are credited with creating them in 1964 as a snack for friends of their son who dropped by the restaurant one busy Friday night. Others say the wings were a local staple, but Teressa added the celery stalks and blue cheese dressing. Sauce choices include plain or mild, medium, medium-hot, hot, or suicidal. Open daily.

>> **Charlie the Butcher's Kitchen,** 1065 Wehrle Dr., Williamsville (**716-633-8330;** www.charliethebutcher.com): This small, casual lunch counter near the Buffalo airport specializes in *beef on weck,* a sandwich with sliced roast beef slapped with horseradish sauce and piled into a *kummelweck,* a Kaiser roll topped with coarse salt and caraway seeds. ***Note:*** If you really fall in love with this sandwich, they even ship a fresh kit of beef, rolls, and the proper sauces anywhere in the 48 continental United States. Open daily.

>> **Cuba Cheese Shop,** 53 Genesee St., Cuba (**800-543-4938** or **585-968-3949;** www.cubacheese.com): The shop carries a hundred varieties of imported and domestic cheeses, including some made on the premises. Fresh cheese curds are a big seller; taste a free sample. Open daily.

>> **DiCamillo Bakery,** 811 Linwood Ave., Niagara Falls (**800-634-4363** or **716-282-2341;** www.dicamillobakery.com): DiCamillo's has been turning out Italian breads, including flatbread and biscotti, since 1920. Fourth-generation members of the family continue to run the bakery today. Their retail outlets pride themselves on their beautiful displays and packaging in addition to the goodies inside. Open daily.

>> **Schwabl's,** 789 Center Rd., West Seneca (**716-675-2333;** www.schwabls.com/): Everybody in and around Buffalo claims to have invented the beef on weck sandwich, and these folks at least have longevity in their favor. The Schwabls

emigrated to Buffalo from Germany and opened their first eatery in 1837, but this classic (and small!) 1940s roadside family restaurant opened in 1942. Their unmatched beef on weck boasts tender slices of rare round roast on a kummel-weck roll with sauce and seasonings. (See the full description in the earlier listing for Charlie the Butcher's Kitchen.)

Other favorites include Hungarian goulash, Canadian-style *poutine* (a glorious mess of French fries and cheese curds topped with gravy), and liver dumpling soup. An old-fashioned bar at the entrance serves classic Manhattans, martinis, and a cold weather seasonal drink, the *Tom & Jerry* (dark rum, brandy, and sweetened egg batter, mixed with hot water and a sprinkle of nutmeg). Be sure to take a selfie out back with Beefy the Buffalo. Open Tuesday through Saturday.

» **Ted's Hot Dogs,** 2312 Sheridan Dr., Tonawanda (**716-834-6287;** www.tedshot dogs.com): Ted's started out in 1927 when Greek immigrant Theodore Spiro Liaros bought a wooden vendor shack underneath Buffalo's then-new international Peace Bridge for $100. Today, Ted's Hot Dogs has nine New York locations, plus one in faraway Tempe, Arizona. Order a foot-long hot dog cooked before your eyes over a charcoal grill until it's dark brown, sizzling, and smoky. Add your choice of toppings; try the hot sauce at least once. Don't walk out without a side of Ted's crisp onion rings — crunchy outside, chewy and sweet inside. Open daily.

Fast Facts about Western New York

Area Code
The following area codes are in effect in this part of New York state: **315, 585, 607,** and **716.**

Driving Laws
In New York state, seat belts must be worn. The speed limit on interstates and controlled-access roads is 65 mph, or lower posted speeds. New York state highways have a speed limit of 55 mph. Speed limits in urban areas are lower.

Emergency
Call **911.**

Hospitals
Along the route, major hospitals are located in Syracuse, Rochester, and Buffalo, among other places.

Information
For tourism information, call **800-225-5697** or go to www.iloveny.com. Call **511** for traffic or transportation information.

Road and Weather Conditions
For road and weather advisories, call the New York State Thruway (**800-847-8929**) or go to www.dot.ny.gov/index.

Taxes
Sales tax is 4 percent; county taxes can add another 4.75 percent. The state fuel taxes are 46.19 cents per gallon for gasoline, and 44.64 cents for diesel, plus local and state sales taxes averaging an additional 20 cents.

Time Zone
New York state is in the Eastern time zone.

Chapter **8**

The Blue Ridge Mountains: Skyline Drive and Blue Ridge Parkway

A s the title of this chapter suggests, this trip consists of two famous roadways. Skyline Drive is a 105-mile *national parkway* (a designation for a protected area that includes a scenic roadway and surrounding parkland) that runs the length of Shenandoah National Park and is maintained by the National Park Service. In Rockfish Gap, Virginia, Skyline Drive continues on as Blue Ridge Parkway, another national parkway (it's actually considered a linear park), linking Shenandoah with Great Smoky Mountains National Park.

By following these two roadways, you can see some of the most scenic areas of the nation, as well as some incredibly important historical sites. The natural beauty is stunning. These roads meander past mountainside homesteads and stretches of wilderness unchanged since the days of Daniel Boone. Back roads and byways seem to beckon around every curve.

This 643-mile trip cuts through an incredibly important slice of America, both geographically and historically. These roads are in the Appalachian Mountains, an enormous range that runs along the Eastern Seaboard through 13 states and into Canada. In the early 19th century, this range was the nearly impassable wall between the *Tidewater* and the *Piedmont* — the inhabited coastal and farming regions — and the *West*, the vast territory beyond that was virtually unexplored.

Following the trip outlined in this chapter, you get a glimpse of the extent of the Appalachians, a system so vast that it contains other entire mountain ranges, such as the Catskills and the Berkshires. On the Blue Ridge Parkway alone, the drive passes through five mountain ranges — the Blue Ridge Mountains, the Black Mountains, the Craggies, the Balsams, and finally the Great Smoky Mountains in North Carolina. The drive then follows the Cumberland Plateau into Knoxville in eastern Tennessee.

Planning for Your Skyline and Blue Ridge Trip

TIP

For the shortest version of this route, choose one drive (Skyline Drive or Blue Ridge Parkway), depending on where you want to be based. You can travel Skyline Drive and see Shenandoah National Park easily over a weekend from the Washington, D.C., area. Anywhere in western Virginia or western North Carolina allows access to Blue Ridge Parkway for a weekend of touring. One thing that makes Great Smoky Mountains National Park the most-visited national park is its location: It's within a day's drive or so of more than half the population of the U.S.

Try to start the day with a full tank, or gas up as soon as possible if you're low. Some areas of the parkway are lean on gas stations. Don't depend too much on apps such as GasBuddy to find a place to buy gas — cell service can be spotty. Ditto for snacks and drinks: You won't find a 7-Eleven off every exit. Even so, RVers have a great advantage for remedying this lack of easy snacks as long as they stocked up the kitchen (see Chapter 4).

Minding your seasons and your daily schedule

Expect to find long and slow-moving lines of traffic during spring blossom, late summer, and autumn foliage seasons. Here are some seasonal expectations:

>> **Spring really springs forth, and summer offers a shady respite.** Beginning in March, colorful azalea, rhododendron, and mountain laurel decorate the roadside, with some color lingering through summer. In summer, shade trees that follow the roadway provide a cool escape from the lowlands heat.

>> **Autumn is magnificent.** The route becomes a spectacle of crimson-leafed black gums and sourwoods, maples and dogwoods, birch and buckeye, orange sassafras, and purple sumac.

>> **Winter presents challenges.** Often, facilities along the route are closed in winter; the end of October is a popular time to shut down. All seasons are beautiful on these drives, but winter can bring heavy fog, and even light snow or a glaze of black ice on the roadway; it also brings many closed campgrounds.

TIP

You should plan to travel in spring, fall, or summer. Also, plan early-morning starts, when the air is clearest, and stop in early afternoon to set up camp or hike. Check the morning weather report for fog potential before heading out.

These roadways are a popular drive, so look for crowds and slow speeds in summer; that's the downside of popularity. But there are major upsides, and one of them is the amount of information available to you at the planning stage. This site, `www.blueridgeparkway.org/rv-the-parkway` — operated by the Blue Ridge Parkway Association — is great for general information. You also find helpful RV-specific info such as a list of all campgrounds with RV hookups.

REMEMBER

Because this region, especially the Great Smoky Mountains, is one of the most visited in the U.S., you need to make campground reservations wherever possible between Memorial Day and Labor Day. Spring and autumn weekends can also be busy in Shenandoah and Great Smoky Mountains national parks. It can get dark earlier and become colder than you expect, even in summer. You don't want to be stranded without a destination campground, particularly if you're not prepared to shelter in place and boondock.

Preparing to enjoy history, nature, and recreational activities

Take your time and enjoy the drive and your surroundings. Plan to spend at least a week (two if time permits) and get in some hiking, biking, golfing, or fishing, and some historical sightseeing. You should pack a variety of clothing weights, even in summer. The mountains can be cool and rainy, and you'll want a jacket or sweater. Always take rain gear. Hiking boots are preferable to jogging shoes on mountain trails, but take along both.

Your best tool for wildlife spotting along the route is a decent set of binoculars that you wear around your neck; they're great for birding, and you can keep your distance from the wildlife.

WARNING

If you're hiking or camping in a deep-woods area, you may come across a bear. If you spot a bear, stay at least 50 yards away. There's no reason to be extremely fearful; the overwhelming majority of black bear encounters in this area end with both camper and bear going on about their business. Also, most people know this by now, but it doesn't hurt to say it again: *Never feed the bears!* And keep your campsite clear of food or scraps that may easily attract bears. You can find other bear safety tips for unusual situations. The National Park Service has a great web page and short video at www.nps.gov/grsm/learn/nature/black-bears.htm.

Also, make sure to have good guidance for your drive through the mountain ranges. Apps and websites and Google Maps are all great, but they have limits, especially when phone signals fail. Google Maps can leave you confused in the planning stage, with constantly shifting and disappearing points of reference at each and every click, in an area you don't know. State borders, another vital point of reference, can get lost in computer maps.

TIP

We have four or five books with travel information that we like to keep in the camper, along with some maps. When talking to other RVers, we were surprised to find that we aren't necessarily old fogies in this practice, and we encourage you to take along some helpful references. We find that a hard copy of our Good Sam Campground Guide (see Chapter 5) comes in handy. And on this trip — through two national parks — our battered copy of *Your Guide to the National Parks*, by Michael Joseph Oswald (Stone Road Press), justifies its hefty weight by including maps and campground info for all 63 national parks. It lists all services, location of entrances, length and difficulty of hiking trails, and just about anything else you'd like to know.

Driving Skyline Drive and Blue Ridge Parkway

This north-to-south journey begins just south of the Washington-Baltimore urban area in **Front Royal, Virginia,** at the beginning of Skyline Drive in **Shenandoah National Park.** The route follows Skyline Drive to where it merges with **Blue Ridge Parkway** and then continues along the parkway through Virginia and North Carolina, all the way to **Great Smoky Mountains National Park.** For convenience — in case you want to fly in and rent an RV for the drive — we've made the southern terminus **Knoxville, Tennessee.** But this itinerary is flexible; you're welcome to chop it up into smaller pieces that suit your needs. Or, if you have more time rather than less, it's an easy drive onward from Knoxville to Pigeon Forge, Gatlinburg, and the heart of Great Smokies National Park. The distance of this drive shown in Figure 8-1, without detours into adjacent towns, is 643 miles.

TIP

Skyline Drive mileposts are numbered from north to south, beginning with 0.6 at Front Royal's toll entrance station and ending with 105 at Rockfish Gap and the entrance to Blue Ridge Parkway. At this point, the parkway begins numbering its own mileposts north to south at 0 again, ending with mile 469, where the parkway intersects U.S. 441 in **Cherokee** at the entrance to Great Smoky Mountains National Park. Although frequent turnouts are found along the way, few are long or wide enough for a motor home or a vehicle towing a trailer.

Starting off in Front Royal

The beginning of **Skyline Drive** in Shenandoah National Park is only an hour away from the Washington-Baltimore area; zoom west on I-66 to Exit 6 to Front Royal, Virginia, where Skyline Drive begins just 2 miles south of I-66. Skyline Drive parallels the Appalachian Trail, a famous hiking and riding trail that wends along the crest of the mountains more than 2,000 miles from Maine to Georgia. It also skirts many of the Civil War battlefields, including **Manassas National Battlefield Park**, 40 miles east of Front Royal and the beginning of Skyline Drive.

The first 28 miles of the route, **Front Royal** to **Beahms Gap,** climbs more than 1,000 feet, past several overlooks. **Dickey Ridge Visitor Center** at milepost 4.6 is a good place to pick up maps, postcards, books, and all sorts of information about your upcoming drive. You also can purchase pocket-size identification guides for birds, trees, wild animals, and wildflowers at the center. At **Elkwallow,** milepost 24, you can buy food, ice, gasoline, and souvenirs between May and October, and picnic in a designated area year-round. If you missed stocking up on any snacks or drinks, be sure to stop here.

At **Thornton Gap,** milepost 31.5, U.S. 211 to Luray and Warrenton crosses the parkway, and a restaurant and gift shop are open in season. At milepost 41.7, **Skyland,** at 3,680 feet, is the highest point on Skyline Drive. It features a lodge with a dining room and gift shop. The **Limberlost Trail** at milepost 43 is accessible to wheelchairs, but some assistance is needed. This 1½-mile loop makes an easy circle through an abandoned orchard and a grove of old hemlocks. You may see deer and even wild turkeys throughout much of this area.

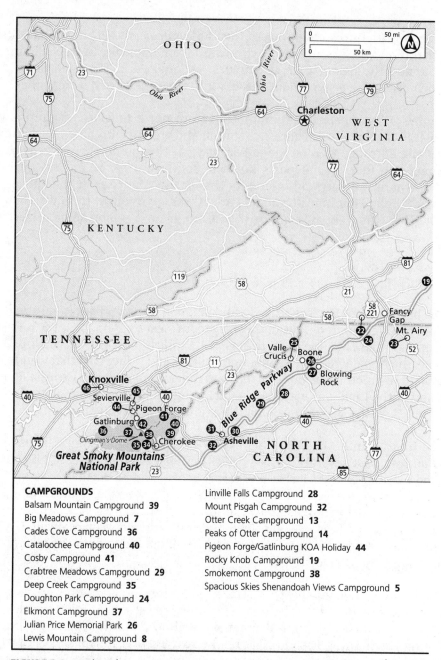

CAMPGROUNDS

Balsam Mountain Campground **39**

Big Meadows Campground **7**

Cades Cove Campground **36**

Cataloochee Campground **40**

Cosby Campground **41**

Crabtree Meadows Campground **29**

Deep Creek Campground **35**

Doughton Park Campground **24**

Elkmont Campground **37**

Julian Price Memorial Park **26**

Lewis Mountain Campground **8**

Linville Falls Campground **28**

Mount Pisgah Campground **32**

Otter Creek Campground **13**

Peaks of Otter Campground **14**

Pigeon Forge/Gatlinburg KOA Holiday **44**

Rocky Knob Campground **19**

Smokemont Campground **38**

Spacious Skies Shenandoah Views Campground **5**

FIGURE 8-1: *continued*

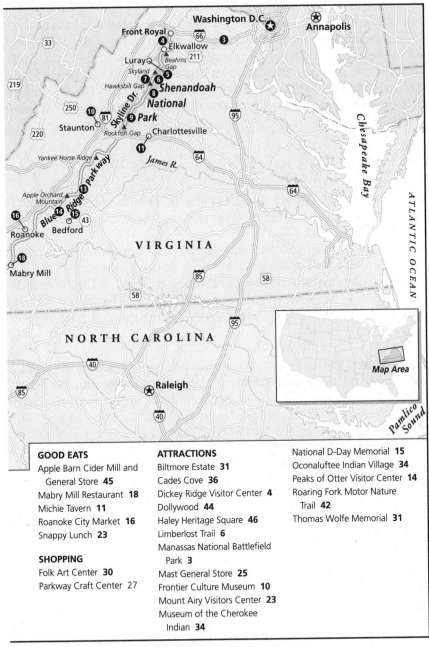

GOOD EATS
Apple Barn Cider Mill and
  General Store **45**
Mabry Mill Restaurant **18**
Michie Tavern **11**
Roanoke City Market **16**
Snappy Lunch **23**

SHOPPING
Folk Art Center **30**
Parkway Craft Center **27**

ATTRACTIONS
Biltmore Estate **31**
Cades Cove **36**
Dickey Ridge Visitor Center **4**
Dollywood **44**
Haley Heritage Square **46**
Limberlost Trail **6**
Manassas National Battlefield
  Park **3**
Mast General Store **25**
Frontier Culture Museum **10**
Mount Airy Visitors Center **23**
Museum of the Cherokee
  Indian **34**

National D-Day Memorial **15**
Oconaluftee Indian Village **34**
Peaks of Otter Visitor Center **14**
Roaring Fork Motor Nature
  Trail **42**
Thomas Wolfe Memorial **31**

FIGURE 8-1: Skyline Drive and Blue Ridge Parkway route.

REMEMBER

From **Hawksbill Gap** at milepost 45.6 to **Big Meadows** at milepost 51.9, you see low stone fences along the parkway and can camp at **Big Meadows Campground** (reservations usually are required; there are first-come, first-served campsites and a ranger station). Two other campgrounds, **Lewis Mountain** at milepost 57.5 and **Loft Mountain** at milepost 79.5, don't accept reservations. Loft Mountain is our favorite of the three — the largest in the park, with waterfalls and hiking trails, and incredible vistas and sunsets.

Picking up the parkway in Virginia

At **Rockfish Gap,** milepost 105.4, Skyline Drive runs right into **Blue Ridge Parkway,** where milepost numbers revert to 0.

Twelve miles west of the parkway via I-64 is **Staunton** (pronounced *stan*-ton), birthplace of Woodrow Wilson and home of the **Frontier Culture Museum.** This excellent living history park explores the origins of the Shenandoah Valley's first settlers — who came from farms in England, Germany, Ireland, and West Africa — and shows how they adapted architectural and farming methods to the new world.

Travel 30 miles east of Rockfish Gap and you come to **Charlottesville,** home of the University of Virginia and Thomas Jefferson's **Monticello,** the magnificent (but not grandiose) home that he designed and built for himself. His gardens are also on display. An avid vegetable gardener, Jefferson introduced eggplant to the U.S., so you probably either love him or hate him for that.

If you're around Charlottesville at lunchtime, the historic **Michie** (pronounced *mik-ee*, like the Disney mouse) **Tavern** is famous for its fried chicken and biscuits, black-eyed peas, and cornbread; it also serves local Virginia wine. Thomas Jefferson, a noted wine lover, cultivated some of the earliest wine grapes in this area of Virginia.

Making it through the ups and downs

While on this section of the drive, you get an instant introduction to the scenery and the type of uphill and downhill climbs and curves that you must negotiate on Blue Ridge Parkway. The road climbs dramatically from 1,900 feet at Rockfish Gap past Wintergreen Ski Resort to **Yankee Horse Ridge** at 3,140 feet. (This overlook at milepost 34.4 is a popular place to stop and stretch your legs. Pretty country vistas, even waterfalls, are a 2-minute walk from the small parking lot; there's also an old narrow-gauge railroad.) Then it starts downhill again to the **James River** — at 649 feet, it's the lowest elevation on the parkway. Then you ascend in only 12 miles to the highest elevation on the Virginia stretch of parkway — **Apple Orchard Mountain** at 3,950 feet, milepost 78.4. The mountain's name comes from the shapes into which the winter wind has twisted the northern red oaks, making them resemble apple trees.

The **Peaks of Otter Visitor Center,** at milepost 85.6, features a lodge with a restaurant that's open year-round, a seasonal store, a gift shop, and a service station. It's another relaxing stop. Just past the center, at mile 86, State Road 43 turns east to **Bedford,** the location of the **National D-Day Memorial**.

The junction of SR 43 with U.S. 220 at milepost 121.4 leads to the city of **Roanoke,** the largest urban area along the parkway. The short detour to see the **Roanoke City Market,** a historic farmers market still offering fresh produce and baked goods, is worthwhile.

Mabry Mill at milepost 176.1 is a must-see for the colorful old mill that still grinds corn into cornmeal and the adjacent **Mabry Mill Coffee Shop,** which serves pancakes made out of the cornmeal with its wonderful country ham and eggs breakfasts.

Heading into and through North Carolina

At **Fancy Gap,** milepost 199.5, the parkway intersects U.S. 52. A 14-mile detour south takes you into the town of **Mount Airy, North Carolina,** birthplace of TV's Andy Griffith, said to be the real-life inspiration for the town of Mayberry in *The Andy Griffith Show.* Check out the new statue of Andy and Opie and get more info from the **Mount Airy Visitors Center,** 200 N. Main St. (**336-786-6116;** www. visitmayberry.com). Fans of the popular TV show will be in hog heaven. The fried pork chop sandwich at **Snappy Lunch** (a café referred to once on the show) is worth the detour.

At milepost 291.9, the parkway intersects U.S. 221 to **Boone** and **Blowing Rock.** Eight miles west of Boone is the great-granddaddy of country stores in the tiny hamlet of **Valle Crucis** — the original **Mast General Store,** opened in 1883.

The flower-filled community of **Blowing Rock** was a big tourist attraction at the end of the 19th century for The Blowing Rock, an outthrust ledge of stone with updrafts of wind that return lightweight objects such as a handkerchief dropped over the edge of the gorge. (No, your pesky kid brother isn't lightweight enough, so don't even think about it.) The rock even has its own lovers' legend. Today's more sophisticated travelers tend to bypass it in favor of the natural scenery of the region.

TIP

Back on the parkway at milepost 294 is the Moses Cone Memorial Park and the beautiful **Moses Cone Manor**, a 13,500 square-foot historical mansion. Then at milepost 382, is the fine **Southern Highland Craft Guild Folk Art Center,** just the place to pick up a handcrafted rocking chair, homemade quilt, or distinctive hand-thrown pottery. The gift shop in the Moses Cone Manor house sells some items from the Folk Art Center.

In **Asheville,** you can visit native son Thomas Wolfe's childhood home, which he portrayed as a fictional Dixieland boardinghouse in *Look Homeward, Angel.* Fire damaged the interior in the late 1990s, but a reconstruction that took nearly six years (1998–2004) has restored it. Writer F. Scott Fitzgerald also is associated with Asheville, because his wife, Zelda, spent the last years of her life in a hospital near there.

REMEMBER

The most-visited attraction in Asheville, however, is the palatial **Biltmore Estate**. The largest private home in the U.S. is now a museum. Commissioned by George W. Vanderbilt in 1895, the 250-room mansion may be familiar to moviegoers who've seen the 1979 Peter Sellers film *Being There* or the 1994 Macaulay Culkin flick *Richie Rich.*

Finding the end of the parkway at Great Smoky Mountains National Park

Milepost 469, **Cherokee, North Carolina,** is near the entrance to Great Smoky Mountains National Park. Skip the touristy side of town, with the "Indian chiefs" who hang around outside curio stands in feathered headdresses borrowed from the Great Plains tribes, waiting to pose for a souvenir photo. Instead, discover the history of the Cherokee and their arts and crafts at the **Museum of the Cherokee Indian** and the **Oconaluftee Indian Village**.

Choose one of several ways to see **Great Smoky Mountains National Park.** You can take

>> The quick tourist drive from Cherokee to Gatlinburg across **Newfound Gap Road,** with the option of a side trip up to **Clingmans Dome,** the highest point in the park.

>> A slower version of the same tourist route with side driving, biking, or hiking trips to Cades Cove and **Roaring Fork Motor Nature Trail.**

>> An in-depth camping stay to spend more time enjoying sightseeing and nature.

TIP

The nearest city on the Tennessee side of the park is **Knoxville,** where a 13-foot bronze statue in **Haley Heritage Square** (in Morningside Park) honors native son Alex Haley, author of the novel *Roots.*

SAFE DRIVING ON THE SKYLINE AND BLUE RIDGE ROUTE

A few tips about safe driving along the mountainous route:

- **You have no need for speed.** Remember at all times that this isn't the Autobahn. The smooth, two-lane roads of Skyline Drive, Blue Ridge Parkway, and Newfound Gap Road across Great Smoky Mountains National Park are closed to commercial vehicles, and posted speed limits are *strictly* enforced. The fastest legal limit is 45 mph, and you'll often be going slower on twisting roads with no shoulder. If you've got a bit of a lead foot, take a deep breath and relax. We've found Lou Rawls tunes helpful.

- **Watch out for low tunnels.** Make yourself aware of the tunnel issue because low tunnels are common on the parkway. Most tunnels have a clearance of 13 feet, but a few are problematic, with the lowest having a clearance of just 11 feet, 3 inches. The edge-to-edge width of these arched tunnels is also an issue, with the height at the centerline being higher than either side. We're driving a Chevy Suburban pulling an Airstream, so we can take all of them, with care. But a high-profile vehicle such as a Class A or tall fifth-wheel trailer may have problems. Some RVers have to skip sections where the lowest tunnels are located. For more info on this, consult the website www.blueridgeparkway.org/rv-the-parkway/, which contains lists of heights for all tunnels, their mile markers, and advice for navigation. Another excellent info site is published by the National Park Service (https://tinyurl.com/2p9vxavj). Look over both sites and size it all up based on your RV's real-life height and width (not just the manufacturer's printed specs). If you utter the words "I think I can make it through there," there's a pretty good chance that you really can't.

- **Steer clear of fog.** Fog can occur during any season in the mountains. When you encounter fog on Skyline Drive or Blue Ridge Parkway, turn on your headlights, slow down, try to exit, and drive to a lower elevation to get out of it. *Remember:* If you're driving too slowly, you may become a hazard to other drivers, who may not see you until they're on your rear bumper. When you get to lower ground, take a break and do some shopping or sightseeing, or drive in your intended direction parallel to the parkway. The narrow two-lane roads have no guardrails, so maneuvering an RV (especially one that's towing a trailer) can be particularly tricky when it gets foggy.

Must-See Skyline and Blue Ridge Attractions

Biltmore Estate
Asheville, North Carolina

Many places deserve a visit, and this attraction is near the top of the list. As grand as any Loire Valley château, the massive 250-room Biltmore mansion and its gardens, craft shops, and winery paint a picture of how America's one-percenters once lived. The Vanderbilts were considered American royalty, and in the late 1800s, with the help of architect Richard Morris Hunt and landscape designer Frederick Law Olmsted, they created a kingdom in the mountains. Today, for the price of a ticket, anyone can tour this splendid estate. Allow a half-day to a full day; there's a long list of restaurants, shops, activities, and special exhibitions. Open daily with extended hours seasonally. *Note:* Order tickets in advance for any Christmastime event, because sellouts are common. Hours are extended seasonally, particularly at Christmas.

1 Approach Rd.; **800-411-3812;** *https://www.biltmore.com.* **RV parking:** *Designated lots. Admission varies by age and season. Annual passes are also available.*

Cades Cove
Great Smoky Mountains National Park, North Carolina and Tennessee

An auto or bicycle tour to Cades Cove (an isolated mid-19th-century community) down an 11-mile, one-way road off Newfound Gap Road is a must for any visitor to the Great Smokies. The road is flat and easy for older kids to bike; it's closed to auto traffic Wednesday and Saturday mornings until 10:00 to allow bikers full use of the roadway. You can rent bicycles at the Cades Cove Campground store for riding around the 4,000-acre valley. The road is closed from sundown to sunrise. Passing isn't allowed, so if you're an impatient driver, plan an early-morning start for your trip. You can make a leisurely drive through the park in an hour; or take time to do some hiking.

25 miles west of Newfound Gap Road via Little River Road and Laurel Creek Road. **865-436-1200;** *https://www.nps.gov/grsm/planyourvisit/ cadescove.htm.* **RV parking:** *Some turnouts are large enough for RVs. Admission is free, but camping has fees.*

Frontier Culture Museum
Staunton, Virginia

Scenic Skyline Drive and Blue Ridge Parkway take you past typical mountain farmhouses, but where did the settlers of this region come from? The Frontier Culture Museum features exhibits of old-world farmsteads from England, Ireland, Germany, and West Africa, to show the origins of the area's early settlers and their influence on an increasingly American way of life. Some buildings are reconstructions; others were moved from Europe and reassembled, giving visitors a sweeping view of American history. Heirloom plants and rare breeds of farm animals are on display alongside costumed inhabitants who work the farms and talk with today's visitors. We're big fans of America's living history museums, and this is one of the best, a great experience for kids. Open daily; closed Thanksgiving, Christmas, and New Year's days. Allow two and a half hours for a guided visit and three hours for a self-guided visit **Note:** Check out the website for many special events and tours throughout the year as well as a detailed description of terrain and challenges for elderly visitors and visitors with disabilities. Golf carts are available for rent. December Lantern Tours are priced separately; you must purchase tickets in advance.

1290 Richmond Ave. **540-332-7850;** *www.frontiermuseum.org.* **RV parking:** *Designated lot. Admission is by age.*

Manassas National Battlefield Park
Manassas, Virginia

Known as Bull Run to the Union forces and Manassas to Confederates, this famous Civil War battlefield was the scene of two Southern victories in the early days of the war, cementing the reputation of General Stonewall Jackson as a strategist and hero. A visit to the 4,500-acre park includes an audiovisual presentation of the battles, an electronic map tracing the fighting, and guides for auto tours through the battle sites, with an excellent museum in the Henry Hill Visitor Center. Knowledgeable and helpful rangers can guide you to the miles of hiking trails and various outbuildings, including the Methodist Church, Stone House (which was the battlefield hospital), and particularly Brawner Farm (closed in winter), with more interpretive history exhibits. An eerie stillness to so many of America's national park battlefields (from Gettysburg to Little Big Horn, as well as Manassas) can leave a far deeper impression than you expect. Open daily; closed Thanksgiving and Christmas days. Allow three hours or longer.

6511 Sudley Rd. **703-361-1339;** *https://www.nps.gov/mana.* **RV parking:** *Designated area at the visitor's center. Admission is free.*

Mast General Store
Valle Crucis, North Carolina

A genuine piece of Americana, the original Mast General Store has been in operation since 1883, and some of the charming stock looks just the same as what was sold to the original shoppers. Once known for peddling everything "from cradles to coffins," the store sells more than 500 types of candies, some from giant barrels, and 5-cent cups of coffee from a potbellied stove.

SR 194. **828-963-6511;** *https://www.mastgeneralstore.com.* ***RV parking:*** *Street parking.*

Monticello
Charlottesville, Virginia

This gracious home of our third president, Thomas Jefferson, along with its original furnishings, his gardens, and his grave, tells a great deal about the man and the statesman. The house is elegant but on a human scale, designed by Jefferson himself, who hated the 18th-century brick buildings of Williamsburg. Lewis and Clark brought back the moose and deer antlers in the entry hall from their expedition, and Jefferson's inventions for better living are all over the house. Some guides and exhibits at the museum present a negative image of the Founding Father. You may want to brush up on the story of Jefferson in a more even-handed source. To supplement your visit, check out the book *Saving Monticello,* by Marc Leepson (University of Virginia Press), a fascinating story of a house mired in debt and decay after Jefferson's death and the long road to saving it. The book gives a rich understanding of what you see in this remarkable historical mansion. Open with seasonal hours. Allow three hours to tour.

1050 Monticello Loop. **434-984-9800;** *https://www.monticello.org.* ***RV parking:*** *Designated lot.* **Note:** *You find many layers of ticket prices and many different types of tours. Consult the website when planning your visit, and then call the reservations desk at* **434-984-9880.**

More Cool Things to See and Do along Blue Ridge Parkway

The Blue Ridge Mountains offer many other activities, from walking through the Oconaluftee Indian Village, to braving the rides at Dollywood.

» **Go home again.** Novelist Thomas Wolfe wrote about his childhood in Asheville in *Look Homeward, Angel,* not troubling to disguise the details much. For many years, he was snubbed or ignored by his hometown. Today, the family home (his mother's boardinghouse) is open to the public as the **Thomas Wolfe Memorial.** A destructive fire in 1998 resulted in a lengthy restoration that left the home in better shape than ever. House tours are available. Closed on state holidays. Allow two hours.

   52 N. Market St., Asheville, NC. **828-253-8304;** http://wolfememorial.com. *RV parking is on the street. Admission is by age.*

KID FRIENDLY

» **Hooray for Dollywood!** Once a tiny village of farmers and potters 25 miles outside Knoxville, Tennessee, Pigeon Forge has been turned into Disneyland Southeast by native daughter Dolly Parton. Despite its humble beginnings in the 1980s, when stand-up comics treated it as a punch line, **Dollywood** has grown into a thriving amusement park complex that hosts more than 3 million visitors during a typical season, from March to the Christmas holidays, and is the biggest ticketed tourist attraction in Tennessee. The amusement park features thrill rides, traditional Smoky Mountains crafts and music, and special events and concerts throughout the season. There's also a water park, resort, and spa. Various discounts are available for children and seniors, as well as for packages, so call ahead to get current prices and to make reservations for your visit. The park is closed January through March and on certain days of the week, depending on the season.

   1020 Dollywood Lane, Pigeon Forge, TN **800-365-5996;** www.dollywood.com. *RV parking is available in a designated lot. Don't plan on driving by for a look-see; the road funnels the traffic into the parking lot, and getting back out the entrance in an RV can be tricky. Admission is by age and length of stay.*

» **Visit the first Americans.** The **Museum of the Cherokee Indian** uses everything from "hear phones" to holographic images to tell the story of this tribe that occupied these hills for 10,000 years until the U.S. government forced its people to relocate to Oklahoma along a route that became known as the Trail of Tears. Open daily, except major holidays. Allow two hours.

   589 Tsali Boulevard (U.S. 441 and Drama Road), Cherokee, NC. **800-438-1601** *or* **828-497-3481;** https://mci.org. *RV parking is available in a designated area. Admission is by age.*

» **Splash toward victory.** The **National D-Day Memorial,** off I-81 and Blue Ridge Parkway, commemorates the Allied troops who landed on the Normandy beaches on June 6, 1944, in an unequaled military action under the command of

General Dwight D. Eisenhower. Open daily. Save on tickets by purchasing online. Allow 30 to 60 minutes.

3 Overlord Circle, Bedford, VA. **800-351-3329** *or* **540-586-3329;** https://www. dday.org. **RV parking** *is available on the street. Admission is by age.*

>> **Travel to the 1750s.** The **Oconaluftee Indian Village** is a living history museum that recreates community life in an authentic 18th-century village populated by craftspeople who demonstrate the basketwork and beadwork typical of the Cherokees. The museum closes seasonally, but is usually open April through October; check the website for the most up-to-date info. Allow two to three hours.

564 Tsali Boulevard (U.S. 441 and Drama Road), Cherokee, NC. **828-497-2111** *or* **800-438-1601;** https://cherokeehistorical.org/oconaluftee-indian-village/. **RV parking** *is available in a designated area. Admission is by age.*

Our Favorite Campgrounds along Skyline Drive and Blue Ridge Parkway

As you can see in the following sections, plenty of campsites are close to the mountain drives in this chapter. In fact, this may be the most campground-rich environment of any itinerary in this book. Almost every exit from Blue Ridge Parkway and Skyline Drive leads to private RV parks where, even in peak season, you may be able to find an overnight campsite. It's the same with other services: You find a few lodges and restaurants spaced along Skyline Drive and Blue Ridge Parkway, but most exits lead some miles into small towns where you can often find a fast-food outlet, restaurant, or grocery store.

REMEMBER

If full hookups and higher-end amenities are important to you, you may have to drive a little farther off the parkway to reach them. This isn't just a shallow hunt for personal comfort; remember that these National Park Service campgrounds were built before World War II, in the days when little canned-ham trailers reigned supreme. Many campgrounds have a hard time accommodating large rigs with slides.

TIP

Of course, you can always find the full-service campgrounds; look near the bigger towns such as Roanoke and Asheville or Boone and Blowing Rock, to find a variety of options. Take advantage of Google and apps such as Campendium to track down these campgrounds. *Note:* Preplanning is a good idea if only because you may have trouble getting phone signals on the parkway.

If you've never been *boondocking* (camping without hookups), taking a trip to the Blue Ridge may be an excellent opportunity to master new camping skills. The more primitive national park campgrounds have scenic beauty nailed down. We love camping in the state and national parks, for the beauty and for the great price. But even in the best public parks, you may have only water and electrical hookups, and you may have to uproot from your camping space more often in order to fill your freshwater tanks or dump the wastewater from your greywater/blackwater tanks.

In most of the national park campgrounds listed in these sections, you must do without electricity as well as water. You usually find restrooms and showers, and a communal dump station, but that's it. For more on the boondocking skills needed to stay in these types of parks (and the fun to be had doing it), check out Chapter 5.

Table 8-1 contains helpful information about the following amenity-rich private campgrounds in each segment of the Skyline Drive and Blue Ridge Parkway route:

» **Spacious Skies Shenandoah Views Campground** is a scenic mountain resort near Luray Caverns and a great starting point for the drive. It's a place to relax and reconnoiter 75 minutes from D.C., and to treat yourself to the many amenities before you rough it in the Blue Ridge Mountains.

» **Pigeon Forge/Gatlinburg KOA Holiday** is considered a high-end resort destination KOA. It's very family-friendly, and kids will love the amenities, including a serpentine lazy river swimming pool. But one of the best things going for this KOA is its location, two miles from Dollywood. If you've decided to close out your Smoky Mountains itinerary by enjoying Dollywood and Gatlinburg, this is a great final location.

Shenandoah National Park campgrounds

The three campgrounds along Skyline Drive within Shenandoah National Park (listed in Table 8-2) operate May through October, with facilities such as gift, book, and craft shops; restaurants; gas stations; and hiking trails. Sites are available for RVs, but there are no hookups. Drinking water, restrooms with flush toilets, pay showers, and a laundry are available.

Dump stations exist for RVs. Some sites are paved and accessible for people with disabilities. Reservations are recommended for the busiest seasons; however, three-quarters of the campsites are first-come, first-served. Backcountry camping for hikers requires a free permit. The maximum stay is 14 days. You can reserve a site online through www.nps.gov/shen/planyourvisit/campgrounds.htm or call **877-444-6777**.

TABLE 8-1　Luxury Camping on Your Drive

Name and Location	Contact Info	Cost	What to Know
Spacious Skies Shenandoah Views Campground; Luray, VA	3402 Kimball Road; **504-743-7222;** https://campatshenandoahviews.com	$$$ - $$$$	82 sites with water and 30/50-amp electric; 82 full hookups; 34 pull-throughs. Wi-Fi, laundry, and spa. Accessible for people with disabilities. Open all year. Operated by Spacious Skies Campgrounds, which currently owns 13 campgrounds in the eastern U.S. Well-tended, full-service, and kid-friendly. Playground, two pools, jumping pillow, gem mining, and a decent camp store.
Pigeon Forge/ Gatlinburg KOA Holiday; Pigeon Forge, TN	3122 Veterans Boulevard; **865-453-7903** or **865-509-8821** (reservations); https://koa.com/campgrounds/pigeon-forge/	$$$ - $$$$	Total of 118 full-hookup sites, with 80 pull-throughs; 59 sites with 50-amp electric. Laundry, pool, Wi-Fi, picnic tables, fire rings, and tickets to local attractions. Open all year with lots of niceties such as seasonal movie nights and petting zoo.

TABLE 8-2　Shenandoah Campgrounds along Skyline Drive

Name and Location	Contact Info	Cost	What to Know
Big Meadows Campground; milepost 51.3	**540-999-3500**	$$	Total of 227 sites, with 32 pull-throughs; some paved, some gravel. Stream for fishing. $30 per night. Reservations required during peak season.
Lewis Mountain Campground; milepost 57.5	**540-999-3500**	$$	Total of 31 sites, with 3 pull-throughs. Paved, mostly shaded. $30 per night. No reservations.
Loft Mountain Campground; milepost 79.5	**540-999-3500**	$$	Total of 221 sites, with 140 pull-throughs. Paved. $30 per night. No reservations.

Blue Ridge Parkway campgrounds

The eight campgrounds along Blue Ridge Parkway (see Table 8-3), open May through October, offer facilities such as gift, book, and craft shops, as well as gas stations, hiking trails, and ranger talks. *Note:* Not all campgrounds have all facilities. These are considered developed campgrounds by the park service, with RV spaces, but sites don't have full hookups. Camping sites can handle RVs up to 30 feet long, but may be narrow. Each campground has a dump station.

Restroom facilities and drinking water are provided, but showers and laundry facilities are nonexistent. Each campsite has a table and fire ring; some are accessible for people with disabilities. Rates are $20 per night for all sites. You can stay at these campgrounds for a maximum 21 days between June 1 and Labor Day. Online reservations for some sites are accepted at www.recreation.gov and at 877-444-6777; other sites within each campground are first-come, first-served. For more information, check out www.nps.gov/blri/planyourvisit/index.htm, the National Park Service website for Blue Ridge Parkway.

TABLE 8-3   Campgrounds along Blue Ridge Parkway

Name and Location	Cost	What to Know
Crabtree Meadows Campground; milepost 339.5	$	Total of 22 sites, with 10 pull-throughs. Paved, mostly shaded.
Doughton Park Campground; milepost 231.5	$	Total of 25 sites. Narrow back-ins. No slideouts, gasoline, or food.
Julian Price Memorial Park; milepost 296.9	$	Total of 68 sites, with 30 pull-throughs. Paved, mostly shaded, narrow sites; accessible for people with disabilities; bad cell reception; fishing and boat rentals on Price Lake. No store, gasoline, or food.
Linville Falls Campground; milepost 316.5	$	Total of 20 sites, with 5 pull-throughs. Paved, some shaded; fishing access on Linville River. No gasoline or food.
Mount Pisgah Campground; milepost 408.6	$	Total of 67 sites, with 13 pull-throughs. Paved, patios, mostly shaded. Mount Pisgah has the highest elevation of all the parks on the Blue Ridge, nearly 5,000 ft. Stunning views at nearby Cradle of Forestry Overlook.
Otter Creek Campground; milepost 60.9	$	Total of 24 sites. Paved, narrow back-ins, some shaded. No gasoline.
Peaks of Otter Campground; milepost 86.0	$	Total of 53 sites, with 25 pull-throughs. Paved and shaded. Freshwater fishing in Abbott Lake.
Rocky Knob Campground; milepost 167.0	$	Total of 28 sites. Paved, some shaded. Fishing. No slideouts or gasoline.

Great Smoky Mountains National Park campgrounds

Ten developed campgrounds are in Great Smoky Mountains National Park, but not all are suitable for big RVs because of the access roads. Those listed in Table 8-4 are the most suitable for RVs. Visitors with smaller vehicles can check out the other campgrounds listed on the map that you receive as you enter the park. Park campgrounds have no hookups, but they do provide fire rings, picnic tables, restrooms, and water. Some sites are suitable only for tent camping. Leave your firewood at home; you're welcome to gather downed wood for your fire in the park or buy it in one of the local camp stores.

Between May 15 and October 31, stays are limited to 7 days; the rest of the year, stays can be 14 days. During the summer period, it's wise to make reservations at the Cades Cove, Elkmont, and Smokemont campgrounds; call 877-444-6777 for reservations or 865-436-1200 for information. Most sites are $25 a night. For more information, check out www.nps.gov/grsm/planyourvisit/frontcountry-camping.htm.

TABLE 8-4   Campgrounds in the Smokies

Name	Cost	What to Know
Balsam Mountain Campground; Heintooga Ridge Road, SE corner	$	Total of 46 sites, with 30-foot length limit. $17.50 per site. No reservations. Open late May–Oct.
Cades Cove Campground; Entrance of Cades Cove Loop	$	Total of 159 sites. Paved, some shaded; back-ins can handle up to 35-foot RVs. Dump station. $25 per site. Open year-round.
Cataloochee Campground; East side off Cove Creek Road	$	Total of 27 unpaved (dirt) sites. Back-ins can handle up to 31-foot RVs. No slideouts. Stream nearby. $25 per site. No reservations. Open Mar 15–Nov 15.
Cosby Campground; NE corner, just south of TN-73	$	Total of 165 sites. Some shaded; back-ins only, with 25-foot length limit. No slideouts. $17.50 per site. No reservations. Open mid-Mar–early Nov.
Deep Creek Campground; North of Bryson City	$	Total of 92 sites, with 26-foot length limit. Paved, mostly shaded, narrow; back-ins; dump station. Stream nearby. $25 per site. No reservations. Open early Apr–Oct.

Name	Cost	What to Know
Elkmont Campground; Near Sugarlands Visitor Center	$	Total of 220 sites. Gravel, some shaded; back-ins can handle up to 35-foot RVs. No slideouts. $25 per site. Open mid-Mar–late Nov.
Smokemont Campground; Near Oconaluftee Visitor Center	$	Total of 142 sites, with 45 pull-throughs and 40-foot length limit. Paved, shaded, narrow; accessible for people with disabilities; dump station. Fishing and swimming in Oconaluftee River. $25 per site. Open year-round.

Good Eatin' along the Blue Ridge Route

Although all the classic Southern dishes — from fried chicken to collard greens, black-eyed peas, and biscuits — abound throughout the region, the culinary theme that ties together the mountains of Virginia, North Carolina, and Tennessee is *country ham*. If your previous acquaintance with ham is the supermarket kind, or spiral-cut honey-baked ham on Super Bowl Sunday, the mahogany-colored, chewy, salty meat called country ham may surprise you. It comes from the pioneers' tradition of preserving meats without refrigeration. They did so by rubbing the fresh meat with salt, sugar, and perhaps saltpeter, and then covering it in salt for four to six weeks. They would then hang the hams in a smokehouse to be infused with hickory smoke flavor.

Many of the homestyle restaurants in the following list offer country ham. They also offer a variety of other things, including a lot of history, some great shopping, eccentric local color, and some really first-class Southern eats.

>> **Apple Barn Cider Mill and General Store,** 230 Apple Valley Rd. (off U.S. 441), Sevierville, Tennessee (**800-421-4606** or **865-453-9319;** www.applebarncidermill.com): What began as a barn where cider was made from the orchard's apples is now a food-production complex that's open to visitors. Apples are mashed into cider and mixed into butter, pies, and dumplings. You find a little village of stores that sell tasty treats, including the Apple Barn winery and the Candy Factory for homemade candies, ice cream, and baked goods. A restaurant and grill are on the premises, and there's a craft shop selling baskets and birdhouses, as well as a Christmas and candle store. The restaurant and stores are open daily. Contact them directly for updated information.

>> **Mabry Mill Restaurant and Gift Shop,** 266 Mabry Mill Rd. SE (Blue Ridge Parkway milepost 176), Meadows of Dan, Virginia (**276-952-2947;** https://mabrymillrestaurant.com): Cornmeal and buckwheat pancakes made with stone-ground grains from the mill next door accompany rainbow trout, country ham, eggs, and homemade biscuits. Breakfast delights are served all day long, and you can buy grains at the mill or in the coffee shop. The coffee shop is open seasonally, from late April through early November.

>> **Michie Tavern,** 683 Thomas Jefferson Pkwy., Charlottesville, Virginia (**434-977-1234;** www.michietavern.com): This historic tavern serves traditional Southern lunches at moderate prices, and bus tours sometimes fill the place. Offerings include fried chicken, black-eyed peas, stewed tomatoes, and Virginia wines. The 1784 tavern was moved in the 1920s to a location near Monticello in order to save it; it's now part of a little complex of beautiful historic buildings, including the pub and inn, a general store, and a tavern shop. A unique experience.

>> **Snappy Lunch,** 125 N. Main St., Mount Airy, North Carolina (**336-786-4931;** www.thesnappylunch.com): A famed breakfast-and-lunch café. Andy once suggested to Barney on *The Andy Griffith Show* that they go down to Snappy Lunch to get a bite to eat, the only time Griffith mentioned a place from his old hometown on the show. The recommended order is the pork chop sandwich — a crunchy, juicy pork chop dipped in batter and fried. Try it with lettuce, tomato, and mayonnaise. Open Monday through Saturday.

TIP

If you're not an Andy Griffith fan and you end up in Mount Airy, check out this blog: https://lauradenooyer.com/sheriff-andy-taylor-recommends-the-snappy-lunch-in-mayberry. It explains much of the town's lore (as well as its lure). If you're a fan, and someone implies it's dumb, shoot back that it was J.D. Salinger's favorite TV show. That'll fix them.

Shopping along Blue Ridge Parkway

REMEMBER

The Blue Ridge Mountains were once America's western frontier, and the resilient Scotch-Irish settlers who built homesteads with logs and chinking were pioneers in the same mold as those who later set out in covered wagons to cross the Great Plains to Oregon. The men split chestnut trees into rails, calling the zigzag fence patterns snake, buck, or post–and–rail. The women made quilts from cloth scraps and named the patterns they created Double Wedding Ring, Flower Garden, and Crazy Quilt — traditional patterns you can still find in shops selling mountain crafts today.

One pleasure of touring the Southern mountains is finding high-quality crafts made in the age–old ways, elegantly handcrafted, but not inexpensive. The Southern Highland Craft Guild has promoted the crafts of this region since 1930. The guild operates four retail stores and galleries in the area, including shops in the following locations:

» **Folk Art Center,** 382 Blue Ridge Parkway, Asheville, North Carolina (**828-298-7928;** `www.southernhighlandguild.org/folkartcenter/`): Craft demonstrations are presented at the center from April through October, and juried shows are scheduled throughout the year. Handcrafted pottery, quilts, rocking chairs, baskets, toys, weavings, and other works of skilled craftspeople are on display; most are for sale. Open daily.

» **Moses Cone Manor,** 294 Blue Ridge Parkway, Blowing Rock, North Carolina (**828-295-7938;** `www.southernhighlandguild.org/mosesconemanor`): The shop at this location, like the Folk Art Center store, sells premium examples of genuine mountain crafts. Open daily April through November; check the website for hours.

Blue Ridge Fast Facts

Area Code
You find the following area codes in the Blue Ridge Mountains: **828** in North Carolina; **423** and **865** in Tennessee; and **434**, **504**, and **804** in Virginia.

Driving Laws
All vehicle occupants must wear seat belts in North Carolina and Tennessee; front-seat passengers must wear them in Virginia. The maximum speed limit on interstate highways in North Carolina, Tennessee, and Virginia is 70 mph; the speed limits on all roads are as posted. Speed limits in urban areas are lower in all three states.

Emergency
Call **911** in all states. Cell phone users can touch ***47** in North Carolina and ***847** in Tennessee.

Hospitals
Major hospitals along the route are located in Roanoke, Virginia, and Asheville, North Carolina.

Information
For North Carolina, go online to www.nc.gov or www.visitnc.com, or call for information on Blue Ridge Parkway (**828-298-0398**) or Great Smoky Mountains National Park (**865-436-1200**).

For Tennessee, contact the Department of Tourist Development (**615-741-8299**; www.tn.gov/tourism.html).

For Virginia, visit www.virginia.gov or www.virginia.org, or call for information on the Travel Guide (**800-742-3935**) or Blue Ridge Parkway (**704-271-4779**).

Road and Weather Conditions
For North Carolina, resources include **919-733-2520** and www.ncdot.gov.

For Tennessee, call **800-342-3258** (weather conditions) or go to www.tn.gov/tdot.

For Virginia, call **800-367-7623** (roadway assistance) or go to www.virginiadot.org.

Taxes
North Carolina state sales tax is 4.5 percent; local taxes can raise rates to 7.5 percent. Tennessee state sales tax is 7 percent; local taxes can raise rates to 9.750 percent. Virginia state sales tax is 4.3 percent; local taxes can raise rates to 5.3 percent.

State gas taxes are 38.5 cents per gallon in North Carolina, 27.4 cents per gallon in Tennessee, and 28 cents per gallon in Virginia.

Time Zone
North Carolina, the eastern half of Tennessee, and Virginia are in the Eastern time zone.

3

Seeing Sights in the South

IN THIS CHAPTER

» **Getting set for your Gulf Coast adventure**

» **Driving from Tallahassee to New Orleans**

» **Taking in the various Gulf Coast attractions**

» **Camping close to the beach or in state parks**

» **Finding fresh foods along the Gulf**

Chapter **9**

The Gulf Coast: Tallahassee to New Orleans

Sugary white-sand beaches, scrumptious shrimp, antebellum gardens bathed in scarlet and pink azaleas, and oak trees dripping Spanish moss are just some of the sights along the U.S. coast of the Gulf of Mexico. When you just want to enjoy good value for your vacation dollar, head on down to this lovely area. This nearly-always-sunny strip of vacation land runs from Tallahassee across Florida's Panhandle, along the Gulf shores of Alabama and Mississippi, and ends at the nonstop party town of New Orleans.

The Florida Panhandle, where Mickey Mouse never paraded and Cuban coffee is hard to find, is a world apart from the central and southern Florida regions most tourists have visited. Here, old-timers who relish smoked mullet and swamp cabbage mix, sometimes reluctantly, with the hotshot jet pilots at Pensacola Naval Air Station and the chic residents of Seaside (the Panhandle equivalent of the Hamptons). Endless platoons of college students notoriously invade the Gulf

Coast every year — especially around Panama City, Florida — between March and April to celebrate a pause in the academic year with their legendary raucous spring break partying.

The fashionable coast between Apalachicola and Pensacola boasts some of the top-ranked beaches in America, according to Dr. Stephen Leatherman (also known as Dr. Beach), a coastal geologist who puts out a listing of the nation's best beaches. After a few years of his listings, the area's tourist offices began to call this region the Emerald Coast. An affectionate, less tourist-conscious nickname for the region is the Redneck Riviera. Alabama and Mississippi serve up the lush romance of their own Gulf Coast regions in an economical 150 miles or so, with oceanside golf courses, Vegas-style casinos, and RV parks and campgrounds so close to the beach that you're lulled to sleep by the sound of the waves. A few more miles down the road and you're in New Orleans, the Big Easy, where you can let the good times roll.

In this chapter, we introduce you to the Gulf Coast drive, the campgrounds, the food, and interesting attractions along the way.

Planning Ahead for Your Gulf Coast Drive

You're in sun-worshipping country here. This Gulf of Mexico coastal drive can be made any time of year, but be aware of weather reports. Dedicated beach lovers may opt for summer, when the water is bathtub-warm (85 degrees F) for swimming, but the air temperatures and humidity levels are too high for taking long hikes and exploring. July is the hottest month of the year, averaging 84 degrees F. But be aware that the Gulf Coast's heat is NOT "a dry heat" by any measure — high humidity is the usual state of the weather here.

The combination of tropical flowers in bloom and a flock of hot pink flamingoes just screams picture-postcard vacation. Flower fanciers love the route in early to late spring, when the azaleas and camellias are blooming everywhere and the days are mild and sunny. In early fall, the weather is warm enough for sunning and swimming (Gulf of Mexico water averages 75 degrees F in November). In winter, the weather is mild, encouraging beachcombing, bird watching, and exploring small towns for antiques and local color. December is the "coldest" month, averaging 61 degrees F. Just makes you shiver, doesn't it?

REMEMBER

Along this route, reservations for RV camping are a good idea during summer, but especially during spring break and around holidays. (Truth be told, Florida's and Alabama's coastal towns should be completely avoided during spring break season in March and April — unless that's the reason you're going.) You should be able to find a spot without reservations in winter and during weekdays in early spring and late fall. Just be aware that many privately owned beachside campgrounds have a no cancellations/no refund policy.

TIP

Here are some tips to keep in mind as you traverse Florida and the Gulf Coast:

» **Go casual with plenty of light clothing.** Pack swimming apparel and light cotton clothes for spring, summer, and fall, and add a light jacket or sweater for most winter days and evenings. In the dead of summer when the sun is hottest, you probably can't bring enough shorts and T-shirts or golf shirts, unless you're prepared to do a lot of hand-washing of your coolest outfits. Dress is casual everywhere along the coast, so don't plan on bringing jackets and ties or fancy dresses and high heels unless you're taking some time off from the RV to visit one of the expensive coastal resort hotels. Always carry sunglasses, a wide-brimmed sun hat or ball cap, and sunscreen. If you intend to do any beach walking, be sure you've got sandals or other shoes you can easily wash the sand out of.

» **Bring rain gear.** You need a waterproof jacket (ideally with a hood) because this coast gets wind and lots of rain periodically throughout the year. Some areas get a daily cloudburst for a few minutes every afternoon.

» **Keep it clean.** Be sure you've got a broom and dustpan on board, unless your rig is equipped with a central vacuum cleaner system. Anytime you walk on the ground in this part of the country, you're going to drag sand into the house with you. Sand gets into everything.

» **Be weather aware.** Stay tuned to weather forecasts from May through November, and if a tropical storm or big wind is forecast, it's smart to consider heading inland with your RV. Always keep a wary eye on daily wind speed forecasts and never leave your RV awnings open if you're away from the campsite for any reason. Wind gusts over 20 mph can quite literally yank the awning right off the side of your rig and scatter your outdoor folding chairs across the campground.

» **Avoid spring break.** If you happen to be driving near Panama Beach and Mexico Beach at any time during college spring break season, the area is bound to be jam-packed, and the beaches will belong to the college-age visitors. Once you're beyond this stretch of the road, you can expect a more sedate populace.

» **Bring the bug juice.** With a hot, humid tropical climate, Florida and the rest of the Gulf states grow some creepy doozies of the bug kingdom. Locals often suggest that the mosquito be named the state bird of Florida and always keep a wary eye out for black widow spiders and red fire ants. Having plenty of insect repellent is a good idea, and so are glue traps for the floor of your RV.

Fire ant mounds are easy to mistake as just a small pile of loose dirt, and the mounds aren't always easy to see in grassy areas. They can literally pop up overnight. You likely won't see any of these savage fiends unless you step on or kick over their mound. That can send hundreds of them pouring out, all determined to have their revenge on you, their big-booted attacker. Their painful, stinging bites aren't usually dangerous in small numbers (unless you're allergic), but suddenly being swarmed and bitten by scores or even hundreds of them can be a terrifying experience.

Campgrounds will often post reassuring signs about a particular indigenous critter called the *palmetto bug,* urging tourists not to confuse them with cockroaches. News flash: They're still cockroaches, just with better press agents, and they can easily slip into cracks under your door or window frames, and up through tiny crevices in the floor around water, sewer, and gas pipes or furnace ducts. They love nesting in palm trees. So it's worth putting a few glue traps down in your rig's corners and closets, and in cabinets under sinks.

Driving the Gulf Coast

Our Gulf Coast adventure is a 610-mile trip that begins in **Tallahassee,** Florida (the state capital), runs southwest to **Apalachicola,** turns northward into the **Florida Panhandle**, runs through the oceanside cities and towns along Alabama and Mississippi's Gulf coastline, and ends at **New Orleans,** Louisiana.

TIP

We present a route that follows the slower oceanside roads (see Figure 9-1), but anytime you need to make up for lost time and mileage, you can jump onto I-10, which parallels much of the drive.

Fabulous Florida history

Tallahassee, in the center of northern Florida on I-10, is a good starting point for a drive through the Gulf Coast region. The state's capital can be a surprise for anyone familiar with Miami, Fort Lauderdale, or Orlando because it's a romantic Southern city — not a tropical Florida resort. It was chosen as the capital of the Florida Territory in 1823 because back then, when Miami was still a swamp, Tallahassee was equally distant from the two most important cities in the territory, Pensacola and St. Augustine. Magnolia trees and azaleas surround the graceful old capitol building, erected in the 1840s. The Spanish- and Moorish-influenced architecture throughout the area makes spending extra time here worthwhile, if you've got it.

Perhaps the most unusual museum in the city, even the state, is the **Black Archives Research Center and Museum** on the campus of Florida A&M University in Tallahassee. The museum houses 5,000 artifacts from slave days and the post–Civil War period, one of the nation's largest collections of African–American artifacts.

From Tallahassee, we drive south, leaving town on U.S. 319 and almost immediately turning off on SR 363 to **Wakulla Springs State Park,** where the classic 1954 monster film *Creature from the Black Lagoon* was shot in the deep, still waters of the springs. The beautiful **Lodge at Wakulla Springs** serves regional dishes, including breakfast with biscuits, gravy, and grits, and luncheon fried chicken with sawdust pie for dessert.

Five miles farther south on SR 363 is **St. Marks,** notable today for the excellent **St. Marks National Wildlife Refuge** and historic remnants from 17th-century Spanish explorers. If lighthouses fascinate you, check out the restored 1800s **St. Marks Lighthouse** at the end of CR 59 (Lighthouse Road).

Starting the Florida Panhandle trek

From St. Marks, we turn west on U.S. 98 and follow it to **Panacea** and then **Carrabelle.** Here, you can relax across from the beach and do some fishing while staying at the **Carrabelle Beach RV Resort.** Just southwest of town off U.S. 98 is the **Crooked River Lighthouse** and heritage museum.

Stay on U.S. 98 until you reach **Eastpoint,** which is 6 miles east of Apalachicola. CR 300 and a toll bridge both extend across the bay to **St. George Island** and its state park. If you cross over to the island, stop in and see the reconstructed **Cape St. George Light** and its museum before you head back to Eastpoint.

Follow U.S. 98 on to **Apalachicola,** famous around the world for its oysters. But pescatarians placating their palates don't ignore the local grouper, blue crab, and clam chowder at places such as the **Owl Cafe.** The **John Gorrie Museum** State Park salutes the inventor of ice cubes, refrigeration, and air-conditioning — without which much of Florida and the Gulf states would still be a hot, humid swampland no one in their right mind would voluntarily visit.

ATTRACTIONS

Bellingrath Gardens and Home **25**
Biloxi Lighthouse **28**
Cape St. George Light **7**
Gulf Islands National Seashore **13**
INFINITY Science Center **29**
John Gorrie Museum State Park **8**
Meek-Eaton Black Archives
   Research Center and Museum **2**
National Naval Aviation Museum **16**
Ohr-O'Keefe Museum of Art **28**
St. Mark's Lighthouse **5**
St. Mark's National Wildlife Refuge **5**
USS Alabama Battleship
   Memorial Park **24**
Walter Anderson Museum of Art **27**
Wakulla Springs State Park **3**

FIGURE 9-1: *continued*

Traveling west from Apalachicola

West of Apalachicola, take CR 30 and then CR 30 East to the **T.H. Stone Memorial St. Joseph Peninsula State Park.** The peninsula curls out and up into the Gulf like a skinny lobster claw, creating a sheltered bay around **Port St. Joe.** For many years, the park has been a great spot for beach camping. Hurricane Michael, a destructive Category 5 storm, made landfall here in 2018 and severely damaged the beach and surrounding park. But much of the area is now open, with campsites anticipated to reopen in summer 2023. Meanwhile, you find **Aqua Bay RV Park** and **Port St. Joe RV Resort** just north of town, and they both overlook the bay and face the western sky, offering up beautiful sunsets.

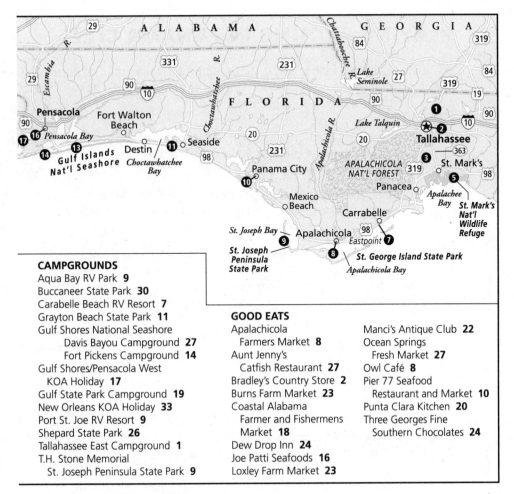

FIGURE 9-1: A map of the Gulf Coast route.

CAMPGROUNDS
Aqua Bay RV Park **9**
Buccaneer State Park **30**
Carabelle Beach RV Resort **7**
Grayton Beach State Park **11**
Gulf Shores National Seashore
     Davis Bayou Campground **27**
     Fort Pickens Campground **14**
Gulf Shores/Pensacola West
  KOA Holiday **17**
Gulf State Park Campground **19**
New Orleans KOA Holiday **33**
Port St. Joe RV Resort **9**
Shepard State Park **26**
Tallahassee East Campground **1**
T.H. Stone Memorial
  St. Joseph Peninsula State Park **9**

GOOD EATS
Apalachicola
  Farmers Market **8**
Aunt Jenny's
  Catfish Restaurant **27**
Bradley's Country Store **2**
Burns Farm Market **23**
Coastal Alabama
  Farmer and Fishermens
  Market **18**
Dew Drop Inn **24**
Joe Patti Seafoods **16**
Loxley Farm Market **23**

Manci's Antique Club **22**
Ocean Springs
  Fresh Market **27**
Owl Café **8**
Pier 77 Seafood
  Restaurant and Market **10**
Punta Clara Kitchen **20**
Three Georges Fine
  Southern Chocolates **24**

WARNING

Return to U.S. 98 and continue west, driving past the almost empty stretches of perfect sand at **Mexico Beach** and then on into **Panama City,** the thriving capital of the Redneck Riviera. If you should happen to be driving through here anytime during the college spring break season between March and April, don't stop, don't pause, and don't linger — detour around it up to SR 20. The beaches and coastal towns belong to the kids, especially **Panama City Beach** across the Hathaway Bridge. It isn't a pretty sight — unless that's what you're here for, in which case it's college student Valhalla.

After you're safely past Panama City Beach, you can slow down again. Don't miss taking the back road off U.S. 98 through **Seaside** (a marked left turn just past **Point Washington**) to get a quick look at the award-winning architecture of the local beach houses. If you're an old movie fan, you may recognize the town from the Jim Carrey movie *The Truman Show* (1998), some of which was filmed in Seaside.

PLAYING AROUND IN PANAMA CITY

While the local population is about 15,000, some 4.5 million tourists flock to Panama City annually, mostly during spring break. This is a heavily developed city with lots of high-rise condos and apartments, and loads to do.

- If shopping is your passion, head over to **Pier Park,** where you also find kid-friendly attractions like an **IMAX theater, Dave & Buster's** entertainment center, and the Emerald Coast **Mirror Maze & Laser Craze.**

- If free drinks are your jam, stop in at **Coyote Ugly,** where you're rewarded with a complimentary libation if you climb up on the bar and dance with sufficient, um, enthusiasm.

- Take a shuttle boat over to **Shell Island** and **St. Andrews State Park** for swimming, snorkeling, and shell hunting, or to enjoy just being a sun-broiled layabout. Between May and October, the gigantic 1,000-pound sea turtles make their way onto the island's beaches to lay their eggs. Enjoy the sight, but give the poor girls a little privacy.

- Take a sightseeing boat trip out to find **pods of bottlenose dolphins** frolicking in the Gulf — make it a sunset cruise to make it even more memorable.

While you're close to Seaside, consider checking out **Grayton Beach State Park,** which was named America's Best Beach by Dr. Beach back in the '90s. The park allows RV camping in designated campgrounds.

TIP

Don't attempt to stop in Seaside; streets are narrow, traffic is heavy, and parking for RVs is unavailable anywhere. If you're a shopper, you're in better luck — the modern malls that line the highway from Panama City to Pensacola, especially around Destin and Fort Walton Beach, have big parking lots that can handle your vehicle.

Making your way to Pensacola

From Seaside, find your way back to U.S. 98 and stay the course through **Destin** and on to Pensacola. Parallel to this drive, **Gulf Islands National Seashore** extends 150 miles from Destin to Gulfport, Mississippi. Established in 1971, the park protects the long chain of barrier islands along this coast from Pensacola westward to Mississippi, many of them undeveloped and unreachable except by boat.

RESPECT THE FLAGS!

Colored flags flying on a beach aren't posted there to cheer on the local sports team, organize a protest march, or advertise a used car lot. When you're enjoying the beaches of the Gulf Coast, especially during hurricane season between June and November, *always* pay attention to the flags that denote current water conditions.

- **A green triangular flag:** Calm water safe for swimming.

- **A yellow triangular flag:** Moderate surf or currents — use caution in the water.

- **A single red triangular flag:** Rough conditions, strong currents, and gale-force winds between 39 mph and 54 mph — don't go in the water!

- **A single square red flag with a black square in the middle:** Tropical storm warning with winds 55–73 mph.

- **Two square red flags with black squares in the middle:** Hurricane warning with winds over 74 mph — get the hell off that beach!

Pensacola is a charming surprise of a city with a lovely old historic district downtown and the headquarters of the Navy's ace flying team, the Blue Angels. (See the later sidebar about Pensacola's **National Naval Aviation Museum.**) If you've got time, catch the 2-hour, hop-on/hop-off guided tour of the city on board a restored 1930 Ford bus.

You can discover plenty of history in Pensacola: The town began as a Spanish colonial settlement in 1559, and (like most of the real estate on this itinerary) was held at varying times by the Spanish, French, and British. Pensacola was also the site of the longest siege of the American War of Independence, lest you think our revolution was solely fought and won by a bunch of snooty New Englanders prattling on about their tea party.

Pensacola also has **Joe Patti Seafoods,** the biggest and best fresh indoor seafood market we've ever seen.

Crossing Alabama

After you explore Pensacola, we suggest that you drive south to see more of Gulf Islands National Seashore; take SR 292 to **Perdido Key** and across into Alabama, where it becomes SR 182, to **Gulf Shores.** If you want to stick close to the water, you can take U.S. 98 across Perdido Bay into Alabama and then follow it to **Barnwell,** where the road turns straight north, tracking the coast of **Mobile Bay.** If you're in more of a hurry, you can pick up either I-10 or U.S. 90 north of Pensacola and head west for Mobile. Regardless of how you go, you're passing across a narrow, 80-mile strip of Alabama that dangles down into the Gulf between Mississippi and Louisiana to give the state its saltwater port at Mobile.

We like **Gulf State Park** at Gulf Shores, Alabama, for beachfront camping and plenty of shrimp sellers.

EATIN', PARTYIN', AND ANTIQUIN', MOBILE-STYLE

More than three centuries old, Mobile was the French capital of Louisiana in America before there was a New Orleans, and the city logo proudly shows off a historic home, the battleship USS *Alabama*, an azalea in full bloom, and a shrimp. What does it all mean? The historic home is a reminder that Mobile offers tours of antebellum houses. The ship, open daily for tours in **USS *Alabama* Battleship Memorial Park,** was operational during World War II. The azalea stands for world-famous **Bellingrath Gardens and Home,** a glorious splash of seasonal flowers year-round. And if shrimp and Alabama make you think of *Forrest Gump,* you won't be surprised to discover that its author, the late Winston Groom, had a home just outside Mobile, in Fairhope.

Depending on your feelings about huge crowds, you may or may not want to visit during **Carnival** and **Mardi Gras** season. Like the New Orleans extravaganza, Mobile's Mardi Gras celebration (a movable Christian holiday held 46 days before Easter) is a huge, nonstop party and parade that draws visitors from all over the world. Campground reservations are a must during Mardi Gras week, and you won't get anywhere near downtown with a big rig. But Mobile starts its Carnival season a whole lot sooner than most other places — wild masquerade parties begin as early as November with the International Carnival Ball, and kick into high gear after New Year's on January 6. Mobile's unique *mystic societies* are secret membership clubs that run these celebrations, and the city's customs are unlike anyone else's.

RVers seeking other gratifications in the area need to make the scenic drive on U.S. 98 and 98A along the eastern shore of Mobile Bay. En route, you can visit the Bloody Mary capital of the eastern shore, **Manci's Antique Club,** in downtown **Daphne. Fairhope** is lined with antiques shops and art galleries, and punctuated with a long pier jutting out into the bay.

Point Clear is home to the **Grand Hotel Golf Resort and Spa,** "the Queen of Southern resorts" and one of the famed Historic Hotels of America. The hotel opened in 1847, served as a hospital during the Civil War, and hosted military training operations during World War II. It's also the home of **Punta Clara Kitchen,** where homemade candies abound.

On the western side of the bay, SR 193 leads to **Bellingrath Gardens and Home** and beyond to **Dauphin Island** and **Fort Gaines,** where you can look across to **Fort Morgan,** the Civil War fortress barricaded with a string of underwater mines across the channel that inspired Admiral David Farragut's famous command, "Damn the torpedoes — full speed ahead!"

In Mobile, on the northwestern edge of the city on Old Shell Road, a super snack-time stop, the **Dew Drop Inn,** has been serving up great hot dogs since 1927.

Moseying across Mississippi

From Mobile, it takes only minutes to get into Mississippi. Cross over the bay on either I-10 or U.S. 90, and then head back south to the coast on 90 toward Pascagoula. Whereas Alabama's Gulf Coast consists of quiet towns and fishing villages on dead-end roads, Mississippi's stretch of coastline is four-lane U.S. 90, brightened by intervals of glitz.

From the moment you cross the causeway from **Ocean Springs** to **Biloxi,** the casinos — a dozen of them — pop up like glittering psychedelic mushrooms. (So you won't be taken for a Yankee, pronounce the town's name buh-*lux*-ee, not bill-*ox*-ee.) As far back as 1900, this section of Mississippi was nicknamed America's Riviera. This Las Vegas of the Deep South is the second-largest gaming region in the U.S., after Vegas itself.

If you're hunting historic lighthouses, you'll find two very different styles here: the cast-iron 1848 **Biloxi Lighthouse,** just west of Ocean Springs at the Biloxi visitor's center, and a replica of the wooden 1853 lighthouse at **Sea Ship Island,** halfway between Mississippi City and Long Beach. But if UFOs are more your interest, there's a historical marker in Lighthouse Park at the site of the famed 1973 Pascagoula Abduction, where Charlie Hickson and Calvin Parker, Jr. claimed to have been abducted by aliens in 1973.

At **Bayside Park,** take a detour north of U.S. 90 onto S.R. 607 toward I-10 and visit **INFINITY Science Center,** which acts as the visitor's center for NASA's John C. Stennis Space Center. The space agency has developed and tested its rockets at Stennis since the 1960s, but the rocket-testing facility is off-limits to civilians. INFINITY displays many of these innovative launch vehicles, along with showing off new technology for both outer space and undersea exploration. Be sure to walk through the full-size module from the International Space Station.

Last stop: Louisiana

From **Gulfport,** following U.S. 90, it's 34 miles to the Louisiana border; but just before you get to the border, you pass **Buccaneer State Park**. If you're in a hurry to get to the Big Easy, **New Orleans,** head north to take I-10.

Exploring New Orleans by navigating your RV through its city streets is not enjoyable or recommended. Camp outside the city and explore by shuttle or car.

Weekend wandering

The full distance for this drive is about 480 miles. If you have only a couple of days and want to take a shorter drive, confine yourself to Florida. Go from Tallahassee southwest to Apalachicola, and continue west along the Emerald Coast to Pensacola — a 270-mile trip — pausing at whatever beaches and campgrounds strike your fancy. Or skip the bulk of Florida and concentrate on the Gulf Coast entirely by starting at Pensacola and following U.S. 90 and U.S. 98 along the beach cities, west to New Orleans. That route is just 210 miles.

WARNING

NEW ORLEANS: EASING INTO THE BIG EASY

Generally speaking, New Orleans is one of the friendliest cities on Earth — that is, to everybody except RVers. It's not that the good folks of "Nawlins" don't welcome us; they do. But their roads, even the interstates, are bumpy and rough, causing our pots and pans to rattle as we bounce through.

Equally troubling are the confusing roadway markings for the interstate, expressway, and surface-street system, which can catapult an innocent RVer into the traffic-clogged French Quarter or the Superdome before you can say, *Laissez les bon temps roulez!* ("Let the good times roll," the traditional Cajun partying cry).

We highly recommend staying at an RV campground in an outlying area (preferably one that has frequent shuttle service to and from downtown if you don't have your own car). Park and secure your living quarters and then set out to have footloose fun in a city that never sleeps.

The obvious attractions in New Orleans usually begin on **Bourbon Street** in the **French Quarter,** with its unique architecture lining the narrow streets and the many clubs and bars around every corner. If you're hunting live music venues in the French Quarter (jazz, blues, or otherwise), the city has a regularly updated website of **French Quarter music clubs** at www.neworleans.com/plan/neighborhoods/french-quarter/music-clubs/.

But plenty of other attractions outside the Quarter can keep you exploring for as much or as little time as you've got. Check out the following:

- **Visit the world-class Audubon Zoo** (https://audubonnatureinstitute.org/zoo). This outstanding zoo is home to animals from all over the world.

- **Swim with the fishes at the Audubon Aquarium of the Americas** (https://audubonnatureinstitute.org/aquarium). One of the best aquariums in the U.S., the Audubon Aquarium has more than 250 species of animals. Visitors can don masks and snorkels and swim the Great Maya Reef habitat to get eye to eye with the fish. At press time, the aquarium was closed for renovation, but was expected to be open in summer 2023.

- **Tour the National WWII Museum** (www.nationalww2museum.org/). Originally opened in 2000 as the D-Day Museum, this museum is dedicated to explaining the vital contributions of the United States in the Allied victory of World War II. It was the pet project of the late historian Stephen Ambrose, who lived in New Orleans.

- **Ride the historic New Orleans streetcars** (www.neworleans.com/plan/itineraries/streetcar-itinerary/). There are four main historic electric streetcar lines in the city still operating with their iconic antique cars, and still being fed electricity by overhead wires. The St. Charles Avenue Line is the oldest continuously operating street railway system in the world, and each of its 1920s-era cars is designated as a historic landmark. (There really were street-cars named "Desire" — they plied the Desire Line in the Bywater District until it shut down in 1948. A deteriorating car with the Desire route sign is parked at the Carrollton Station in the repair shop, if you really must have that perfect selfie. Be sure to smile and scream *"Stella!"*)

- **Discover haunted New Orleans.** Explore at least one of the fascinating and distinctive aboveground cemeteries with their spooky mausoleums. (Belowground burials are almost impossible here because of the city's shallow water table — dig a hole, and it immediately fills with water.) Day or night, there are lots of haunted ghost, voodoo, and vampire walking tours, and at least one bus tour. Many advertise themselves as kid-friendly. Check out Haunted History Tours (https://hauntedhistorytours.com/). Their Cities of the Dead bus tour is the only one with nighttime access

(continued)

(continued)

to the oldest (and creepiest) cemeteries like St. Louis and Charity Hospital. There are also several haunted pub crawls.

- **Hop on a New Orleans airboat tour** (www.neworleansairboattours.com). The tour boards about a half-hour's drive from downtown New Orleans in the town of Marrero and winds through the mossy cypress swamp close to Jean Lafitte National Historical Park and Preserve, named for the 19th-century pirate and smuggler. You'll likely see alligators, turtles, snakes, egrets, herons, ibis, and other wildlife. Just remember that airboats are wet, windy, and LOUD (hearing protection is provided). You and your companions will spend lots of time shouting, "WHAT?!"

- **Visit one of the many old plantations.** These historic sites along the Mississippi near New Orleans include the 1837 Oak Alley Plantation, Houmas House and Gardens, Laura Plantation, and Whitney Plantation. For details, see www.cajunen counters.com/tours/plantations/

- **Roll down the river on the *Natchez* or the *Creole Queen* paddle wheelers.** Take a harbor tour or dinner cruise on the paddle-wheel boat *Natchez* (www.steamboat natchez.com/). Cruise the river on the Creole Queen (www.creolequeen.com/) and hear about the 1815 Battle of New Orleans. Or just hang out by the Mississippi River and watch the nonstop parade of ships coming from and going to the harbor.

- **Hit the jackpot.** If gambling is your idea of fun, the New Orleans area should more then satisfy your tastes. According to the Casinos.us website (https://www.casinos.us/louisiana/new-orleans/), New Orleans and the surrounding communities in southeast Louisiana feature 47 gambling establishments and a horse race track. That list counts truck stops and off-track betting locations, so it's kind of a fudge on numbers, but you still find several upscale places. The best is probably Harrah's New Orleans (www.caesars.com/harrahs-new-orleans). Churchill Downs operates the Fair Grounds Race Course & Slots (www.fairgroundsracecourse.com), touted as America's third-oldest racetrack.

HEEDING HURRICANE AND TROPICAL STORM WARNINGS

It's a fact of life that much of this scenic region is periodically whacked by hurricanes and tropical storms that can blow through anytime between May and November. Reconstruction can be slow, and state-run parks and beaches can sometimes take years to recover: Hurricanes Katrina in 2005 and Michael in 2018 hit the Florida Panhandle hard, and some parks, campgrounds, and businesses have taken time to recover or never rebuilt at all.

But tropical storms that become hurricanes or cause damage are actually rare from the panhandle westward to New Orleans in any given year. Most RVers don't bother to watch local TV news broadcasts, listen to local radio, or pick up any of the few local newspapers that remain in the world, so you may not always be aware of an impending weather emergency in time to alter your route. *Hint:* If you see the locals suddenly nailing plywood over their windows, you can confidently expect something's coming. The sidebar figure shows a sign that marks a hurricane evacuation route.

We'll repeat ourselves here: **Hurricane and tropical storm season in the southeastern Atlantic and Gulf states lasts from May through November,** and coastal areas where you'll be driving on this trip can be hammered by high winds and storm surge flooding during these events.

Be sure you have at least one smartphone weather app that can be set to loudly notify you of local National Weather Service warnings and watches. Our favorites include **AccuWeather,** the **Weather Channel,** and especially **Weather Underground.** And **CARROT Weather** is both informative and a little entertaining — you can set it to have different personalities so it delivers the weather with a dose of smart-assery. May as well have a chuckle while a deadly storm bears down on you, we always say.

(continued)

(continued)

It can't hurt to have a portable **NOAA weather radio** on board as well (check the batteries before leaving home). These special radios scan the public emergency radio bands silently in the background 24 hours a day and only spring to life when they detect a signal from the Emergency Alert System.

The wireless phone industry has its own warning system, and if you have a smartphone newer than 2012, the ability to receive these warnings with their distinctive alarm tone should be built in. Called *Wireless Emergency Alerts (WEAs)*, these warnings are emergency messages issued by authorized government agencies through your mobile carrier. Government WEA partners include local and state public safety agencies, FEMA, the Federal Communications Commission, the Department of Homeland Security, and the National Weather Service. WEAs may include:

- **Extreme weather warnings** alerting of approaching storms.

- **Local emergency alerts** requiring evacuation or immediate action.

- **Presidential Alerts** issued during a national emergency.

- **AMBER Alerts** regarding missing or abducted children when the public's assistance is sought.

- **Silver Alerts** regarding missing, abducted, or otherwise endangered adults.

- **Blue Alerts** regarding suspects who have killed, seriously injured, or pose an immediate, credible threat to law enforcement or first responders. These include bulletins about police officer attacks or killings, missing members of law enforcement, at-large criminal suspects, or other crimes in which police seek the public's immediate assistance in spotting or identifying dangerous suspects.

- **Other immediate alerts** conveying information for protecting lives and property.

WEAs are location-specific — they're broadcast from local cell towers to all cell phones in the immediate vicinity, so you'll only get alerts for the area you happen to be in at the moment. You won't get an alert from back home in Des Moines if you happen to be in Biloxi. Unlike the hundreds of push notifications from pizza places, credit card companies, Amazon, and CVS going off in your pocket every five minutes, *you cannot turn off WEAs*. The only downside is, if you're in an area with no cell service (which can happen a lot on RV trips), you won't receive them.

If local authorities do declare an evacuation emergency, Gulf Coast area highways are marked with **evacuation route** signs (see the sidebar figure) that will direct you to the best way out of the area you're in. Authorities will often turn both sides of major highways into one-way-out emergency routes to handle as much traffic as smoothly as possible. They've had a lot of experience here.

Must-See Attractions along the Gulf Coast

USS Alabama Battleship Memorial Park
Mobile, Alabama

The USS *Alabama* is a decommissioned World War II battleship that carried a crew of 2,500 into action in both the North Atlantic and the South Pacific, where she led the American fleet into Tokyo Bay in 1945. The ship opened as a museum and the state's official veterans' memorial in 1965, and is Alabama's most popular tourist attraction. She was the ship in the 1992 Steven Seagal action pic *Under Siege*. Most recently, the "Mighty A" starred as the ill-fated USS *Indianapolis* in the 2016 Nicolas Cage movie *USS Indianapolis: Men of Courage.*

The USS *Alabama* is on stationary display, along with the submarine USS *Drum* (launched in 1941 and the oldest U.S. submarine currently open to the public), a B-52 bomber, a P-51 Mustang fighter, cannons, tanks, armored personnel carriers, and helicopters, including a Bell 212 helicopter used as "Marine 1" that transported presidents Nixon, Ford, Carter, Reagan, and George H.W. Bush. Kids love to climb all over the military hardware and explore the hidden corners of the ship. Open daily; closed on Christmas. Allow two to three hours to tour the ship.

Battleship Parkway, Mobile Bay., AL; **251-433-2703** *or* **800-GANGWAY (4264929);** www.ussalabama.com. **RV parking** *fee per vehicle. Admission varies with age.*

Bellingrath Gardens and Home
Theodore, Alabama (south of Mobile)

Six themed formal gardens are strung together with a series of bridges, walkways, pools, and streams to create one of the most appealing floral displays in the world. In spring, 250,000 azaleas blaze with color; in summer, everything comes up roses; in autumn, chrysanthemums bloom by the thousands; and winter's poinsettias and camellias glow in the semitropical landscape. The 15-room Bellingrath family home (he was the first Coca-Cola bottler in the Mobile area) houses collections of antique china and glass, including 200 pieces of Edward Marshall Boehm porcelain. A café is also on the estate. Open daily; closed on Thanksgiving, Christmas, and New Year's days. Allow two hours for the gardens only and three hours for the gardens and house.

*12401 Bellingrath Gardens Rd., Theodore, AL; **251-973-2217;** https://*
*bellingrath.org. **RV parking:** Large designated parking areas. Admission*
varies by age.

Gulf Islands National Seashore
Florida and Mississippi

Extending 160 miles from Destin, Florida, to Gulfport, Mississippi, Gulf
Islands National Seashore is divided into 11 sections, 6 of them in Florida
and 5 in Mississippi. The park features barrier islands, maritime forests,
historic forts, bayous, and marine habitat. Miles of uncrowded beaches
famous for acres of soft white sand and sea oats attract day visitors and
overnight campers in modest numbers. Two campgrounds, Florida's Fort
Pickens and Mississippi's Davis Bayou, usually have campsites available on
a first-come, first-served basis. Much of the parkland consists of offshore
islands reachable only by boat. Areas accessible by motor vehicles offer hiking trails, bike paths, and nature trails. There's a good book and gift store at
Fort Pickens. Open daily year-round.

Headquarters: 1801 Gulf Breeze Pkwy., Gulf Breeze, FL, or 3500 Park Rd.,
*Ocean Springs, MS. **850-934-2600** (General campground questions) or **228-***
***875-9057** (William M. Colmer Visitor Center, MS);* https://www.nps.gov/
guis. ***RV parking:** Designated off-road areas. Admission by age or vehicle.*
Free with an annual America the Beautiful Pass.

INFINITY Science Center
Pearlington, Mississippi

Since the 1960s, NASA has developed and tested its rockets and increasingly powerful engines at the John C. Stennis Space Center, but that facility
has been closed to the public for decades. INFINITY acts as the visitor's
center for the Stennis Space Center and displays many of NASA's innovative launch vehicles, along with showing off new technology for both outer
space and undersea exploration. Highlights include the Apollo 4 command
module, the first stage of the Saturn V rocket built for the canceled Apollo
19 mission, an advanced deep ocean exploration vehicle, the carnivorous
plants conservatory (always a kid favorite, with 200 species of hungry
plants!), the space suit technology gallery, and the hurricane prediction
lab. Be sure to explore the full-size Destiny laboratory module from the
International Space Station. Open Thursday through Sunday; closed
Thanksgiving, Christmas Eve, Christmas, and New Year's days. Give the
center at least 2½ hours.

*1 Discovery Circle, Pearlington, MS; **228-533-9025;** https://visitinfinity.com. **RV parking** free and available.*

PENSACOLA'S NATIONAL NAVAL AVIATION MUSEUM: CURRENTLY CLOSED TO THE PUBLIC

A longtime favorite attraction in the Florida panhandle has been the National Naval Aviation Museum on the grounds of the Naval Air Station (NAS) at Pensacola (www.navalaviationmuseum.org).

NAS Pensacola is an active military base, and aircraft and ships based there often assist in NASA and SpaceX recovery missions, along with servicing Coast Guard vessels. But most famously, it's the headquarters of the Blue Angels, the Navy's aerial acrobatics team, with their distinctive A-4 Skyhawk fighter jets. The museum and the base were open to the public for decades, and visitors could see the Blue Angels practicing their skills almost every week.

But in 2019, a Royal Saudi Air Force pilot training at NAS Pensacola went on a shooting spree in what was described as a self-radicalized terrorist attack, killing three sailors and wounding eight other military and civilian personnel before he was shot by base security. As of press time in 2023, NAS Pensacola is still mostly closed to nonmilitary visitors, but frustrated base commanders continue to seek ways to reopen the museum to the public.

The National Naval Aviation Museum is still open Monday through Sunday from 9:00 a.m. to 4:00 p.m., but only to current Department of Defense (DoD) ID card holders. Visitors can climb into a cockpit trainer, observe a flight simulator in action, see A-4 Skyhawks like those flown by the Blue Angels, discover the history of flying, from wooden planes to the Skylab module, experience the Apollo 11 moon mission via virtual reality, and see big-screen aviation films with a pilot's point of view in the adjoining IMAX theater. Allow three hours; real buffs spend a whole day. If you're interested in seeing the Blue Angels practice their aerial acrobatics, they usually fly on Tuesdays and Wednesdays from March through November.

Access to NAS Pensacola is also limited to DoD ID card holders (active duty service members, retirees, and their families). If you have a Veterans Health Identification Card, visit https://cnrse.cnic.navy.mil/Installations/NAS-Pensacola/ for base access information. DoD ID card holders can escort guests to the museum but must remain with them at all times.

NAS Pensacola has a special visitor information line at 850-452-8450 for answers to questions about visiting the museum. They want it reopened to the public as much as we do.

Walter Anderson Museum of Art
Ocean Springs, Mississippi

This museum displays the astonishing works of an eccentric loner named Walter Anderson. A master artist who painted plants, animals, and people of the Gulf Coast, he sometimes isolated himself in primitive conditions on an uninhabited barrier island for months at a time. After his death in 1965, his family went into the small cottage he used as a studio and discovered the "little room," every inch of its floor, walls, and ceilings covered with paintings of plants, animals, and an allegorical figure thought to represent the Mississippi River. The little room, Anderson's paintings and murals, and ceramic pieces from the family's Shearwater Pottery collection are on display here. Open daily. Allow two hours.

510 Washington Ave.; **228-872-3164;** *www.walterandersonmuseum.org.*
RV parking: *Use street parking because the museum lot is small. Admission varies by age.*

More Cool Things to See and Do along the Gulf Coast

Fascinating attractions line the Gulf Coast. A few more of our favorites follow, although you'll no doubt make your own discoveries.

KID FRIENDLY

» **Explore Black history.** With 5,000 objects and 500,000 documents, one of the most extensive collections of African-American artifacts in the U.S., the **Meek-Eaton Black Archives Research Center and Museum** at Florida A&M University in Tallahassee, displays everything from slave-era implements and old, decidedly un-woke Aunt Jemima pancake-mix packages, to the first ironing board, built in 1872 by a servant named Sarah Boone, who got tired of ironing on the floor and propped a board up on legs. A hands-on Underground Railroad exhibit fascinates the kids. Open Monday through Friday; closed on holidays. Allow two hours.

445 Robert and Trudie Perkins Wy, Tallahassee, FL; **850-599-3020;** *www.famu. edu/academics/libraries/meek-eaton-black-archives-research- center-and-museum/index.php.* ***RV parking*** *is available in a designated guest parking area or on the street. Admission is free.*

>> **Meet the mad potter of Biloxi.** The **Ohr-O'Keefe Museum of Art** honors the mad potter of Biloxi, George E. Ohr, who had a knack for self-promotion. The museum has 130 pots of his creation, along with other collections of Black art, Mississippi folk art, and ceramics. Open Tuesday through Saturday; closed on major holidays.

>> *386 Beach Blvd., Biloxi, MS;* **228-374-5547;** `https://georgeohr.org`. *Admission varies by age.*

>> **See where ice cubes were invented.** In 1851, Dr. John Gorrie invented a machine to cool the rooms of malaria and yellow fever patients, but when pesky ice blocks kept clogging its pipes, it suddenly dawned on him that he was onto something bigger, and he invented ice cubes, the artificial ice maker, and air-conditioning. Before Gorrie's innovations, ice had to be cut from natural ice deposits in mountains or chopped from icebergs, brought to ports by ship, and then stored in warehouses with no means of preserving them. Gorrie's process quite literally changed the entire world. You can see a replica of the machine in the **John Gorrie Museum State Park;** the original is in the Smithsonian. Open Thursday through Monday; closed on Thanksgiving, Christmas, and New Year's days. Allow one hour.

>> *46 Sixth St., Apalachicola, FL;* **850-653-9347;** `www.floridastateparks.org/parks-and-trails/john-gorrie-museum-state-park`. *No restrooms.* **RV parking** *is available on the street. Admission varies by age.*

>> **Look out for alligators!** Bike, hike, and canoe numerous trails and streams in **St. Marks National Wildlife Refuge,** bordering Florida's Apalachee Bay. An excellent visitor's center has maps and advice.

>> *1255 Lighthouse Rd., Wakulla County, FL;* **850-925-6121;** `www.fws.gov/refuge/st_marks`. *The refuge entrance is south of Newport on SR 59.* **RV parking** *is available in designated lots at the visitor's center and on trailheads. If you want more information, contact the U.S. Fish & Wildlife Service, Box 68, St. Marks, FL 32355.*

KID FRIENDLY

>> **Trail Tarzan and the Creature.** Many of the early Tarzan movies of the 1930s with beefy Johnny Weissmuller and Maureen O'Sullivan (moviedom's most perfect Jane) were filmed at Florida's **Wakulla Springs State Park**, and so was the 1954 3-D horror classic *The Creature from the Black Lagoon.* The clear, almost bottomless freshwater springs and lush jungle foliage with its spooky cypress trees and dangling moss make this area a popular family vacation site. Take a jungle cruise down the Wakulla River, and chances are, you'll spot manatees and alligators, along with wading birds like herons and flamingoes. Or take a glass-bottom boat across the crystal clear springs and see ancient mastodon remains

in their sandy basin. You can also go swimming in the springs, which stay a constant 70 degrees F even on the most sweltering days. Stop in and see the classic 1930s Spanish-style lodge with its beautiful murals and have breakfast, lunch, or dinner in the Edwin Ball Dining Room.

*State Park Lodge, 550 Wakulla Park Dr., Wakulla Springs, FL; **855-632-4559**; https://thelodgeatwakullasprings.com or www.floridastateparks.org/ parks-and-trails/edward-ball-wakulla-springs-state-park. **RV parking** is available in designated areas in the park and at the lodge. Park admission per vehicle; river boat tours by age. Make jungle cruise, glass-bottom boat ride, and overnight lodge reservations online.*

Our Favorite Campgrounds along the Gulf

The Gulf Coast is a popular destination for RVers — whether they're family vacationers, snowbirds, or full-timers — and plenty of RV parks, state parks, and recreation areas with camping line the way. Supermarkets, country stores, restaurants, cafés, and national fast-food outlets also generously dot the route.

RVers love the opportunity to camp right on the beaches in many locations. Unfortunately, Mother Nature can be a bad-tempered old battle-ax some days, especially in this part of the country. Recent hurricanes have severely damaged or closed a couple of our favorite beach camping sites, but plenty of newly built or rebuilt campgrounds, and many reliable favorites, are up and running.

All campgrounds listed in Tables 9-1 and 9-2 are open year-round and have public flush toilets, showers, and sanitary dump stations unless otherwise noted.

TABLE 9-1 Our Favorite Gulf Coast Campgrounds

Name and Location	Contact Info	Cost	What to Know
Davis Bayou Campground; Gulf Islands National Seashore, Ocean Springs, MS	3500 Park Rd; **228-230-4136;** www.nps.gov/ guis/planyourvisit/ db-campground.htm	$	Operated by the Army Corps of Engineers at the western end of Gulf Islands National Seashore. Shaded, paved back-in sites are narrow, though a few can accommodate RVs up to 45 feet. First-come, first-served. Accepts the National Park Senior Pass for half off. Visitor's center on-site shows a film about the national seashore.

Name and Location	Contact Info	Cost	What to Know
Fort Pickens Campground; Gulf Islands National Seashore, Pensacola Beach, FL	1400 Fort Pickens Rd; **850-934-2622;** www.nps.gov/guis/ planyourvisit/ fortpickens- campground.htm	$$	Inside Gulf Islands National Seashore at the east end of Santa Rosa Island. One of the ten busiest campgrounds in the national parks system. Reserve up to six months in advance online. All sites have a paved pad, fire pit, and picnic table. Tour nearby historic Fort Pickens, built in 1834 to help defend the port of Pensacola.
Gulf Shores/ Pensacola West KOA Holiday; Lillian, AL	11650 Co Rd 99; **251- 961-1717** or 800-562- 3471; https://koa. com/campgrounds/ gulf-shores	$$–$$$	A quiet rural waterfront campground just a short walk uphill from a swimming beach with a fishing pier. Sites with full hookups and pull-through access. Saturday night ice cream socials. Famous Flora-Bama beach bar next to the bay bridge (www.florabama.com) within walking distance.
Gulf State Park Campground; Gulf Shores, AL	22050 Campground Rd; **251-948-7275;** www. alapark.com/parks/ gulf-state-park/ rv-and-primitive- campground	$$	Almost 500 full hookup sites with big, paved 65-foot pull-throughs and 45-foot back-ins. A limited number of beachfront sites. Many amenities (11 bathhouses, camp store, laundry, swimming pool, tennis/pickle ball courts, horseshoes, volleyball, nature center, and weekly activities). A mile and a half away from the park's beach, fishing pier, boating, and nature trail. The Lodge at Gulf State Park serves all-you-can-eat buffets. Reservations are a good idea in spring and summer.
New Orleans KOA Holiday; River Ridge, LA	11129 Jefferson Hwy; **800-562-5110** or **504-467- 1792;** https://koa. com/campgrounds/ new-orleans	$$–$$$$	Well-kept facilities and friendly management. A daily shuttle bus is available, and a city bus that goes into downtown New Orleans stops at the campground entrance. Car rentals available. Large sites, mostly shady back-ins, but no pull-throughs. About 15 minutes from the French Quarter.

TABLE 9-2 **Runner-up Gulf Coast Campgrounds**

Name and Location	Contact Info	Cost	What to Know
Carrabelle Beach RV Resort; Carrabelle, FL	1843 Hwy 98 W; **850-697-2638;** www.carrabelle beachrv.com	$–$$	Find white-sand beaches and great fishing in the Gulf of Mexico along Florida's Forgotten Coast. Park is freshly renovated and has new sites for big rigs, a new pool, new bathhouses, and a convenience store on-site with bait and tackle.
Grayton Beach State Recreation Area; Santa Rosa Beach, FL	357 Main Park Rd; **800-326-3521;** www.floridastateparks.org/graytonbeach	$$	The recreation area beach provides saltwater fishing, swimming, and boating. Campsites are comfortably sized; some are shaded. A few have sewer hookups, but most don't.
Shepard State Park; Gautier, MS	1034 Graveline Rd; **228-497-2244;** https://shepardstatepark.com/rv-camping/	$	Large, heavily wooded campsites for a low price. Recent hurricanes damaged the area, and the bathhouse is currently under construction, but the campsites are in fine shape. Maximum 14-day stay.
T.H. Stone Memorial St. Joseph Peninsula State Park; Port St. Joe, FL	8899 Cape San Blas Rd; **850-227-1327;** www.floridastateparks.org/parks-and-rails/th-stone-memorial-st-joseph-peninsula-state-park	$$	A remote park with sandy beaches, boardwalks for exploring, and even alligators inhabiting ponds near the campground entrance. Fairly narrow sites with side-by-side hookups, but most are large enough for big RVs. Maximum 14-day stay.
Tallahassee East Campground; Monticello, FL	346 KOA Rd; **850-997-3890;** www.goodsam.com/campgrounds-rv-parks/florida/monticello/tallahassee-east-campground-740002114/	$$$$	A handy overnight stop at the beginning of the Gulf Coast drive. Day canoe trips, horseback riding, and freshwater fishing (in Lake Catherine) available. Sites are large; some are shaded.

Good Eats along the Gulf Coast

When hunting food and supplies along the Gulf Coast, you'll find the most common supermarket chains are **Publix** (in Florida and the short stretch of Alabama you're going through), **Piggly Wiggly, Winn-Dixie,** and the occasional **IGA. Walmart** originated in the South (in Arkansas), and they have a huge presence all along this route.

Southern cooking has a well-deserved reputation worldwide, and the Gulf Coast provides the best examples anywhere. In this section, you can find out more than you ever wanted to know about fresh shrimp and delicious home-style, all-you-can-eat dining. And the prices are great!

Gulf Coast markets

Farmers markets are always great for picking up the very freshest foods, along with discovering a few local surprises. Some of our favorite locally sourced markets along the route include:

» **Apalachicola Farmers Market,** 479 Market Street, Apalachicola, Florida, in the Mill Pond Pavilion (www.facebook.com/ApalachicolaFarmersMarket/): Open Saturday.

» **Bradley's Country Store,** 10655 Centerville Rd., Tallahassee, Florida (**850-893-4742;** www.bradleyscountrystore.com/): This isn't a farmers market, but a good old authentic country store that opened in 1927 (the sort that Cracker Barrel tries to emulate in the front of their establishments). Bradley's makes their own smoked sausages, along with a line of packaged cornmeal and grits. The home-made smoked sausages and special sausage biscuits hot off the griddle are the attractions at this store's lunch counter. Open daily.

» **Burris Farm Market,** 3100 N Hickory St. S, Loxley, AL; **251-964-6464.** Stock up on fruits, vegetables, and breads. Open daily.

» **Coastal Alabama Farmers & Fishermens Market,** 781 Farmers Market Lane; Foley, AL (**251-709-4469;** https://coastalalabamamarket.com): Located just north of Gulf Shores between Hwy. 59 and the Foley Beach Expressway, this huge 30-acre market is one of the top farmers markets in the U.S., selling fruits, vegetables, seafood, and other agricultural products. Open Saturday.

» **Loxley Farm Market,** 5201 S. Hickory Lane, Loxley, AL (**251-964-4602**; www.facebook.com/loxleyfarmmarket/): The market features fresh fruits and vegetables, including vine-ripened tomatoes. Open daily.

» **Ocean Springs Fresh Market,** 1000 Washington Ave., Ocean Springs, MS (**228-257-2496;** www.oceanspringsfreshmarket.com): This Ocean Springs market features locally grown fruits, vegetables, plants, and flowers. Open Saturday.

For statewide guides to farmers markets, consult the following websites:

» **Alabama:** https://agi.alabama.gov/farmersmarket/

» **Florida:** www.fdacs.gov/Agriculture-Industry/State-Farmers-Markets

» **Mississippi:** https://agnet.mdac.ms.gov/msFarmersMarkets/FarmersMarkets

Seafood markets

Delectable fresh shrimp in big, bigger, and jumbo sizes are for sale all along the Gulf Coast at fair prices. The finest local shrimp are called Royal Red — ask for them by name. For tips on preparing fresh shrimp, see the nearby sidebar "Put another shrimp on the barbie." Although you'll find several good seafood sellers along the route, here are two of our favorites:

>> **Joe Patti Seafoods,** 524 S. B St., Pensacola, FL (**850-432-3315 or 800-500-9929;** https://joepattis.com): Open daily.

>> **Pier 77 Seafood Restaurant and Market,** 3016 Thomas Dr., Panama City, FL (**850-235-4099;** http://pier77seafood.com): Stop here for super-jumbo shrimp and frozen clam strips. Open daily. You sometimes find live music on Friday and Saturday nights.

PUT ANOTHER SHRIMP ON THE BARBIE

Although you can buy boiled, fried, or grilled shrimp in every little restaurant and takeout along the route, the most delicious are those that you buy fresh and cook yourself. In only a few minutes, they turn pink and are ready to eat. What follows are some favorite ways to serve 'em up.

- Steam them in their shells in boiling salted water or beer with a little bit of shrimp-boil seasoning (bay leaves and dried herbs).

- Grill them in the shell on your barbecue grill or over a campfire.

- Peel them and thread them on skewers to lay over the coals.

- To turn out instant shrimp scampi, sauté peeled shrimp quickly in a frying pan with a little butter or olive oil and plenty of chopped garlic and herbs.

- Peel them, leaving the tail part of the shell for a handle. Dip shrimp in flour that's been salted and peppered, then dip them in egg beaten with a little water, and dip them in dry bread crumbs. (Japanese panko crumbs are best; you can find them in the Asian food section of the supermarket.) Finally, deep-fry them in a half inch of hot oil for a few minutes on each side. Yummy!

- Put ¼ cup Cajun spice and ¼ cup white flour in a bag and shake. Add 6 to 8 peeled shrimp and shake the bag some more. Take the shrimp from the bag, add to the deep fryer one at a time, and cook about 2 to 3 minutes after the last shrimp is in the fryer.

Snacks and full-meal deals along the Gulf

Along the Gulf of Mexico, you find great seafood and other tasty treats, as well as some of the best bars in the nation.

KID
FRIENDLY

- » **Aunt Jenny's Catfish Restaurant,** 1217 Washington Ave., Ocean Springs, Mississippi; **228-875-9201;** http://www.auntjennyscatfish.com. Obviously, fried catfish filets — *all you can eat!* — are the main meal here, along with fried okra, fried green tomatoes, and turnip greens. This is about as traditional as Southern food gets, served up in a historic 1852 home surrounded by centuries-old spreading oak trees. Open daily.

- » **Dew Drop Inn,** 1808 Old Shell Rd., Mobile, AL; **251-473-7872;** www.facebook.com/DewDropInn.Mobile.AL. The proprietors claim the Dew Drop Inn, open since 1924, is the oldest restaurant in Mobile. Stop here for hot dogs topped with chili, sauerkraut, mustard, ketchup, and pickles. Mobileans claim Jimmy Buffett's famous anthem "Cheeseburger in Paradise" was inspired by the burgers at the Dew Drop Inn. You can get a burger (chili included) for under $4, hand-battered onion rings, or a fried pork chop or hamburger steak, or seafood like the shrimp and okra gumbo, crabmeat omelet, or fried catfish dinner. Open Monday through Saturday.

- » **Manci's Antique Club,** 1715 Main St., Dauphine, AL; **251-375-0543;** www.mancisantiqueclub.com. Originally opened as a gas station and speakeasy in 1924, Manci's calls itself the Bloody Mary capital of the Eastern Shore. They also claim to have the largest collection of Jim Beam decanters outside the distillery's own. *Esquire* magazine named Manci's one of the 21 best bars in America. Open daily.

- » **Owl Cafe,** 15 Avenue D, Apalachicola, FL; **850-653-9888;** www.owlcafeflorida.com. A favorite with the locals, the Owl serves excellent clam chowder, real crab cakes, and fried grouper. Adventurers try the gator sausage creole over grits. Open Tuesday through Sunday.

KID
FRIENDLY

- » **Punta Clara Kitchen,** 17111 U.S. Hwy. 98, Point Clear, AL; **800-437-7868;** www.puntaclara.com. A candy and gift shop in an 1897 gingerbread house delights visitors and sells pecan butter crunch, pralines, bourbon balls, and *buckeyes* (peanut butter balls dipped in chocolate). Open since 1952, the company is still run by the founder's great-grandchildren. Open daily.

- » **Three Georges Fine Southern Chocolates,** 226 Dauphin St., Mobile, AL; **251-433-6725;** https://3georges.com. Three Greek friends, all named George, established this confectionary in 1917, and their descendants turn out hand-dipped chocolates and tasty handmade Southern sweets such as divinity, pralines, and heavenly hash. Open Monday through Saturday.

Fast Facts for Gulf Coast Travelers

Area Codes
Area codes along this drive include **251** for Alabama, **850** for Florida, **504** for Louisiana, and **228** for Mississippi.

Driving Laws
Maximum speed limit on interstate highways in Alabama, Florida, and Mississippi is 70 mph; top speed on some rural interstates in Louisiana is 75. Speed limits in urban areas are lower. **However**, all vehicles towing trailers are restricted to a top speed of 55 mph in Alabama and 65 mph in Florida, Louisiana, and Mississippi. Double towing is prohibited in Florida, which means you can't drive your Class A motorhome towing a car behind it, **plus** a motorcycle trailer behind that. In Alabama, Florida, Louisiana, and Mississippi, all riders in the front seats must wear seat belts.

Emergency
Call **911** in all states.

Hospitals
Major hospitals along the route are in Tallahassee, Pensacola, Mobile, Biloxi, and New Orleans.

Information
Helpful resources in the individual states include the Alabama Tourism Department (**800-252-2262;** https://tourism.alabama. gov/group-and-international-travel/), Visit Florida (**888-735-2872;** www.visit florida.com), Louisiana Office of Tourism (**800-227-4386;** www.louisianatravel.com), and Mississippi Division of Tourism (**800-927-6378;** https://visitmississippi.org).

Road and Weather Conditions
Call the following numbers for road and weather advisories. For Alabama: **334-242-4128;** www.dot.state.al.us. For Florida: **888-558-1518;** www.fdot.gov. For Mississippi: **601-987-1211;** www.dps.ms.gov. In Louisiana, cell phone users can dial ***577** for state police assistance, or http://wwwsp.dotd. la.gov/Pages/default.aspx.

Taxes
Alabama state sales tax is 4 percent; local taxes can raise it to 11 percent. Florida state sales tax is 6 percent; local taxes can raise it to 8 percent. Louisiana state sales tax is 4.45 percent; local taxes can raise it to 11.45 percent. Mississippi state sales tax is a flat 7 percent; local rates can add another 1 percent.

State gasoline taxes are as follows: Alabama, 29.2 cents per gallon; Florida, 42.6 cents per gallon; Louisiana, 20.01 cents per gallon; and Mississippi, 18.79 cents per gallon.

Time Zones
Eastern Florida is on Eastern time. Western Florida from Apalachicola as well as Alabama, Mississippi, and Louisiana are on Central time.

Chapter **10**

The Natchez Trace: Natchez to Nashville

The Natchez Trace meanders nearly 450 miles from a point northeast of Natchez, Mississippi, to a point southwest of Nashville, Tennessee, passing the birthplaces of megastar Oprah Winfrey, rock idol Elvis Presley, and blues musician W. C. Handy. The path also passes the location where Meriwether Lewis (of Lewis and Clark fame) died under mysterious circumstances.

An 8,000-year-old Native American trail, the *trace* — an old-fashioned term for a path or road — was turned into a scenic highway in the 1930s. The route preserves some 300 segments of the improved roadway along the old trace that was commissioned in 1806 by President Thomas Jefferson. In spring and summer, the route is green with thick, lush grass and plenty of leafy hardwood trees, and you get the occasional glimpses of small farms and villages through the foliage. The highway is easy and undulating, but not wide. Most, but not all "overlook turn-offs" are spacious enough for large motorhomes or vehicles pulling trailers.

In this chapter, we encourage you to consider leaving the clogged arteries of crowded interstates behind to enter a shaded, curving rural highway with no commercial traffic or speeding — 50 mph is the limit. But don't worry about the speed limit — it's so peaceful and scenic along the way that you won't even be tempted to rev up your RV. Along the way, you find campgrounds, craft shops, picnic tables, and nature trails to explore, including a boardwalk through an eerie swamp with lime-green water and spooky sunken trees.

Planning Your Natchez Trace Adventure

The Natchez Trace is unlike interstates or major highways — it's a limited-access scenic parkway deliberately designed to keep commercial businesses and services out of view. You won't find many food outlets, restaurants, or big national chain stores alongside the route, but this itinerary frequently detours off the trace through a number of towns and villages.

TIP

There's a great website that lists all 18 towns you pass through on the Natchez Trace, with links to the events, festivals, and stuff to do in each one of them. The site helps you be on the lookout for local farmers markets and wine festivals. Find this great resource at www.scenictrace.com/communities.

Favoring early spring and fall

Although the Natchez parkway is comfortable to drive year-round, the best times are in early spring and fall when the weather is mild (and less humid), the flowers are in bloom, and the pilgrimage tours through *antebellum homes* (built before the Civil War) are on the agenda. Winter usually is mild but can be rainy and sometimes chilly; summers are hot.

TIP

To get jazzed for your trip, and to better understand the beauty and history of this road, check out the short YouTube video *Traces Through Time*, narrated by Grammy-winning pop music star Amy Grant (https://youtu.be/i0myhkMCKqc). She lives on a farm in Franklin, Tennessee and is proud to show off this part of the country.

Taking it easy

In any time of year, we're usually big believers in not hitting the road for the day without a campground reservation for that night. However, you shouldn't need campground reservations for most of the places mentioned in this chapter. But if you're in high season, wanting to get into a popular place such as **Ross Barnett Reservoir** campgrounds, do yourself a favor and make reservations. Remember that any major event, like the annual **Country Music Association Music Festival** in Nashville in June, can make reservations an absolute necessity. If you can dry camp without hookups, many of the primitive campgrounds we list later in the chapter are a good choice at crowded times, not only for a free or low-cost campsite, but for one that needs no reservation.

REMEMBER

This trip is deliberately designed to be slow-moving and relaxing, so give yourself three to seven days for the drive. And plan on spending a day or two exploring the Natchez area before you set out on the trace. It's a charming Mississippi city and was once the richest town in America. Numerous historic homes are open all year, with hoop-skirted hostesses to show you around.

JEFFERSON'S ROAD: A 19TH-CENTURY TRADE, MAIL, AND MILITARY ROUTE

In 1806, President Thomas Jefferson ordered a roadway "12 feet in width and passable for a wagon" to be built along the trade routes originally used by flatboat men returning upriver after delivering their furs, tobacco, pork, and farm products in Natchez and New Orleans. Although traveling downriver was easy, the *Kaintucks,* as they were called, were unable to row or pole their boats upstream against the current.

After selling their goods, and maybe their rafts, too, they had to walk or ride horseback to get back home. The traders had little enough remaining from their profits after the gamblers, cutthroats, and prostitutes of Natchez-Under-the-Hill had finished with them, but the toughest part of the trip was yet to come — protecting themselves and their money from the highwaymen who lurked along the trace. Jefferson was thinking about not only the traders but also the postal service riders who used the roadway to deliver mail and the military troops who might need the wide, clear pathway for wagons and cannons.

Ladies and gentlemen of fashion, circuit-riding preachers, frontier prostitutes, pioneer families, medicine peddlers, and flatboat men — everybody used the Natchez Trace. A despondent Meriwether Lewis died mysteriously along the trail in 1809, and in 1815, a triumphant Major General Andrew Jackson, better known as Old Hickory, marched his Tennessee militia along the trace on their way back home from the Battle of New Orleans.

But in 1812, the first steamboat arrived in Natchez, and by 1820, steamboats dominated the rivers. Eventually, except for a brief period during the Civil War, the little-used Natchez Trace was neglected and reverted to woods. Only in the 1930s, under the administration of Franklin D. Roosevelt, did restoration of the historic trace begin; today's road closely follows the contours of the original.

Driving the Natchez Trace

Our drive begins in **Natchez,** Mississippi, and goes north to **Nashville,** Tennessee, but it's just as easy to begin in Nashville and drive south to Natchez. If you have extra time planned for your RV trip, also check out the Gulf Coast drive between New Orleans, Louisiana, and Tallahassee, Florida, in Chapter 9.

The trace begins northeast of Natchez off U.S. 60, with a well-marked beginning and a couple of short unfinished spots. At **Jackson,** Mississippi, you have to exit the parkway at the junction of I-20, follow I-20 to I-220 North, and then continue on I-55 to Exit 105, which reconnects you to the parkway.

At the northern terminus of the trace, you exit by a dramatic bridge (past milepost 440) that swoops you down onto SR 100 about ten miles west of Nashville. The total drive is around 450 miles. See the route in Figure 10-1.

TIP

The easiest way to make a shorter version of the drive covered in this section is simply to follow the 444-mile trace and overnight at one of the campgrounds along the way, without turning off to see the attractions in Port Gibson, Vicksburg, Jackson, and Nashville — or the state of Alabama.

Characteristics of the route

The **Natchez Trace Parkway,** like the Blue Ridge Parkway and Skyline Drive (described in Chapter 8), is a federally designated scenic drive along a two-lane road with a 50-mph speed limit and no commercial traffic permitted. Frequent pull-offs and turnouts are indicated with signs shaped like arrowheads that tell you whether the spot ahead is of historic interest, a trailhead, or a segment of the original roadway.

Also like Skyline Drive and the Blue Ridge Parkway, the Natchez Trace has well-marked entrances and exits that take you onto commercial highways and in and out of towns and villages. And the trace has numbered mileposts that double as addresses for sites along the route. The route begins at milepost 8 near **Natchez** and finishes past milepost 440 near **Nashville**.

This parkway is a winding ribbon of road that's probably narrower than you're used to — and without a shoulder, so safe driving is key. The route has a length restriction for RVs over 55 feet, and — even more important — a height restriction of 14 feet. Tall Class A motorhomes with rooftop accoutrements, take note. Remember as well that the trace is a designated bicycle route; so *watch for cyclists*. Unlike at a deep wilderness park such as Yellowstone, wildlife isn't much of a threat on the trace, though deer do stray across the road and can be an obstacle to safe navigation. (Deer frequently travel in pairs, so slow down if you see the first one.)

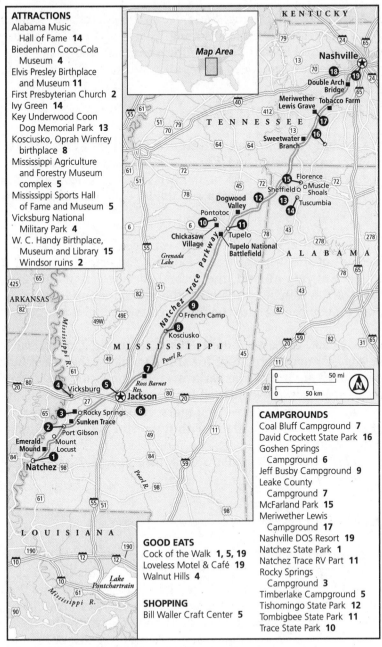

ATTRACTIONS
Alabama Music
  Hall of Fame **14**
Biedenharn Coco-Cola
  Museum **4**
Elvis Presley Birthplace
  and Museum **11**
First Presbyterian Church **2**
Ivy Green **14**
Key Underwood Coon
  Dog Memorial Park **13**
Kosciusko, Oprah Winfrey
  birthplace **8**
Mississippi Agriculture
  and Forestry Museum
  complex **5**
Mississippi Sports Hall
  of Fame and Museum **5**
Vicksburg National
  Military Park **4**
W. C. Handy Birthplace,
  Museum and Library **15**
Windsor ruins **2**

GOOD EATS
Cock of the Walk **1, 5, 19**
Loveless Motel & Café **19**
Walnut Hills **4**

SHOPPING
Bill Waller Craft Center **5**

CAMPGROUNDS
Coal Bluff Campground **7**
David Crockett State Park **16**
Goshen Springs
  Campground **6**
Jeff Busby Campground **9**
Leake County
  Campground **7**
McFarland Park **15**
Meriwether Lewis
  Campground **17**
Nashville DOS Resort **19**
Natchez State Park **1**
Natchez Trace RV Part **11**
Rocky Springs
  Campground **3**
Timberlake Campground **5**
Tishomingo State Park **12**
Tombigbee State Park **11**
Trace State Park **10**

FIGURE 10-1: A map of the Natchez Trace route.

Keep a cautious eye on the ground when you walk in the woods or tall grass and steer clear of the three types of poisonous snakes along the trace: rattlesnake, Southern copperhead, and Western cottonmouth. The family dog will likely spot them before you do, so keep your four-legged buddy on a leash.

REMEMBER

One more safety note on driving the trace; a good, reliable smartphone weather app is a necessity. Weather is a big RV issue: If you're in the South in summer, you need to know if a darkening sky means a tornado's coming; when traveling in winter, you need ice reports, and so on.

Taking in the first 20 miles

TIP

When you're ready to hit the road, drive northeast from Natchez on U.S. 60 about eight miles to the designated entrance of the Natchez Trace. Just before the entrance to the parkway, stop at the **Mississippi Welcome Center** and pick up an official Natchez Trace map and guide — handy materials to keep with you.

Almost immediately after entering the parkway, you come to the spot where you can see a section of the original trace; look for the arrowhead-shaped sign. At milepost 10.3 is **Emerald Mound,** the second-largest ceremonial mound in the U.S. Ancestors of the Natchez tribe built the mound around 1400 C.E. It covers some eight acres; you can walk to the top if you want.

At milepost 15.5, you come to **Mount Locust,** a restored historical house that served as a *stand,* or overnight stop, for travelers along the trace. Built in 1779, it's the oldest surviving inn on the parkway and is now run by the National Park Service. President Jefferson encouraged innkeepers to open these primitive lodging establishments to care for travelers; more than 20 were in operation by 1820, when the trace was at its peak. Along with the restored inn, you find restrooms, an information center, and a bookstore. Admission is free. Check the website for events and historical demonstrations (www.nps.gov/places/mount-locust-historic-house.htm).

Noting the history that runs deep

Exit on U.S. 61 near milepost 37 to drive a short loop detour into **Port Gibson,** Mississippi. Union general Ulysses S. Grant reportedly said this town was "too pretty to burn," and so Port Gibson survived the Civil War intact and was the first town in Mississippi to be designated a National Historic District. What initially strikes visitors today is the huge golden hand atop the 1859 **First Presbyterian Church** at Walnut and Church streets, the index finger pointing heavenward. Southwest of town are the haunting **ruins of Windsor mansion,** the largest antebellum house ever built in Mississippi; 23 Corinthian columns are all that's left. The site was used in a memorable scene with Alec Baldwin in the 1996 film *Ghosts of Mississippi.*

Back on the Natchez Trace at milepost 41.5 is the **Sunken Trace,** a five-minute walk along a deeply eroded section of the original trace. A designated parking turnout is nearby. In the right light, this is one of the spookiest parts of the trace. For more information, check out the **Historical Marker Database** at www.hmdb.org/m.asp?m=87313.

At milepost 54.8, you come to **Rocky Springs ghost town,** formerly a thriving metropolis with a population of 2,616. Take a short uphill trail from the upper parking area to the site of the notorious Red House Inn, where highwaymen sized up travelers and then robbed them later. The town fell into decline during the Civil War, when first the war, and then the boll weevil, yellow fever, and soil erosion wiped it out. The only building still standing is the church, with its fascinating graveyard. For info on the town, go to www.legendsofamerica.com/ms-rockysprings/. A campground without hookups, **Rocky Springs Campground,** and a foot trail are located along a section of the old road.

Making it to and through Vicksburg

Around milepost 67 is the exit to **Vicksburg,** SR 27. You can also go to Vicksburg from Port Gibson at milepost 37, but you'd miss the points of interest on the parkway.

REMEMBER

The Civil War seems to be the main preoccupation of Vicksburg, with **Vicksburg National Military Park** on its northern boundary. Comparable to Gettysburg as a major turning point in the war, Vicksburg is known not only for its fine old houses, but also for the bravery and endurance of its citizens during a 47-day siege in 1863, when General Grant's troops bombarded the city almost constantly. As if to add insult to injury, the Mississippi River itself abandoned Vicksburg in 1876, changing its course to cut across the neck of land that Grant had worked so hard to take. Years later, the waters of the Yazoo River were diverted into the Mississippi's old channel with a canal built by the Army Corps of Engineers so Vicksburg could have its harbor back.

Vicksburg is famous for two beverages: It was the first city to bottle Coca-Cola, and the **Biedenharn Coca-Cola Museum** displays replicas of the original bottling equipment; and the mint julep was supposedly invented in Vicksburg.

A family-style restaurant in Vicksburg, called **Walnut Hills,** is the epitome of Southern home cooking, serving help-yourself bowls and platters filled with fried chicken, pork chops, a dozen different vegetables, salads, corn muffins, biscuits, and sweet iced tea.

The Jackson interruption at milepost 87

Back on the Natchez Trace, the drive is interrupted just past milepost 87, taking you through **Jackson**. To return to the trace, follow the parkway detour signage along I-20 to I-220, and then to I-55, rejoining the trace at milepost 102. For current conditions or closures, check the Natchez Trace page on the National Park Service website: www.nps.gov/natr/index.htm.

If you have a few hours, however, spend some time in Jackson, the state capital. The expansive and excellent **Mississippi Agriculture and Forestry Museum** — much more interesting than it sounds for adults and children — features a 1920s town with costumed inhabitants and craftspeople (and hand-pumped gas for 15¢ a gallon), a museum about crop dusting, and an entire working farm that was moved here from southern Mississippi.

KID FRIENDLY

The **Mississippi Sports Hall of Fame and Museum** shares the same big parking lot as the Mississippi Agriculture and Forestry Museum. Here, you can broadcast play-by-play action from a replica press booth that's stocked with videos of outstanding game highlights; walk through a museum salute to Dizzy Dean, Mississippi's own baseball great; stroll into a locker room housing uniforms and equipment used by local sports heroes; and test your skills in golf, baseball, soccer, or football.

Rejoining the parkway's attractions

When you reenter the parkway at milepost 101.5, look for the sign for the **Bill Waller Craft Center,** for some great shopping along the way. The center is at 950 Rice Road, **Ridgeland**, Mississippi (**601-856-7546;** https://mscrafts.org/the-bill-waller-craft-center/). It sells handicrafts created by local artists and craftspeople, including weavers from the local Choctaw and Chickasaw tribes. Items are attractively arranged in a spacious gallery inside the 20,000-square-foot center. Standouts include quilt-work handbags, pottery, Choctaw baskets, and books about the region. Prices range from affordable to expensive. The center is open Tuesday through Saturday. Take exit 105A from Trace Road to Ridgeland.

At milepost 105.6, a road from a turnoff to the **Ross Barnett Reservoir** follows the Pearl River and parallels the parkway for eight miles, accessing four campgrounds with hookups.

One of the prettiest spots along the route is a **tupelo and bald cypress swamp** at milepost 122 with boardwalks leading across yellow-green, algae-covered water so smooth it looks like a chartreuse mirror that you can walk on. The nature trail takes about 20 minutes to walk — first across the swamp, then along the other side through the woods, and back across the swamp on a second walkway. Nearby at milepost 123.8, you find Ratliff Ferry Road. If you're hungry, turn right and follow for a half-mile to the **Ratliff Ferry Trading Post**, founded in 1849. You can stock up on goods at the convenience store or have a hamburger and a beer in the restaurant; the post has live music on Friday and Saturday nights, and a patio looking out over the Pearl River.

REMEMBER

When you drive past **Kosciusko** (pronounced koz-ee-*esk*-ko) at milepost 159.7, take a moment to remember that this is where Oprah Winfrey was born on January 29, 1954. Liberty Presbyterian Church has a sign outside pointing out that "she said her first piece here" — in other words, made her first public appearance.

French Camp, a historic village at milepost 180.7, comes to life every fall when it's time to demonstrate how sorghum molasses is made from sugar cane. The parkway's only bed-and-breakfast is here, along with a craft shop, exhibits, and a lunch café.

History and celebrity near Tupelo

One mile east of milepost 259.7 is **Tupelo National Battlefield,** a National Park Service historical site for a major Civil War battle in 1864. Here, Union general A. J. Smith trapped Confederate general Nathan Bedford Forrest, famous for quick strikes and tough fights. General William Tecumseh Sherman ordered Smith to "follow Forrest to his death."

LOUISIANA PURCHASE: THE DEAL OF THE CENTURY

In the annals of real estate coups, few can match the 1803 Louisiana Purchase, ordered by President Thomas Jefferson and negotiated by future president James Monroe. Three years earlier, Napoleon had traded land with Spain, swapping the Italian kingdom of Parma, home of Parmesan cheese, for the territory of Louisiana in America — in those days it stretched from the banks of the Mississippi River westward to the Rocky Mountains, and from Canada in the north to the Gulf of Mexico in the south.

Monroe paid Napoleon around $15 million, or 4¢ an acre. In truth, all Jefferson wanted was to regain the port of New Orleans and the land along the Mississippi so Americans could continue to use the river for trade.

Turn off the Natchez Trace on SR 6 for the Tupelo National Battlefield and for the **Elvis Presley Birthplace** in downtown Tupelo. The rock icon was born in a simple two-room house that his father built; sometimes a relative or friend of Elvis is on hand to share personal memories. **Tombigbee State Park,** with RV camping, is just east of Tupelo.

TIP

Return to the parkway by the same route you took to go off into Tupelo, so you don't miss any of the highlights.

A **Chickasaw village** site at milepost 261.8 presents exhibits on Native American life, and a nature trail displays plants that were commonly used for food and medicine. The **Parkway Visitors Center,** milepost 266, also offers a 20-minute nature walk showing forest regrowth. At milepost 269.4, a short walk along the old trace leads to the graves of 13 unknown Confederate soldiers. A nature trail into **Dogwood Valley** at milepost 275.2 takes about 15 minutes to explore a grove of dogwood trees.

Crossing into Alabama

Tishomingo State Park at milepost 302.8, shortly before the parkway crosses from Mississippi into Alabama, offers camping, swimming, canoeing, and picnicking. At milepost 310, the parkway crosses into Alabama.

Although the parkway traverses only a 38-mile corner of northwestern Alabama on its way north, this little stretch of land is full of fascinating discoveries. Just past milepost 320, turn east on U.S. 72 to **Tuscumbia,** which, with its nearby sister towns of **Sheffield, Muscle Shoals,** and **Florence,** offers a great place to eat down-home Southern cooking.

Plan to spend a day in lively northwestern Alabama, where attractions include the following:

>> **Ivy Green,** birthplace of Helen Keller, immortalized in the play and film *The Miracle Worker.* Here you find the world's most famous backyard pump, where Keller learned to say "Water!"

>> **Alabama Music Hall of Fame,** a splendid museum saluting Alabamians from Jimmie Rodgers and Tammy Wynette, to Nat King Cole and Jimmy Buffett.

>> **W. C. Handy Museum and Library,** celebrating the blues composer and musician who wrote "St. Louis Blues," "Memphis Blues," and other classics.

> » **Key Underwood Coon Dog Memorial Graveyard,** the only graveyard in the world dedicated solely to coonhounds, dating from 1937.

Ending your drive in Tennessee

At milepost 341.8, the parkway crosses the border from Alabama into Tennessee. Another section of the **Sunken Trace** is open for walking at milepost 350.5, and a nature trail along **Sweetwater Branch** crosses a section of wildflowers in spring and early summer. The walk takes 20 minutes.

You find the grave of **Meriwether Lewis,** of Lewis and Clark fame, at milepost 385.9, along with a campground, picnic area, ranger station, restrooms, and a reconstruction of the log inn called **Grinder's Stand,** where Lewis died under curious circumstances. The famous explorer, only 35 years old, was on his way back to Washington, D.C., on government business when he died mysteriously here on the night of October 11, 1809, of gunshot wounds; historians have never determined whether the incident was suicide or murder.

At milepost 401.4 is a tobacco farm with a barn and field on exhibit, and a two-mile drive along the old trace.

The Natchez Trace ends with a dramatic soaring double-arch bridge at SR 100, some ten miles southwest of Nashville.

Must-See Natchez Trace Attractions

Alabama Music Hall of Fame

Tuscumbia, Alabama

KID
FRIENDLY

From the first touring motorhome used by the band Alabama, to artifacts from jazz innovator Sun Ra, this modern, interactive museum salutes the great musicians who were born in or lived in Alabama. The list includes Hank Williams, Nat King Cole, Jimmie Rodgers, Jimmy Buffett, Tammy Wynette, Emmylou Harris, Big Mama Willie Mae Thornton, Odetta, Martha Reeves, Bobby Goldsboro, Dinah Washington, Lionel Richie, Toni Tennille, and Wilson Pickett.

The museum was built here instead of in a major Alabama city because nearby Muscle Shoals, in the 1960s and 1970s, housed popular recording studios where Percy Sledge recorded the rhythm-and-blues classic "When a Man Loves a Woman," Aretha Franklin cut early soul records, and a young Duane Allman was a studio guitarist. Listening on individual earphones, kids of all ages groove to original music tracks performed by artists spanning decades. Open Tuesday through Saturday. Allow two to three hours.

612 U.S. 72 West. **256-381-4417;** *www.alamhof.org.* **RV parking:** *Large parking lot. Admission varies by age.*

Elvis Presley Birthplace
Tupelo, Mississippi

This little two-room cottage was built by Elvis's father, Vernon, who borrowed $180 and had the house finished in time for the birth of Elvis Aaron and his stillborn twin brother, Jesse Garon. The family was evicted two years later when they couldn't repay the loan. Besides the birthplace, you can see a small memorial chapel and pick up the map for a local driving tour that takes you past other Elvis shrines, such as the local Tupelo Hardware, where his mother bought him his first guitar for $12.98. Some Tupelo relatives say Elvis really wanted a BB rifle instead. Open daily; closed Thanksgiving, Christmas Eve, and Christmas days. Allow one to two hours.

306 Elvis Presley Dr. **662-841-1245;** *www.elvispresleybirthplace.com.* **RV parking:** *Small parking lot, adequate street parking.*

Mississippi Agriculture and Forestry Museum
Jackson, Mississippi

KID FRIENDLY

Far more fun than it sounds, this sprawling complex includes a 1920s rural Mississippi town, complete with craftspeople and shopkeepers, and a working farm (moved here in its entirety from southern Mississippi) that includes several Mississippi mules, a breed famous for its stubbornness. Kids enjoy wandering about the area and experiencing "the olden days" and then ending up at a general store that sells cold soft drinks and a staple of Southern snack fare, the Moon Pie.

Inside the main building is a well-arranged historical museum, and around the complex in separate buildings are the Craftsmen's Guild of Mississippi's display area and shop, the museum café, and the National Agricultural Aviation Museum and Hall of Fame, saluting crop dusters. All these attractions can be entered on the same ticket. The adjacent Mississippi Sports Hall of Fame and Museum (see the next listing) requires a separate admission ticket. Open Memorial Day through Labor Day, Monday through Saturday; closed on major holidays. Allow three hours.

1150 Lakeland Dr. **800-844-8687** *or* **601-432-4500;** www.msagmuseum.org. ***RV parking:*** *Large parking lot. Admission varies by age.*

Mississippi Sports Hall of Fame and Museum
Jackson, Mississippi

KID FRIENDLY

This museum salutes sports heroes of Mississippi and automatically makes all fans who enter (young and old) into heroes, too. With interactive machines, visitors can play golf, check the speed and impact of their baseball pitch, or take penalty kicks against a soccer goalie. A press box mock-up lets wannabe sports announcers call the play-by-play for a game, and the locker room displays uniforms and equipment that famous players have used. A special second-floor museum salutes Mississippi baseball great Dizzy Dean, and touch-screen kiosks let visitors look up archival sports information and interviews. Open Monday through Saturday. Allow three hours.

1152 Lakeland Dr. **800-280-3263** *or* **601-982-8264;** https://msfame.com/. ***RV parking:*** *Large parking lot adjacent. Admission varies by age.*

Vicksburg National Military Park
Vicksburg, Mississippi

The park commemorates one of the most decisive battles of the Civil War. General Ulysses S. Grant and 50,000 men held the city under siege for 47 days. The national cemetery contains the graves of some 17,000 Union soldiers. A 16-mile auto tour around the park passes markers, monuments, and recreated breastworks. In the museum, you can see the gunboat Cairo, which was pulled from the Yazoo River 100 years after it sank in 1862. Park and visitor center open daily.

3201 Clay St. **601-636-0583;** www.nps.gov/vick. ***RV parking:*** *Visitor lot at center, turnouts along Park Road. Admission per vehicle, bike, or pedestrian.*

More Cool Things You Find along the Natchez Trace

Culturally rich and sometimes quirky attractions line the Natchez Trace, from antebellum ruins to a coon dog cemetery and the hometown of a well-known media mogul.

BARGAIN ALERT

>> **Swig down a cheap Coca-Cola.** You can see the original bottling machinery from the world's first Coca-Cola bottling plant, used from 1894 to 1924, in Vicksburg at **Biedenharn Coca-Cola Museum.** Open daily. Allow one hour.

1107 Washington St., Vicksburg, MS. **601-638-6514;** *www.biedenharncoca-colamuseum.com.* **RV parking** *is available on the street. Admission varies by age.*

>> **Sip a mint julep.** While in Vicksburg, sample one of the hallmarks of Southern hospitality in the place of its birth. According to local historians, it was at Mint Springs (now located in Vicksburg National Military Park) that a sprig of mint was first stirred into a cup of bourbon, and the legendary drink was born.

TIP

Don't be a heretic by buying a "mint julep" from some street vendor who's likely going to hand you a snow cone with some miserable booze-and-syrup concoction in a plastic cup. Go to a tavern or restaurant and order a *proper* mint julep — made with shaved ice, fine bourbon, powdered sugar, and a sprig of fresh mint, served in a frosted silver cup.

>> **Meet Helen Keller at Ivy Green.** The birthplace and childhood home of Helen Keller, a lecturer and essayist who lost her sight and hearing at 19 months of age, has been restored to the way it looked during her childhood. A production of *The Miracle Worker*, the play depicting how she overcame her disabilities, is presented here every summer. In the backyard is the famous water pump where, as a child, she first made the connection between words and sign language. Open Monday through Saturday. Allow two hours.

300 W. North Commons, Tuscumbia, AL. **256-383-4066;** *https://helenkeller birthplace.org.* **RV parking** *is available in a large parking lot and on the street. Admission varies by age.*

>> **Howl with the hounds. Key Underwood Coon Dog Memorial Graveyard** is the only cemetery in the world dedicated to the raccoon-hunting hound. More than 160 champions are buried here, some with elaborately carved granite tombstones like Doctor Doom's, which lists his awards. Others have simple

wooden markers with handwritten sentiments such as, "He wasn't the best coon dog there ever was, but he was the best I ever had." The cemetery is open year-round during daylight hours. Allow at least 30 minutes.

4945 Coon Dog Cemetery Rd., Cherokee, AL. **256-383-0783;** `www.coondog cemetery.com`. **RV parking** *is plentiful. Admission is free.*

» **Check out Oprah's birthplace.** The little Mississippi town of Kosciusko, named for a Polish general in the American Revolutionary War, was the birthplace and early childhood home of Oprah Winfrey, and a road named for her goes past her first church, her family cemetery, and the site of her birthplace. Allow one hour.

For information, stop by the Kosciusko Information Center. Milepost 160 on the Natchez Trace Parkway; **662-289-2981;** `https://tinyurl.com/yruus4h3`.

» **Sing the blues and all that jazz.** Florence, Alabama, is the home of the **W. C. Handy Museum and Library**. The blues genius, a trained musician with his own brass band, wrote a campaign song for Memphis political boss Edward R. Crump that introduced jazz breaks into a musical composition for the first time. Retitled "Memphis Blues," it's the first composition recognized as jazz. Open Tuesday through Saturday. Allow two hours.

620 W. College St., Florence, AL. **256-275-3128;** `www.wchandymuseum.org`. **RV parking** *is available on the side street. Admission varies by age.*

» **Revisit Gone with the Wind.** The 23 Corinthian columns are all that's left of a formerly grand Greek Revival mansion, now known as the **Windsor Ruins,** on Rodney Road in Port Gibson, Mississippi. The mansion still evokes the ghost of the antebellum South. It survived the Civil War but succumbed to a fire in 1890 caused by a cigarette, a newly fashionable way to use tobacco at that time. It's open from dawn to dusk. Allow 30 minutes; photographers may want more time.

To get there, take U.S. 61 south from Port Gibson, turn right on SR 552, and follow the signs. There's plenty of open area at the site for **RV parking,** *but a short, narrow dirt road with bushes leads to it. Admission is free.*

Sleeping along the Natchez Trace

The Natchez Trace provides plentiful overnight camping opportunities all along the route, either directly on the parkway or a few miles off on a side road. Few public campgrounds accept reservations, so if you're making the trip during a busy season, such as spring, plan to stop earlier in the day than usual to be sure you have an overnight spot, or reserve sites a day or two in advance at privately owned campgrounds near the parkway.

All campgrounds listed in Table 10-1 or Table 10-2 are open year-round and have public flush toilets, showers, and sanitary dump stations unless they're otherwise designated as primitive camping areas. Toll-free numbers, where listed, are for reservations only.

TABLE 10-1   Our Favorite Natchez Trace Campgrounds

Name and Location	Contact Info	Cost	What to Know
David Crockett State Park; Lawrenceburg, TN	Off U.S. 64; **931-903-2323**; https:// tnstateparks.com/ parks/campground/ david-crockett	$$	Natural beauty and newly renovated RV sites (52 sites; no pull-throughs; 50-amp electric; water). Full hookups are lacking, so campers must dump at a central station.
Nashville KOA Resort; Nashville, TN	2626 Music Valley Dr.; **800-562-7789** or **615-889-0282**; https:// koa.com/campgrounds/ nashville/	$$$$$	Kid-friendly; 244 sites with full hookups, pull-throughs, Wi-Fi, accessible facilities; laundry; pool. A concierge arranges tickets and transportation for shows and events, and a coordinator offers daily tours to local attractions. Seasonal live entertainment.
Tishomingo State Park; Tishomingo, MS	Off CR 90; **662-438-6914**; www.mdwfp.com/ parks-destinations/ state-parks/ tishomingo	$$	Total of 62 sites, paved and mostly shaded; 30- and 50-amp hookups. Haynes Lake offers fishing and boating, a ramp, dock, and boat rentals. Bargain prices and a 14-day maximum stay.
Tombigbee State Park; Tupelo, MS	Off Veterans Boulevard; **662-842-7669** www.mdwfp.com/parks-destinations/ state-parks/ tombigbee	$$	Total of 20 sites; water and 20- and 30-amp electric; 18 full hookups; no pull-throughs. Medium-size paved sites with patios, some with shade. Bargain prices. Near Elvis's birthplace and the Tupelo battlefield for sightseeing. Freshwater fishing, boating, ramp, dock, and boat rentals on Lake Lee.

Name and Location	Contact Info	Cost	What to Know
Trace State Park; Belden, MS	2139 Faulkner Road; **662-489-2958;** www.mdwfp.com/parks-destinations/state-parks/trace/	$$–$$$	Total of 52 large sites, most shaded and paved; water and 30- and 50-amp electric; 3 pull-throughs. Convenient location near Tupelo and the Natchez Trace. Freshwater fishing, boating, boat ramp, dock, and boat rentals on Lake Trace. Bargain price for full hookups.

TABLE 10-2   Runner-up Natchez Trace Campgrounds

Name and Location	Contact Info	Cost	What to Know
McFarland Park Campground; Florence, AL	1000 Jim Spain Dr; **256-740-8817;** https://florenceal.org/departments/parks_&_recreation	$$	Total of 60 paved full-hookup sites with patios; water and 30- and 50-amp electric; 12 pull-throughs. On the Tennessee River with freshwater fishing, boating, boat ramp, and dock. A bargain price for full hookups. *Note:* The area is subject to flooding in heavy rains, so check availability before arriving if they've had recent rainstorms.
Natchez State Park; Natchez, MS	230-B Wickliff Road; **601-442-2658;** www.campsitephotos.com/campground/ms/natchez-state-park/	$$	Total of 50 sites with water and 30- and 50-amp electric; 6 full hookups. Wide paved sites with patios; many are shaded. Reservations suggested in summer.
Natchez Trace Parkway National Park Campgrounds (next three campgrounds)	Along the Natchez Trace; follow signs from the relevant milepost; **800-305-7417;** www.nps.gov/natr/planyourvisit/camping.htm	$	All campgrounds are primitive. No charge and no reservations; first-come, first-served, with a 15-day maximum stay. Some small amenities such as maps or freshwater stations; some nearby attractions. See Chapter 5 for info on finding dump stations.
Jeff Busby Campground	Milepost 193.1		Total of 18 sites, all pull-throughs, all paved.
Meriwether Lewis Campground	Milepost 385.9		Total of 32 sites, some pull-throughs. Near Meriwether Lewis museum and gravesite.
Rocky Springs Campground	Milepost 54.8		Total of 22 sites; 12 pull-throughs.

(continued)

CHAPTER 10 The Natchez Trace: Natchez to Nashville   223

TABLE 10-2 *(continued)*

Name and Location	Contact Info	Cost	What to Know
Natchez Trace RV Park; Shannon, MS	189 CR 506 between mileposts 251 and 252; **662-767-8609**	$$	Total of 32 comfortably wide sites with water and 30- and 50-amp electric; 21 full hookups; 14 pull-throughs. A Good Sam Park that can handle big rigs. Amenities include a pond with freshwater fishing and tackle for rent. No credit cards.
Ross Barnett Reservoir; Greater Jackson, MS (next fourcampgrounds)	115 Madison Landing Circle in Ridgeland; **601-856-6574;** https://www.therez.ms.gov	$$	Four campgrounds around the Ross Barnett Reservoir perimeter; reservations suggested for weekends. All campgrounds offer hookups; all are back-ins; all provide access to freshwater fishing.
Coal Bluff	Coal Bluff Rd.; **601-654-7726**		Total of 39 sites with water and 30- and 50-amp electric; 11 with full hookups.
Goshen Springs	SR 43 off Natchez Trace; **601-829-2751**		Total of 68 full hookups with 30- and 50-amp electric; laundry.
Leake County Water Park	Park Rd.; **601-654-9359**		Total of 34 full hookups with 30- and 50-amp electric.
Timberlake Campground	Timberlake Dr.; **601-992-9100**		Total of 108 full-hookup sites with 30- and 50-amp electric; Wi-Fi; laundry.

Good Eats along the Natchez Trace

Unfortunately, the plentiful options you find for camping along the trace don't apply to your eating choices. You'll be happy to have a well-stocked refrigerator and your own kitchen. At some exits, a simple convenience store may be hard to find. Even when a town is near the parkway, that doesn't mean any special treats await. Some small communities in Mississippi, for example, don't have any fast-food places, so take that as either good or bad, depending on your culinary sensibilities. A convenience market or small-town drugstore may be the only place to find something already prepared for lunch.

REMEMBER

Rural America is suffering from a severe shortage of grocery stores, with few options for shoppers apart from Walmarts and various discount dollar stores, where meat and fresh fruits and vegetables are not available. "Food deserts" is a common term for these grocery-starved areas, and Mississippi, unfortunately, is one of the worst; 70 percent of SNAP eligible households in this, our poorest state, must drive more than 30 miles to reach a grocery store. The situation is not as dire in Tennessee or Alabama, but overall it's something you need to be prepared for, partially by staying well-stocked in your RV. Take a look at Chapter 4 for some tips on eating well off the beaten path.

Enjoying veggies and drinks Southern-style

You find plenty of vegetables in this part of the world, but don't expect them to be cooked *al dente*. Southern vegetables are cooked until they're very well done, as a rule, and made tastier by the addition of seasonings — often butter, bacon fat, pot juices, or even sugar. Don't expect to find fresh herbs and olive oil or a judicious sprinkle of balsamic vinegar on your veggies, but if you're willing to be open-minded, you may find some unfamiliar side dishes that you like. Take a chance and order fried green tomatoes, fried pickles, corn pudding, collard or turnip greens, yams, hominy, black-eyed peas or field peas, okra, squash, lima beans, or green beans (often called *snap beans*) cooked in water with a little chopped bacon or bacon fat until tender and succulent.

TIP

You can always find a wedge of lemon to squeeze over everything, because lemon is an essential condiment in this land of iced tea. By the way, iced tea usually comes as *sweet tea* (loaded with sugar) throughout the South; if you don't want sugar, ask for yours unsweetened. If ordering tea at breakfast, be sure to specify *hot tea*, or you'll get iced tea. Don't ask for a soda; carbonated drinks are called *pop* or *soda pop* in the South.

Minding your carbs and portions

Hot breads, usually biscuits or cornbread, are the general rule as well. By the way, unlike the cornbread and corn muffins in other parts of the U.S., Southern cornbread rarely contains sugar. You won't find hot breads at barbecue joints; there, multiple slices of soft white bread straight from the plastic bag come as a side dish.

Servings are large in this part of the country; we find that one takeout meal often is enough for both of us. If it seems skimpy when we open the takeout box, we add a green salad or a dessert.

Finding fun regional cooking

The following restaurants are some of our favorites for regional cooking. These are iconic restaurants with great Southern food. Remember that a Southern family-style restaurant often serves no beer or wine; but you won't lack for sweet iced tea, the house wine of the South. Hours listed are the latest available; always phone or check the web for updated hours.

>> **Cock of the Walk,** 2624 Music Valley Dr., Nashville, Tennessee (**615-889-1930**; www.cockofthewalkrestaurant.com/): An easy stroll from the Nashville KOA campground, this popular casual eatery provides sit-down and takeout service; the latter, with its own order window, is much quicker. The fried catfish is delectable, and so are the fried shrimp and a sampler dinner that adds fried chicken. Side dishes include fried dill pickles (don't laugh 'til you taste them), fried onions, and a cooking pot of beans or greens. Cocktails, beer, and wine are also served. (Two other locations are in Mississippi, in Ridgeland and Pocahontas.) Open Tuesday through Sunday.

>> **Loveless Motel & Cafe,** 8400 SR 100, Nashville, Tennessee, about 10 miles southwest of town (**615-646-9700**; www.lovelesscafe.com): A motel by the side of the road with a pink and green neon sign that says "Loveless" serves the world's best breakfasts — country ham, grits, gravy, eggs, homemade biscuits, and homemade jams and jellies. Lunches and dinners are great too, with meals built around country ham or fried chicken. (Get one of each and trade bites.) The same generous servings of hot biscuits, butter, and homemade jams come with every meal, and they sell jars of the jam to go. Open daily.

>> **Walnut Hills,** 1214 Adams St., Vicksburg, Mississippi (**601-638-4910**; https://walnuthillsms.com/): Since 1868 this restaurant, in a grand house in Old Town Vicksburg, has been offering large portions of great Southern dishes: fried chicken, ribs, catfish, chicken-fried steak, crab cakes, gumbo, grits and corn muffins, not to mention iced tea and Creole cream cheesecake. A Vicksburg institution. Open Wednesday through Monday.

SOUTHERN COOKING, STATE BY STATE

In northwestern Alabama, breakfast can be a feast, with grits, ham, biscuits, sausage, eggs, and gravy. Fried chicken stars at lunch and dinner (the former sometimes called dinner and the latter supper in the rural South), and you may run across dessert curiosities such as Coca-Cola cake and mile-high meringue pies.

Mississippi cuisine is heavy on fried catfish — hardly unusual, as the state turns out 58 percent of all the catfish farmed in the U.S. In fact, the catfish capital of the world is Belzoni, a few miles west of the Natchez Trace. Fried fish of all sorts is usually served with hot tamales and *hush puppies,* which are deep-fried balls of cornbread seasoned with onions. The hot tamales are a mystery; nobody is sure where they originated, but most Mississippi restaurants, especially in the Delta, serve them as appetizers or side dishes. Rolled in parchment paper rather than cornhusks and ordered by the half dozen or dozen, Mississippi hot tamales are smaller and spicier than the Mexican version.

Down-home Tennessee restaurants around Nashville serve what they call *meat and three,* meaning your choice of a main dish of meat and three sides. Country ham on a Southern menu, especially in Tennessee, describes a smoked or dry-cured ham that spends weeks in a bed of salt and turns out as a salty, densely textured, and intensely flavored meat that can be sliced and fried for breakfast or boiled whole and then baked and served cold in paper-thin slices. A classic Southern snack is a Moon Pie (two round graham crackers with a marshmallow filling in between, dipped in chocolate) served up with an RC Cola. And don't miss Nashville's famous Goo Goo Cluster candy bars, with peanuts, chocolate, marshmallow, and caramel.

Stocking the pantry for your trace trek

The national craze for eating locally fits right in along the path of the Natchez Trace, so keep your eye open for discoveries. Ask at fuel stops where the best market or diner in town is, and you may be pleasantly surprised by what you find.

The most common supermarket chains you'll encounter near the Natchez Trace Parkway are **Aldi's**, **Stop and Shop**, **Save-A-Lot**, and **Piggly Wiggly**. There's also a **Kroger** at Tupolo, MS. There's an upscale **Fresh Market** and a large **Mac's Market** just off the intersection of the Natchez Trace and I-55 in Ridgeland, just north of Jackson, MS.

The South is Walmart country, and you find **Walmart Superstores** just off the Trace Parkway in Natchez, Jackson, Ridgeland, Kosciusko, Houston, Tupelo, and at Fairview in Tennessee, south of Nashville.

To find the farmers markets along the Trace, check the following websites for each state:

>> **Alabama Department of Agriculture:** Farmers Market, Farmers Stand and U-Pick Locations (https://agi.alabama.gov/farmersmarket/locations/)

>> **Mississippi Department of Agriculture and Commerce:** Farmers Markets
(https://agnet.mdac.ms.gov/msFarmersMarkets/FarmersMarkets)

>> **Tennessee Association of Farmers Markets** (https://tnfarmersmarkets.org)

Whenever you exit the parkway, keep your eyes open for fresh produce as you pass through small towns in the South during spring, summer, and fall. Vegetable and fruit growers often put up produce stands in their farmyards or even on their front lawns during harvest time. The prices are always low, and the food can't be any fresher.

"WHAT DO YOU HAVE TO DO TO GET A DRINK AROUND HERE?!"

If you imbibe alcohol, take special note that the sale of booze is prohibited in many counties along the Natchez Trace. Nine U.S. states, located mostly in the South, have counties that prohibit the sale of alcohol; these are referred to as *dry counties*. Two of these states are Tennessee and Mississippi, where you'll be traveling. (Alabama has no completely dry counties, but there are various restrictions in 26 counties.) And since all three states allow municipalities to have their own dry laws, it can result in confusion for a tourist. In other words, just shrug and be polite about it. America's 13-year experiment with a national prohibition on alcohol ended with the passage of the 21st Amendment in 1933, but you'll still encounter pockets along the Natchez Trace where municipal and county laws restrict or prohibit the sale of booze. These restrictions can include total bans, specific restrictions on sales of hard liquor or beer and wine, and variations on Sunday or weekend sales.

If you need to replenish your beer supply or grab a bottle of bourbon, do it in another state or ask what the rules are at the local gas station or grocery store. Locals are usually well-versed in where and how far you need to travel to get to a *bottle shop* (liquor store). And don't be surprised if a waitress says you need to become a member of the restaurant's "private club" if you want to enjoy a drink — you usually pay a nuisance fee of a dollar or two in order to exploit a loophole in the local law.

Fast Facts

Area Code
The following area codes are in effect along the Natchez Trace: in Alabama, **251**; in Tennessee, **931**, **615**, and **256**; in Mississippi, **601** and **662**.

Driving Laws
In Alabama, Mississippi, and Tennessee, riders in the front seats must wear seat belts. The maximum speed limit on interstate highways in Alabama, Mississippi, and Tennessee is 70 mph. Speed limits in urban areas are lower.

Emergency
Call **911**. Cell phone users can dial ***847** in Tennessee.

Hospitals
Major hospitals along the route are in Vicksburg, Mississippi; Jackson, Mississippi; and Nashville, Tennessee.

Information
Helpful resources in the individual states include the Alabama Tourism Department (**800-252-2262**; www.tourism.alabama.gov); Mississippi Division of Tourism (**800-927-6378**; https://visitmississippi.org); and Tennessee Department of Tourist Development (**615-741-2159**; www.tnvacation.com).

For information on fishing licenses in Mississippi, call **800-546-4868**. Tennessee prefers you get a license online; the info is at www.takemefishing.org/tennessee. If you have any trouble on the website, call **888-891-8972**.

Road and Weather Conditions
To get the latest on traffic and road construction in Mississippi, including the trace, go to MDOTtraffic.com and sign up for the free service. You can then type in "Natchez Trace" for all updates. For a road emergency in Mississippi, call the Natchez Trace emergency line, **800-300-7275**. In Tennessee, you have the 511 system — just dial 511 on any phone for information on road conditions, closings, and weather. If you need to report a road hazard in Tennessee, dial THP (847) on any cell phone to alert highway patrol officers. For an emergency, dial 911. For your 33 miles in Alabama, the highway patrol is at **251-660-2500**.

For road conditions all along the parkway, and loads of other valuable information, go to NatchezTraceTravel.com, a great website.

Taxes
Alabama state sales tax is 4 percent; local taxes can raise it to 8 percent. Mississippi state sales tax is 7 percent. Tennessee state sales tax is 7 percent; local taxes can raise it to 8.35 percent.

State gasoline taxes are as follows: Alabama, 28¢ per gallon; Mississippi, 18¢ per gallon; and Tennessee, 27.4¢ per gallon, including local taxes.

Time Zone
Alabama, Mississippi, and western Tennessee are on Central time.

4
Meandering through Mid-America

IN THIS PART . . .

Find the Wright stuff and rock on with the rock 'n' roll greats in Ohio.

Soak in hot springs, savor down-home foods, and tap your toes to some Ozark Mountain music

Chapter **11**

The Heart of Ohio: A Circle around Circleville

Get down and get real — the Buckeye State is the heart of America! "Why, oh why, oh why, oh/Why did I ever leave Ohio?" sang the unhappy-in-New York heroine of the Broadway musical *Wonderful Town*. You can't blame her. Ohio is the best of the Midwest; seven presidents were born in Ohio, and eight have lived there. So much that's quintessentially American came out of this state — not to mention some great food, from Skyline chili to Buckeye candy (the original peanut butter cup). And nobody does a hall of fame with the panache of heartland Ohio. Is any place cooler than the Rock and Roll Hall of Fame (designed by world-class architect I. M. Pei) in Cleveland?

You find a fascinating blend of rural and urban: small-town charm alongside the busy cities of Cincinnati, Cleveland, and Columbus, as well as Toledo, Akron, and Dayton. Ohio gave us the Wright brothers, Thomas Edison, and astronauts Neil Armstrong and John Glenn. The state was a major player in the birth of the auto industry, but on the quiet back roads around Millersburg, the world's largest

Amish community still tends huge family farms without using electricity or the internal combustion engine.

Ohio has a richly diverse past. It was the home of the mighty Tecumseh, chief of the Shawnee, and many other Native American tribes, including the Lenape and the Wyandot. They left their mark on the land in the form of mounds (more than a thousand of them), including several famed mound sites you can visit today.

In Ohio, you also find a rich German immigrant history and many European connections going back to the days when the area was part of the vast Northwest Territory. Historically, Ohio was also the linchpin of the Underground Railroad, with more stations than any other state in the Union. Dreamers, reformers, and immigrants with a vision flocked to the Ohio River Valley, where they founded towns and churches, communal villages and newspapers, and factories and colleges. This influx helped forge what quickly became the richest and most populous state carved out of the new West.

In this chapter, you find out why Ohio is a surprise to people who are visiting for the first time. You discover that it's heaven for RVers, with much to see and do, great roads, splendid parks and campgrounds, and very nice people.

Planning Ahead for an Ohio Excursion

Summer months are the prime season in Ohio, but that's also when Midwestern families take their camping trips and vacations, so you may consider visiting in late spring or early fall. Here are some thoughts on timing a spring or fall visit:

>> **In May,** rain threatens quite often, but temps are mild. That said, April through June is a less crowded time to visit Amish country.

>> **Late September and early October** are practically perfect weather-wise but can be crowded in Amish country because harvest season is the most popular time to visit.

Watching for weather and traffic

Winters can be rough in northern Ohio. Freak weather conditions governed by the Great Lakes, called "the lake effect," can make for tough travel in this area. When a snowstorm hits any of the northernmost Snowbelt cities like Cleveland, Ohio, along the Great Lakes, vacationers are wise to stay far, far away.

WARNING

RVers always need to be weather-aware, and should be especially cautious about Midwestern tornadoes. When you're in Ohio, spring can pose weather dangers, particularly in May and early June. As Hoosiers, we're used to this situation, but other travelers can be taken by surprise. Local TV and radio stations are a great source of information, often better than a smartphone app, but you need to be aware of which county you're camping or driving in. A statement like "superstorm cells are running east/northeast of a line from Strongsville to Canton" can be confusing anyway, and may as well be Greek to an out-of-stater. Always keeping track of your location helps. In ominous weather, know what county you're in (just ask your phone) and know the name of the nearest town.

Watch for darkening greenish skies, heavy air and afternoon doldrums, the still calm before the storm. Know where in your campground to go in case a tornado is spotted — most have a safe area. In fact, we've never encountered a campground in the Midwest that didn't have a designated safe area. If an alarm sounds, leave your RV and make your way to the designated shelter — often a cement-block recreation hall or laundry room, or even a storm cellar or concrete vault — where you need to remain until the alert is over. During tornado season, you may run into severe thunderstorms with driving rain while you're on the road. When the rain gets too powerful, pull over at the first opportunity and wait for it to subside.

REMEMBER

On Ohio back roads, drive slowly and exercise caution. You may round a bend and run up behind a large, slow-moving tractor, a horse-drawn Amish carriage, or even a herd of cattle crossing the road and heading for the barn. Also look out for sharp turns. Country roads in the Midwest are famous for making sudden right or left turns at a property boundary where a farmer didn't want their land bisected for the sake of a straight road.

Reserving a spot and packing

TIP

Most of the RV parks recommended in this chapter shouldn't require campsite reservations, but they're still a good idea. Especially in high summer, we try to have a reservation for the next stop before leaving the campground in the morning. You definitely need to reserve ahead for big holidays such as Memorial Day, Independence Day, and Labor Day.

Pack a variety of clothing weights and options because weather can change suddenly. Out in the country in hot weather, relaxed clothing such as lightweight cotton shorts, shirts, and T-shirts is acceptable, but have a sweater or jacket handy in case it cools off. Take moderate rain gear. And give RVing a touch of class: If you plan to go to a nice restaurant, or attend a church service, pack long pants for men and dressy but relaxed slacks or skirts for women.

Touring the Buckeye State

Our circle drive around the heart of Ohio (the Buckeye State) begins in **Dayton,** swings east to **Springfield** along I-70, then south into the lush countryside, through **Xenia** and toward the antique shops of **Waynesville** and **Lebanon,** following US 42 all the way down into **Cincinnati.** From there we follow the broad Ohio River along winding, scenic US 52 to **Ripley,** to discover the route of escaped slaves to freedom across the river. We then turn north into the hilly midsection of Ohio and the state capital of **Columbus.** Then it's eastward into Amish country for home cooked food and a slower way of life. Finally, we head north to **Canton** and **Cleveland** and their must-see stops for football and rock and roll fans.

The total distance of the route, as shown in Figure 11-1, is approximately **680 miles.** Allow a week to ten days for this leisurely drive around the back roads of Ohio and more if you're a dedicated antiques shopper or museumgoer.

Heading from Dayton to Cincinnati

The drive begins in **Dayton,** where you can hobnob with the Wright stuff — the **Dayton Aviation Heritage National Historical Park** has museums and displays commemorating the Wright brothers and their part in the history of flight, including their restored bicycle shop where they built their first prototype flying machines.

Not far from Dayton is **Wright-Patterson Air Force Base,** which is where you find the **National Museum of the United States Air Force**, the largest museum of its kind in the world, displaying more than 300 airplanes in its gigantic hangars.

From the Air Force Museum, drive northeast on SR 4 to I-70, then head east a few miles to Exit 52, and turn south on U.S. 68 to **Yellow Springs** and **Xenia.** The pretty town of Yellow Springs, home of Antioch College and Young's Jersey Dairy, is at the junction of U.S. 68 and SR 343. Hikers find good trails in nearby **John Bryan State Park** and **Glen Helen Nature Preserve.**

From Xenia, U.S. 42 continues south to Waynesville and Lebanon. These towns are 10 miles apart but have some 250 shops between them, and are almost always spoken of in tandem as the antiques capitals of Ohio. Stop at the renowned **Golden Lamb** for a lunch break. Waynesville, at the junction of U.S. 42 and SR 73, also is home to the **Ohio Sauerkraut Festival** every October, where you can sample sauerkraut candy and sauerkraut pizza, among other offbeat offerings.

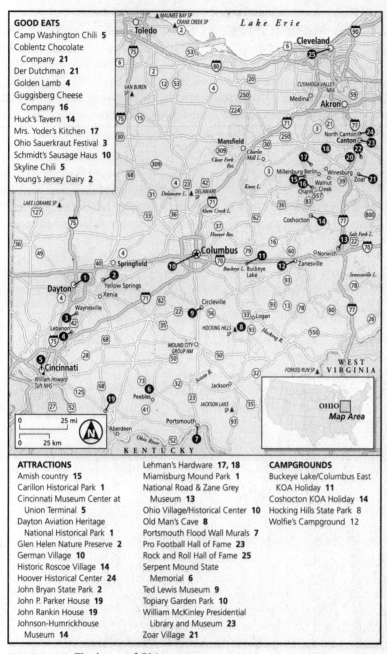

GOOD EATS
Camp Washington Chili **5**
Coblentz Chocolate
   Company **21**
Der Dutchman **21**
Golden Lamb **4**
Guggisberg Cheese
   Company **16**
Huck's Tavern **14**
Mrs. Yoder's Kitchen **17**
Ohio Sauerkraut Festival **3**
Schmidt's Sausage Haus **10**
Skyline Chili **5**
Young's Jersey Dairy **2**

ATTRACTIONS
Amish country **15**
Carillon Historical Park **1**
Cincinnati Museum Center at
   Union Terminal **5**
Dayton Aviation Heritage
   National Historical Park **1**
Glen Helen Nature Preserve **2**
German Village **10**
Historic Roscoe Village **14**
Hoover Historical Center **24**
John Bryan State Park **2**
John P. Parker House **19**
John Rankin House **19**
Johnson-Humrickhouse
   Museum **14**

Lehman's Hardware **17, 18**
Miamisburg Mound Park **1**
National Road & Zane Grey
   Museum **13**
Ohio Village/Historical Center **10**
Old Man's Cave **8**
Portsmouth Flood Wall Murals **7**
Pro Football Hall of Fame **23**
Rock and Roll Hall of Fame **25**
Serpent Mound State
   Memorial **6**
Ted Lewis Museum **9**
Topiary Garden Park **10**
William McKinley Presidential
   Library and Museum **23**
Zoar Village **21**

CAMPGROUNDS
Buckeye Lake/Columbus East
   KOA Holiday **11**
Coshocton KOA Holiday **14**
Hocking Hills State Park **8**
Wolfie's Campground **12**

FIGURE 11-1: The heart of Ohio route.

Cincinnati is 34 miles down U.S. 42. Mark Twain used to say he wanted to be in Cincinnati when the world ended because it was always 20 years behind the times, but today, the city that was once called Porkopolis (because it was the center of the U.S. pork-packing industry) has laid on the charm with a refurbished river-front. The splendid art-deco **Cincinnati Museum Center** at **Union Terminal** would make Twain change his tune. The city's unique **Cincinnati chili,** sold at numerous **Skyline Chili** franchises, is an Ohio lunch of choice.

Cruising along the Ohio River

From Cincinnati, head south on U.S. 52 for a scenic drive along the Ohio River; stop in at **Ripley** to see the station on the **Underground Railroad** and then continue on this picturesque river route into **Portsmouth.** This colorful town is where the late cowboy star Roy Rogers, born Leonard Slye in Cincinnati in 1911, lived with his family on a houseboat for several years. The walls along the town's riverfront are covered with the **Portsmouth Floodwall Murals,** depicting each era of the city's history.

From Portsmouth, continue east on U.S. 52 along the Ohio River to SR 93 and follow that north to Jackson. Then turn north on SR 93 and west on SR 56 into the Hocking Hills. Numerous campgrounds, caves, waterfalls, and hiking areas color this rugged, scenic section of Ohio, particularly around the area off SR 56 known as **Old Man's Cave** (look for signs), named for hermit Richard Rowe, who lived in and is buried in the cave.

From **Hocking Hills State Park,** return to SR 56 and continue west to **Circleville,** where a small museum is dedicated to Jazz Age entertainer and Big Band leader **Ted Lewis.** ("Is everybody happy?!")

Turning toward Columbus and Zanesville

From Circleville, continue north on U.S. 23 to **Columbus,** Ohio's capital and a city that has many quirky attractions, including **Thurber House,** birthplace of humorist James Thurber; **Topiary Garden,** which replicates the figures from Georges Seurat's classic painting *A Sunday Afternoon on the Island of La Grande Jatte* in clipped boxwood topiary; and a **German village** with an October beer festival and good German restaurants.

From Columbus, drive 56 miles east on I-70 to Zanesville, where the delightful **National Road and Zane Grey Museum** is 10 miles east at Exit 164. U.S. 40, which parallels I-70 at this point, was the first attempt at building a National Road when people still traveled by horseback and oxcart. Detailed dioramas depicting the road at different stages of travel history fill the museum.

From Zanesville, follow SR 60 north 16 miles to its junction with SR 16, and then turn northeast on SR 16 to **Coshocton** and **Historic Roscoe Village,** a restored canal town where craft shops offer beautiful handmade pottery, furniture, baskets, and weavings, and the bar food at **Huck's Tavern** is a great way to end your day.

Appreciating Amish country

SR 83 leads north from Coshocton to **Holmes County** and Amish country around **Millersburg.** If you have time, set aside a day or two to explore. In nearby **Mount Hope** and **Kidron,** the worthwhile stops include **Lehman's,** a hardware store with a full range of nonelectrical appliances, from hand-cranked wringer washing machines, to wood-burning stoves.

From the Millersburg area, drive east on U.S. 62 to **Berlin** (pronounced *burr*-lin) and **Walnut Creek.** North of Walnut Creek on SR 515 at U.S. 62 is the town of **Winesburg,** which gave its name to a book of short stories by native son Sherwood Anderson. The real model for Winesburg, however, was probably **Clyde,** 20 miles southwest of Sandusky, where Anderson actually grew up.

Next, follow U.S. 62 east for 5 miles to **Wilmot.** Turn right on Main Street, which is U.S. 250, and continue east, hopping onto SR 212 for 12 miles to Zoar.

Exploring Zoar and on to Cleveland

Zoar, a communal town founded in 1817 by a group of German separatists, is now **Historic Zoar Village,** one of our favorite places in Ohio. On Mondays and Tuesdays, the historic buildings are closed to the public; costumed interpreters occupy them the rest of the week. You can wander the town at will anytime, and enjoy the peace and quiet, but you may want to stop by when the buildings are open.

Leave Zoar by driving west on SR 212, following the signs to I-77, which you take north through Canton and Akron to Cleveland. In **Canton,** the **William McKinley Presidential Library and Museum,** next door to the tomb of this third American president to be assassinated, has animated figures of McKinley and his wife, who "chat" with visitors about life in Canton and the White House.

North Canton is where you find the **Hoover Historical Center,** not another presidential home but rather the home of William Henry Hoover, founder of the vacuum cleaner company of the same name.

From here, continue north on I-77 to its junction with I-90 on the Cleveland lakefront, home of the **Rock and Roll Hall of Fame.** The drive ends in Cleveland.

Enjoying a couple of side trips

TIP

If you're into Native American history, consider visiting two ancient mound sites near two spots on our Ohio itinerary:

>> **Serpent Mound State Memorial:** After seeing the town of **Ripley,** you can detour north at nearby Aberdeen onto SR 41 to **Peebles,** and the location of **Serpent Mound.** The striking snake-shaped mound was made famous in the 19th century when a Harvard archeologist saved it from being plowed under for crops, but it's impossible to get the famed aerial view of it, even if you climb the viewing tower. Still, the earthwork, constructed between 800 BCE and 44 CE, is fascinating. A pathway enables you to explore the perimeter of the mound, and the museum on-site discusses theories of how and why it was built. Afterwards, SR 73 carries you back down to U.S. 52 at Portsmouth.

WHERE SOME ICONIC RVs ARE MADE

More than 80 percent of the RVs in America are manufactured in and around the city of Elkhart, in northern Indiana, and with its RV museum and factory tours, it's a favorite destination for shoppers and RV fanatics. But some first-rate RVs are made right next door in Ohio, and their factories can be toured as well. In fact, America's oldest and most iconic travel trailer — Airstream, the eye-catching "silver bullet" with the retro 1930s style — is built north of Dayton in the little company town of Jackson Center.

Airstream was founded in 1931 by engineer and entrepreneur Wally Byam, who was without question the greatest force in crafting an aspirational image for RVing in America, leading well-publicized adventure caravans of Airstreams across America, Europe, and Africa. Byam's story, and that of the trailer he built, is told in the **Airstream Heritage Center**, which opened in June 2022. The factory tour and museum make for a nice side trip, even if you aren't thinking of buying an Airstream, and the town of Jackson Center is welcoming. The Heritage Center (www.airstream.com/heritage-center) is open Monday through Friday, but if you'd like a tour of the factory, you need to make a reservation in advance (www.airstream.com/company/factory-tours). The tour is free, and the museum's admission fee goes to the Airstream Foundation.

Another charming town in Ohio is the little Swiss village of Sugarcreek, less than 20 miles east of Millersburg on the Amish Country Byway. This is the location of nüCamp, the American company behind the return of the teardrop trailer, and the factory where the popular TAB and TAG teardrop trailers are made. You can take a tour Monday through Friday, but you need to call to schedule it (**330-852-4811**).

>> **Miamisburg Mound Park:** This famous mound site near our stop in Dayton features a pyramid-like conical earthwork; it's only about 15 minutes south of the Dayton Aviation Heritage historical sites on the itinerary.

Must-See Ohio Attractions

Amish Country

Centered around Millersburg

Ohio's Amish country offers enough attractions to fill a week of sightseeing. Pick up one of the free Amish Country maps (found in most tourism-related businesses in the area) that carry ads for shops, restaurants, and sightseeing along what's called the Amish Country Byway. Charming towns like Millersburg and Berlin have loads of antique and gift shops, as well as bakeries and stores selling Amish goods, locally made items from soap to ice cream. For the best part of the journey, however, strike out along the back roads to glimpse farm families at work — men plowing fields, women hanging out washing, and children on their way to school.

U.S. 62 becomes the scenic Amish Country Byway, running for 164 miles through many of the Amish communities of Holmes County. Also, SR 77 between Berlin and Mount Hope is a colorful back road lined with big farms and horse-drawn Amish buggies going to and from town.

Cincinnati Museum Center at Union Terminal

Cincinnati

KID FRIENDLY

In a magnificently restored 1933 Art Deco railway station, the city has built three excellent museums: the **Cincinnati History Museum,** the **Museum of Natural History and Science,** and the hands-on **Children's Museum.** You can walk through the Ice Age, explore a limestone cavern inhabited by live bats, and step onto a vintage steamboat from the Cincinnati Public Landing. Because sightseeing can make you hungry, you also find a food court that includes a Skyline Chili stand. Allow three to four hours. Open Thursday through Monday.

1301 Western Ave.; **800-733-2077** *or* **513-287-7000;** www.cincymuseum.org. ***RV parking:*** *Parking garage with height limits; try street parking or take public transportation to the museums. Admission varies; see website for the latest info and packages available.*

Dayton Aviation Heritage National Historical Park
Dayton

This four-part museum complex spread around the city salutes the Wright brothers and their contemporary and friend, Black poet Paul Laurence Dunbar. From 1895 to 1897, the brothers operated Wright Cycle Company, which has been restored and furnished with period bicycles and machinery. The **Wright-Dunbar Interpretive Center** and **Aviation Trail Museum and Visitor's Center**, are adjacent to the Cycle Company.

You also find

>> **Paul Laurence Dunbar House Historic Site,** the home Dunbar lived in with his mother from 1904 until his death in 1906. He was a successful poet and author, newspaperman, and lifelong friend of Orville Wright; exhibits include a bicycle the Wright brothers built for him.

>> **Huffman Prairie Flying Field,** where the Wright brothers tested and refined their planes, and built the first permanent flying school. Allow one hour for each museum and 15 minutes for the **Wright Brothers Memorial,** which overlooks the flying field.

If you're wanting still more of the Wright stuff, the **Wright Flyer III**, the brothers' first aircraft capable of controlled flight, is on display at **Carillon Historical Park**, a separate 65-acre park within the campus of the University of Dayton that showcases the city's industrial, scientific, and transportation achievements.

Wright Brothers Memorial: 2380 Memorial Road. No admission fee. Open daily.

*Wright Cycle Company: 22 S. Williams St.; **937-225-7705.** No admission fee. Open daily in summer.*

*Dunbar House Historic Site: 219 Paul Laurence Dunbar St.; **937-224-7061;** www.nps.gov/places/dunbar-house.htm. Admission is free. Open Friday, Saturday, and Sunday.*

*Huffman Prairie Flying Field: Gate 12A at Wright-Patterson AFB off SR 444; **937-425-0008.** The historic field is run by the National Park Service.*

*Carillon Historical Park: 1000 Carillon Blvd.; **937-293-2841;** www.dayton history.org/. Admission fees by age. Open daily.*

*For additional info, visit Wright-Dunbar Interpretive Center: 16 S. Williams St. **937-225-7705;** www.nps.gov/places/wdic.htm. Admission is free. Open daily.*

Historic Roscoe Village
Coshocton

An 1850s restored living history village along the Ohio and Erie Canal, **Historic Roscoe Village** is like a miniature Colonial Williamsburg. Artisans demonstrate weaving, pottery making, and broom making in the shops along the main street, while a horse-drawn canal boat takes visitors through a restored section of the historic canal. There's charm at every turn in this lovely village frozen in time. You can create period crafts at the Hay Activity Center, take the walking tour, and visit the Gardens of Roscoe in summer. You find frequent seasonal celebrations, from May's Dulcimer Days to October's Apple Butter Stirrin' Festival, not to mention the Christmas Candlelighting. And don't forget a visit to the **Johnson-Humrickhouse Museum,** with its Historic Ohio Exhibit.

The major attractions, restaurants, and shops are within an easy walk from one another. Allow three to four hours. Visitor's center open daily; canal boats run on weekends, May to October. ***Note:*** Various events and tours are priced separately. Call for group and educational tours info.

*Visitor's center at 600 Whitewoman St.; **800-877-1830** or **740-622-7644**; https://roscoevillage.com. **RV parking:** Designated parking area at site.*

Historic Zoar Village
Zoar

All over the Midwest, particularly in Ohio and Indiana, are the remains of communal societies where visionaries, from socialist reformers to religious figures, settled after crossing over from Europe to build a new world in the freedom of the Northwest Territory. In 1817, German separatists from the Kingdom of Württemberg, proponents of an offshoot of Lutheranism known as Radical Pietism, founded the communal town of Zoar. Named for Lot's biblical town of refuge, Zoar flourished as one of America's most successful Christian communal societies until it disbanded in 1898.

Both men and women had voting power on the town board, and they produced their own food and other goods, operating blast furnaces, a blacksmith shop, a tin shop, a garden and greenhouse, and a wagon shop. They sold what they didn't need, and had a million dollars in assets by 1852. There are ten restored historic buildings in the village, including a general store, blacksmith's shop, hotel, and town hall. Weekends in summer season often feature volunteer reenactors in the various buildings.

The visitor's center is open Wednesday through Sunday; visitors are free to walk the area and see building exteriors at any time, open or closed. Check in advance for seasonal hours.

The Zoar Store & Visitor's Center is at 198 Main Street; **800-262-6195** *or* **330-874-3211;** https://historiczoarvillage.com/. ***RV parking:*** *Street parking or designated lots off the main route.*

John P. Parker House
Ripley

John Parker was a very important figure in Ohio history, an inventor and iron industrialist. He was also an escaped slave, born in Virginia. He first settled in Jeffersonville, Indiana, another "across the river" town with a large Free Black community, but he later moved to Ripley, where he became a prominent businessman as well as an abolitionist. He had the astonishing courage to cross into the slave state of Kentucky in order to aid other escaping slaves. After the Civil War, Parker told his story to a journalist; the interviews were eventually published as his autobiography, *His Promised Land*. The house was his private home; at one time, he also used it for manufacturing for his iron business. Open Friday, Saturday, and Sunday; May–October. Allow one hour.

300 North Front Street; **937-392-4188** *or* **937-344-3145;** http://johnparker house.net. ***RV parking*** *on nearby streets. Admission varies; call for information on hours and group tours.*

John Rankin House
Ripley

As you cruise down U.S. 52 along the scenic Ohio River, you reach the little town of Ripley. It doesn't seem as if it was ground zero for such an earthshaking civil rights battle. Here, on a hill above town, is the home of Presbyterian minister John Rankin, a famed abolitionist and "conductor" on the Underground Railroad. From this hill, the river (and any pursuers) could be seen, and the home faces a section of the river that's relatively shallow and slow-moving. These factors helped it become one of the busiest crossing points and a crucial stop on the Underground Railroad, ferrying escaped slaves across the Ohio River to freedom; Rankin had as many as a dozen escaped slaves in the house at any given time. Many of the greatest abolitionists, including Harriet Beecher Stowe, author of *Uncle Tom's Cabin,* knew

Rankin and were influenced by his writings. His sons became equally prominent in the movement. Open Wednesday through Sunday, May–October.

6152 Rankin Hill Road.; **937-392-1627;** *www.ohiohistory.org/visit/ browse-historical-sites/john-rankin-house.* **RV parking** *is available in the lot. Admission varies.*

National Museum of the United States Air Force
Dayton

Wear comfortable shoes if you plan to see all of this museum — it's the world's largest of its kind, filling 10 acres and displaying more than 360 aircraft, missiles and more, both inside and outside. From observation balloons to the B-1 bomber, from the plane that dropped the "Fat Man" atomic bomb on Nagasaki in 1945 to the plane that took President Kennedy's body from Dallas to Washington, D.C., in 1963, air history is here. Even NASA spacecraft are displayed, like the Command Module *Endeavour* from the Apollo 15 Moon mission.

There are four hangars of aircraft and displays on the museum grounds. The museum also has a theater, café, and museum store. Allow at least three hours — a full day is better. Open daily; closed on major holidays.

1100 Spaatz St. **937-255-3286;** *www.nationalmuseum.af.mil.* **RV parking:** *Free in designated areas. Admission is free.*

National Road and Zane Grey Museum/John and Annie Glenn Museum
Norwich/New Concord

This museum contains a historical overview of the first National Road, a salute to native son Zane Grey, and a display of art glass and pottery made in the area. Road warriors love the dioramas depicting various stages of the National Road from 1811 to the present day. You can follow the progress of travelers from early inns to early campers with tents and *tin lizzies* (small, cheap Ford cars), and then take in a panoramic view of a trolley, a biplane, and some Model Ts. You see Conestoga wagons displayed with toll-road signs and other vintage vehicles. Another room houses a full-size replica of the studio used by Zanesville-born Western writer Zane Grey.

Five miles away in New Concord, the **John and Annie Glenn Museum** — a living history experience about the astronaut and future senator's boyhood home — is run by the same entity. Your ticket purchase gives you admission to both museums. Open May–October, Wednesday through Sunday. Allow two hours.

National Road and Zane Grey Museum: 8550 E. Pike, Norwich; **800-752-2602;** `http://nationalroadandzanegreymuseum.org/`. **RV parking:** *Large open lot capable of handling big rigs.*

John and Annie Glenn Museum: 72 West Main, New Concord. **RV parking** *is on street.*

Portsmouth Floodwall Murals
Portsmouth

The pretty little river town of Portsmouth is where cowboy star Roy Rogers was born and cruise boats sailing the Ohio River frequently call. The waterfront is lined with huge murals depicting an awesome panorama of town history, from prehistoric days to the present. Yes, Roy Rogers and his horse Trigger are in one of the murals, but our favorite is an evening depiction of the town during the days of World War II, with a movie house, vintage cars, and soldiers in uniform. The murals are quite lovely, and many are historical in theme. The evocative shops in the Historic Boneyfiddle District are appealing. Always open. Allow one hour.

The murals line Front Street in downtown Portsmouth. Portsmouth-Scioto County Visitors Bureau, 342 2nd St. **740-353-1116;** `www.portsmouth.org/travel-tourism/`. **RV parking** *is on the street.*

Pro Football Hall of Fame
Canton

Ohio is "hall of fame" country, and Canton's Pro Football Hall of Fame doesn't disappoint. Exhibits include: busts depicting every Hall of Fame member; the **Lamar Hunt Gallery** chronicling the history of the Super Bowl, where championship rings designed for each year's winner are on display; and a holographic theater featuring the film *The Game of Life*. The museum also showcases many traveling artifacts and temporary special exhibits; check the website for a list of upcoming events. Open daily. Allow 3 to 4 hours.

2121 George Halas Drive NW; **330-456-8207;** `www.profootballhof.com/`. **RV parking** *is available in the lot for a fee. Admission varies.*

Rock and Roll Hall of Fame
Cleveland

Cleveland's wonderful rock museum, designed by innovative architect I. M. Pei with a glass pyramid (reminiscent of the entrance he created for the Louvre Museum in Paris), is a great place to spend a day. Some of the most important exhibits are underground in the Ahmet M. Ertegun Exhibition Hall, a large, darkish area housing all sorts of displays and interactive exhibits, such as "One Hit Wonders," saluting now-forgotten artists who had one big hit, and then vanished from view. Life-size mannequins display John Lennon's collarless Beatles jacket, Alice Cooper's bondage outfit, David Bowie's exaggerated 1970s fashions, Michael Jackson's sequined glove, Lead Belly's 12-string guitar, Jim Morrison's Cub Scout uniform — you get the idea. Open daily.

1100 Rock and Roll Blvd.; **888-764-7625;** *www.rockhall.com.* **RV parking:** *A big problem because the museum parking garage has a height limit that prohibits most RVs; point your rig to the right toward Burke Lakefront Municipal Airport, and when you reach the intersection facing the museum, look for a spot in the airport parking lot, a block from the museum. Admission varies by age.*

OHIO: A CRUCIAL STATION ON THE UNDERGROUND RAILROAD

The Underground Railroad was a complex network of secret routes and safe houses used by abolitionists in the early to mid-1800s to get escaped slaves north, to be resettled there or aided in eventually fleeing as far as Canada or Mexico. Perhaps a hundred thousand slaves were ferried to freedom this way, helping set off the American Civil War.

Ohio, bordered by two slave states, was the most active state in the network, with more than 3,000 miles of underground routes. When Congress established the Northwest Territory in 1787, abolitionist lawmakers fought for and won an agreement to forbid slavery in this vast area north of the Ohio River (which eventually became the five states of Ohio, Indiana, Illinois, Michigan, and Wisconsin, and the northeastern part of Minnesota), though they gave in on something else to achieve this: It was a federal crime to aid any runaway slave who made it into a free state. Over the decades, as northerners began to actively ignore this law and opinion increasingly hardened into uncompromising abolitionism, it became the South's major justification for seceding from the Union.

(continued)

(continued)

Small farmers who immigrated into Ohio and the Wabash Valley of Indiana were for the most part antislavery; proponents of the new religious faiths gaining popularity in the territory in what was called the Great Awakening, including Presbyterians, Methodists, and a growing Quaker population, were also a powerful force for abolition. The John Rankin House on our itinerary was the home of a Presbyterian minister and ardent abolitionist who organized the movement in southern Ohio and influenced it nationally. Another home on the route belonged to entrepreneur, abolitionist, and escaped slave John Parker.

There are many museums and sites telling the history of the abolitionist movement in Ohio. And in Cincinnati you can visit the **National Underground Railroad Freedom Center** (https://freedomcenter.org), which is open Wednesday through Saturday.

More Cool Things to See and Do in Ohio

Ohio's roadside attractions run the gamut from the world's largest cuckoo clock to the birthplace of humorist James Thurber. You can have fun and/or get informed at several spots along the way.

Visit neighborhoods and nature

Here are just a few places to take a walk and maybe pick up some of the area's history (along with a few souvenirs):

>> **Sprechen sie Ohioan? German Village** in **Columbus** is one of Ohio's best-loved destinations. Saved from demolition in the 1950s, the 19th-century neighborhood is home to microbreweries, restaurants, antique shops and art galleries, and its brick streets are perfect for wandering. One of the best neighborhoods in Columbus, it's a charming place to stroll, shop, and dine. Stay as long as you like.

   The visitor's information center is at 588 S. Third St., Columbus; **614-221-8888;** *https://germanvillage.com.* **RV parking** *is available on the street. For more on Columbus neighborhoods, visit* www.experiencecolumbus.com.

>> **Grind your own grist. Lehman's Hardware,** an institution in Ohio's Amish country, is located about 20 miles north of Millersburg in Kidron. It's a country store extraordinaire, a treasure trove of nonelectrical appliances, from hand-cranked wringer washing machines to wood-burning cookstoves, all brand-new.

Heaven for anyone living off the grid. Butter churns, stone crockery, hand-cranked gristmills (to make coarse meal out of dried grain), carpenter's adzes, solid oak furniture, handmade quilts, washboards, and apple peelers are only a small part of what's available. The store features a garden shop, a year-round holiday room, and a candle and historic oil lamp room. Allow one hour or more. Open Monday through Saturday. Call for more information or to schedule a group tour.

Located on the square at 4779 Kidron Road, Kidron; **800-438-5346;** *www. lehmans.com. Plenty of on street* **RV parking.**

KID FRIENDLY

>> **Meet woolly mammoths. Ohio Village** recreates an Ohio town in the 1890s with costumed interpreters and artisans, keeping kids and adults interested in the past. In the **Ohio History Center,** you can meet woolly mammoths and hear some hair-raising ghost stories. Allow two hours. Open Wednesday through Sunday, November–April; special holiday hours for Dickens of a Christmas.

1982 Velma Ave., Columbus; **800-686-6124;** *www.ohiohistory.org/visit/ ohio-village.* **RV parking** *is available in the lot. Admission varies by age.*

>> **Step into a painting.** Sundays in the park (with or without George) come alive in Columbus's **Topiary Garden** in the **Old Deaf School Park.** The garden is a replica in pruned shrubbery of Georges Seurat's painting *A Sunday Afternoon on the Island of La Grande Jatte* (which inspired the Stephen Sondheim musical *Sunday in the Park with George*). It has 50 topiary people, 8 boats, 3 dogs, a monkey, and a real pond to represent the Seine. Open daily.

480 E. Town St. at Washington Avenue, Columbus; **614-645-0197;** *https:// tinyurl.com/ytn973w6. Admission is free.*

Discover famous Ohio folks

You meet an eclectic group of folks when you're traveling around this state. Some notable stops include:

BARGAIN ALERT

>> **Clean up your act.** Contrary to what you may think, **Hoover Historical Center** is not a museum devoted to a former president but, instead, educates the public about the famous vacuum cleaner company. When invented, the vacuum was considered a miracle because "it beats as it sweeps as it cleans." In many parts of the English-speaking world, "Hoover" came to mean both the cleaner and the cleaning action. This museum contains decades of cleaning history

(including an early "portable" that weighed 100 pounds) plus a gift shop. Allow one hour. Open Thursday through Saturday, March–October.

*1875 E. Maple St., North Canton; **330-490-7435;** www.walsh.edu/hoover-historical-center.html. **RV parking** is available in a small lot or on the street. Admission is free; donations are appreciated. Reservations needed for group tours.*

» **Chat with a dead president.** The **William McKinley Presidential Library and Museum** honors the 25th U.S. president, William McKinley, who was assassinated in 1901. The animated figures of McKinley and his wife occupy the museum and talk about their life in the White House. The **McKinley National Memorial,** where the president is interred, is reached by a flight of 108 terraced steps that fitness buffs often climb on the run. Allow two hours. Open Tuesday through Saturday. The tomb is closed November 1 to April 1.

*800 McKinley Monument Dr. NW, Canton; **330-455-7043;** https://mckinley museum.org. **RV parking** is available in a designated lot. Admission varies by age.*

» **"Is everybody happy?"** That was the signature phrase of Jazz Age entertainer **Ted Lewis** from Circleville, who is remembered in his hometown with a pleasant little museum showcasing his battered top hat and clarinet, along with the sheet music for his hits "Me and My Shadow" and "When My Baby Smiles at Me." Allow one hour. Open on Saturday or by appointment.

*133 W. Main St., Circleville; **740-477-3630;** www.tedlewismuseum.org. **RV parking** is available on the street. Admission is free.*

BARGAIN ALERT

» **Chuckle with a humorist.** A unicorn stands in the garden across from **Thurber House,** birthplace of the eccentric and beloved humorist and cartoonist whose short stories and drawings graced the pages of the New Yorker for so many years. **James Thurber** was famous for drawing unicorns, clocks, bossy wives, and mournful dogs, and the house in Columbus is where "the ghost got in" in one of his famous stories. A fine bookstore is on-site, and you also find literary events, ranging from readings by distinguished authors, to literary picnics, to a Birthday Gala for Thurber every December. Open Tuesday, Thursday, Saturday, and Sunday. Allow a half hour to an hour.

*77 Jefferson Ave., Columbus; **614-464-1032;** www.thurberhouse.org. **RV parking** is available on the street. Admission is free for self-guided tours. Contact them online two days in advance for guided tours.*

Weekend wanders

You can't cover everything Ohio has to offer in one weekend, but if that's all you've got, concentrate on the section that interests you most.

>> **For crafts collectors and folks with hearty appetites,** Amish country fills the bill nicely. Start and end your trip in Columbus, driving north to Millersburg and Berlin and overnighting in that area.

>> **Scenery, hiking, and camping fans** need to drive along the Ohio River from Cincinnati and then go up into the Hocking Hills, where campgrounds abound.

>> **Sightseeing for the whole family** includes one of our favorite Ohio weekend getaways, which starts in Dayton (for all the airplane history), heads south through the antiques mecca of Waynesville and Lebanon for a little shopping, pauses for a meal at the famous old Golden Lamb, and then finishes up in Cincinnati with the trio of great museums at the Cincinnati Museum Center at Union Terminal.

Campgrounds in Ohio

In Ohio, you're in God's country — as far as campgrounds are concerned. In Table 11-1, we recommended a few of our favorites in some areas where you may not have lots of campground choices.

REMEMBER

KOA has a large presence in the state, and sometimes a KOA is your best bet for a campground, particularly if you want full hookups or pull-throughs out in the hinterlands. A KOA is great, for example, in Coshocton, when you're visiting Historic Roscoe Village. We've always had good experiences at the KOAs in Ohio, and in fact, the Coshocton KOA is a standout in the system, as is the Sunbury KOA Resort north of Columbus. Also, a Good Sam membership (see Chapter 5 for details) gets you discounted access to more than 30 great RV parks from Akron to Zanesville.

But there are more choices in RV-friendly Ohio. Only one national park graces the state, Cuyahoga Valley National Park near Cleveland, and though it has waterfalls and a scenic railway, it no longer has any campsites; they were shut down in 2019. However, you find 75 state parks in Ohio, with more than 50 of them offering camping as well as boating, fishing, and so on at reasonable prices. Most are open year-round. Several of the best state park campgrounds are near sites on this itinerary (for example, the Hocking Hills). On the U.S. 52 Ohio River route,

Shawnee State Park offers camping at their Turkey Creek campground. You also find private campgrounds available all along the route.

TIP

A terrific tool for finding the state parks of Ohio — in fact, it works for every state — is America's State Parks website (www.americasstateparks.org/). You put your cursor on the state you plan to visit and bring up a map showing the location of every park, with names and addresses listed. The map icons link to info for that particular park. The site is invaluable, and state park camping is a real money-saver to make your trip easier and more fun.

TABLE 11-1 **Our Favorite Ohio Campgrounds**

Name and Location	Contact Info	Cost	What to Know
Buckeye Lake/ Columbus East KOA Holiday; Buckeye Lake, OH	4460 Walnut Rd.; **800-562-0792** or **740-928-0706;** https://koa.com/campgrounds/buckeye-lake/	$$–$$$	Total of 209 sites with water and 30/50-amp electric; 131 full hookups; 98 pull-throughs. CATV, laundry, heated pool, Wi-Fi. Pretty, wooded area, with a camp store and loads of kid-friendly amenities. Convenient to all the attractions in Columbus, an area that can be a bit dry on campgrounds. Open April 2–October 31.
Coshocton KOA Holiday; Coshocton, OH	24688 County Road 10; **800-562-1633** or **740-502-9245;** https://koa.com/campgrounds/coshocton/	$$– $$$$	Total of 41 sites; 3 pull-throughs; 30/50-amp electric. Near Historic Roscoe Village, small but well-run campground with camp store, level sites, friendly staff, swimming pool, and playground. Hosts many local events, from wine tastings to fall festivals, including a sunflower festival. Open April 1–November 1.
Hocking Hills State Park; Logan, OH	Off SR 664; **866-644-6727;** https://tinyurl.com/3tcynvxf	$$	Total of 156 paved RV sites, all with 20-, 30-, or 50-amp electric; some with full hookups; all can accommodate a 50-foot rig. Laundry, pool, playground, camp store. Recent upgrades for RVers include more hookups and longer sites. All sites must be reserved. Great scenery, hiking, and lake for swimming and fishing. Open year-round.

Name and Location	Contact Info	Cost	What to Know
Wolfie's Campground; Zanesville, OH	101 Buckeye Dr.; **740-454-0925;** www.wolfiescampground.com	$$	Total of 54 sites with water and 30/50-amp electric; 49 full hookups; 18 pull-throughs. Wi-Fi, laundry, heated saltwater pool, propane exchange. A long-standing local favorite, this Good Sam campground offers big sites with gravel pads and some with shade. Conveniently located near the National Road and Zane Grey Museum. Open all year.

Good Eats along the Ohio Route

Travelers in the Buckeye State can eat around the clock, from snacks to traditional Midwest meals with enormous Amish-style servings, and sweets in between.

Chili, sauerkraut, and Amish cooking

Prices are modest, portions are large, and cooking is hearty in many of our recommended Ohio restaurants, unpretentious eateries that win the balloting in Ohio Magazine polls under headings such as "Best Restaurant Values" and "Favorite Neighborhood Restaurants."

» **Camp Washington Chili,** 3005 Colerain Ave. at Hopple, Cincinnati (**513-541-0061;** https://campwashingtonchili.com):This restaurant is probably the most colorful purveyor of Cincinnati's famous chili, an acquired taste for any chili-head who has come to love Southwestern chili. Greek Americans created the Cincinnati version — a mild, soupy chili richly seasoned with cinnamon, cumin, and allspice, poured over a plate of spaghetti, and piled high with shredded cheddar cheese. That's *three-way* chili. Add some chopped onions and it's *four-way* chili; if you ladle beans over the top, it's *five-way*. Don't say we didn't warn you! Or skip the spaghetti and have a couple of mini-sized Coney Dogs smothered in chili, mustard, onions and cheese. Burgers, specialty sandwiches and wraps, fries, and salads round out the menu. Most important, they're open 24-hours, Monday through Saturday.

» **Der Dutchman,** 4967 Walnut St., Walnut Creek (**330-893-2981;** https://
dhgroup.com/restaurants/der-dutchman-walnut-creek-oh): With five Ohio
locations, Der Dutchman is an Amish eatery with its own bakery and family-style
dinners. Broasted chicken, roast beef, country cured ham, Swiss steak, plenty of
mashed potatoes and noodles, and a huge variety of "pies made from scratch"
highlight the offerings. Closed Sunday and Monday.

» **Golden Lamb,** 27 S. Broadway, Lebanon (**513-932-5065;** www.goldenlamb.com):
This venerable inn usually wins the vote as the state's favorite restaurant in
Ohio Magazine. Since 1803, the Golden Lamb has hosted Charles Dickens, Mark
Twain, and ten American presidents, plus assorted ghosts. While Dickens com-
plained loudly about the inn not serving spirits, today you can order a bottle of
wine to enjoy with the meltingly tender lamb shanks, fried chicken, and lemon
curd cheesecake at lunch or dinner. Open daily.

**BARGAIN
ALERT**

» **Mrs. Yoder's Kitchen,** 8101 SR 241, Mount Hope (**330-674-0922;** https://
mrsyoderskitchen.com/): At this Amish restaurant, family-style dinners are
on the menu and the buffet, all of which is available for carryout. This is the
ultimate comfort food, so come hungry. Fried chicken, roast turkey, salmon,
perch, prime rib, and pork chops, along with fresh local vegetables and a salad
bar. And, of course, wonderful homemade pies. A very Amish experience.
Open Monday through Saturday.

» **Ohio Sauerkraut Festival,** Old Main Street, Waynesville (**513-897-8855;**
https://sauerkrautfestival.waynesvilleohio.com): Held the second
weekend in October, the festival draws more than 200,000 visitors with its live
music, craft vendors, and, most of all, traditional pork-and-sauerkraut dinners,
cabbage rolls, hot dogs with sauerkraut, sauerkraut candies, and sauerkraut
pizza.

» **Schmidt's Sausage Haus,** 240 E. Kossuth St., Columbus (**614-444-6808;**
www.schmidthaus.com): At this restaurant in the colorful German Village
section of town, look for bratwurst, wiener schnitzel, pork and sauerkraut,
red cabbage, German potato salad, and the house special dessert, a jumbo
cream puff. And live oompah music! Open Sunday through Saturday.

» **Skyline Chili** (www.skylinechili.com): This big local chain has locations all over
Ohio, as well as Indiana, Kentucky, and, yes, Florida, because Midwesterners like
to know we can order up our favorites even when we go south for the winter.
If you've never tried it, you really should. Skyline often wins the title for the best
version of the local chili, seasoned with cinnamon, cumin, and allspice. Oyster
crackers are served on the side. Their Cheese Coney hot dogs, tiny and tender,
can easily become your next passion. Hours vary from location to location;
check individual stores.

Snacks of chocolate, cheese, and ice cream

Ohio has its priorities straight: Along our drive are several havens for lovers of chocolate and dairy treats.

>> **Coblentz Chocolate Company,** 4917 Walnut St., Walnut Creek (**800-338-9341;** https://coblentzchocolates.com): In a charming Victorian house in the heart of Amish country, Coblentz displays its homemade candies in gorgeous wood-and-glass cases. A company Jason and Mary Coblentz started in their kitchen in 1987 has become an Amish country tradition. The Walnut Creek store is open Monday through Saturday. Their candies are available online.

>> **Guggisberg Cheese Company,** 5060 SR 557, Millersburg (**330-893-2500;** www.babyswiss.com): You can't miss this place, appropriately enough near the tiny village of Charm. Just look for the big Swiss chalet with stainless-steel silos and a cuckoo-clock tower. Come inside, and during cheesemaking hours, you can see the giant copper vat where they make the delightful, slightly creamy Baby Swiss cheese that was born here. Wander the store while you sample the cheeses; be sure to buy a whole Baby Swiss to go, along with other picnic makings from the deli. Open Monday through Saturday; cheese making is Monday through Friday.

>> **Young's Jersey Dairy,** 6880 Springfield-Xenia Road, Yellow Springs (**937-325-0629;** https://youngsdairy.com): Young's does quadruple duty as a bakery, soda fountain, restaurant, and cheese shop, as well as a sort of amusement park, with miniature golf, batting cages, and various kids' rides. Extra-thick shakes, every flavor imaginable of homemade ice cream, waffle cones and banana splits, in addition to regular breakfast and lunch fare and packaged ice cream you can take home. Open daily.

Finding Ohio's supermarkets and farmers markets

The most common supermarket chains in Ohio are Kroger, Save A Lot, IGA and Giant Eagle. Kroger's national headquarters are in Cincinnati, and they are the biggest player in the state. Ohio is a huge agricultural state, and farmers markets and roadside food stands are plentiful here. Best place to start hunting these are at the Ohio Proud website (https://tinyurl.com/FMOhio).

There are also some outstanding local markets across Ohio:

>> **Jungle Jim's International Market** (https://junglejims.com) is located at 5440 Dixie Highway, Fairfield, which is a northern suburb of Cincinnati. (A second location is in Eastgate, on the east side.) Jungle Jim's is like a massive

Trader Joe's with a seriously overactive thyroid condition. It has fresh meat, fruit and vegetables, a huge international section, aisles of wine and beer selections, along with being a massive, traditional supermarket. Extremely kid-friendly, there's plenty for them to do while you go stock up your pantry. Jungle Jim's is a destination in and of itself and draws shoppers from nearby states. Must be seen to be believed. Open daily. **RV parking** on-site.

>> **North Market** at 59 Spruce Street, Columbus (https://northmarket.org). Almost 150 years old, it's consistently ranked among the best markets in the nation. Open daily. Being in a downtown location, **RV parking** can be a major problem. If possible, park your rig and take a car or an Uber.

>> **2nd Street Market**, 600 E. 2nd Street, Dayton (**937-228-2088;** www.metroparks. org/places-to-go/2nd-street-market). More than 40 vendors located in an historic freight house selling fresh produce, flowers, and baked goods. Open Fridays, Saturdays and Sundays until 3 pm. Located in a downtown area, call in advance to arrange for parking an RV in their adjacent lot.

Shopping along the Ohio route

All of Amish country is a constant shopping delight: It has potters, basket makers, weavers, quilt makers, and artists of all sorts. Outside the Amish area, artisans staff historic villages and sell goods at every special event. Antiques also are a main attraction in Ohio. In fact, Ohio boasts two antiques centers, a sort of twin cities of shopping. The website www.ohioslargestplayground.com/ lists the individual shops in both towns.

>> **Lebanon,** on U.S. 42 at the junction of SR 63, about 33 miles north of Cincinnati, has much history — Charles Dickens slept here — and is home to 70 antique shops and boutiques in its downtown area, along with Ohio's oldest inn, the Golden Lamb.

>> **Waynesville,** at the junction of U.S. 42 and SR 73, about halfway between Dayton and Cincinnati, has trademarked the title "Antiques Capital of the Midwest" for its 35-plus antique shops, along with art galleries, specialty shops, and boutiques. To tell the truth, we planned a special antique-hunting trip to Vermont, and though it was great, nothing there was as bountiful as this cornucopia of antiques.

Slightly off of our suggested route, two other big antiques markets outside of Springfield are worth mentioning, and they're considered to be among the best antique malls in the country. Shoppers come here from all over the world because of the mind–boggling selections of antique furniture, objects and much more:

>> **Springfield Antique Center**, 1735 Titus Road (Building 1: **937-322-8868**; Building 2: **937-324-8448**; www.springfieldantique.com). Two massive warehouses host more than 1,000 dealers inside. They even welcome your leashed pets. Open daily; closed Easter, Thanksgiving, and Christmas days. **RV parking** is free, and there's plenty of it.

>> **Heart of Ohio Antique Center**, 4785 E. National Road, Springfield (**937-324-2188**; https://heartofohioantiques.com). Hosts 1,425 booths inside, along with a massive area outside that features outdoor furniture, statuary, and architectural items. Open daily; closed Easter, Thanksgiving, and Christmas days. RV parking is free.

Fast Facts for the Ohio Route

Area Code
You find the following area codes in Ohio: **216, 234, 330, 380, 419, 440, 513, 614, 740,** and **937.**

Driving Laws
In Ohio, seat belts must be worn in the front seats. The maximum speed limit on interstates and controlled-access roads is 65 mph. Speed limits in urban areas are lower, and can go up to 70 mph on rural interstates.

Emergency
Call **911.**

Hospitals
Major hospitals along the route are located in Akron, Canton, Dayton, Cincinnati, Columbus, and Cleveland.

Information
For tourism information, go online to https://ohio.gov/tourism or https://

ohio.org, or call **800-BUCKEYE (282-5393)** for maps and travel info.

Road and Weather Conditions
Resources include the Ohio Transportation Information System online (https://gis.dot.state.oh.us/tims) or the Ohio Highway Patrol by phone (**877-7-PATROL [772-8765]**). In Ohio or adjacent states, call **888-264-7623** for road conditions. You can also call the Ohio Department of Transportation at **614-466-7170.**

Taxes
Sales tax is 5.75 percent to 7 percent, depending on the county. The state gasoline tax is 28¢ per gallon.

Time Zone
Ohio is on Eastern time.

IN THIS CHAPTER

» **Planning when to hit the Ozarks and what to bring along**

» **Driving through the Ozarks**

» **Toe-tapping to mountain music**

» **Canoeing the Buffalo National River**

» **Seeing the stars in Branson**

» **Frying up catfish and hush puppies**

Chapter **12**

The Ozarks and Branson: Hot Springs to Springfield

I f you see the word *Ozarks* and think only of feudin' barefoot cartoon hillbillies or songs by the Ozark Mountain Daredevils, like "If You Wanna Get to Heaven, You Got to Raise a Little Hell," you're missing the mark on a truly beautiful and unique part of America.

The Ozark mountain range covers almost all of Arkansas and the southern half of Missouri. For all their craggy remoteness, the Ozark Mountains are only about 2,300 feet high. "Our mountains ain't so high," goes an old local saying, "but our valleys sure are deep." Even deeper are the subterranean caves that hide their beauty from plain sight throughout this whole area. You find every stage of geological evolution in the Ozarks: Water from streams and underground springs eats away at the limestone rock, the fissures open up and become caves, and more water flows through and weakens the rock until it collapses and leaves behind deep gorges, streams become rivers, and the gorges become valleys.

But the Ozarks aren't just an interesting geographical area — you also find a culture that's different from anywhere else in the country. The region roughly bounded by the Missouri, Arkansas, and Mississippi rivers is the heart of American folk music and crafts, preserved primarily because so much of the area was remote and poor until the last half of the 20th century. And a chunk of the area is *still* hard to access, even today. During the Depression of the 1930s, many people from the region migrated to industrial cities in the North to make a living, leaving great swaths of the Ozarks to revert to wilderness. In the 1950s, when so many Southern cities were tearing down their Victorian buildings to put up modern facades, lovely but declining old resort towns that fed off the Ozarks' tourist trade — for example, Hot Springs and Eureka Springs in Arkansas — kept theirs, mostly because they couldn't afford modernization. Today, they are unique time capsules of that earlier time.

But not all of the Ozarks region was left behind by the mid-20th-century economy. In the 1960s, in what had originally begun as a lakeside industrial community, a small town on the shores of Lake Taneycomo in Missouri called Branson transformed itself into what would become one of the top vacation spots in the country for fans of live music. By the 1980s, music stars flocked to Branson to build their own theaters, and the town is still hugely popular among music tourists and families alike.

In this chapter, you explore the mountains and valleys of one of America's most unique mountain ranges, with some of the country's oldest and most hidden resorts. You also find the wildest sporting goods shop anywhere on Earth and discover one of the most popular travel destinations in the United States for music lovers from all over the world.

Planning and Packing for the Ozarks

Lots of the tourism-based businesses on the Ozarks itinerary are seasonal, open only from late April or early May until September or October. Of course, Branson is always open, but even it is brimming with the most events and shows between April and the end of October. During the off-season, many theaters and campgrounds close, but some theaters do put on shows during the Christmas season.

The Ozarks are beautiful in spring — when the dogwoods, redbuds, lilacs, and May apples are blossoming and the weather is mild — and in autumn — when fall temperatures color the leaves, and good weather is likely through October. In summer, days can be hot and humid, and traffic is heaviest.

Allow about two weeks for your Ozarks vacation, depending on how many activities you schedule and the number of shows you take in.

Making the reservations you must

Once you know when you want to take your Ozarks excursion and where you want to stay, make campground reservations in or around Branson ahead of time. Making show reservations doesn't seem to be as important. Check the **Explore Branson** website (www.explorebranson.com/shows) to see who's playing when. Unless there's one particular show they *absolutely MUST see or they will just DIE(!)*, seasoned visitors usually wait until they arrive and then make reservations or purchase tickets.

Branson has more than 100 shows to choose from, with 16,500 seats across an array of live-music theaters that offer daily matinee and evening shows; some even offer breakfast shows. Don't expect a late night — in most cases, evening shows start at 8:00 p.m., although you can find a few late shows offered after 10:00 p.m. during the busier seasons.

Packing the right clothing and gear

Dress is casual in this part of the world, so pack jeans, shorts, T-shirts, and light-weight cotton clothing if you're coming in summer. For spring and fall, add a sweater or jacket, some lightweight rain gear, and hiking boots. If you're the outdoorsy recreation type of vacationer, bring along the gear for your favorite sport. You can easily arrange mountain biking, canoeing, whitewater rafting, hiking, fishing, and horseback riding when you're in the area. And be sure to pack bathing suits for everyone, even if you don't swim, because lots of area attractions involve water.

Anticipating Ozarks driving challenges

Some of the most colorful and picturesque roads through the Ozarks are narrow, steep, and winding. The size of your rig and your comfort with challenging roads can help you decide the specific routes to take. Be courteous to the drivers behind you by pulling aside and letting them pass your rig if you're having trouble keeping up with the speed limit.

The Arkansas Scenic 7 Byway can be harrowing for RVers because it is a slow, twisting, turning climb over the mountains between Hot Springs and Jasper, Arkansas. It's a gorgeous drive (especially in the fall), but if you're behind the steering wheel, you won't see much of it — your eyes will be glued to the road most of the time. Take it slow and take advantage of the many pull-offs and scenic overlooks.

Traffic jams often occur on the streets of Branson, where you can spend extra time inching your way along State Road 76 through the middle of town during the summer season. Locals tell stories about visitors who hop out of their RV (leaving a driver behind, of course!), go shopping, and meet back up with their vehicle a block or two farther along. The best way to avoid the jam-ups and not consign your driver to a very dull day of cussing about pedestrians and other drivers is to leave your RV at the campground and take a local shuttle.

Exploring Ozarks Country in Your RV

The recommended itinerary begins at Hot Springs, Arkansas, with its many charms. Our rambling loop drive heads north on the Arkansas Scenic 7 Byway, passes through **Ouachita National Forest** (pronounced *wah-shee-tuh* — you're welcome), crosses the Arkansas River, and winds through **Ozark-St. Francis National Forests** to **Harrison, Missouri.** Then you turn west to **War Eagle** and **Rogers via** U.S. 412, SR 23, and SR 12. Next, you drive north to **Bentonville** and follow U.S. 62 to the picturesque Victorian town of **Eureka Springs**, east to **Bear Creek Springs,** and then north to **Branson** and **Springfield, Missouri,** on U.S. 65.

After Branson, you head back into Arkansas on U.S. 65, turning east at **Leslie** on SR 66 to **Mountain View,** home of **Ozark Folk Center State Park** and scenic **Jacksonport State Park,** with its spacious, appealing campground. A short jog south on U.S. 67 finally takes you into the Arkansas state capital of **Little Rock** to wind up your journey. The total distance of this trip is approximately **700 miles.** See the mapped route in Figure 12-1.

WARNING

Parts of this route are hilly and curvy on state and county roads through the mountains, and that can pose challenges to RVers who have big rigs or are inexperienced drivers. Never be in a hurry, and be sure to pull off and take regular breaks. Also, we always recommend starting with a tank full of premium fuel to prevent engine knocking on trips with steep inclines.

Starting at Hot Springs

Spend some time in the very first spot on the itinerary. **Hot Springs, Arkansas,** may be best known these days as the town where former President Bill Clinton grew up (he was born in the nearby town of Hope), but it's also home to **Hot Springs National Park.** This unique place once was the most fashionable watering hole in the Midwest, in more ways than one.

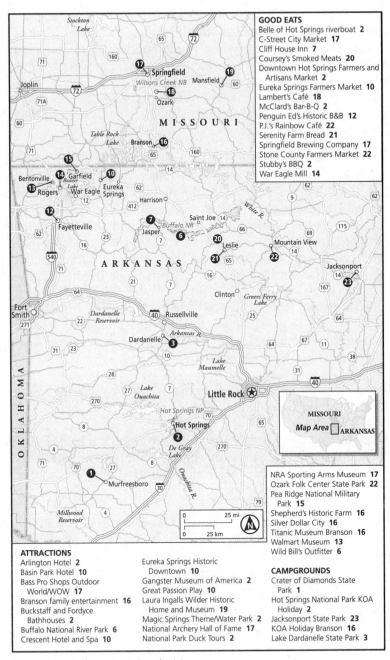

FIGURE 12-1: The scenic Ozarks itinerary.

Some 65 miles south of Hot Springs via U.S. 70 and SR 27 is **Crater of Diamonds State Park.** This park includes America's only publicly accessible diamond mine, where you not only can dig for the elusive gems for a modest fee but also get to keep any diamonds you unearth.

Hotfooting it hill-ward

The most scenic mountain drive from Hot Springs north to Jasper and Harrison is the 157-mile stretch of SR 7 — also known as Arkansas Scenic 7 Byway — a winding two-lane road that meanders over the mountains, past **Lake Ouachita State Park,** the **Ouachita Mountains** (which can be dazzling in autumn), **Ozark-St. Francis National Forests, Nimrod Dam and Lake,** and **Lake Dardanelle State Park.** This drive is a big hit with motorcycle riders, as you can probably imagine. Along the way, you have plenty of opportunities to shop for country ham, local arts and crafts such as handmade quilts, and the very kitschiest in hillbilly souvenirs.

WARNING

The 137-mile drive from Hot Springs to Jasper is absolutely breathtaking, but you *must* take it slowly — give yourself at least three to four hours, and make plenty of stops to calm your nerves. Be aware that gas stations are few and far between, so gas up at Hot Springs before leaving.

TIP

If the notion of a white-knuckle drive on the Scenic Byway unnerves you, see "Taking alternate routes" at the end of this section.

North of **Dardanelle,** SR 7 winds its way up through Ozark-St. Francis National Forests past hillbilly trading posts and pretty mountain villages such as **Pelsor** (also known as Sand Gap), home of Hankins Country Store, dating from 1922, and **Cowell.**

The **Buffalo River,** the only major river in Arkansas without a dam, courses its way for 153 miles through the Ozarks between **Buffalo City** and **Boxley.** The lower 135 miles, managed by the National Park Service and known as **Buffalo National River,** is a favorite destination for canoeing. SR 7 crosses the national river at **Pruitt.** You can rent recreational gear at several outfitters along the river.

Turning west from Harrison and meandering

From **Harrison,** a major junction and gateway to Branson, Missouri, the drive turns west to **War Eagle,** off SR 12 near Rogers. **War Eagle Mill,** a working gristmill, has a general store and a tiny café where you can buy their stone-ground grits, cornbread, pancake, and waffle mixes, along with grains, flours, and more. A few miles west is **Bentonville,** where Sam and Helen Walton opened their first five-and-dime in 1945. Enshrined on the main square in town, the original store, now the **Walmart Museum,** was the modest beginning of the Walmart empire.

From Bentonville, SR 72 leads northeast to **Pea Ridge,** site of **Pea Ridge National Military Park** and one of the American Civil War's most unusual battles.

Continuing east on U.S. 62 from Pea Ridge leads you to **Eureka Springs,** probably the most charming town in the Ozarks. Downtown Eureka Springs is one of those rare places that looks too art-directed to be real, as though Disney Imagineers created it. Block after block of Victorian houses are listed on the National Register of Historic Places. Hillsides are so steep that some houses can be entered on the first floor on one street and on the fifth floor on the next street uphill. This town is worth a full day of exploring.

Heading east and north to Branson and Springfield

The Ozarks route continues east along U.S. 62 to its junction with U.S. 65 and then turns north to **Branson.** This little town that nobody ever heard of before the 1980s now claims to be "the country music capital of the *UNIVERSE*," in case a few banjo- and mandolin-strumming Martians try to horn in on the act. Today, it purportedly attracts more visitors every year than Yellowstone or the Grand Canyon.

From Branson, **Springfield** is only 40 miles north via U.S. 65. On the way, stop halfway between Ozark and Springfield for an all-you-can-eat meal at **Lambert's Café,** an offbeat restaurant known as "the home of throwed rolls." Springfield is home to the incredible **Bass Pro Shops headquarters/Wonders of Wildlife National Museum and Aquarium**, one of Missouri's major tourist attractions. While in Springfield, consider a Jeep tour through the aptly named **Fantastic Caverns.** Or if you came of age in the 1980s and miss those halcyon days of Pac-Man gobbling power pills, relive your misspent youth at the **1984** arcade downtown.

TIP

Famous **Route 66** passes through Springfield — visit the **Route 66 Car Museum** while you're there and see both classic cars and some Hollywood star cars from *Transformers* and *Ghostbusters*. If you're so inclined, you can turn west onto this historic Mother Road toward **Joplin,** and then head on into Oklahoma to combine this trip with the Route 66 itinerary (see Chapter 16).

Fans of the *Little House* books and long-running TV series *Little House on the Prairie* may want to drive the 35 miles east from Springfield on U.S. 60 to **Mansfield,** where **Laura Ingalls Wilder's** home has been turned into a museum. Wilder wrote the popular series at this location.

Circling back to Arkansas

The route returns to Arkansas and the Ozarks via U.S. 65 to Harrison and south-east across **Buffalo National River** at **Silver Hill.** We like to stop in the pleasant little town of **Leslie** for some delectable baked goods from **Serenity Farm.**

From Leslie, cut across SR 66 to **Mountain View** and **Ozark Folk Center State Park.** The cultural traditions of the mountain regions — the music, dancing, handicrafts, foods, and folkways — are cherished and preserved at the center. Folk musician Jimmy Driftwood probably best described the music at the center. When asked the difference between the folk music at Ozark Folk Center versus the hillbilly and country music shows staged elsewhere in Arkansas, he said, "We don't allow counterfeit cornpone around here."

From Mountain View, follow scenic SR 14 east to **Jacksonport State Park.** From Jacksonport, you can easily swing south along U.S. 67 to **Little Rock** and the end of the tour.

Taking alternate routes

WARNING

If you aren't comfortable maneuvering your rig on the back roads, you can stick to the less curvy SR 9 or I-30 to Little Rock, I-40 west to Fort Smith, and U.S. 71 north to Bentonville. U.S. 62 from Eureka Springs to U.S. 65 at Bear Creek Springs also is easy to drive, and so is U.S. 65 north to Branson and Springfield. Class B and C motorhomes and most travel trailers other than fifth-wheels should be no problem, as long as you drive carefully through the Ozarks on the routes suggested. But RVers in big Class A motorhomes and giant fifth-wheels may have a nerve-wracking drive. Be honest with yourself about your confidence level and choose your route accordingly.

TIP

The path you follow on SR 7 (Arkansas Scenic 7 Byway) out of Hot Springs goes through a rugged stretch of mountains in Ozark-St. Francis National Forests. If you want a more relaxing change of pace from this demanding road, detour onto I-40 west from Russellville to Fort Smith and then head north on I-540 to Bentonville, where you can return to the tour route.

Another alternative route takes you from Little Rock north on I-40 to U.S. 65; turn east at Clinton on SR 16 to Mountain View for a visit to Ozark Folk Center State Park. Follow scenic SR 14 northwest across the Buffalo National River at Buffalo Point. Then go on to Yellville, where you turn west on U.S. 62/U.S. 412 to join U.S. 65 for the short trip north to Branson. This detour runs around 230 miles.

TIP

If you want to condense this scenic Ozarks drive and Branson entertainment holiday into a weekend, start in Hot Springs, Arkansas; follow SR 7 north through the Ozarks into Harrison; and go on to Branson, Missouri. The drive itself is slightly less than 200 miles but may take all day on the narrow, curvy roads.

Must-See Ozarks Attractions

Bass Pro Shops Outdoor World/Johnny Morris' Wonders of Wildlife

Springfield, Missouri

KID FRIENDLY

Bass Pro Shops' massive outdoors-themed experience is one of the top tourist destinations in Missouri, attracting hundreds of thousands of visitors. If you've ever shopped at Bass Pro Shops or Cabela's, you may think their location in Springfield is just one more massive store full of hunting, fishing, and camping gear. But Springfield is the headquarters of the company, and this place is affectionately known as "the Grandaddy of All Outdoor Stores" (or just "the Grandaddy").

Sure, you find a store to visit in this complex with nearly 500,000 square feet of retail fun: The Grandaddy offers visitors one of the largest assortments of outdoor gear, apparel, guns, ammo, and gifts under one roof. It holds 4-story waterfalls surrounded by craggy rock cliffs and mounted masterpieces of taxidermy. (Drop by the camping area and see if there's anything you need for the RV — outdoor cooking supplies are big here.) You can even test your new rifle at the indoor shooting range.

But the store is just one component of this humongous complex known as *Johnny Morris' Wonders of Wildlife*. (That's *WOW* for short; Morris is Bass Pro Shops' visionary founder.) WOW has been named the Best Aquarium in North America several times in *USA Today* polls. This incredible indoor attraction has a mile and a half of immersive exhibits and dioramas featuring some 800 species of birds, mammals, and reptiles. The 1.5 million–gallon aquarium is home to 35,000 fish, sharks, penguins, and more. Don't miss the daily fish feeding! Open daily. Allow at least two to three hours.

1935 S. Campbell Ave. **800-227-7776**; *general information:* **417-887-7334**; *store:* **417-890-9453**; *museum:* https://wondersofwildlife.org. *RV parking: Huge parking lot with plenty of RV spaces. Overnight parking is okay, but no hookups or dump sites are available.*

Besides the store and WOW, you also can visit:

» **The National Rifle Association Sporting Arms Museum** displays hunting firearms used in the U.S. from colonial times to the present day, and is home to an incredible collection of sporting arms, including Teddy Roosevelt's favorite hunting rifle.

» **The National Archery Hall of Fame** has more than 1,500 artifacts, including a handmade bow created by the famous Apache leader Geronimo.

» **Hemingway's Blue Water Café** is a full-service restaurant inspired by author and legendary fisherman Ernest Hemingway. In addition to seafood, freshwater fish, and traditional family dining fare, the menu contains more adventuresome items involving bison and alligator meat.

Branson: Music, museums, and other amusements
Branson, Missouri

Legendary guitarist Roy Clark opened the first celebrity-built Branson theater in 1983. Now, with almost 40 live-music theaters putting on more than 100 shows (see the current list at www.branson.com), the huge entertainment center of Branson claims to have more theater seats than Broadway, as much musical excitement as Nashville, and a wholesome atmosphere for the entire family. Shows in Branson cover just about any variety of popular music. Live appearances by major stars tend to be seasonal (May–October), but the holidays bring some great Christmas shows, and some live shows still happen from January through March.

Currently, the incredibly talented Haygood family has the most popular show in Branson, and they've been at it for more than 30 years. You can find many tribute shows with impersonators filling in for legendary stars. For example, you may see Elvis, Dean Martin, Willie Nelson, Reba McEntire, or the Blues Brothers, along with several Motown-sound groups. Then throw in a spectacle like Dolly Parton's Stampede dinner show, which is a kid-friendly crowd-pleaser.

Visit the Branson/Lakes Area Convention & Visitors Bureau at 4100 Gretna Rd. **800-214-3661;** *www.explorebranson.com.*

But Branson isn't just about theatrical shows and music. Tons of other attractions far too numerous to list are all over the area. Here are a few to whet your appetite for fun:

KID FRIENDLY

» **Silver Dollar City** (www.silverdollarcity.com) is an amusement park with an 1880s theme. The original park grew up around Marvel Cave in the 1960s, but today's visitors tend to skip the cave (the 500 steep steps leading down into it may be one reason) and partake of the rides, shops, craft venues, and country music groups that perform daily throughout the park. Kids love the White Water water park, roller coasters, and rides on the stern-wheel riverboat, the *Branson Belle.*

» *The Shepherd of the Hills* (https://theshepherdofthehills.com) is an outdoor play based on a popular novel published in 1907 by Christian minister Harold Bell Wright. Strictly G-rated, the exciting, action-packed melodrama, written in mountain dialect, features a cast of 90, live animals, horse-drawn wagons, and a real burning cabin. The property also has its own adventure park, which features the Copperhead Mountain Coaster.

» **Titanic Museum Branson** (https://titanicbranson.com) features a life-size (yes, really) replica of the massive ship, including many of its most famous interior rooms. It tells the story of the doomed passenger liner with more than 400 artifacts salvaged from the wreck at the bottom of the sea.

Hot Springs: Fordyce Bathhouse
Hot Springs, Arkansas

The Renaissance Revival style Fordyce Bathhouse, the most splendidly restored bathhouse along the famous Bathhouse Row in Hot Springs National Park, doubles as the visitor's center for the park, and as a museum of thermal-bathing history. Go in, get park information from the rangers, and see the lineup of marble bathtubs and showering stalls for the bathers. An 8,000-piece stained glass skylight illuminates the De Soto Fountain, with its Art Deco statue of a Native American woman offering a bowl of water to explorer Hernando De Soto. In the 1915 gymnasium, a fitness center displays punching bags, vaulting horses, and acrobatic rings. Open daily. Allow one hour.

369 Central Ave. **501-620-6715;** *https://www.nps.gov/hosp/index.htm.* ***RV parking:*** *Limited number of dedicated long RV spaces behind the Hot Springs Visitor Center at 629 Central Ave. Admission is free.* **Note:** *Vehicles longer than 30 feet are not permitted to drive up Hot Springs Mountain Drive.*

Throughout the 19th and 20th centuries, people came to Hot Springs from far and wide to "take the waters" that bubbled up from the area's natural thermal springs. Soaking in various combinations of hot and cold baths from the different mineral springs was believed to have great health benefits for just about any ailment. Baseball legend Babe Ruth was a frequent visitor, and in fact, several baseball teams made this their off-season headquarters so that players could rejuvenate their aching muscles in the baths. Here are some other interesting ideas for what to do around Hot Springs:

» **Gamble like the gangsters.** Notorious gangster Al Capone loved to soak in the hot sulfur springs and booked the entire 4th floor of the **Arlington Hotel** (www.arlingtonhotel.com) whenever he came to take the waters. This hotel was considered one of the top gambling palaces in the country from 1927 until after World War II — all illegal, of course.

   If you wanted the legal kind of gambling back then, you could bet on the ponies at Oaklawn racetrack (www.oaklawn.com), which is still open today.

» **Soak in the waters.** Modern visitors wanting to take the waters as it was done a century ago can go soak themselves at **Buckstaff Bathhouse** (www.buckstaffbaths.com), a historic bathhouse a few steps from Fordyce Bathhouse. It's the only public bathhouse that still uses its original tubs and other fixtures and equipment.

» **Enjoy a kid-friendly amusement park.** If the kids are unnerved by all this talk of bathtubs, visit **Magic Springs Theme and Water Park** (www.magicsprings.com) on the northeast side of town for thrill rides, waterslides, and a full day of family fun.

» **Dine on the river.** When it's time to eat, book a lunch or dinner cruise on the **Belle of Hot Springs** riverboat (www.belleriverboat.com).

Historic Downtown Eureka Springs
Eureka Springs, Arkansas

The downtown area of Eureka Springs, with its colorful Victorian "painted lady" stone houses lining the steep, narrow streets, is on the National Register of Historic Places. Limestone walls mark boundaries, and streets cross at diagonals, none making a perfect right angle. A leisurely stroll through Eureka Springs makes you wonder if the town was originally founded by mountain goats — some houses that appear to be single-story with an entrance on one street turn out to have four more floors below when you get to the next block downhill. You enter St. Elizabeth Catholic Church through its bell tower.

Craft shops, art galleries, superb inns, and several outstanding restaurants make Eureka Springs a popular romantic getaway for honeymooners, with a generous collection of upscale bed-and-breakfast inns. Like Hot Springs, Eureka Springs was founded to exploit its 63 therapeutic hot springs, with bathhouses and boardinghouses springing up to soothe and accommodate health-seeking soakers. The arrival of the railroad in 1883 spurred the building of more than 50 plush hotels over the next three decades.

Two hotels are especially worth visiting:

>> **Crescent Hotel and Spa** (75 Prospect Avenue; `https://crescent-hotel.com`): If ghost hunting is on your bucket list, this beautifully restored 1886 hotel is billed as "America's most haunted hotel" and is the site of the annual Eureka Springs Paranormal (ESP) Weekend ghost hunt.

>> **Basin Park Hotel** (12 Spring Street; `www.basinpark.com`): This 1905 hotel is another restored architectural gem and the tallest building in the downtown area.

This jewel of a town delighted even as tough a character as Carrie Nation, famed fiery opponent of alcohol, who settled here in 1908, naming her home Hatchet Hall after her favorite saloon-smashing tool. Allow at least two to three hours for sightseeing.

Get info from the Greater Eureka Springs Chamber of Commerce. **800-6-EUREKA** *(638-7352); `www.eurekaspringschamber.com`.* **RV parking:** *Do not attempt to drive your RV within downtown Eureka Springs! Streets are extremely narrow, steep, and twisty, and on-street parking can be a nightmare. Instead, leave the rig at the campground if you're staying in the area. Or park in one of the open-air lots at the base of town (before the main roads climb uphill) and use the town's trams.*

Ozark Folk Center State Park
Mountain View, Arkansas

The first folk cultural center in the U.S. sprang up here in 1973 to preserve the music, dancing, handicrafts, and folkways of the Ozarks. Dulcimers, fiddles, banjos, guitars, mandolins, autoharps (another word for *zithers*), and jaw harps (which make a completely unique "boing" sound) are all hallmarks — or earmarks — of Ozark Mountain music traditions. A 1,000-seat theater hosts concerts and music festivals, and the weekly NPR program *Ozark Highlands Radio* is recorded onstage. The center offers special gospel music concerts on Sunday evenings.

Cloggers often dance to the tunes of musicians who play frequent sets throughout the day at Blacksmith Stage in the Craft Village. (*Clogging*, done with wooden- or hard-soled shoes to deliberately make noise, is what they mean when they call bluegrass or other traditional mountain-style music *foot-stompin'* music — think *Riverdance* with Bluegrass instead of Irish tunes.) Two dozen craftspeople work inside the center's Craft Village and sell their handcrafted wares Tuesday through Saturday during the tourism season. The center's restaurant serves honest Arkansas food, and a snack bar offers barbecue sandwiches and fried peach and apple pies. The visitor's center is open daily all year; the folk center is open daily April–October. Allow a half day to a full day.

1032 Park Ave. **870-269-3851;** *www.arkansasstateparks.com/parks/ozark-folk-center-state-park.* **RV parking:** *Large lot at the base of the center; free tram uphill to the center.*

More Cool Things to See and Do in the Ozarks

The Ozarks region is a haven of American innovations and creations that reflect earlier eras. Sometimes, you may think you've entered not only another time zone but also another century.

>> **Paddle away the day.** During winter and spring, the **Buffalo National River** reaches its peak flow for canoeists and rafters. The Buffalo River, the first designated national river in the U.S., is a natural stream that's truly unique in a state with multiple man-made fishing streams and lakes created by the U.S. Army Corps of Engineers.

At **Wild Bill's Outfitter,** you can rent canoes, rafts, and kayaks. You can find additional outfitters in Jasper, where the Arkansas Scenic 7 Byway crosses the river; in Ponca, where SR 43 crosses the river; in Tyler Bend and Silver Hill, where U.S. 65 crosses the river; and in Buffalo Point, where SR 14 crosses the river.

23 SR 268 No. 1, Yellville, AR. **800-554-8657** *or* **870-449-6235;** *www.wildbill soutfitter.com.* **RV parking** *is available on the road.*

>> **Meet the gangsters, youse mugs.** Hot Springs ran one of the biggest illegal gambling rackets in the country between 1927 and 1967, with more than 100 gambling houses, big and small, along with a burgeoning prostitution business. At the **Gangster Museum of America,** you can meet up with the most notorious gangsters of the Depression era and find out why the mobsters and mugs of New York, Chicago, and Miami liked to hang up their fedoras and

relax in this quiet little valley deep in the Ozarks. Seven galleries include a period re-creation of a small gambling parlor where you and your mob can safely wager without getting fleeced, nabbed, or treated to a nickel stretch at Sing Sing. Open daily. Just tell 'em we sent ya.

*510 Central Ave., Hot Springs, AR. **501-318-1717;** www.tgmoa.com. **RV parking** is scarce; your best bet is to leave your rig at the campsite.*

» **Ride the duck boats.** While in Hot Springs, check out **National Park Duck Tours** to enjoy riding an amphibious World War II landing craft converted to tourist transportation — and bop around Lake Hamilton over land and water. Tours run daily.

*418 Central Ave., Hot Springs, AR. **501-321-2911;** www.rideaduck.com. **RV parking** is scarce in town; look for parking lots across from Bathhouse Row on Bath and Exchange streets.*

» **Catch the Ozarks' own religious spectacle.** More than 8 million people have come from all over the world to see **The Great Passion Play,** the story of the last week in the life of Jesus, with a massive cast and many special effects. This popular outdoor Eureka Springs production is performed by 250 actors, 40 sheep, 12 horses, 5 donkeys, and 3 camels. Other attractions at the same location include the **Bible Museum,** with 6,000+ bibles in 625 languages (including a 1st edition King James Bible from 1611), the **Sacred Arts Museum,** with more than a thousand pieces of Christ-centered art, **Noah's Ark Park** petting zoo, and the giant **Christ of the Ozarks,** a 70-foot concrete sculpture. The play runs from May through October; special shows run during Easter week, including a sunrise performance Easter Sunday.

*935 Passion Play Rd., Eureka Springs, AR. **800-882-7529** or **479-253-9200;** www.greatpassionplay.com. **RV parking** is available in designated lots.*

» **Visit the little house in the Ozarks.** The **Laura Ingalls Wilder Historic Home & Museum** was the author's home from 1894, when she moved to Missouri with her husband and daughter, until her death in 1957. She wrote all nine of her *Little House* books here. The house is preserved as she left it, and handwritten manuscripts of the books are on display. It's open daily from March 1 through mid-November. Allow two hours.

*3060 State Highway A, Mansfield, MO. **877-924-7126** or **417-924-3626;** http://lauraingallswilderhome.com. **RV parking** is available in a large lot.*

» **Flip for Missouri. Pea Ridge National Military Park** commemorates the 1862 battle that decided whether Missouri would become a member of the Union or secede with the Confederacy. Some 23,000 federal and Confederate troops clashed here, and the battle ultimately led to Missouri remaining in the Union. This was also the first sizable battle in the Civil War to involve Native Americans — two regiments of Cherokees on the Confederate side. A driving tour takes about 30 minutes, but allow two hours so you can tour the visitor's center and museum, and stop throughout the park. The park is open daily but closed on major holidays.

On U.S. 62, 2 miles west of Garfield and 10 miles northeast of Rogers, AR. **479-451-8122;** `https://www.nps.gov/peri/index.htm`. **RV parking** *is available in a lot.*

» **Count sheep, catch a morality play, and find inspiration. Shepherd's Historic Farm** presents *The Shepherd of the Hills,* a rustic outdoor melodrama based on Harold Bell Wright's 1907 best-selling novel of the same name. (The book was made into a 1941 film starring John Wayne.) With a cast of 90 actors, a covey of animals, and a roaring cabin fire onstage, the play holds your attention in the farm's 2,000-seat amphitheater.

The more lighthearted seasonal dinner shows feature down-home fare such as smoked turkey breast, pulled pork, corn on the cob, and cobbler. Also at the site is Shepherd's Adventure Park, home of the Copperhead Mountain roller coaster; Missouri's highest zip line, which launches from 140 feet in the air and is more than half a mile long; and a very cool zip line/rope challenge course for younger kids. **Note:** This park was named best Aerial Adventure Park in America every year since 2019 by *USA Today.* Check the website for days and hours of operation.

5586 W SR 76, Branson, MO. **417-334-4191;** `https://theshepherdofthe hills.com`. **RV parking** *is available in designated lots.*

KID FRIENDLY

» **See the cave and hit the midway.** Silver Dollar City is an amusement park near Branson with an 1880s theme. More than 40 rides and shows, a 13-acre water park called White Water, 18 restaurants, 60 shops, and an on-site RV campground are all located here. Of the park's several great coasters, we like the steampunk-styled Time Traveler, touted as the world's fastest, tallest, steepest spinning coaster. (**Note:** Ride it *before* lunch!) The whole complex is built on top of one of Missouri's deepest caves, Marvel Cave, which was the original attraction that led to the park's creation in the 1940s. You can still descend 500 steps and visit the cave today.

More than 100 artisans demonstrate the crafts, skills, and workmanship of the 19th century, and you can buy many of the handcrafted pieces of jewelry, furniture, and other items made here. You can even take in an evening show and dinner cruise on Table Rock Lake aboard the *Belle of Branson* stern-wheel showboat. Open daily from mid-April to late December.

> *399 Silver Dollar City Pkwy., Branson, MO.* **417-336-7100;** www.silverdollar city.com. ***RV parking*** *is available in a large lot.*

» **Witness the dawn of Walmart.** In Bentonville, Arkansas, Sam and Helen Walton opened their first five-and-dime store in 1945. Today, that store is the **Walmart Museum,** filled with 1950s and '60s merchandise, 35 electronic historical displays, and Sam's original desk. You can even ask questions and hear anecdotes from "Mr. Sam the Hologram," a computer re-creation of Sam Walton himself. The visitor center is open from March through October, Monday through Saturday. Allow one hour.

> *105 N. Main St., Bentonville, AR;* **479-273-1329;** https://www.walmartmuseum. com. ***RV parking*** *is available on the street. Admission is free.*

TIP

At press time, the Walmart Museum, including the five-and-dime and the Spark Café, is undergoing extensive renovation, which is scheduled to finish in spring 2024. A temporary exhibit is set up in the **Walmart Museum Heritage Lab** at 240 S. Main Street in Bentonville.

Our Favorite Ozarks Campgrounds

Arkansas state parks are especially RV-friendly and are almost uniformly excellent. Most have water and electric hookups (15 state parks have full water/sewer/electric hookups available), and all are in scenic areas. With 9,700 miles of streams and rivers and 6,000 acres of surface water, the state promises plenty of fishing, boating, floating, and canoeing in public and private campgrounds.

TIP

For July and August and spring weekends, we recommend that you make reservations, especially around Branson and crowded Eureka Springs. However, Arkansas's state parks online reservation system (www.arkansasstateparks. com) can be finicky, and it's incredibly slow. We recommend phoning the park office and dealing with a human, if possible.

All campgrounds in this section are open year-round and have public flush toilets, showers, and sanitary dump stations unless designated otherwise. Toll-free numbers, where listed, are for reservations only. Table 12-1 lists our favorite campgrounds.

SLEEP CHEAP AS GUESTS OF THE ARMY

Arkansas and Missouri have plenty of land around rivers and lakes designated as recreation and camping areas by the **U.S. Army Corps of Engineers** (sometimes abbreviated in camp guides as ACOE or COE sites). Since most ACOE RV campsites are around lakes, they're automatically in the places with great water views. These sites are often the cheapest you find anywhere — usually $30 for water/sewer/electric hookups (less if you just want electric and water) — and even cheaper with an **America the Beautiful National Parks and Federal Recreational Lands Pass.**

Bear in mind that campsites closest to the water often have no freshwater or sewer hookups to prevent contamination of the lake or stream itself. Payment is usually on the honor system because there are no offices or rangers around. Check for locations and make reservations at https://corpslakes.erdc.dren.mil/visitors/visitors.cfm.

TABLE 12-1   **Our Favorite Ozarks Campgrounds**

Name and Location	Contact Info	Cost	What to Know
KOA Holiday Branson; Branson, MO	397 Animal Safari Rd.; **417-334-4414;** https://koa.com/campgrounds/branson/	$$$–$$$$	140 full hookups with water and 30/50-amp electric; 120 pull-throughs. CATV, laundry, pool. Paved sites with picnic tables and barbecue grills. Kid-friendly pool and playground. Only a half mile from the busy Branson strip; free shuttle transportation to select shops and shows in season. Just 15 minutes from Silver Dollar City amusement park. Free pancake breakfast served daily. Open year-round. **NOTE:** Avoid approaching from the west which has steep grades and tight turns on Animal Safari Road west of the park. Come from the east side through the town of Branson via CR W76 (Country Boulevard) and SR 165.
Crater of Diamonds State Park; Murfreesboro, AR	209 State Park Rd.; **870-285-3113;** www.arkansasstateparks.com/parks/crater-diamonds-state-park	$$	47 sites; all have full hookups with 20/30/50-amp service and concrete pads; no pull-throughs. Laundry and new bathhouses. 14-day maximum stay. In this top-notch park, the eroded surface of a volcanic crater is the only publicly accessible diamond mine in the U.S. You can also fish in the Little Missouri River.

Name and Location	Contact Info	Cost	What to Know
Hot Springs National Park KOA Holiday; Hot Springs, AR	838 McClendon Rd.; **800-562-5903** or **501-624-5912;** https://koa.com/campgrounds/hot-springs-national-park/	$$–$$$$	Total of 70 sites with water and 30/50-amp electric; all full hookups; 15 pull-throughs. CATV, laundry, pool, Wi-Fi. Call for latest rates. Terraced sites with landscaping offer privacy. Weekend pancake breakfasts and free shuttles to downtown Hot Springs, Oaklawn racetrack, and Magic Springs Theme and Water Park.
Jacksonport State Park; Jacksonport, AR	205 Avenue St.; **870-523-2143;** www.arkansasstateparks.com/parks/jacksonport-state-park	$$	20 sites with water and 20/30/50-amp electric; no full hookups; no pull-throughs. Wheelchair accessible. 14-day maximum stay. A charming park and peaceful campground with an 1872 courthouse/museum/visitor's center. Offers big grassy sites on the White River with fishing and mature shade trees.
Lake Dardanelle State Park; Russellville, AR	2426 Marina Hill Road; **479-967-5516;** www.arkansasstateparks.com/parks/lake-dardanelle-state-park	$	Total of 57 sites with water and 20/30-amp electric; 30 full hookups; 4 pull-throughs. 14-day maximum stay. Three campgrounds with shade trees and picnic tables. Boat, fish, or water-ski on Lake Dardanelle; equipment rental available. An official Trail of Tears National Historic Site with visitor's center.

Good Eatin' in the Ozarks

Penny-pinchers are in hog heaven in the Ozarks because prices, especially for restaurant meals, are generally lower than in many other areas of the country. Big, family-style meals and all-you-can-eat buffets are available in places such as Branson. Keep an eye out for roadside stands and rural markets along this route, as they are often unexpected delights. You may find some areas of the Ozarks route lack easy access to supermarkets, but we clue you in to the chains you run across along the way.

Dining Ozarks style

Here are our favorite places to pick up some down-home cooking and Ozark-area specialties. Most are open for lunch and early dinner, but don't arrive fashionably late, because they'll probably be closed.

» **Penguin Ed's Historic B&B**, 200 S. East Ave., Fayetteville, Arkansas (**479-521-3663;** https://penguineds.com/): The barbecue pit at this joint is fired with hickory, and the bread is homemade. You place your order from an orange phone in your booth, and when the phone lights up, your food is ready. Beef, chicken, and pork barbecue, batter-dipped fries, fried dill pickles, and fried peach or apple pies dusted with cinnamon and sugar make a generous meal. Open daily.

» **Cliff House Inn,** SR 7, 6 miles south of Jasper, Arkansas (**870-446-2292;** https://cliffhouseinnar.com): This is a convenient spot on the Scenic 7 Byway with a balcony that offers a great view of the valley known as "Arkansas's Grand Canyon" (with the deepest valley in the Ozarks). Cliff House serves main dishes such as catfish, fried chicken and steak, as well as burgers, sandwiches and homemade pies. Open Wednesday through Sunday but closed from mid-November to mid-March.

» **Coursey's Smoked Meats**, 152 Courseys Dr., St. Joe, Arkansas (**870-439-2503;** www.facebook.com/profile.php?id=100063587473586): Hickory-smoked, salt-cured ham is an Ozarks specialty. Coursey's is a family-owned retail store and smokehouse with a deli in the back, and they cure hams and bacon here the old-fashioned way (their original log-built smokehouse from 1943 sits out in front of the store). This rich, salty ham lasts for months without refrigeration in a cool, dark place, so you can buy one to take home and store it in the RV. Walk in to the store and you'll see rows of these football-sized hams hanging from the rafters. Grab a sandwich from the deli and be sure to pick up a slab of bacon, along with locally-produced cheeses, jams, jellies and honey. Open March through December, but it's best to call them directly before trying to visit. Closed Tuesday and Wednesday.

KID FRIENDLY

» **Lambert's Café,** 1800 W. Highway J, off U.S. 65, Ozark, Missouri (**417-581-ROLL** [7655]; https://throwedrolls.com): Despite their slogan, "home of throwed rolls," Lambert's doesn't pelt you with your entire dinner — just certain parts of it. Only the fluffy, slightly sweet dinner rolls are tossed at you as the servers make their rounds. Good main-dish selections include fried chicken, chicken and dumplings, ham, steaks, and ribs. But for some real Ozarks cuisine, try the hog jowls, or order the all-you-can-eat white beans with fried bologna, which includes an after-dinner King Edward cigar or a stick of Big Red chewing gum. Open daily but closed on major holidays. ***Note:*** Located halfway between Ozark and Springfield, Missouri, Lambert's Café has their own on-site RV park with 34 pull-through, full-hookup, 30/50-amp sites, so you can be there for both dinner *and* lunch the next day.

»» **McClard's Bar-B-Q,** 505 Albert Pike, Hot Springs, Arkansas (**501-623-9665;** www.mcclards.com): Established in 1928 and known for their "world's greatest hot sauce," McClard's is in their fourth generation of family ownership. Travel Channel has voted them one of its Top Ten Bar-B-Q Restaurants. (A little on the hot side for our list, but still a fine entry.) This was a favorite hangout for young Bill Clinton when he was growing up in Hot Springs, wistfully recalling the tamale spreads — one or two tamales topped with corn chips, beans, chopped beef, cheese, and onions. Open Tuesday through Sunday.

»» **P.J.'s Rainbow Café,** 216 W. Main Street, Mountain View, Arkansas (**870-269-8633;** www.facebook.com/Pjsrainbowcafe): Not far from Ozark Folk Center State Park, P.J.'s serves up classic Southern home-cooked comfort food such as fried chicken, meat loaf, open-face beef sandwiches with *real* mashed potatoes, chicken-fried steak, catfish, rainbow trout, and homemade soups; the menu changes daily. But more than just loving the food, patrons say over and over that, by the time you leave, you'll feel like a special part of the family too. Fellow diners talk to each other instead of staring into their phones, and it's common for owner Robbie Baker to sit down and chat, show you his family photos, and make you feel like the returning prodigal siblings. Open Tuesday through Sunday, and breakfast is available all day.

»» **Serenity Farm Bread,** 423 Main Street and 805 U.S. 65, Leslie, Arkansas (**870-447-2211;** https://serenityfarmbread.com): Serenity Farm Bread has two locations in Leslie. The bakery on Main Street is open Monday, Friday, and Saturday. The separate pastry shop on U.S. 65 offers a huge selection of pastries, sandwiches, snacks, and desserts made on-site and is open daily. Proprietors Adrienne Freeman and Daniel Burlison bake authentic sourdough bread without yeast or sugar, using only freshly milled flour from organically grown wheat, sea salt, and filtered water. Other tasty loaves include French, whole wheat, focaccia, and fruit-filled breads.

»» **Springfield Brewing Company,** 305 S. Market Ave., Springfield, Missouri (**417-832-TAPS** [8277]; https://springfieldbrewingco.com): This nostalgic brewpub — with a rooftop beer garden, live music, and a Sunday brunch buffet — is a few blocks from Bass Pro Shops Outdoor World/Wonders of Wildlife. Serves traditional pub food with loads of deep-fried appetizers, pizzas, burgers, and sandwiches — even a decent Quebec-style *poutine* (French fries and cheese curds smothered in gravy). Open daily (Tuesdays are bar service only).

»» **Stubby's BBQ,** 3024 Central Ave., Hot Springs, Arkansas (**501-624-1552;** https://stubbys.com): Stubby's has been here since 1952, and their barbecue is described as a mix between Texas and Tennessee style. All meats are hickory-smoked, and even the smoky baked potatoes are cooked in the barbecue pit. Ham, beef brisket, chicken, and both pork and beef ribs are coated with a rich, dark sauce. We highly recommend the pot-o-beans with big hunks of smoked ham mixed in. Open daily.

» **War Eagle Mill,** 11045 War Eagle Road, Rogers, Arkansas (**479-480-4449;** https://visitwareaglemill.com/): From Eureka Springs, take SR 23 south to SR 12E, and turn south on SR 98 to the mill. This operating gristmill on the War Eagle River sells organic, non-GMO stone-ground grits, cornmeal, flour, waffle and pancake mix, hush puppy mix, and fish-fry coating. These are made on-site, the old-fashioned way, with a water-powered stone grinding wheel. Their jams, jellies, syrups, salsas, and mustards are also made locally and sold in the on-site general store. A tiny café in the store serves up bakery items, meals like traditional beans and cornbread, and other homemade dishes. Closed Mondays.

Farmers markets

In this section, we list a few large, organized farmers markets in some of the bigger towns you'll be visiting.

» **Eureka Springs Farmers Market,** Eureka Springs, AR. 44 Kings Hwy. (www.facebook.com/ESFarmersMarket). Open Tuesday and Thursday from April through November; Thursday only from December through April.

» **Downtown Hot Springs Farmers and Artisans Market,** Hot Springs, AR. 121 Orange Street (www.hotspringsfarmersmarket.com). Open Tuesday and Saturday from May through October; Saturday only from November through April.

» **Stone County Farmers Market,** Mountain View, AR. 1103 Main Street (www.facebook.com/stonecofarmersmarket/). Open Tuesday and Saturday from June through November.

» **C-Street City Market,** Springfield, MO. 321 E. Commercial Avenue, beneath the Jefferson Street pedestrian bridge in the C-Street Historical District (www.cstreetcitymarket.com). Open Thursday and Saturday from April through October.

Ozarks supermarkets

Arkansas is Walmart's backyard. Their superstores are in Fort Smith, Harrison, Hot Springs, Little Rock, Ozark, Russellville, and other places we're forgetting. At Hot Springs, you can find several **Krogers, Harps,** and **Walmart Neighborhood Markets.** In Harrison, you find **Aldi, Harps,** and **Hudson's.** Fort Smith has several **Harps** and **Aldi** stores, along with some **Walmart Neighborhood Markets.** It's not a supermarket, but stop at **The Eureka Market** in Eureka Springs at 121 E. Van Buren just because it's so darling a place.

Supermarkets are few and far between in this part of Missouri, apart from Springfield, which has stores from several chains. We usually hit the **Hy-Vee**, but you can also find **Price Cutter, Food 4 Less, Harter House, Save A Lot,** and several **Walmart Neighborhood Markets** in town. **Walmart Supercenters** can be found in Branson and Springfield.

Fast Facts for Your Ozarks Vacation

Area Codes
The area codes along this route are as follows: Arkansas **479, 501,** and **870;** Missouri **417** and **573.**

Driving Laws
In Arkansas and Missouri, all passengers must wear seat belts. The speed limit on interstates and rural state highways is 70 mph in both Arkansas and Missouri. Speed limits in urban areas and secondary roads are lower.

Emergency
Call **911** in both states. Other emergency resources include the Arkansas State Police (**501-618-8100**) and the Missouri Highway Patrol (**573-751-3313**).

Hospitals
Major hospitals along the route are in Hot Springs, Branson, and Little Rock.

Information
Contact the Arkansas Department of Tourism (**501-682-7777** or **800-NATURAL**

[628-8725] for a vacation-planning kit; https://www.arkansas.com) **or the Missouri Division of Tourism (573-751-4133;** https://www.visitmo.com).

Road and Weather Conditions
Contact the Arkansas State Highway and Transportation Department (**800-245-1672** or **501-569-2374;** www.arkansashigh ways.com) **or the Missouri Department of Transportation (573-751-2551;** https://www.modot.org).

Taxes
Sales taxes are 6.5 percent (local taxes can add 2.125 percent) in Arkansas, and 4.225 percent (local taxes can add 3.888 percent) in Missouri. State gasoline taxes are 21.8 cents per gallon in Arkansas and 17 cents per gallon in Missouri.

Time Zone
Arkansas and Missouri are on Central time.

5

Wandering the Wild West

IN THIS PART . . .

Track Buffalo Bill through Montana and Wyoming, and roam the wilderness of Yellowstone.

Hunt UFOs, chomp into some chiles, and go bats in the caverns of New Mexico.

Cruise California's Central Coast for butterflies and barbecue.

Get your kicks on Route 66, from Oklahoma to L.A.

Traverse the Oregon coastline, taking in the majestic Columbia River and Pacific Ocean views.

IN THIS CHAPTER

» Rustling up some plans for a Montana and Wyoming tour

» Conquering the Beartooth Highway, or not

» Trailing Custer at Little Bighorn

» Camping in Yellowstone

» Feasting on fish and bison burgers

Chapter **13**

Montana and Wyoming: Tracking Buffalo Bill

They call the area in this chapter Big Sky country for a reason. Many years ago, on a trip to Portugal, we were astounded by the biggest sky we'd ever seen, an ice blue vista with brilliant, in-your-face stars at night. We say now with a healthy dose of American pride that Portugal's got nothing on Montana and Wyoming.

The moniker is fairly old: A. B. Guthrie wrote his famed Western novel *The Big Sky* in 1947. It tells the story of the early settlement of Montana and Wyoming. But you find lots of other nicknames for these two states. For example, Montana is sometimes known as the Treasure State (for its trove of gold and silver), High, Wide, and Handsome, or the Cowboy State. Some people call Wyoming the Equality State, and Native Americans call the area the Land of the Shining Mountains.

People in Big Sky country have long prided themselves on being a bit more rugged, able to survive and thrive in this harsher, more demanding environment. They're also proud of their arts and their history, and justly so. And for the typical RVer who wants to pay homage to all this majesty and take advantage of our great national parks system, these states offer a pristine-feeling experience.

Despite the crowds in the gift shops on a summer day in Yellowstone National Park, you're still going to find the vast wilderness that lures campers to this area.

In this chapter, you discover a scenic path through mountains, national parks, and forests, get an introduction to the Wild West environment, uncover unique camping opportunities, and face a welcome dearth of fast food. An RV vacation into Yellowstone National Park requires a unique collection of insider info to avoid disappointment or frustration, so you get that in this chapter, too. Enjoy the journey!

Planning your Montana–Wyoming Trip

The best time to take the Montana and Wyoming drive is in **late spring, summer, or early fall.** In winter, snow closes many of the scenic highways, most of the entrances into Yellowstone Park, and a majority of the campgrounds. The only road generally open year-round to automobiles is from the North Entrance at Gardiner, Montana through the park to Cooke City, Montana (via Tower Junction). Most of the other park roads are closed to regular vehicles from early November to late April.

Early spring brings snowmelt and mud, and wildflowers don't start blooming until June. July and August usually offer the warmest weather and always have the biggest crowds, with sometimes maddening traffic in Yellowstone National Park. Autumn, from Labor Day until early October, is probably the best time to visit because the weather is mild, although days may be rainy. If you can't visit at that time, we've also had some luck with smaller crowds in mid-May and early June.

TIP

Consider grabbing a copy of Norman Maclean's moving novella of Montana, *A River Runs Through It.* It's a great companion on a trip to Big Sky country. The paperback edition from University of Chicago Press includes Maclean's stories, as a very young man, of working for the even younger U.S. Forest Service. Actor/director Robert Redford made a wonderful film version of this novella.

For the entire drive, including exploring Yellowstone, and a relaxed trip, allow **ten days to two weeks.**

Prepping for your Yellowstone visit

Planning is everything for a trip to Yellowstone. A good place to start is the **National Park Service** website (www.nps.gov/yell/index.htm) where you can browse through tons of information about the park.

A BRIEF HISTORY OF BIG SKY DEVELOPMENT

One nickname for Montana — the Last Best Place — makes some residents a little nervous these days, because the Montana experience is changing quickly. Consider that the Jackson Hole valley in Wyoming has been considered hip for some time, especially for skiers. This hipness had people wringing their hands about the "Aspenization" of the area three decades ago. But, beginning in the 1980s, everyone from movie stars to oil sheiks began discovering Montana; it's a fad that didn't burn out. Recently, especially in the wake of the popularity of the Kevin Costner TV series *Yellowstone*, Montana has become *the* place for the elite class to go to play cowboy, setting off a land rush and a buying frenzy by some cosseted Hollywood types who'd yet to experience their first winter in Kalispell. In their wake, Bozeman has picked up the nickname *Boz Angeles*.

But the truth is, the natural beauty is still there, still intact, and both states feel like there is, for the moment, plenty of room for people seeking the solace of placid waters and isolated valleys. When you're driving the Beartooth Highway between Red Lodge and Yellowstone, it's tough to worry about the specter of development. That doesn't mean we turn off our radar and stop paying attention. But, with one Missoula real estate agent comparing the buying frenzy to the toilet paper–hoarding nuttiness at the beginning of the COVID pandemic, we should probably see it as a blessing that the federal government owns about a third of Montana and nearly half of Wyoming. These lands, at least, will be kept safe from development.

In fact, Wyoming has always been underpopulated compared to neighboring states; it's still the least populous state in the union. It glories in being the Equality State, the first to grant women the right to vote and hold political office, though one of the reasons for doing so was less than political: With a six-to-one ratio of men to women, lonely men were hoping women would see Wyoming as a welcoming place to settle. The state never had a gold or silver boom, but it did have a cattle boom in the 1860s, and the ranches tended to be big — several thousands of acres, many of them owned by Europeans. Even today, cattle outnumber people by more than two to one.

On the whole, any time is a busy time in Yellowstone, so you need to make **campground reservations** six months in advance if you intend to stay in the park itself; that's also not bad advice for some of the more popular campgrounds just outside one of the Yellowstone entrance gates. Towns like Billings, Buffalo, and even Red Lodge aren't as busy, though special events can affect this; for example, the midsummer motorcycle madness in Red Lodge — the Beartooth Rally — will see big crowds.

If you plan to drive the Yellowstone National Park's **Grand Loop Road** (141 miles) on one long day of sightseeing, you probably don't need campground reservations.

You can just stay in one of the outside-the-gates towns like Gardiner or West Yellowstone, or even Cody, and do a drive-through to get a taste of the park. This is how we saw Yellowstone our first time. It's arguably a more relaxed way to do it, but it left us wanting more. We went back for a longer trip later.

REMEMBER

If you're taking a leisurely trip, with more than two weeks to spend in Big Sky country, Grand Teton National Park is near Yellowstone and, combined with it, another great experience. On every geographic side of Yellowstone National Park are a huge number of national forests: 27 in the greater Yellowstone region, including 9 in Montana, 6 in Wyoming, and 12 in Idaho. In other words, no matter where you are on this itinerary, you're not far from a national forest — for example, **Shoshone, Custer-Gallatin,** and **Bridger-Teton.** Go to the U.S. Forest Service's website (www.fs.usda.gov) and click on the Visitor Map. It will carry you to every gorgeous national forest in the country, and all their opportunities for reasonably priced wilderness camping.

TIP

If you're 62 or older, be sure to look into *America the Beautiful* passes for seniors — you can save a bundle. Twenty bucks buys a year's pass not only into Yellowstone but into all the national parks and national forests, and you get discounts in many places, including Army Corps of Engineer campgrounds. For $80, you get a lifetime pass. You can buy it in person at a Yellowstone park gate or visitor center; you can also call **888-ASK-USGS (275-8747)** or visit https://store.usgs.gov/recreational-passes.

Gearing up for potentially bad roads

Many of the roads in Yellowstone National Park are rough and bumpy because of winter freezes that buckle the pavement. Roadwork goes on constantly every summer, so you may encounter gusts of dust (or stretches of mud, if it's been raining) and closed sections of roadway. You also run into frequent traffic jams around sightings of bear, bison, and elk.

REMEMBER

Even on a good day, the speed limit in Yellowstone National Park is just 45 mph. Allow twice as much time as you'd expect to negotiate Yellowstone's roads (and pack some sandwiches). You also find that many of the park's turnoffs that work well for cars don't allow enough space for motorhomes or vehicles towing trailers. For maximum efficiency, consider leaving your RV in the campground and taking your own car or a rental around the park. We towed a 23-foot Airstream trailer all through the park with ease, but wouldn't want to take the 30-footer we tow now.

Packing and taking along preventatives

When you pack, keep in mind that Big Sky country attire is casual, and you need to include garb for all kinds of weather. Rain gear is essential, as are hiking boots, jeans, jackets, and sweatshirts or sweaters. We advise taking a lightweight packable puffer jacket, in any season. The days can get hot, with temperatures around Little Bighorn Battlefield sometimes topping 100 degrees F in summer, but during the same week, you can drive over Beartooth Pass in below-freezing weather.

TIP

Here's a twofer tip for dealing with the Montana and Wyoming environments:

>> **The mosquito and tick problem is real.** Mosquitoes and ticks are plentiful in summer, especially on scrubby hiking trails. You may have no problem at all, but we still advise taking along your favorite mosquito repellent. And consider trying repellent-treated camping clothes; we've had good luck with them, especially No Fly Zone camp pants and leggings from L.L. Bean. We tried these because Alice reacts badly to repellent containing DEET (Deep Woods OFF! has a high concentration of DEET). Don't forget to shake out your pants legs after a hike in the woods and check yourself over for ticks.

>> **Yellowstone breeds *killer* pollen.** In early summer, Yellowstone is blanketed with some of the worst pollen you've ever seen. Much of it is from the lodgepole pines that are the most common tree in the park. It's not at all unusual, in June or July, to walk out to your car or truck and find it covered in a thick layer of bright yellow pollen (an oversize feather duster will sweep it off without scratching your paint). It also can coat the surface of lake water. If you have a bad allergy problem set off by pollen, take along whatever you need to fight it.

Driving Buffalo Bill's Montana and Wyoming

Setting out from **Billings, Montana,** and driving south on U.S. 212 to **Red Lodge,** this tour follows the curves of spectacular Beartooth Highway (named for a rocky outcropping at the summit shaped like a bear's tooth) across a pass with a 10,947-foot summit that drops into **Wyoming** and **Yellowstone National Park.** Next, you make a circle tour of Yellowstone highlights, and then drive east along little-traveled Chief Joseph Scenic Byway into **Cody.** From Cody, go east on U.S. 14 to **Greybull,** then travel south on U.S. 16 to **Worland,** and head east on U.S. 16 to **Buffalo** across the Powder River Pass. From Buffalo, return to Billings by driving north on I-90 back into Montana and pausing at **Little Bighorn Battlefield National Monument.** The distance traveled is **772 miles.** See the route in Figure 13-1.

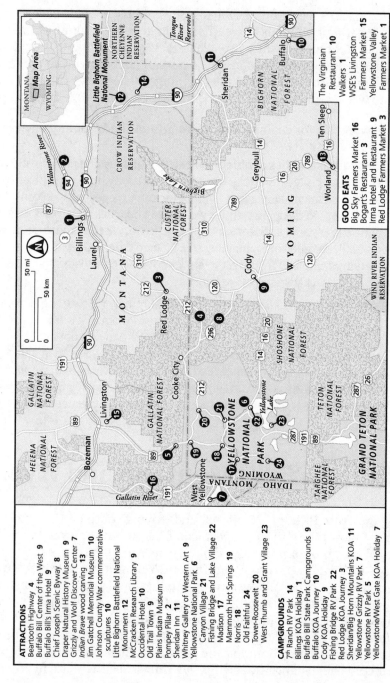

FIGURE 13-1: The route through Buffalo Bill country.

ATTRACTIONS
Beartooth Highway 4
Buffalo Bill Center of the West 9
Buffalo Bill's Irma Hotel 9
Chief Joseph Scenic Byway 8
Draper Natural History Museum 9
Grizzly and Wolf Discover Center 7
Indian Brave wood carving 13
Jim Gatchell Memorial Museum 10
Johnson County War commemorative sculptures 10
Little Bighorn Battlefield National Monument 12
McCracken Research Library 9
Occidental Hotel 10
Old Trail Town 9
Plains Indian Museum 9
Pompey Pillar 2
Sheridan Inn 11
Whitney Gallery of Western Art 9
Yellowstone National Park 6
Canyon Village 21
Fishing Bridge and Lake Village 22
Madison 17
Mammoth Hot Springs 19
Norris 18
Old Faithful 24
Tower-Roosevelt 20
West Thumb and Grant Village 23

CAMPGROUNDS
7th Ranch RV Park 14
Billings KOA Holiday 1
Buffalo Bill State Park Campgrounds 9
Buffalo KOA Journey 10
Cody KOA Holiday 9
Fishing Bridge RV Park 22
Red Lodge KOA Journey 3
Sheridan/Big Horn Mountains KOA 11
Yellowstone Grizzly RV Park 7
Yellowstone RV Park 5
Yellowstone/West Gate KOA Holiday 7

GOOD EATS
Big Sky Farmers Market 16
Bogart's Restaurant 3
Irma Hotel and Restaurant 9
Red Lodge Farmers Market 3
The Virginian Restaurant 10
Walkers 1
WSE's Livingston Farmers Market 15
Yellowstone Valley Farmers Market 1

Note: For a shorter loop that covers many of the highlights, see "Alternative weekend wanderings" at the end of this section. Later in the chapter, we provide details on some of the attractions mentioned in the overview of the longer drive.

Trekking from Billings to Yellowstone

Before setting out from Billings, take a look around town and then head to a unique landmark called **Pompeys Pillar**, 28 miles east of town on I-94. The Lewis and Clark expedition passed this spot in 1806, and William Clark paused to carve his name in the sandstone tower that later acquired other 19th-century graffiti left by fur trappers, missionaries, soldiers, and settlers on their way west.

From **Billings,** head west on I-90, which is also U.S. 212, driving 18 miles to Exit 434 at **Laurel,** and continue to follow U.S. 212 southwest to **Red Lodge.** The pretty town of Red Lodge is a good place to take a rest break; the next 61 miles to Yellowstone are difficult to drive but spectacular to see.

The **Beartooth Highway** is usually open from the end of May or beginning of June, when the snowmelt is sufficient for crews to clear the road, until early to mid-October, when the snowfall begins again in earnest. The switchback twists and turns climb out of Red Lodge at 5,555 feet to the summit of Beartooth Pass at 10,947 feet and then wind downhill to **Cooke City,** elevation 7,651 feet, near the entrance to Yellowstone. Here, the white-knuckled RVer can stop for a break before forging on to **Yellowstone National Park.**

WARNING

The Beartooth Highway is not for the fainthearted or the inexperienced RV driver. Once the switchbacks begin, drivers dare not take their eyes off the road. For RVers in large rigs who don't want to tackle this narrow, twisting road (particularly in dicey weather or high winds), you have an optional route that you find in the section "Must-See Montana and Wyoming Attractions," later in this chapter.

In Yellowstone, the figure-eight-shaped Grand Loop Road enables you to see the major highlights — from **Tower-Roosevelt** to **Mammoth Hot Springs,** south to **Old Faithful,** around **West Thumb** to **Fishing Bridge,** and north again to **Tower Junction** — in a 141-mile circuit.

Heading for Cody and on east

If you've already visited Yellowstone, and don't relish the idea of crawling along in an August traffic jam, you can turn southeast on SR 296 to Cody, Wyoming, before you get to Cooke City. Doing so cuts about 200 miles off the route, allowing you more time for the uncongested parts of Montana and Wyoming. The **Chief Joseph Scenic Byway,** SR 296, runs 46 miles between the Beartooth Highway and SR 120 into Cody. Although paving was completed in 1995, this wonderfully scenic roadway still is deserted, and numerous Forest Service campgrounds — some of them large enough for big RVs — are spread out along the way. You can find primitive camping, incredibly low prices (as little as ten dollars per night), and some of the most spectacular scenery you've ever seen.

Cody is the city most associated with Buffalo Bill because it's where he spent some of his last years. The immense museum of Western history called the **Buffalo Bill Center of the West** is the town's most outstanding sight.

BUFFALO BILL: AN AMERICAN LEGEND

William F. Cody was born in a log cabin in Iowa, signed on as a bullwhacker driving teams of oxen for 50¢ a day when he was 11, and by age 14 was the youngest Pony Express rider ever hired. During the Civil War, too young to be a soldier, he volunteered as a scout, ranger, and messenger with the 7th Kansas Cavalry on the Union side. His nickname, Buffalo Bill, came in the late 1860s, when he was hired to kill buffalo to feed workers building the Kansas Pacific Railroad.

But Buffalo Bill turned out to be bigger than life, thanks to dime novelist Ned Buntline, who told heroic stories about him in cheap paperbacks during the 1870s and 1880s. Cody cashed in on the publicity and created a successful touring show about the Old West with cowboys and Indians, roping and shooting, and stagecoach races around the ring.

Buffalo Bill's Wild West show toured America and Europe for 30 years at the end of the 19th century and the beginning of the 20th. Queen Victoria wrote in her diary that she loved it. (She saw it twice.) The show starred at times such diverse Western characters as crack shot Annie Oakley, Buck Taylor ("King of the Cowboys"), and Chief Sitting Bull, who was paid $50 a week and all the oyster stew (his favorite dish) he could eat.

City fathers of a newly developing town near Yellowstone in western Wyoming persuaded Cody to head up their company because he was "the best-advertised man in the world." He agreed, but with the stipulation that they name the town after him. Cody built a luxury hotel in his namesake town and called it Hotel Irma after his daughter. He moved to Cody after the Wild West show folded in 1913. He died during a visit to his sister in Denver, where he was buried in 1917.

From Cody, drive 47 miles east on U.S. 14 to **Greybull,** and then drop south to **Worland** on U.S. 16, where a wood carving by Peter Toth called Indian Brave, part of his *Trail of the Whispering Giants* collection, adorns the courthouse lawn. The Hungarian sculptor created 50 Native American–style carvings between 1972 and 1988, donating one to each state, and then continued to create them across the U.S. and Canada. His most recent Whispering Giant, #74, dedicated to Tecumseh, was completed in 2009 in Vincennes, Indiana.

The route from Worland continues east, still on U.S. 16, to **Ten Sleep,** a town named for the way local tribes measured the distance between places by how many nights of sleep, along with days of riding, it took to travel between them.

Enjoying the charm of Buffalo

From Ten Sleep, the next 69 miles takes you over the Powder River Pass to the town of **Buffalo,** named not for the bison that used to congregate in this area but for the town of Buffalo, New York. As the story goes, five settlers dropped names into a hat and the winner was a man from Buffalo. The town is worth a visit of several days if you have the time.

Take a walk along Main Street in the historic district for a look at some charming antiques shops, small cafés, and a drugstore with an old-fashioned soda fountain. At the intersection of Main and Angus streets, notice the two wrought-iron **Western sculptures** commemorating the 1892 Johnson County War, a skirmish between big ranchers who wanted to keep the range open and small ranchers and farmers who wanted to fence their lands. One is called *Ridin' for the Brand*; the other, *Living on the Edge.*

Completing the circuit

From Buffalo, drive north on I-25 to the junction with I-90 and continue to **Sheridan,** where Buffalo Bill owned the **Sheridan Inn.**

From Sheridan, I-90 zips north back across the Montana border, where, in about 50 miles, you find **Little Bighorn Battlefield National Monument,** commemorating a battle between 1,500 Sioux and Cheyenne warriors, and 210 troops led by George Armstrong Custer. From the battlefield, drive 50 miles back to Billings on I-90 to complete the tour.

Alternative weekend wanderings

Buffalo Bill country is a little distant for a weekend stopover for most people, but if you're in the vicinity in summer and have a yen to see the best part in a couple of days, plan a driving tour from **Billings** to **Red Lodge,** Montana, over the Beartooth Highway to the Chief Joseph Scenic Byway and into **Cody,** Wyoming, a beautiful drive. In Cody, you can spend relaxing quality time at the Buffalo Bill Center's quintet of museums. There are other fun things to do in Cody, from fly-fishing to hang gliding. Check out this website: www.codyyellowstone.org/see-do.

If you're heading back east to go home, you're not terribly far from **Mount Rushmore** in the Black Hills of South Dakota. You're also near the famous Western town of **Deadwood,** South Dakota, and **Devil's Tower,** Wyoming (made instantly recognizable in the classic science fiction movie *Close Encounters of the Third Kind*). Or head north from Livingston up U.S. 89 to visit **Glacier National Park,** along the Canadian border. As with Yellowstone and Grand Teton, it's possible to visit both Yellowstone and Glacier on one trip.

Must-See Montana and Wyoming Attractions

Beartooth Highway
Red Lodge, Montana

Driving over the 10,947-foot Beartooth Pass is one of America's great thrill rides, especially for an RVer. Even the curves have names like Mae West and Frozen Man. Have your camera ready for once-in-a-lifetime views and be prepared for some roadside snow play, even in warm months. After you hit the road, tackle the switchbacks with caution, especially when you're towing a larger vehicle. Most turnouts along the way are big enough for any RV, so if your courage fails, you can always turn around and go back. The highway is open from late May or early June until early to mid-October, depending on local snow conditions. Driving time is three hours.

REMEMBER

In marginal weather and at the fringes of the late-May-to-early-October season, check the road conditions before setting out by calling the U.S. Forest Service office in Red Lodge at **406-446-2103**.

The alternate route to Yellowstone from Red Lodge is to return to I-90 West and travel to Livingston (which has a fun downtown worth visiting), then south on U.S. 89 to Gardiner and the north entrance to the park near Mammoth Hot Springs. It's a pretty drive, and it parallels the Yellowstone River for much of the way.

Another alternate route is to follow I-90 West to Bozeman, then follow U.S. 191 south to the town of West Yellowstone and the West Gate entrance to the park.

U.S. 212 between Red Lodge and the northeast entrance to Yellowstone National Park, a distance of 68 miles. **406-446-2103** *for road conditions;* www.redlodge.com/beartooth-highway.asp *is loaded with links to great info.*

Buffalo Bill Center of the West
Cody, Wyoming

In the middle of Cody, five world-class museums and a research library are gathered in one sprawling complex that many call the Smithsonian of the West. The **Buffalo Bill Museum** is particularly lively, with posters from his shows, furniture, jewelry, and gifts that European royalty presented to him. You also find

» The **Plains Indian Museum** is magnificent, with life-size figures in various ceremonial dress. Filling the exhibit areas are cradleboards, painted buffalo robes, medicine blankets, bags for carrying ceremonial pipes, grizzly-bear-claw necklaces, and ceremonial garments used in the religious Ghost Dances of the 1890s.

» The **Whitney Western Art Museum,** named for New York sculptor Gertrude Vanderbilt Whitney, displays a replica of artist Frederic Remington's studio and the original studio of Western illustrator W. H. D. Koerner, along with major Western artwork. The H. Peter and Jeannette Kriendler Gallery of Contemporary Western Art celebrates today's artists.

» The **Cody Firearms Museum,** one of the world's largest, and certainly the most detailed of its kind, includes an engraved gun that belonged to **Annie Oakley,** one of the stars of the Wild West show.

» The **Draper Natural History Museum** is an interactive tour of Yellowstone National Park's geology, including a path displaying slabs from different geologic ages and exhibits about current issues, such as the reintroduction of wolves into the environment.

» The **McCracken Research Library** houses a collection of traditional cowboy songs and range ballads, and extensive archives of photographs, documents, films, books, and original manuscripts relating to the West.

Allow a half day to a full day for the entire complex. Days and hours open vary by season ; closed Thanksgiving, Christmas Day, and New Year's Day.

720 Sheridan Ave. **307-587-4771;** https://centerofthewest.org.
RV parking: *Designated lots adjacent to the center. Two-day admissions vary by age.*

Chief Joseph Scenic Byway
Cody, Wyoming

The Chief Joseph Scenic Byway, SR 296, was a favorite of intrepid travelers who didn't mind the gravel roadway. But now this scenic route is completely paved, lightly traveled, and breathtakingly beautiful. Running 46 miles between the turnoff from Beartooth Highway (U.S. 212) to SR 120, 17 miles northwest of Cody, the road is named for the Nez Perce chief who led his tribe through this area in 1877 while fleeing the U.S. Army. The route follows Clarks Fork of the Yellowstone River for the first part of the journey and then turns into a corkscrew of switchbacks as it climbs to Wyoming's highest bridge (8,060 feet) at **Dead Indian Summit**. The road construction, finished in 1995, completed Wyoming's goal to pave all its state highways and links the town of Cody with the Beartooth Highway and the northeast gate of Yellowstone Park. The highway is open year-round. Allow two hours.

SR 296, between U.S. 212 (Beartooth Highway) and SR 120 (17 miles northwest of Cody), a distance of 46 miles.

Jim Gatchell Memorial Museum
Buffalo, Wyoming

With 15,000 artifacts arranged in three interconnected buildings, this museum tells the real story of the Wyoming range wars and the Indian Wars, set out in miniature dioramas. Gatchell was a druggist who collected historical artifacts from the day he opened his drugstore in 1900. Among the collections are dolls, firearms, Crow and Cheyenne beaded deerskin garments, buffalo and horsehide winter coats, and homemade knives confiscated from prisoners in the Johnson County Jail. Allow two hours. Open daily in summer; Monday through Friday in winter.

*100 Fort St. **307-684-9331;** https://jimgatchell.com. **RV parking:** Free city parking lot across from the museum sometimes has space; otherwise, use street parking. Admission varies by age.*

Little Bighorn Battlefield National Monument
Crow Agency, Montana

The famous battle at Little Bighorn lasted less than an hour on June 25, 1876, when a force of at least 1,500 Sioux and Cheyenne warriors, under the leadership of Sitting Bull, Crazy Horse and other chiefs, wiped out

George Custer's troops while two other battalions of the 7th U.S. Cavalry waited on a distant ridge for word to join him. The Sioux Wars against the Plains Indians were the apex of America's treaty betrayals, when the Black Hills that had been given to the Lakota Sioux in 1868 were simply taken back by the federal government, handed over to the waves of miners arriving for the Black Hills gold rush. The cocky, courageous and hot-tempered Custer — underestimating the Plains Indian forces he'd been sent to crush — had rashly decided to divide his 700 troops into thirds to create a pincer action, and then attacked without waiting for the others. All 210 soldiers were killed, in what became known as Custer's Last Stand.

From the visitors center, you walk uphill to a fenced cemetery with tomb-stones that document the soldiers' names, insofar as they were known, and where the men were believed to have fallen. Although accounts vary, estimates put the number of Native American casualties at 150, and 268 cavalry. For non-historians who would like a brief but solid explanation of what happened that June day in 1876, History Channel has an excellent article, *What Really Happened at the Battle of Little Bighorn,* which you can access at www.history.com/news/little-bighorn-battle-facts-causes.

The battlefield is open daily; hours are seasonal, so check online. Allow two hours.

WARNING

Signs caution visitors wandering around the battlefield to watch out for rattlesnakes.

I-90 Frontage Rd. **406-638-2621;** *www.nps.gov/libi.* **RV parking:** *Large lot at visitor's center. Admission charged per vehicle.*

Yellowstone National Park
Yellowstone National Park, Wyoming

On our first visit to Yellowstone, we arrived expecting large doses of natural splendor. But we were overwhelmed by a feeling that we were no longer on planet Earth, like a pair of space travelers scoping out a new planet being born in the steaming cauldron around us. Yellowstone is like a time machine, the biggest ecosystem on Earth containing the plants and animals of a temperate zone before humans arrived. Half the active geysers in the world are here. It's an area of incredible natural beauty, surrounded by five national forests. Yellowstone National Park is unique; it's a bucket-list site you shouldn't miss.

Yellowstone is also quite large — well over 2 million acres and roughly 3,500 square miles. The park is bigger than the states of Delaware and Rhode Island combined. Still, it's pretty easy to find your way around.

There's one main road, the 141-mile-long **Grand Loop Road,** or **GLR,** often described as a figure eight. From this loop road, five roads leading to the five park entrances extend like spokes on a double wheel. The roads are imaginatively named North Entrance Road, South Entrance Road, Northeast Entrance Road, and so on. Even for those who are directionally challenged, it's tough to get lost. An old-fashioned, inexpensive paper map is extremely handy and will help you get your initial bearings.

Visiting the developed areas

You'll find eight developed areas in the park, like small villages, where you have access to hotels and restaurants, convenience stores, gas stations, and a visitor center. These are:

>> **Mammoth Hot Springs,** five miles from the North Entrance, with its technicolor terraces of colored limestone boiling up from the earth, is the area open all year, as is Mammoth Campground. On cold days, large elk congregate around Mammoth, where it's warm. Along with gas, lodging and shopping, you find a post office and medical station.

>> **Tower-Roosevelt,** at the northeast corner of GLR near the famous Tower Fall waterfall and Roosevelt Lodge, has the usual gas, lodging, and convenience store.

>> **Canyon Village,** near the center of GLR and the Grand Canyon of the Yellowstone, is a popular developed area, with several places to eat and the **Canyon Visitor Education Center**. The village was part of Mission 66, a burst of construction in the 1950s to improve roads and visitor facilities. At Canyon village, you're near **Canyon Campground**, which makes an excellent central location for RVers to stop.

>> **Norris,** opposite Canyon Village in the eastern center near the thermal areas of Norris Geyser Basin, is home to **Steamboat**, the world's tallest geyser. **Norris Campground** is here, and so is the Museum of the Park Ranger.

>> **Madison,** southwest of Norris is half a mile from the **Firehole Falls** waterfall. **Madison RV campground** is here, as well as a nice bookstore/information center. This area isn't far from the busy West Yellowstone entrance.

>> **Old Faithful,** at the southwest corner of GLR, is the location of the park's famed geyser. The exhibits in **Old Faithful Visitor Education Center** do much to enrich the whole experience. You find good shopping and lots of services at the equally-famous **Historic Old Faithful Inn and Visitor Center**, with lots of services.

>> **West Thumb** and **Grant Village,** sitting on Yellowstone Lake at the southern end of GLR is a gorgeous area with six stories of excellent lodging, a lakeside restaurant, and a scenic lake cruise. **Grant Village campground** is here.

>> **Fishing Bridge** and **Lake Village** is on the opposite side of the lake from Grant Village. The **Fishing Bridge campground,** with full hookups available, is here. **Bridge Bay Campground,** a medical station, and a ranger station are all near Lake Village.

TIP

Yellowstone's developed areas quickly become the anchors to finding your way around. If you need cell service, hang near one of these areas. Only about half of Yellowstone has cell service, and there's no Wi-Fi park-wide. Wi-Fi is available for purchase in a few spots; ask a park worker where to find the nearest one. On the whole, Yellowstone encourages you to spend a few relaxing days being less connected.

Looking for wildlife

Lamar Valley, in the northeast section of the park, offers good, if distant, animal spotting for herds of bison; we've shot good close-ups during the fringe seasons at **Sylvan Lake** and along the Firehole River at **Lower Geyser Basin.** Bears are a long shot; you may glimpse one from the highway, but sightings from the road are rare now due to the incredibly successful 1970 program to stop bear feeding, which resulted in bears returning to their natural forage. Ask a park ranger where they've seen a bear recently and polish up your long lens.

Everyone's looking for Yellowstone's newest inhabitants, the famed wolf packs. We haven't been lucky yet, but we're told to hang out in Lamar Valley, **Hayden Valley,** or near the canyon, at dawn or dusk. Autumn, just before the park closes for the season, is the best time to see wolves, when they come down from higher elevations. They're not easy to spot; we're told you have to be dogged. No pun intended.

Enjoying Yellowstone activities and seasons

Fishing and canoeing are encouraged at Yellowstone, though you'll need a fishing permit, available at any of the ranger stations or visitor centers. Swimming is not encouraged. It's not really a safe place to swim, with too many rapids and too many rivers or lakes that can be dangerously sulfurous or hot. Actually, **Yellowstone Lake** is forbidden to swimmers for the opposite reason, being dangerously cold. The park does have several recommended swimming holes; ask any ranger or park worker.

Wilderness hiking is another matter. Even if you're an old hand, consult a ranger before you start, and pick up some trail maps in one of the many shops that sell them. You find about 900 miles of trails, sorted into six types, and they sometimes close. Some trails can be steep, unmarked, and unmaintained. You don't want to get lost hiking in Yellowstone, where the cell service is nothing if not undependable.

The park can suffer from "Disney-itis": summer crowds that clog the roads, and restaurants that are expensive and have a long wait, with food that's at best so-so. Grin and bear it, and try to take advantage of outposts that are there to help you. For example, we liked the books and maps and helpful people at the **West Yellowstone Visitor Information Center,** and the **Grand Canyon of the Yellowstone** has plenty of RV parking at a large lot that's a short walk to a dramatic viewpoint. Follow the signs to Canyon Village, where any park worker can help you, or consult the park service site: www.nps.gov/yell/planyourvisit/canyonplan.htm.

Officially, Yellowstone National Park is open all year. In reality, a winter trip is one you've got to do battle for, though the results are worth it for the right person. Only the north entrance is open to autos; the others are closed to non-snow-vehicle traffic, as are many roads and services. This northern area around Mammoth Hot Springs is the winter zone. Some companies specialize in arranging winter travel for Yellowstone and Grand Teton, providing guided tours, snow vehicle rentals, and so on. A winter visit can be a bit pricey, but also a once-in-a-lifetime experience. If you're interested, check out the information at https://travelwyoming.com/article/winter-guide-yellowstone.

Open year-round. Road access is all year from the north entrance, U.S. 89 at Gardiner, Montana; other park entrances are open seasonally but usually closed November through May.

Yellowstone National Park is in the northwestern corner of Wyoming, with spillover into Idaho and Montana. For road and general park information, **307-344-2117;** *www.nps.gov/yell/index.htm. For lodging, dining, and camping reservations,* **307-344-7311;** *www.yellowstonenationalpark lodges.com/.* **RV parking:** *Some designated RV parking in commercial areas and 12 campgrounds with RV camping. Admission varies by vehicle and age.*

YELLOWSTONE IS A WILDERNESS

A few years ago, we bought a book called *Death in Yellowstone,* by Lee H. Whittlesey, one-time park ranger. Maybe a depressing purchase, but it was a fascinating one. We came away with much information that's already on signs posted all over the park. It never hurts to reiterate these basic safety rules, with a reminder: Yellowstone is a wilderness. It isn't Disney's Jungle Cruise, nor is it a state park. On top of that, it's an unusual wilderness, with features you won't find at Great Smoky Mountains, where the common causes of rare deaths are climbing accidents, along with lightning strikes and drownings. At Yellowstone, death can come in a more exotic fashion.

- **Never approach a wild animal on foot.** Don't leave your vehicle when you see wildlife. It's hard to remember, because you get so excited, but realize that you can easily be maimed, or even (rarely) killed. A bored, slow-moving, grass-chewing bison can be bigger than a lot of SUVs and can get spooked and charge you without warning — that's more than a ton of angry pot roast going 35 mph that can leap up or out six feet.

- **If you're a hiker, buy some bear spray and keep it handy, in a "quick draw" position on your body, and don't hike alone.** Before your hike, check with a ranger for the most recent bear info. Stay 25 yards away from wildlife such as elk, but stay 100 yards or more away from a bear. The most dangerous situation is to come upon bear cubs unexpectedly. Back away, and stay away. Momma Bear is nearby and will see you as a threat. If possible, avoid hiking at dawn or dusk, when bear activity is high. Don't run from a bear; you'll set off their chase instinct, and a grizzly can sprint at 35 mph — they will catch you. And RVers, keep all food locked up tight in bear country, or you're liable to have an unexpected guest. Before arriving, go over the bear safety info at the park website (www.nps.gov/yell/planyourvisit/bearsafety.htm).

- **Be very cautious in thermal areas.** People think grizzlies are the most dangerous things in the park (and they are dangerous), but more people have been killed by walking or falling into thermal springs. Never step off designated walkways or boardwalks onto the fragile ground; it can be a very thin, brittle crust with hyperthermal water below. Pets are now prohibited from all thermal spring areas; too many accidents occurred because people were rescuing their dogs. When we visit the hot springs, we leave Sophie comfortably ensconced in the Airstream. (You need to be very careful with pets in Yellowstone. For so many residents of this wilderness, pets are juicy prey.) There are famous geothermal wonders all over Yellowstone: Old Faithful; Norris, Midway, and West Thumb geyser basins; Mammoth Hot Springs. But how hot is hot? The temperature of the water averages between 160 and 200 degrees. Water boils at 212 degrees. In other words, you can easily cook a chicken in this water. Keep that image in mind.

More Cool Things to See and Do in Montana and Wyoming

Montana and Wyoming are full of fascinating sights, activities, and outdoor pursuits. See the following list for some of our favorites; you'll find many more on your driving tour.

>> **Shoot the gunslingers.** Bring a camera, because the photogenic Cody Gunslingers congregate and shoot it out in and around Buffalo Bill's Irma Hotel. Shootouts occur Memorial Day through Labor Day, Monday–Saturday.

   Sheridan and 12th streets, Cody, WY. For reserved seats, call **307-527-7043**; `https://codytrolleytours.com/cody-gunfight/`. *Free, but Cody Trolley Tours offers reserved seats for a small fee.*

>> **Greet a grizzly.** The closest you can safely get to a live grizzly bear is at the **Grizzly and Wolf Discovery Center,** just outside of the Yellowstone West Entrance gate. Here, in a natural habitat, this nonprofit center takes care of aggressive bears, orphaned bears, or bears that just plain got hooked on eating out of garbage cans and have become a problem. You also find a resident wolf pack, some adorable otters, and other wild creatures who need shelter. Allow two hours. Open daily.

   201 South Canyon St., West Yellowstone, MT, near the west entrance to Yellowstone National Park. **800-257-2570** *or* **406-646-7001**; `www.grizzly discoveryctr.org`. *RV parking is available in a designated lot. Admission varies by age.*

>> **Mosey up to the bar.** The first classic Wild West confrontation, or *walk down,* in the pages of Owen Wister's novel *The Virginian,* is said to have taken place in front of the **Occidental Hotel.** The log hotel was opened in 1880 and still welcomes visitors and overnight guests. It contains a gift shop and small museum. Named Best Hotel in the West three times by True West magazine.

   The Virginian Restaurant at the hotel is open Wednesday through Saturday. Or drop in and see the historic bar, The Saloon, which is open daily.

10 Main St., Buffalo, WY. **307-684-0451** *for the hotel,* **307-278-0205** *for the restaurant, and* **307-684-0451** *for The Saloon; www.occidentalwyoming.com/.* **RV parking** *is available on the street or in a free city lot at the corner of Main and Fort streets.*

» **Carve it in stone.** The big, loopy handwriting still is clear behind the framed section of the sandstone pillar: "W Clark, July 25, 1806." William Clark of Lewis and Clark fame couldn't resist leaving his name and the date of his visit carved on what's now **Pompeys Pillar National Monument,** a 700-foot sandstone plug sticking up from the flats along the Yellowstone River east of Billings, Montana. A wooden staircase with handrails leads up 500 steps to the top of the pillar. Allow one hour. Open daily from May through September; visitors may still walk the park in daylight hours when it's closed.

On I-90 at Exit 23, 28 miles east of Billings, MT. **406-875-2400;** *www.blm.gov/ visit/pompeys-pillar-national-monument.* **RV parking** *is available for a fee in a large lot by the visitor's center. Admission is free.*

» **Set 'em up, Bill.** Established in 1893 and now a National Historic Landmark, the **Sheridan Inn** was owned and run by Buffalo Bill; he once auditioned acts for his famed Wild West show on the lawn. Today, the revitalized hotel has 22 rooms, each dedicated to Buffalo Bill and a major figure from his life and our history, from Wild Bill Hickock to the Grand Duke Alexis. At present, the restaurant and **Buffalo Bill Saloon** are closed but scheduled to open in summer 2023.

856 N. Broadway, Sheridan, WY. **307-674-2178;** *www.sheridaninn.com.* **RV parking** *is available on the street.*

KID FRIENDLY

» Brave **an encounter with** Butch Cassidy. Historic buildings from across Wyoming are preserved in a photogenic Western setting at **Old Trail Town.** Mountain man Jeremiah Johnson's grave is in the cemetery, and they've got some original outlaw hideout cabins, such as the **Sundance Kid's Mud Spring Cabin** and **Butch Cassidy's Hole in the Wall Gang Cabin**. Open daily mid-May through September.

1831 Demaris Dr., at the edge of Cody, WY. **307-587-5302;** *www.oldtrailtown. org/.* **RV parking** *is available in a large lot. Admission varies by age.*

Camping Out in the Wild West

Montana and Wyoming are **RV-friendly states** with plenty of public and privately owned campgrounds, good, lightly traveled roads, and wide-open spaces. Although state park and national forest campgrounds don't usually offer RV hookups, the scenery is so great and the vistas so wide that it may be worth the hassle of doing without, at least for a couple days.

Thanks to the brutal winters, most of the campgrounds listed in Table 13-1 (our favorites) are open only seasonally, usually early May to the end of October; a few are year-round. All have flush toilets, showers, and sanitary dump stations unless designated otherwise. Toll-free numbers, where listed, are for reservations only.

Note: If this list seems to have a few too many KOAs, with 6 out of the 11 in Table 13-1, there's a reason. This is KOA country. Even many of the independent private campgrounds are former KOAs.

REMEMBER

KOAs tend to be more expensive. (Those listed as Journey cost less; Holiday and Resort campgrounds cost more.) KOAs also tend to be a bit closer to the highway, which is convenient if you're only stopping for the night. They offer pull-throughs for larger rigs, and various amenities like full hookups that are often missing from public and smaller private campgrounds. We don't use the pool ourselves, but many families have told us their kids love to be able to swim, and all the listed KOAs have pools.

But if saving money is the most important aspect of your trip, see our recommendations for finding great campgrounds on a budget in Chapter 5.

We like the campgrounds we list in Table 13-1. But one problem tends to be universal in this area, not just within Yellowstone, and that's short, narrow campsites. Anything in or near Yellowstone was probably built 50 years ago or more, when the typical RVer was in a car or truck pulling a trailer no bigger than 25 feet. We all know how much has changed since then.

TIP

Many of the campgrounds we cover have pull-throughs and large spaces. If having a large campsite is important to you, make reservations, and try to call the campground itself rather than using online services. That way, you can talk to someone at the desk. They'll do their best to get you into a larger site. To their credit, many old KOAs are attempting to ease this problem by building some high-end sites that have a private patio with a table and chairs. These cost more, but for anyone in a 42-foot Tiffin with five slides towing a Jeep Wrangler, it's probably well worth the cost to upgrade.

TABLE 13-1   **Our Favorite MT and WY Campgrounds**

Name and Location	Contact Info	Cost	What to Know
Billings KOA Holiday; Billings MT	547 Garden Ave.; **800-562-8546** or **406-252-3104;** https://koa.com/ campgrounds/ billings/	$$$–$$$$	Total of 118 sites with water and 30/50-amp electric; 40 full hookups; 90 pull-throughs. CATV, laundry, pool, spa, mini golf, Wi-Fi. This very first KOA opened in 1962. It offers shady sites with gravel or grass, and is well-run and friendly. A spot on the Yellowstone River has freshwater fishing and long pull-throughs with patios. You can buy breakfast and evening barbecue dinners in summer. Open April–Oct.
Buffalo Bill State Park: Lake Shore, North Fork, and Stagecoach campgrounds; Cody, Wyoming	4192 N Fork Hwy; **307-587-9227** or **877-996-7275** for reservations; www. reserveamerica. com/explore/ buffalo–bill– state–park/ WY/1220022/ overview	$–$$	Three campgrounds belong to Buffalo Bill State Park: Two are 9 and 14 miles west on U.S. 14/16/20. Some sites have electric or electric/water hookups. Bargain-priced sites are narrow but attractive, each offering fishing and boating, gorgeous scenery, and abundant wildlife. Reservations required and accepted 4 months in advance; can rent unreserved sites in person. The new Stagecoach Campground is on a first-come, first-served basis. Open May–Sept.; 14-day maximum stay. Lake Shore is open year-round.
Buffalo KOA Journey; Buffalo, WY	87 U.S. 16; **800-562-5403** or **307-684-5423;** https:// koa.com/ campgrounds/ buffalo–wyoming/	$$–$$$	58 sites with water and 30/50-amp electric; 45 full hookups; 37 pull-throughs. Laundry, pool, Wi-Fi, camp store. Great location halfway between Mount Rushmore and Yellowstone. Some larger pull-throughs and 22 private patio sites along the banks of Clear Creek. Freshwater fishing, fenced dog park, kid-friendly playground, and blueberry pancake breakfasts with bacon and sausage in summer. Open all year.
Yellowstone National Park/ West Gate KOA Holiday; West Yellowstone, MT	3305 Targhee Pass, off U.S. 20; **800-562-7591** or **406-646-7606;** https:// koa.com/camp grounds/ yellowstone– park/	$$$–$$$$	Total of 198 sites with water and 30/50-amp electric; 120 full hookups; 64 pull-throughs for large motorhomes. Laundry, indoor pool and spa, large camp store and gift shop. Large sites with patios in a quiet location. Bike rental, tours, nearby horseback riding, and fishing. Daily breakfasts and barbecues in summer. Open May 22–Sept. ***Note:*** A less-expensive KOA Journey is 1½ miles west at 1545 Targhee Pass.

(continued)

TABLE 13-1 *(continued)*

Name and Location	Contact Info	Cost	What to Know
Yellowstone Grizzly RV Park; West Yellowstone, MT	210 S. Electric St.; **406-646-4466;** www. grizzlyrv.com	$$–$$$$	227 full-hookup sites with water and 30/50-amp electric CATV, laundry, Wi-Fi. Wide sites with patios and gravel; deluxe 70-foot pull-throughs. A Good Sam RV park and a good choice for RVers with a car and a desire to spend a few days exploring Yellowstone (the west gate is 4 blocks away). Many nearby attractions, including the Grizzly and Wolf Discovery Center, shops, and restaurants. Open May 1–mid-Oct.
Cody KOA Holiday; Cody, WY	5561 Graybill Hwy.; **800-562-8507** or **307-587-2369;** https://koa. com/campgrounds/ cody/	$$$–$$$$	Total of 101 sites with water and 30/50-amp electric; 62 full hookups; 57 pull-throughs. CATV (some sites), laundry, pool, spa, Wi-Fi. Narrow sites, but some wider with patios. Offers many extras, including free pancake breakfasts daily. Clean, well-run campground with kids' amenities, including pool, playground, and nightly shuttle to rodeo. Great location for seeing the Cody area. Open May– Sept.
Fishing Bridge RV Park; Yellowstone National Park, WY	22 Fishing Bridge RV Park Rd.; **307-344-7311** for reservations; www. yellowstone nationalpark lodges.com	$$$$	Total of 346 spaces, some with full hookups (the only ones in Yellowstone). Laundry and showers. Handy for travelers who want comfort and convenience inside Yellowstone. Nearby gas station and general store. Only hard-sided RVs are permitted; bears and bison wander in at will (so pay attention to posted signs). Some upgraded sites as long as 95 feet. Reserve at least 6 months ahead and choose flexible dates. Open mid-May– early Oct., with dates changeable due to weather.
7th Ranch RV Park; Garryowen, MT	I-90 South Exit 514, Reno Creek Rd.; **406-638-2438;** www. historicwest.com	$$–$$$	52 full-hookup level gravel sites; another 18 water/electric only; all are pull-through. Laundry, showers, playground, self-service RV wash, Wi-Fi that supports streaming. Fishing in Big Horn River, hot tub, walk-up coffee shop, and weekend barbecues in summer. Close to Little Bighorn Battlefield. A Good Sam campground with views of rolling hills and great sunsets. Private horse stalls or corrals available. Open mid-April–mid-Oct.

Name and Location	Contact Info	Cost	What to Know
Red Lodge KOA Journey; Red Lodge, MT	7464 Hwy. 212; **800-562-7540** or **406-446-2364;** https://koa.com/campgrounds/red-lodge/	$$$–$$$$	Total of 49 sites with water and 30/50-amp electric; 25 pull-throughs; 4 deluxe. Laundry, pool, camp store. Restful nights with grass sites, shade trees, and a brook. Trout fishing in nearby Rock Creek. New owners making major upgrades, including deluxe sites, playground, and gem mining. Open May–Sept.
Sheridan/ Big Horn Mountains KOA Journey; Sheridan, WY	63 Decker Rd.; **800-562-7621** or **307-674-8766;** https://koa.com/campgrounds/sheridan/	$$$–$$$$	Total of 97 sites with water and 30/50-amp electric; 43 full hookups; 71 pull-throughs, can accommodate up to 90 feet. Laundry, pool, Wi-Fi. Tree-shaded sites, freshwater fishing, and mini golf. Easy access to interstate, about 150 miles from Cody. Open all year.
Yellowstone RV Park; Gardiner, MT	121 U.S. 89 S; **406-848-7496;** www.rvparkyellowstone.com	$$–$$$	Total of 46 sites full hookups with water and 30/50-amp electric; some pull-throughs. CATV, Wi-Fi, laundry, and showers. At one mile from the north gate, it's convenient when exploring Yellowstone. A Good Sam park with abundant wildlife and sites overlooking Yellowstone River. Use caution when entering campground due to steep grade. Open May–Oct.

Camping in Yellowstone National Park

So, you'd love to stay inside Yellowstone National Park instead of outside the gates. Which is understandable, not just for the natural beauty, but because it can take an hour to drive from the West Entrance to Old Faithful. Pay special attention if you want to book a campsite in Yellowstone, not only because it can be confusing, but because the rules have recently changed. In fact, Yellowstone is, in our experience, the most confusing place to make an RV reservation, with web information that is contradictory.

REMEMBER

Yellowstone has 12 campgrounds that can accommodate RVs (depending on size). For years, many of these were first-come, first-served, but no longer — all 12 now require you to have reservations. There's one exception: Mammoth is the only Yellowstone RV campground open in winter, and the only one for which you need no reservations in winter. The rest of the time, you need to reserve a space. If you want to stay at one of the more developed RV parks during the summer, we'd recommend reserving well in advance of your trip.

Booking with the right operator

Yellowstone has split their 12 campgrounds, and two different entities control reservations. These are your resources for researching and reserving campground space within the park:

>> **The National Park Service** (NPS) website lists (and maps) every Yellowstone campground and its amenities, including length restrictions and costs. (www. nps.gov/yell/planyourvisit/campgrounds.htm).

>> Five campgrounds, the best ones for RVs, are operated by a concessioner called **Yellowstone National Park Lodges,** part of hospitality company **Xanterra Parks and Resorts.** You can reserve these campsites online at www.yellow stonenationalparklodges.com or by contacting Xanterra (**307-344-7311;** www. xanterra.com). These five are **Bridge Bay, Canyon, Fishing Bridge, Grant Village,** and **Madison.**

>> **Seven RV campgrounds** in the park have fewer amenities and shorter spaces. These are operated by the National Park Service and can *only* be reserved online, at www.recreation.gov/camping/gateways/2988. These seven are **Indian Creek, Lewis Lake, Mammoth, Norris, Pebble Creek, Slough Creek,** and **Tower Fall.**

REMEMBER

Only one Yellowstone campground has full hookups, or *any* for that matter: **Fishing Bridge RV Park,** with 346 spaces for around $80 a night. (Refer to Table 13-1 for details.)

WARNING

One warning about Fishing Bridge: No tents and no pop-up RVs with canvas or nylon sides are permitted here. No, the grizzlies haven't been ripping open Coachmen Clippers and devouring the unfortunate inhabitants, but it *is* an area of higher grizzly activity, close to feeding grounds on the Yellowstone River. Hence the long-standing precautions.

RV size does matter

Be sure when you reserve a space at a campground within Yellowstone National Park that your *total* rig's length will fit the available site.

Bridge Bay can accommodate up to 60 feet, and Grant Village 50 feet. But, once you get down to the seven NPS-operated campgrounds, the maximum length of many sites is as short as 25 feet. And remember, you must count the total length of your tow vehicle and trailer, or your motorhome, plus any car you're towing. And no, you can't pay for two spaces and park your truck in the other one. Sorry, them's the rules.

If you're in a small SUV towing a compact TAB teardrop trailer, these restrictions aren't prohibitive, but they're problematic for even medium-sized rigs. So, if you desperately want to camp in Yellowstone, and you either can't get into Fishing Bridge or you'd like a less expensive site, get out your tape measure, go on the NPS website that lists lengths for all 12 campgrounds, and start shopping. Or you may want to take another look at campgrounds outside the park.

Here are a few other facts and tips to consider when selecting your Yellowstone campground:

>> The five Xanterra campgrounds run by Yellowstone National Park Lodges are the superior ones for RVs. For example, all five have dump stations; this is not true of the seven NPS campgrounds.

>> Of all 12 campgrounds, **Pebble Creek, Slough Creek,** and **Tower Fall** are considered primitive campgrounds, without showers or toilets, except a vault toilet. In some areas, designed more for tent campers, you may have trouble even getting an RV in and out. *Note*: due to historic flooding in June 2022, Pebble Creek, Norris, and Tower Fall will probably be closed for the 2023 season.

>> Almost all sites in Yellowstone are back-ins; some of the newest sites at Fishing Bridge are pull-throughs.

>> In all Yellowstone campgrounds (and most of the park), there's *no internet*, and *cell service* is limited.

>> You can't boondock (dispersed camping) with an RV in Yellowstone; only tent campers can get what's called a **backcountry permit** in order to camp outside of the designated campgrounds.

>> If you have a reservation, especially in a shoulder period near the campground's opening or closing dates, check before your arrival to make sure the facilities are open; bad weather can cause late openings, early closings, and, every once in a while, road washouts.

>> Generator use is limited. Only some campgrounds (including Fishing Bridge) permit them, and they enforce quiet time from 8:00 p.m. to 8:00 a.m. Some campgrounds claim to limit you to 60 decibels. On the whole, try to keep generator use limited anyway. People in Yellowstone came for the wonders of nature, and they won't like you much if you're constantly running a generator.

TIP

If you can't get into Fishing Bridge, and you're staying any length of time in Yellowstone, there are dump stations in other campgrounds, like Grant Village; however, these may be only for residents of that campground. There are dump stations at a few other locations throughout Yellowstone — ask a ranger. Potable water is also available in the park, though not always at a dump station. Be sure to use a filter on your hose, which we recommend in all RV parks, especially public ones, with their notorious sandy, rusty, rocky water. Also, most campgrounds outside the five Yellowstone park gates will allow you to dump your blackwater tanks, for a fee. In other words, you may have to drive a bit, but you'll find water and a dump station.

Good Eatin' in the Wild West

Cafés and restaurants in Montana and Wyoming are primarily in towns and cities. If you're craving a Big Mac along the scenic highways, you're going to have a long and hungry wait — best chances for the national chains are at interstate exits. Be thankful that you're carrying your own kitchen and keep the refrigerator well stocked.

Finding a few good restaurants

Here are some restaurants to try out along the way:

>> **Bogart's,** 11 S. Broadway, Red Lodge, Montana (**406-446-1784**; www.bogarts. fun): This spot offers pizza, hamburgers, and Mexican food, along with boutique beer. And bring a bigger-than-Bogart smile. A fan named the restaurant after Humphrey Bogart, whose likeness adorns the place. Fun atmosphere. Open daily.

>> **Hotel Irma,** 1192 Sheridan Ave., Cody, Wyoming (**307-587-4221**; www. irmahotel.com/): The dining room of this wonderful historic hotel serves breakfast, lunch, and dinner. Stop for their famous prime rib, served daily, or lunch and dinner specials such as mountain trout or buffalo burgers. You can even order snacks out on the porch and find buffets throughout the summer. Open daily.

>> **Walkers,** 301 N. 27th St., Billings, Montana (**406-245-9291**; https://walkers grill.com/): Walkers is open only for dinner and serves downright elegant comfort food: meatloaf with gravy and mashed potatoes, rainbow trout, and pork shank. Imaginative takes on down-home classics turn fried bologna and deviled eggs into gourmet delights. You also find great wine, beer, and cocktails. Open daily at 4:00 p.m.

Stocking the pantry and fridge

WARNING

Be sure to stock up on groceries and fuel whenever you see a suitable and convenient spot — don't count on finding another one for quite some time. The rule along this itinerary is, if you see it, buy it, or you may have a long drive to civilization when you run out. With that rule in mind, get started with the ultimate "see it and buy it" food stop.

Farmers markets

There are seasonal farmers markets along our itinerary that are great if their schedule coincides with yours.

>> **Yellowstone Valley Farmers Market,** Billings, MT. 2nd Avenue and N. Broadway (www.yvfm.org/). Open Saturday, July 15 through October 7.

>> **Big Sky Farmers Market,** Big Sky, MT. Town Center at 33 Lone Peak Drive (www.bigskytowncenter.com/farmers-market). Open Wednesday, June 1 through September 28.

>> **WSE's Livingston Farmers Market,** Livingston, MT. Miles Park Band Shell at 229 River Drive (https://westernsustainabilityexchange.org/livingston-farmers-market). Open Wednesday, June 7 through September 13.

>> **Red Lodge Farmers Market,** Red Lodge, MT. Lion's Park, West 8th Street (http://redlodgefarmersmarket.com/ or www.facebook.com/redlodge farmersmarket). Open Saturday, June 24 through September 16.

Supermarkets and not-so-super markets

Plan ahead for grocery shopping because supermarkets, like restaurants, are few and very far between in these areas of Montana and Wyoming. **Billings,** the largest city on the drive, is a good place to stock up. We didn't take this advice seriously enough the first time we did Yellowstone, and we ended up at the **Food Roundup Supermarket** outside the west gate, infamously the only large grocery store near the park; it will remind you of a "supermarket" from 1947. It's okay for a gallon of milk, but our impression was of a small neighborhood market overwhelmed by the masses trying to use it. So, do your level best not to need much of anything, and stock up in the larger towns.

You can find the reliable **Albertsons** supermarket chain (which includes **Safeway** stores) in Billings and in many towns in Montana and Wyoming. There's talk in the wind of a Kroger buyout of the chain at press time, but for now, **Smith's** is the name Kroger operates under in both states.

In **Buffalo,** Wyoming, **DJ's Grocery** on Fort Street (also known as Highway 16) has an adequate selection of bakery items, deli food, groceries, and liquor. Ditto for nearby **Lynn's Superfoods,** which is a small chain in Montana and Wyoming.

If you need them, you also find the big–box stores, including **Walmart,** in Montana at **Billings, Laurel,** and **Livingston;** in Idaho at **Rexburg,** outside Yellowstone; and in Wyoming at **Cody** and **Sheridan,** near **Big Horn.**

DON'T CONFUSE YOUR BISON AND BUFFALO

Give me a home where the buffalo roam. . .

The big, cow-like beasts stomping around in Yellowstone are actually bison, not buffalo.

Buffalo (like water buffalo or cape buffalo) live in Asia and Africa, while *bison* are found in North America and Europe. You don't have to be Jeff Corwin to figure out that they're related, both part of the *Bovidae* family (a scientific Latin term for *great big cow*), though apparently the relationship is fairly distant; bison are closer to yaks, believe it or not. True buffalo look like something from an ancient Egyptian tomb painting, with extra-long curved horns. North American bison have a high hump on their shoulders and back, with bigger heads and shorter horns. They have big shaggy beards, and they shed their thick coats in summer, making them look as if they're molting.

If you don't want to get pegged as a greenhorn, remember that, in Yellowstone, the correct term is bison. And if you don't want to get pegged as an out-of-towner, be aware that buffalo (or bison) turns up on menus and in meat markets all over Montana and Wyoming.

Fast Facts about the Buffalo Bill Route

Area Code
The area codes are **406** in Montana and **307** in Wyoming.

Driving Laws
All RV occupants must wear seat belts in Montana and Wyoming. The maximum speed limit in Montana is 80 mph on some rural interstates (for trucks and RVs, it's 70), with 65 mph posted on urban interstates and two-lane highways. (Montana has lower posted speed limits for night driving.) The maximum speed limit in Wyoming is 75 mph.

Emergency
For road emergencies, call **911** in both states. In Montana, road hazards can be reported to 24-hour dispatch at **855-647-3777**. In Wyoming, to report road hazards anytime, call **800-442-9090**.

Hospitals
Along the route, major hospitals are in Billings, Montana; Cody, Wyoming; and Sheridan, Wyoming.

Information
Resources include the Montana Office of Tourism (**800-847-4868;** www.visitmt.com) and the Wyoming Department of Tourism (**800-225-5996** or **307-777-7777;** https://travelwyoming.com).

Road and Weather Conditions
In Montana, call **800-226-ROAD (7623)** or **511**, or contact the Montana Highway Patrol (**406-444-3780;** www.mdt.mt.gov/travinfo). In Wyoming, call **888-996-7623** or **307-772-0824**, or hit **511** on a cell phone. For conditions in Yellowstone National Park, call **307-344-2117**.

Taxes
Montana does not have sales tax. In Wyoming, sales tax is 4 percent, but local taxes can raise it to 6 percent. State gasoline taxes are 27.8¢ per gallon in Montana and 14¢ per gallon in Wyoming.

Time Zone
Montana and Wyoming are on Mountain time.

IN THIS CHAPTER

» Plotting your New Mexico drive

» Tracking Billy the Kid's path

» X-filing UFO reports in Roswell

» Camping under the stars

» Checking your chile capacity

Chapter **14**

New Mexico: Billy the Kid Meets E.T.

L*and of Enchantment* is New Mexico's longtime license plate slogan, and you can find the natural and cultural magic everywhere. Red rock canyons and mesas meld into blue hills, which, in turn, stand out against snowcapped peaks topping 10,000 feet. *Ristras* (strings of dried red chiles) hang from the eaves of adobe houses, and silver-and-turquoise jewelry twinkles in the windows of battered trading posts. The first inhabitants arrived in the area around 25,000 years ago; their ancient cliff dwellings rest within sheltered rocky overhangs. Native Americans still invoke the spirits of the past with traditional ceremonies, and golden aspen leaves quiver in the first cold puffs of winter wind.

It was here in the 1870s that a slight, cocky New York-born boy named Henry McCarty and nicknamed "the Kid" — also known as Henry Antrim, William H. Bonney and, most commonly as Billy the Kid — entered into Old West legend. In 1945, the world's first nuclear test at the Trinity Site near Socorro broke windows 120 miles away in Silver City, the town where Billy the Kid grew up. And many believe aliens crashed their interstellar spaceship in southern New Mexico in the middle of the 20th century.

In the 21st century, Spaceport America, the world's first purpose-built commercial spaceport, was opened outside Truth or Consequences (60 miles north of Las Cruces); it's home to Virgin Galactic's operations. And southern New Mexico is where, in 1950, a bear cub was rescued from a terrible forest fire, nursed back to health, and sent to live at the National Zoo in Washington, D.C. This cub rose to fame in America's cultural history as Smokey Bear, the animated ranger hat–wearing character who continues to solemnly remind us, "Only you can prevent forest fires."

You can find plenty to see and do all over New Mexico, but this chapter's itinerary concentrates on the southern portion of the state and some of the roads less traveled there. If you want to explore a different part of New Mexico farther north, have a look at Chapter 16, which covers the famed Route 66.

Planning Ahead for a New Mexico Jaunt

Spring and fall are the best seasons to visit New Mexico. Winter brings snow to higher elevations, such as Silver City in the southwest, although the deserts around Carlsbad in the southeast usually have milder winter weather. The portion of our drive between Angus, Sierra Vista, Alto, Ruidoso, and Mescalero on SR 48 and U.S. 70 is ski resort country, with elevations above 7,000 feet, so expect heavy wintertime snowfall. (*Remember:* You may feel occasionally short of breath here, because of the thinner air.)

Keeping seasonal weather in mind

During the winter months, all of New Mexico gets whacked by dangerously high winds, which at times can sideline high-profile RVs. These winds can blow for days at a time. (More than once, we've been trapped for days on end at Las Cruces in early January.) Sustained winds of 30–50 mph are common, and gusts can often hit 70 mph and above — that's hurricane force, and strong enough to roll an average trailer or motorhome! If you plan a trip for this time of year, be sure to check the weather every night and again every morning. *Never* leave your awnings open overnight. And if you see signs along the roadway warning of high winds, take them seriously.

Summer heat sizzles the terrain surrounding Carlsbad Caverns, but the temperature belowground stays steady at 56 degrees F, which is a real treat. Most days are sunny (even in winter). The southern part of the state claims to get 300 days of sunshine per year. But mind the odd differences: The mountains around Cloudcroft get 25 inches of rain a year, while Las Cruces, less than 100 miles away, gets only 8 inches.

Expect to see a torrential late afternoon thunderstorm or two in July and August, and if you're a *boondocker* (off-the-grid camper), never camp in a dry riverbed because of the potential danger from flash floods.

Packing smart and allotting time

When packing, take along sweaters and jackets no matter when you visit. Summer nights are cool — even in the desert. Winter days are cold but usually dry and clear.

Bring plenty of sunscreen when you visit southern New Mexico because the sun's ultraviolet rays can reach your skin instantly through the clear air.

Allow 7 to 14 days to drive this itinerary, with time for visiting Lincoln, and hiking and exploring Carlsbad Caverns.

Exploring the Land of Enchantment

Our trip begins at the farthest tip of West Texas, in **El Paso**. Follow I-10 west and take Exit 6 to SR 28, which winds past pecan groves and chile fields. The route follows the **Rio Grande** north, paralleling I-25 on rural roads to **Hatch**, some 65 miles away. The river that separates El Paso, Texas, from Juárez, Mexico, also irrigates this valley that carries its name. (See Figure 14-1 for a map of our itinerary.)

Throughout this chapter, you encounter multiple spellings of chili/chile/chilli when describing the locally-grown hot peppers and the spicy concoction made from them. We're not illiterate or inconsistent. See the sidebar "How hot is that chile. . ." later in this chapter.

The most famous chile restaurant in this part of the valley is **Chope's Town Bar & Café** in **La Mesa,** favored by the local chile growers for *chiles rellenos* (fresh green chiles filled with cheese, dipped in egg batter, and fried). Chope's also serves the blue-corn version of tortillas, which used to be unique to New Mexico. Look for produce stands selling local chiles, tomatoes, pecans, and melons in season. (*Note*: Many of the eateries and attractions mentioned throughout this section are covered in detail later in the chapter.)

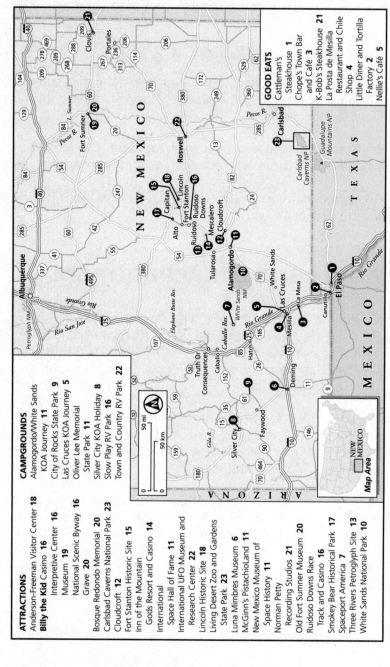

ATTRACTIONS

Anderson-Freeman Visitor Center **18**
Billy the Kid Casino **16**
    Interpretive Center **16**
    Museum **19**
    National Scenic Byway **16**
    Grave **20**
Bosque Redondo Memorial **20**
Carlsbad Caverns National Park **23**
Cloudcroft **12**
Fort Stanton Historic Site **15**
Inn of the Mountain
    Gods Resort and Casino **14**
International
    Space Hall of Fame **11**
International UFO Museum and
    Research Center **22**
Lincoln Historic Site **18**
Living Desert Zoo and Gardens
    State Park **23**
Luna Mimbres Museum **6**
McGinn's PistachioLand **11**
New Mexico Museum of
    Space History **11**
Norman Petty
    Recording Studios **21**
Old Fort Sumner Museum **20**
Ruidoso Downs Race
    Track and Casino **16**
Smokey Bear Historical Park **17**
Spaceport America **7**
Three Rivers Petroglyph Site **13**
White Sands National Park **10**

CAMPGROUNDS

Alamogordo/White Sands
    KOA Journey **11**
City of Rocks State Park **9**
Las Cruces KOA Journey **5**
Oliver Lee Memorial
    State Park **11**
Silver City KOA Holiday **8**
Slow Play RV Park **16**
Town and Country RV Park **22**

GOOD EATS

Cattleman's
    Steakhouse **1**
Chope's Town Bar
    and Café **3**
K-Bob's Steakhouse **21**
La Posta de Mesilla
    Restaurant and Chile
    Shop **4**
Little Diner and Tortilla
    Factory **2**
Nellie's Café **5**

FIGURE 14-1: Map of the New Mexico route.

REMEMBER

Mesilla, the next town north from La Mesa on SR 28, is a must-stop destination, especially for first-time visitors to New Mexico, who can see in one small town all the details — a plaza, a mission-style church, and an abundance of adobe shops and restaurants — that go into creating such tourist meccas as Santa Fe and Taos.

From Mesilla, continue north to Hatch; between here and **Canutillo** to the south, farmers grow most of New Mexico's chiles. This state, where the chile is the official vegetable, leads all the rest in production of the spicy pods. (See the sidebar "How hot is that chile in the chili?" later in the chapter.) From Hatch, turn southwest on SR 26, and then north on U.S. 180, to Silver City.

TIP

An alternative route, if you're driving a small RV and/or traveling in summer, when there's little chance of snow on the roadway, is to continue north on I-25 to **Caballo** and turn west on SR 152 at Exit 63 for a hilly, scenic 86-mile drive into **Silver City**. If you go this way, you won't wind up repeating the drive along U.S. 180 between Silver City and **Deming** on the way back.

Entering Billy the Kid country

Silver City commemorates the youthful Billy the Kid, born Henry McCarty but later known as Henry Antrim (he took the surname of his mother's second husband after she died of tuberculosis). Her grave can be found at 21 Cypress Lane (by the ninth tree from the entrance of the local cemetery on Memory Lane). In 1875, the 16-year-old Kid had the first arrests of his career — for stealing food, and then ten days later for stealing clothes from a Chinese laundry. He was locked up, but he broke out of jail during the night by climbing up a chimney. He ran away to Arizona (making himself a federal fugitive) and severed his ties with Silver City forever. The Kid's legendary status as a Wild West outlaw was cemented over the next five years; he was alleged to have killed at least 21 men (and maybe as many as 24) by his 21st birthday. He didn't live to blow out 22 birthday candles.

Halfway between Silver City and Deming off U.S. 180 is one of our favorite state parks. **City of Rocks** is an eerie collection of gigantic boulders with campsites hidden in, around, between, and under the rocks. These massive rock columns were hurled out of a volcano 34 million years ago, and plopped down in a one-square-mile pile that looks like it was deliberately laid out in lanes and paths. It's a cool place to overnight.

The nearby town of Deming, reached by following U.S. 180 to I-10, is home of the **Luna Mimbres Museum,** said to be the largest free museum in New Mexico, with thousands of exhibits in three different historic buildings.

Exploring the atom, the air, and outer space

From Deming, make the fast trip back east across I-10 to **Las Cruces,** where you join I-25 North and then turn off onto U.S. 70 at Exit 6. About 50 miles up the road is the entrance to **White Sands National Park,** the world's largest gypsum dune field, an improbable 275 square miles of sugar-white sand as fine and soft as powder. You'd be forgiven for thinking it was fresh snowfall.

WARNING

Be aware of occasional closures of Dunes Drive due to active missile testing at nearby White Sands Missile Range. No, we're not kidding.

Alamogordo, where you find the **New Mexico Museum of Space History,** is 10 miles or so up U.S. 70 from White Sands National Park. It's hard to imagine that more than a century ago, this infant town set out as a planned city in 1898 to attract businesses, tourists, and (hopefully) Eastern socialites with plenty of money and culture to throw around on the frontier. When that plan fizzled, Alamogordo — described by one local writer as "miles and miles of nothing but miles and miles" — slept quietly until the 1941 attack on Pearl Harbor plunged America into war. Then all that emptiness was turned into a bombing and gunnery range for training British and American heavy-bomber crews.

Today near Alamogordo, you find **White Sands Missile Range,** the space museum, and nearby **Holloman Air Force Base** (home of several fighter squadrons and unmanned drone programs). Fans of the 2007 *Transformers* movie can spot several locations around town and the base where scenes took place. And for lovers of kitsch, you find a 30-foot-tall concrete sculpture of the World's Largest Pistachio nut outside **Pistachio Land: McGinn's Pistachio Tree Ranch and Country Store,** off U.S. 54/70.

TIP

Ski areas, lavish resorts, golf courses, racetracks, thousand-year-old rock carvings, and museums clustered within a triangular area north of Alamogordo can fill a month-long holiday almost any season of the year — if you're willing to zigzag back and forth to get there. **Cloudcroft,** as cool and romantic a four-seasons town as it sounds, is 19 miles northeast of Alamogordo on U.S. 82.

TIP

If you're interested in archeology or Native American art, follow U.S. 54 north from Alamogordo for 30 miles to find **Three Rivers Trading Post.** Turn east on CR 30 and go 5 miles up the road to the Three Rivers Petroglyph Site, where you find more than 21,000 rock drawings dating as far back as 400 CE, along with a partially excavated prehistoric village. It's considered the best and largest collection of preserved Native American petroglyphs in the country.

Following Billy the Kid National Scenic Byway

It's sometimes odd the people and things we choose to raise to legendary status, and the **Billy the Kid Trail,** tracing the life and exploits of a young killer and outlaw, may be one of the oddest. The official highway route proceeds through the **Lincoln National Forest,** where you're surrounded by the Sacramento Mountains on the south and the Capitan Mountains on the north.

TIP

To get your bearings and plan your stops, first check out the official **Billy the Kid National Scenic Byway** website (https://nsbfoundation.com/nb/billy-the-kid-national-scenic-byway/).

North of Alamogordo at Tularosa, turn east on U.S. 70 for about 30 miles, through the **Mescalero Reservation.** The byway officially begins at **Ruidoso Downs** on U.S. 70, just east of the junction with SR 480 (Sudderth Drive), between Ruidoso and Ruidoso Downs. Just past the **Ruidoso Downs Race Track & Casino,** the **Billy the Kid Interpretive Visitor's Center** (www.billybyway.com/bywaycenter.html) features a museum with a scaled-down, walk-through version of the byway that highlights the various communities and historic sites along its path. At the racetrack, you find the **Billy the Kid Casino,** with 300 electronic slot machines, so you can claim to your friends that you "wuz robbed by Billy the Kid."

Continue east on U.S. 70, and at **Hondo,** the byway turns northwest onto SR 380. (If you choose to skip the byway, you can turn east onto SR 380 from here to Roswell.) Nine miles up the road from Hondo, slow down as you approach **Lincoln,** and watch out for pedestrians as they dart back and forth across the road. Lincoln is the major location for Billy the Kid lore and the site of the **Lincoln County War** (described in the sidebar "Billy the Kid and the Lincoln County War," later in the chapter).

Almost the entire town of Lincoln is a National Historic Landmark and New Mexico State Monument, preserving some 17 structures much as they were in the 1870s when Billy was in his prime. It's considered to be one of the best-preserved frontier towns in the country, even if it doesn't look like the classic saloon-lined ones you remember from old Western movies and TV shows. Pick up a town map and guide at the **Anderson Freeman Visitor Center.**

Eight miles north of Lincoln on U.S. 380, turn southwest onto SR 220 (Kit Carson Road) to visit **Fort Stanton Historic Site.** Many of the players in the Lincoln County War were associated with the fort.

Moving on to bear and alien encounters

Smokey Bear Historical Park in **Capitan** houses the grave of the real-life Smokey, a popular longtime resident at the National Zoo in Washington, D.C. The park features exhibits about forest health and honors the legacy of the bear that warns campers to be sure to put out their campfires before leaving a campsite. Consider overnighting off SR 48, south of Capitan between **Angus, Alto,** and **Ruidoso.** You find almost 20 RV campgrounds and resorts lining this stretch of road back to **Ruidoso Downs,** because you're deep into golf and mountain ski resort country.

Some 50 miles east of Lincoln on SR 380 is the city of Roswell, forever on the map for an alleged UFO incident on or around July 4, 1947. Everything you ever wanted to know about flying saucers and extraterrestrials is on display at the International UFO Museum and Research Center in downtown Roswell.

Getting back to Billy the Kid

Eighty-four miles up the road from Roswell is the village of Fort Sumner, the final resting place of Billy the Kid. Follow U.S. 285 north to SR 20, and then trek another 48 miles through the extremely desolate countryside (be sure to gas up at Roswell first). The gravesite is about 4 miles east of Fort Sumner. The tombstone was stolen twice, taken to Texas for 26 years and to California for 2 years, but it's now securely shackled at the site. Adjacent to the grave is the former Old Fort Sumner Museum, which is now the local Chamber of Commerce office. All of the museum's artifacts were transferred to the extensive **Billy the Kid Museum** at the junction of SR 20 (17th Street) and U.S. 84 (Sumner Avenue). Stop in and see the door he backed through the night he was shot, and the curtains that were hanging in the room.

Just south of the gravesite is the **Bosque Redondo Memorial,** which commemorates the suffering of thousands of Native Americans who were forced to make a 300-mile journey (on foot) — known as the *Long Walk* — to a remote New Mexico reservation. Many died on the walk and afterward on the reservation. The government judged the operation a total failure, and in 1868, the survivors who hadn't died or escaped were permitted to walk back home. There's a museum here.

Follow U.S. 60/84 an hour east to Clovis, where Buddy Holly recorded "That'll Be the Day," "Peggy Sue," and "Maybe Baby" at **Norman Petty Recording Studios,** and then continue south 19 miles on U.S. 70 to Portales, the Valencia peanut capital of the U.S. Another 90 miles driving southwest on U.S. 70 returns you to Roswell.

Completing the route

From Roswell, drive south on U.S. 285 to **Carlsbad,** the site of the incredible **Carlsbad Caverns National Park,** one of the world's largest cave systems, and Living Desert Zoo and Gardens State Park, a wonderful collection of Chihuahua Desert animals, plants, and reptiles.

From Carlsbad, the quickest route back to El Paso is a 165-mile straight shot down U.S. 62/180 past **Guadalupe Mountains National Park,** dominated by 8,749-foot Guadalupe Peak, the tallest mountain in Texas.

This complete drive covers a total of 943 miles.

Weekend wonder

If time is short, you can eliminate parts of this journey to make an accelerated dash to the main attractions. Get an early start from **El Paso,** drive north on I-25 to **Las Cruces,** where U.S. 70 (Exit 8) turns east to **Alamogordo.** Pause to take the Dunes Drive through **White Sands National Monument,** and then continue along U.S. 70 to Ruidoso Downs. The 69-mile **Billy the Kid National Scenic Byway** takes only an hour to cover; allow a second hour for a walking tour around **Lincoln.** If you have kids (or kids at heart) on board, pause at **Smokey Bear Historical State Park** in **Capitan.** And Roswell's **International UFO Museum and Research Center** is a must-stop. Then head south to **Carlsbad Caverns National Park,** allowing a minimum of an hour for a self-guided tour through the Big Room. Return to El Paso via U.S. 62/180.

Without advance reservations, your best weekend bets for campground overnight lodging are around Alamogordo and again around Roswell or Carlsbad.

Must-See Attractions in New Mexico
Carlsbad Caverns National Park
Carlsbad, NM

KID FRIENDLY

Even card-carrying claustrophobics won't mind descending underground to tour the spectacular caverns at Carlsbad, unless the elevator ride from the visitor center down 75 floors spooks them. The general self-guided tour takes an hour (including the elevator ride down and back) and covers a lit circular walkway around a gigantic cavern that's big enough to contain 14 football fields. Highlights include **Hall of Giants, Giant Dome, Lower Cave,** and **Top of the Cross**, with its 255-foot ceiling. **The Bottomless Pit** gave us the shivers, and so did a close encounter with a cluster of sleeping Mexican free-tailed bats.

Touring the caverns

Although kids love the caves, they can't run about freely; all visitors must stay on the pathways. The best tour for preteens is the self-guided tour of the Big Room. Ranger-led tours are more informative, but children may get fidgety, especially with no Wi-Fi or cell service for their smartphones to distract them.

Optional ranger-led tours cover other major areas of the cave system (for extra fees), such as the **Lower Cave, King's Palace, Hall of the White Giant, Left Hand Tunnel** candlelight tour, and **Slaughter Canyon Cave.** Intrepid hikers who want to enter the cavern the same way Jim White first discovered it can skip the elevator down and go in via the steep Natural Entrance.

WARNING

You can't just show up and get into the caverns. Reservations and an assigned entry time are required in advance for all tours. You make reservations online via the Carlsbad Caverns Fees and Passes web page (www.nps.gov/cave/planyourvisit/fees.htm). Making the timed-entry reservation online costs $1, and then you pay the per-person admission fee separately at the visitor's center. If you didn't reserve a tour ahead of time, you can sit in the parking lot and make a same-day reservation online via your smartphone.

Accepting the tour conditions and dress code

REMEMBER

When Mother Nature was doing her thing down in her subterranean laboratory, she had no interest in making the caves family-friendly or ADA-compliant. The main tour of the Big Room is easy for just about everyone, but each optional tour has its own physical requirements, limitations, and restrictions, so be sure you study the details online carefully before reserving. Some are "slip 'n slide" tours, without permanent lighting, trails, or facilities, and some tours may require you to crawl on wet rock floors, in extreme cases.

Other tours involve major hiking or climbing. For example, the Lower Cave has 60 feet of ladders and a knotted rope walk; the entrance to Slaughter Cave is a 30- to 40-minute hike from the parking area. You don't need to be an experienced *spelunker* (cave explorer), but these tours may be strenuous and are not really appropriate for less-limber adults or small kids. Children under 6 are typically not permitted on most of them. Extra tours have separate fees for adults and must be reserved in advance of your arrival.

TIP

Wear low-heeled, nonskid walking shoes, and anticipate a walk of approximately one mile inside the Big Room. Hiking boots are highly recommended — do not wear sandals, flip-flops, or dress shoes in the caves! Take a jacket; even when the outside temperature climbs to 97 degrees F, the temperature inside the caverns always is a cool 56. The Big Room is lit up and safe for visitors, but you're welcome to bring your own flashlights.

Respecting the cave bats and minding the rules

REMEMBER

The cave bats are *not* interested in anything about you; they *don't* want to nibble your neck, and they *won't* lay eggs in your hair and make you go crazy.

Most of the bats hang out far from the main tour routes with one exception: Visitors can gather every evening between May and October at bat flight time in an amphitheater at the Natural Entrance to watch the 300,000-member colony speed out at the rate of 5,000 bats a minute in search of their evening meal, 3 tons of insects. (Think of it this way — that's 3 tons of mosquitoes and flies that won't pester you around the campsite.) Unfortunately, the local bat population has been infected with a disease-carrying mold in recent years, so some sensitive areas may be restricted to the public or require very strict sanitary measures before entering. Don't be surprised if rangers ask you to change into a freshly laundered shirt and wipe your shoes off.

No pets are allowed in the caverns, but kennels are available if it's extremely hot outside and you can't leave your RV's air conditioner running for your little buddies. (Be sure to bring proof of Fido's up-to-date vaccines.)

The visitor center and Big Room are open daily; the last tour by elevator leaves at 3:30 p.m. Closed Thanksgiving, Christmas Day, and New Year's Day. Allow at least a half day here.

3225 National Parks Hwy. **888-900-CAVE (2283)**, **575-785-2232** *for information, or* **877-444-6777** *for reservations;* www.nps.gov/cave. ***RV parking:*** *Designated area in a large lot at the visitor center entrance. Admission varies by age and tour type. An America the Beautiful Pass covers your entrance fee.*

EXPLORING THE WONDERS OF CARLSBAD CAVERNS

Deep beneath the Guadalupe Mountains and the Chihuahua Desert, a magical wonderland of nature unlike anywhere else on Earth awaits you at **Carlsbad Caverns National Park**.

In 1898, a 15-year-old self-described broncobuster named Jim White was riding through the desert one afternoon, mending fences and rounding up stray cattle, when he spotted what he first thought was either a desert whirlwind or smoke from a volcanic explosion on the horizon. It turned out to be a cloud of thousands of bats emerging from a small opening in the ground for their nightly feeding. He later wrote that "any hole in the ground which could house such a gigantic army of bats must be a mighty big cave." He eventually returned with a lantern, a hatchet, and fence wire, fashioned a crude ladder, and descended into what is indeed one of the mightiest, biggest caves in the world.

Some 265 million years ago (give or take a million), this area of New Mexico was beachfront property — part of the rugged coastline of an inland sea rimmed by a limestone fossil reef. Water and wind pounded the coast, wearing at the limestone, but after the sea receded and the water evaporated, rainwater mixed with underground sulfurous spring water kept gushing and running and seeping and dripping, interacting with the minerals in the rock. The result many geological epochs later is an unbelievable variety of stalactites, stalagmites, delicate "soda straw" formations, multicolored mineral deposits, popcorn-shaped outcroppings, and more. The caves you see here today have never stopped changing, but they've looked this way for the last million years or so.

At least 119 different subterranean caves have been found and explored at Carlsbad Caverns. The main area that's open to tourists (the Big Room and some attached chambers) is only a tiny part of more than 40 miles of passages in a single cave. (Nearby Lechuguilla Cave has at least 140 miles of passages — so far!) What you see are most of the areas White discovered and gave evocative names to by the dim illumination of his kerosene lantern.

A huge bat population resides in the caves at Carlsbad today. (A century ago, their poop — known as *guano* — was valuable as both a fertilizer and an ingredient in gunpowder.) Throughout the summer and early fall, you can still see bats erupting out of the cave at sunset and darkening the sky overhead. Because of the very delicate subterranean ecosystems, most of the caves in the park are off-limits to the public and require special permits and supervision to enter. Various tours with many options are available to the public, but Carlsbad Caverns requires advance reservations for all tours.

International UFO Museum and Research Center
Roswell, New Mexico

The **International UFO Museum and Research Center,** opened in 1991, was founded by key figures who were in Roswell and close to the events of July 1947. The museum is located downtown in a 1930s-era Art Deco movie theater, where you find dioramas and displays describing the famous incident, along with the various official explanations given by the U.S. military over the years. For researchers, it's also the repository of the world's largest collection of UFO encounter reports and documentation. A large gift shop does brisk sales in UFO souvenirs and T-shirts. Open daily; allow two hours. (We talk more about this museum in Chapter 19.)

114 S. Main St. **575-625-9495;** *www.roswellufomuseum.com.* ***RV parking:** Street parking; city streets are wide enough for RVs to park comfortably. Admission varies by age*

UFOs: THE ROSWELL INCIDENT

Although the details of the most famous UFO event in history often are confusing or conflicting, it seems irrefutable that *something* happened near Roswell in the hot summer days of 1947. The truth, as they say, is out there.

In June 1947, a pilot named Kenneth Arnold made national news after reporting a sighting of what he described as nine shiny, supersonic "flying saucers" or discs near Mount Rainier in Washington state. Two weeks later, on July 4, a sheep rancher named Mac Brazel came across a pile of odd-looking debris as he was riding through his rural property surveying storm damage from the night before. Without a phone, newspapers, radio, or television at the time, Brazel had heard nothing about Arnold's highly publicized story, or the national craze it had set off. The next evening, he drove from his isolated ranch into the town of Corona, about an hour away, where he heard the flying disc story for the first time.

This part of New Mexico had several important military bases, airfields, and top secret research facilities during and after World War II — the Trinity Site, where the first atomic bomb was exploded, is just outside nearby Alamogordo. Brazel became concerned that the U.S. military would want to know about the odd wreckage he found that had obviously come from the sky, especially if it was from some foreign power's aircraft. So he went home, gathered up the debris, and drove it to the sheriff's office in nearby Roswell,

(continued)

(continued)

where Roswell Army Air Field was. The debris was handed over to Major Jesse Marcel, who visited the ranch and recovered more pieces. After examining everything for several days, Air Force public information officer Walter Haut issued a press release stating that the debris was apparently wreckage from a "flying disc" and it had been passed along to "higher headquarters."

But the next day, the Air Force released a different story, explaining that the tin foil, rubber, thick paper, tape, and wood items recovered from the Brazel ranch had come from a weather observation balloon that was fitted with a reflective, kite-like attachment to study wind currents and make it easier for ground observers to spot and track its progress. In other words, Lieutenant General Roger Ramey essentially told the press and the rest of the world, nothing to see here.

The incident pretty much ended there, but new interest arose in 1978 when Marcel told an interviewer that the recovered wreckage was no balloon, but was, in fact, extraterrestrial in nature. The release of the UFO movies *Close Encounters of the Third Kind* in 1977 and *E.T. - the Extra Terrestrial* in 1982 suddenly put Roswell on the radar screens for UFO believers and investigators. The "Roswell Incident" soon became regular material for the spate of unexplained mystery and ancient alien TV programs that mushroomed in popularity.

Consequently, the town took on a tongue-in-cheek attitude about its flying saucer reputation. One city brochure is headlined "Some of our most famous visitors . . . came from out of state." Indeed, some 200,000 visitors a year come from around the world to find out about the July 1947 "Roswell Incident" and other purported UFO sightings. (It's such a big secret that *everybody* knows about it!)

Lincoln Historic Site
Lincoln, New Mexico

**KID
FRIENDLY**

Don't blink as you arrive in **Lincoln** — the handful of small, primitive buildings snugged right up against U.S. 380 really do make up the whole village. Lincoln is a time capsule, preserving some 17 places much as they were in the 1870s. President Rutherford B. Hayes famously called the town's main street "the most dangerous street in America" during Billy the Kid's lifetime; visitors were in serious danger of dying from .45-caliber "lead poisoning." Fortunately, the biggest danger visitors face today is dodging cars as they cross the highway. Don't bet on Wi-Fi or cell service here.

You can find six different museums in this short stretch of road, and with only one street here, you really can't get lost. If you can't see it all, here are the highlights:

>> **Anderson Freeman Visitor Center** offers a self-guided walking tour map of the town, which features historical exhibits in a timeline starting with Native American prehistory and ending with the Lincoln County War. Operated by the state of New Mexico, this is considered the best-curated museum in the area. Open Thursday through Monday; paid admission.

>> **Tunstall Store** contains displays of 19th-century merchandise in its original 1870s display cases, along with the Tunstall residence next to the store. Today, it's probably the best gift and book shop in town. This was the place of business that was the crux of the Lincoln County War. In fact, the graves of John Tunstall and Alexander McSween are out in the lawn on the side of the store.

>> The museum in the **Old Lincoln County Courthouse** (also known as the Murphy-Dolan store, or the Big House) provides details of the Lincoln County War, along with the building's use as a courthouse, jail, bar, billiard parlor, Masonic hall, and Lawrence Murphy and James Dolan's general store. Billy the Kid made his final escape from here after killing deputies J. W. Bell and Bob Olinger. (Chris was excited to see that the 1870s Masonic hall has been re-created on the top floor and that the Grand Lodge of New Mexico holds a meeting here every year.)

Lincoln's historic landmark designation prevents modernization, which means you find no glitzy signage anywhere, no McDonald's or truck stops, and no giant parking lots, and the front doors of several buildings open right onto the road's shoulder. Here's some additional info you should know:

>> You won't find any restaurants in town, but for liquid refreshments, there's **Annie's Little Sure Shot** coffee and espresso bar (http://annieslittlesure shot.com) across from the courthouse, and **Bonita Valley Brewing Company's** microbrewery and taproom (www.bonitovalleybrewing.com/), which often has live music. The microbrewery is the town's principal hangout, but it's a lot quieter and a whole lot safer than the saloons that were here back in the day. During tourist season, it isn't unusual to find food wagons set up on the street.

>> If you're in the area the first week in August, **Old Lincoln Days** is a big living history event, with re-creations of Billy's last escape, complete with shootouts (referred to as The Last Escape of Billy the Kid folk pageant). And in mid to late October, the **Día de los Muertos** (the Day of the Dead) festival celebrates the Mexican heritage of the town.

*U.S. 380. **575-653-4025;** https://nmhistoricsites.org/lincoln. For recent news, check the **Friends of Historic Lincoln** website (http://www.oldlincoln town.org) and Facebook page (https://www.facebook.com/friendsofhis toriclincoln). **RV parking:** Almost all parking is along the street, but you find a large RV-friendly lot at the north end across from the amphitheater and smaller lots behind the visitor's center and the old courthouse museum.*

BILLY THE KID AND THE LINCOLN COUNTY WAR

When soldiers from nearby Fort Stanton wanted to have a hot weekend, get blasted and forget about their miserable lives out in the middle of nowhere, Lincoln was where they went. Every Western movie cliché you've ever seen about outlaws, gunslingers, family feuds, ride-by shootings, cattle rustling, jail breaks, corrupt sheriffs, cattlemen vs. farmer shootouts, and powerful businessmen killing greedy rivals — all of it happened (and more) in little Lincoln in the 1870s.

The Murphy-Dolan General Store in Lincoln had the corner on lucrative government contracts to provide beef and other supplies for nearby Fort Stanton to the north, and the Mescalero Apache Reservation to the south. Proprietor Lawrence Murphy had been tossed out of having a store in the Fort itself, so he built his new two-story building in nearby Lincoln, and made it big enough to accommodate a bar, a pool hall, a Masonic meeting hall, plus the local jail, courthouse and county offices, along with his own establishment. His building became known as "the Big House." Accusations of ruthless, monopolistic practices against Murphy and his partner James Dolan were plentiful, which is not surprising since they were also the biggest source of credit to local landowners, residents and business people.

Meanwhile, a Texas land baron named John S. Chisum had expanded into Lincoln in 1874, and became a financial and political rival of Murphy's. When two newcomers, a Kansas lawyer named Alexander McSween and a young English adventurer named John Tunstall, opened a rival general store and bank just down the street, Murphy and Dolan figured that Chisum had helped fund the new enterprise to spite them. Their feud over the competition, and the expanding corruption and overall lawlessness, made Lincoln one of the most dangerous towns in America.

Matters came to a head early in 1878 when Sheriff William Brady dispatched a posse to take over Tunstall's ranch, claiming that the Englishman's partner McSween owed Murphy money. In the ensuing argument, Tunstall was shot and killed, and that might have ended the trouble then and there if Tunstall hadn't previously befriended and hired an 18-year-old cow puncher calling himself William H. Bonney. Bonney — the new alias taken by Henry Antrim, also known as Billy the Kid —swore to avenge his friend's death.

The Murphy-Dolan team had Sheriff Brady and his deputies (nicknamed "The Boys") on their side, and it was enormously handy that the Lincoln jail, sheriff's office, and court-house were located inside of their store. Billy the Kid and his "Regulators" had Dick Brewer, the newly appointed Lincoln County constable and former foreman for the Tunstall Ranch on their side. Brewer "deputized" Billy the Kid and some of his friends, and within days they had captured and shot two of Sheriff Brady's posse. On April 1st, Billy and his Regulators crouched in ambush by the Tunstall Store as Brady and his depu-ties walked toward the Wortley Hotel. Shots rang out, Brady keeled over into the street, and the deputies scattered for cover.

After a shootout at the Chisum Ranch, Billy and his men took refuge in the McSween home, next door to the Tunstall Store. The Murphy-Dolan Boys surrounded the house and fired into it from a vantage point atop a nearby hill. At dusk on July 19th, they set fire to the house. Billy the Kid and several others made a successful dash for freedom and escaped into the underbrush.

Finally, an exasperated President Rutherford B. Hayes appointed former Civil War General Lew Wallace (soon-to-be author of the blockbuster novel *Ben Hur*) as Territorial Governor to involve the army and finally bring serious law and order to the chaotic region. Wallace met secretly with Billy and promised him a full pardon if he would give testimony against Dolan and The Boys for murdering the lawyer of McSween's widow. The Kid agreed and appeared at the trial, but his pardon never came.

After three years on the lam, Billy was captured in 1880 by Sheriff Pat Garrett, who had been elected on the promise he would arrest the Kid and bring him to justice. Billy was brought to Mesilla for trial, found guilty of killing Sheriff Brady, and sentenced to be hanged. He was removed to the Lincoln County Jail, where he escaped again, overpow-ering and shooting his two guards. The Kid hid out in the Fort Sumner area at ranches belonging to several different Hispanic families, but in July 1881, Sheriff Garrett finally caught and shot the Kid in a darkened bedroom of one of the houses.

Within six weeks of his death, the dime novelists, including Garrett himself, got hold of Billy the Kid, and an American myth was born.

If you're hunting simplified storytelling about the Lincoln County War and Billy the Kid, John Wayne portrayed cattleman John Chisum in the 1970 film *Chisum,* which tells a fic-tionalized version of the feud. Director Sam Peckinpah's 1973 film *Pat Garrett and Billy the Kid* with James Coburn as Garrett and singer Kris Kristofferson as Billy has more than its

(continued)

(continued)

share of fiction in it. John Wayne's son Patrick Wayne played Sheriff Garrett in the much more historically accurate 1988 film *Young Guns,* which featured Emilio Estevez as Billy, Jack Palance as Lawrence Murphy, and Charlie Sheen as Dick Brewer, along with Kiefer Sutherland, Lou Diamond Phillips, and Terence Stamp.

In 2022, EPIX streaming service released the limited series *Billy the Kid,* which traced the outlaw's life from his family's roots in Ireland, his childhood move from New York to New Mexico, his youth in the American West, and his involvement in the Lincoln County War. It featured Tom Blyth as Billy, Vincent Walsh as Murphy, and Alex Roe as Garrett.

Grab the popcorn, but just remember, these are movies, not necessarily good history.

Living Desert Zoo and Gardens State Park
Carlsbad, New Mexico

**KID
FRIENDLY**

The stars of the show at Living Desert are its birds and animals, all of them native to the **Chihuahua Desert**, most of them brought here because of injury or illness and scheduled to be released back into the wild. Those too ill or too old to return stay on. A pack of endangered Mexican wolves also makes its home here. The setting is a hilltop covered with native cacti and other plants. A well-manicured trail wends its way through the terrain — the design of the path brings surprises at every turn. Kids have a chance to see the animals in a natural environment. In the gift shop, you can buy all sorts of tie-in clothes and toys. Plan to visit in the cooler early morning hours, when the animals are more active. Open daily; final tour at 3:30 p.m. Allow at least two hours.

Skyline Drive off U.S. 285 north of Carlsbad. **575-887-5516;** `https://living desertnm.org/.` **RV parking:** *Large paved lot in front of the museum. Admission charged per vehicle.*

New Mexico Museum of Space History
Alamogordo, New Mexico

**KID
FRIENDLY**

You can't miss this gold-tinted, four-story glass tower as you drive south on U.S. 54. Here you find an outdoor display area with rockets, an Apollo test launch vehicle, the air-powered Daisy Decelerator sled track, and an early test model of the secretive X-37 Air Force space plane. Several exhibits highlight the pivotal role New Mexico played in the space program, and you see displays explaining what life in space is really like. The distinctive museum building also houses the **International Space Hall of Fame, New Horizons Dome Theater and Planetarium,** and **Astronaut Memorial Garden** (the final resting place of Ham the Astrochimp — the first great ape launched into space as part of testing for Project Mercury in 1961). The museum offers year-round Rocketeer Academy classes and summer camp experiences for kids. Open Wednesday through Monday. Allow at least two hours for the museum, more depending on how far out you are.

At the end of SR 2001. **575-437-2840;** *www.nmspacemuseum.org.* **RV parking** *in a lot. Admission by age for the museum and theater.*

White Sands National Park
Alamogordo, New Mexico

KID FRIENDLY

Imagine the lure of 60-foot pure white gypsum sand dunes sparkling in the sunlight. Your first reaction on seeing the gently drifting white mounds is that the sand looks just like snow — and indeed, the gift shop sells sleds in case you want to zip down the slopes on your own Flexible Flyer. For new visitors, all sorts of discoveries await, from the bleached earless lizard, which camouflages itself by turning white, to the handful of plants tough enough to survive the constantly shifting sands. On nights during a full moon, park rangers or special guests present "howling at the moon" evenings.

The **Dunes Drive** goes 8 miles into the heart of the dunes, turns at a circle, and then comes back out the same way. A picnic area, boardwalk, and two hiking trails are reached from turnouts along the drive. Allow one hour for a visit to the dunes and boardwalk, or more if you want to hike or picnic. Visitor's center open daily; closed on Christmas Day. (Note: Dunes Drive may be closed when testing is taking place on White Sands Missile Range.)

WARNING

No one is allowed to drive across the dunes, but hiking is permitted. Be aware that you can get lost *very* easily because few landmarks exist, especially if a windstorm produces a whiteout. The powdery white sand blows easily and can penetrate your RV even when doors and windows are closed. And *please* don't try to take home a jar of sand to show your friends. Leave it for the next visitors to discover.

15 miles southwest of Alamogordo on U.S. 70/82. **575-679-2599;** *www.nps. gov/whsa.* **RV parking:** *Parking lots at visitor's center and at frequent turnouts along Dunes Drive. Admission is per vehicle or individual.*

THE TRINITY SITE: TESTING THE FIRST ATOMIC BOMB

Due north of White Sands National Park, in the middle of White Sands Missile Range — about 50 miles as the crow flies — is the Trinity Site. This closely guarded area is where the world's first nuclear bomb was tested on July 16, 1945. A stone memorial stands at Ground Zero, where the force of the blast melted the dirt in the area into a strange green glassy substance called *Trinitite*.

The site is open to the public just two days a year: the first Saturdays of April and October, when tours are conducted from Alamogordo. Cars line up in single file with headlights on and proceed behind a military escort to Ground Zero. You also can visit the ranch house where "the Bomb" was assembled. Some radiation from the original blast remains at the site. For more information, call the Alamogordo Center of Commerce at **575-437-6120.**

More Cool Things to See and Do in New Mexico

New Mexico is full of fascinating sights. What follows are more of our favorites. In addition, you may want to try your luck at Inn of the Mountain Gods **Resort & Casino (800-545-9011** or **575-464-7777;** https://innofthemountaingods.com/), east of Tularosa on U.S. 70.

>> **Hold the fort.** Just up the road from Lincoln, stop at **Fort Stanton Historic Site,** established in 1855 as a base of military operations against the Apache people. It's considered one of the most intact 19th-century forts in the U.S. Over the years, soldiers here clashed with Apache, Mescalero, and Kiowa tribes, and the fort was briefly seized by the Confederate Army during the Civil War. After the 1890s, the fort became a tuberculosis hospital for sailors in the Merchant Marine. And during World War II, it was used to intern German prisoners of war, as well as people the Justice Department called German and Japanese "troublemakers."

But the fort was also a big part of the Lincoln County War and the saga of Billy the Kid. General Lew Wallace stayed here during his mission to finally bring law and order to the region. The museum covers all eras of the fort's history, including the *Buffalo Soldiers* (Black soldiers) of the 9th Cavalry and the 24th, 57th, and

125th Infantry who were stationed here. Open Thursday through Monday. Allow at least an hour.

> *104 Kit Carson Rd. **575-354-0341;** www.fortstanton.org/. Admission varies by age. **Note:** If you want to overnight close by, you find Rob Jagger Campground on Kit Carson Road on your way to the fort. It's a Bureau of Land Management campground with 27 water/electric RV sites — first come, first served.*

>> **Visit Billy the Kid's grave.** If you have the time and inclination to make the long, arid drive up to Billy the Kid's grave and visitor's center in Fort Sumner, you may appreciate how long it took the outlaw to reach this destination on horseback. The Kid's tombstone is now securely set inside a fenced site after being stolen several times over the years. Open daily. Give yourself at least half a day.

> *3501 Billy the Kid Road (SR 272), Sumner. **575-355-7705.**The former Old Fort Sumner Museum located at the gravesite is now the office for the local Chamber of Commerce, but its artifacts have all been transferred to the Billy the Kid Museum, as noted in the list. **RV parking** is available in a large lot at the gravesite.*

Take the time to poke around and check out the other local museums, including:

- *Bosque Redondo Memorial* tells the tragic story of the enforced removal of almost 10,000 disparate, nomadic Navajo and Apache people from Arizona and New Mexico to this isolated reservation along the Pecos River in the 1860s. The museum is open Thursday through Sunday. Admission varies by age.

- *Billy the Kid Museum* contains an amazingly extensive collection, with more than 60,000 artifacts about Billy and the Lincoln County War, along with displays about buggies, wagons, and the rugged life in the New Mexico frontier of the 19th and early 20th centuries. The collection once housed at the Old Fort Sumner Museum next to his gravesite was recently moved to this location. Billy the Kid's Museum has been operated by members of the Sweet family for over 100 years. Open Monday through Saturday; closed holidays.

> *Bosque Redondo Memorial: 3647 Billy the Kid Rd. **575-355-2573;** www.nmhis toricsites.org/bosque-redondo. No specific **RV parking**, but there's a large, free parking lot, and street parking is also available.*

> *Billy the Kid Museum: 1435 Sumner Ave. **575-355-2380;** www.billythekidmuseum fortsumner.com/index.html. Admission varies by age. **RV parking** on the street. **Note:** The well-regarded Good Sam-rated Valley View RV Park is next door, in case you want to overnight here.*

>> **Take a walk in the clouds.** The town of **Cloudcroft**, at an elevation of 9,200 feet and surrounded by 500,000 acres of Lincoln National Forest, is a cool, pretty spot for a morning or afternoon pause if you tire of the hot valley climate. The lodge, built in 1899, still welcomes visitors to its restaurant, and a ski slope, golf course, and quaint Western-style boutiques provide distraction.

Be aware that snow in winter may require tire chains in this region; check conditions before leaving the Alamogordo area.

1001 James Canyon Hwy (Chamber of Commerce). **575-682-2733;** *www.newmexico. org/places-to-visit/regions/southeast/cloudcroft/.* **RV parking** *is available on the street.*

>> **Wade hip-deep in New Mexico culture.** On the way to or from Silver City, pause at the **Deming Luna Mimbres Museum,** which is housed in a 1917 brick armory, to see some good examples of local black-and-white Mimbreño pottery, one of the most elegant tribal collectibles. The museum also is a starting point for a self-guided walking tour of the historic town (maps are available). This museum claims to have "New Mexico's largest collection of exhibits," and that doesn't seem to be an idle boast: Its almost endless array of artifacts encompasses frontier life, military history, geology, Native American culture and art, legendary Western characters (including Pancho Villa), and local lore and heritage. Open daily. Allow at least one hour; add an hour for the walking tour.

301 S. Silver St. **575-546-2382;** *www.lunacountyhistoricalsociety.com.* **RV parking** *is plentiful on the street. Admission is by donation.*

>> **Help prevent forest fires.** If you didn't know that there's no "the" in Smokey Bear, you discover it right away at **Smokey Bear Historical Park.** When firefighters found a badly singed bear cub clinging to a burnt pine tree near Capitan in 1950, a cartoon Smokey Bear in a ranger costume had already been informing campers about the dangers of forest fires for five years. The young black bear was given the name Smokey, and when his burns healed, he was sent to the National Zoo in Washington, D.C., where he was a visitor favorite. After Smokey died in 1976, he was returned to Capitan for burial. The visitor's center tells Smokey's story and features displays about forestry, wildfires, modern forest ecology, and more. Kids can become Little Rangers through a program about fire prevention. Open daily; closed major holidays. Allow two hours.

118 Smokey Bear Blvd., Capitan. **575-354-2748;** *www.emnrd.nm.gov/sfd/ smokey-bear-historical-park/.* **RV parking** *is available in a designated lot. Admission varies by age.*

>> **Spot the petroglyphs.** At **Three Rivers Petroglyph Site,** you can see some 21,000 petroglyphs (images scratched, carved, or chiseled into a rock face). The pictures of people, animals, fish, and reptiles were carved by the Jornada Mogollon people between 400 and 1400 CE. A path winds for a mile through the hilltop site. Open daily from sunrise to sunset. Allow two hours, or more if you want to do additional hiking.

TIP

Two RV sites with water and 30-amp electric hookups are available if you want to overnight here (first come, first served). Fees are cash or check only; rangers won't make change. This is Bureau of Land Management land, so you can boondock here as well.

455 Three Rivers Rd., Tularosa. **575-525-4300;** *www.blm.gov/visit/three-rivers-petroglyph-site.* ***RV parking*** *is available in a large lot at the site. Admission is per vehicle.*

>> **Sign up for the next spaceflight.** Richard Branson's space tourism operation, Virgin Galactic, is located at **Spaceport America,** which sits in the desert between Las Cruces in the south, Truth or Consequences in the north, and White Sands Missile Range in the east. New Mexico's Spaceport is the first purpose-built commercial space facility in the U.S., and it's here that Virgin develops and launches their spacecraft — the VSS *Unity* mother ship, and the VSS *Imagine*, their space-going passenger vehicle. The first passengers flew in July 2021, and once Virgin begins regularly scheduled flights, this is where you'll be training and departing from. The current reservation price is a trifling $450,000 (sorry, no AARP discounts available).

Because this is an active, secure aircraft construction and testing site, you can't just show up at the gate to tour the spaceport. Guided bus tours operated by Final Frontier Tours (**575-267-8888;** www.spaceportamerica.com/visit/) depart from Truth or Consequences on Saturday and from Las Cruces on Sunday. Tours must be arranged in advance and have a minimum of 8 and maximum of 14 guests. Price is charged per person. Tours take about 4 hours. Reservations for tours often fill up 4 to 8 weeks in advance, so plan ahead!

Spaceport America Visitor Center, 301 S. Foch Street, Truth or Consequences. **575-267-8888;** *www.spaceportamerica.com/.*

Camping in Southern New Mexico

Many of the communities along our driving route have at least one RV campground; most of them have several. You can eyeball the action early in the drive to figure out whether you need to make reservations for the remainder of the trip.

If most campgrounds look full as you drive by in the afternoon, consider calling ahead for a spot. But usually, you'll have no problem finding a spot, except perhaps in the Carlsbad Caverns area during tourist season, which is summer, the Christmas holidays, and Presidents' Day weekend.

WARNING

If you're traveling the route in summer, when temperatures can reach 95° F or more at lower elevations, plan ahead for an electrical hookup capable of running your RV's air-conditioning unit full blast. Daytime boondocking will be miserable unless you have an onboard generator that can run your air-conditioning. And never set up camp in dry streams or riverbeds. Yes, we know they're flat and smooth, and seemingly perfect for a campsite, but frequent summer thunderstorms can cause flash floods miles downstream with no warning.

All campgrounds listed in this section are open year-round and have public flush toilets, showers, and sanitary dump stations unless otherwise noted. Toll-free numbers, where listed, are for reservations only. Table 14-1 gives you a bit of info about our favorite campgrounds along the southern New Mexico route.

TABLE 14-1 **Our Favorite Southern New Mexico Campgrounds**

Name and Location	Contact Info	Cost	What to Know
Alamogordo/ White Sands KOA Journey; Alamogordo, NM	412 24th St.; **800-562-3452** or **575-437-3003;** https://koa.com/campgrounds/alamogordo/	$$-$$$$	Total of 55 full hookups with water and 20/30-amp electric; 17 50-amp sites; 42 pull-throughs. CATV, laundry, pool, Wi-Fi. A tree-shaded, older campground with grass, privacy walls, and narrow sites. Close to White Sands National Park, the Space Museum, and Mescalero Apache Reservation. Right on the edge of town and convenient to shopping. This kid-friendly park is highly favored by families.
Slow Play RV Park; Ruidoso Downs, NM	26514 U.S. 70 E; **575-378-4990;** www.circlebrv.com/	$-$$	Total of 150 full hookups with water, 30/50-amp electric; 63 pull-throughs. Laundry and Wi-Fi. Sites are narrow and some have side-by-side hookups. Large, modern, well-kept Good Sam RV park conveniently located near Ruidoso, which offers much to do. The camping fee is kept low so you can spend your savings at the casino. Walmart is 3 miles away.

Name and Location	Contact Info	Cost	What to Know
City of Rocks State Park; Faywood, NM (near Deming)	327 SR 61; **877-664-7787** or **575-536-2800** for reservations; https://tinyurl.com/mwkuatzr	$	Total of 52 sites, 10 with water and 50-amp electric. ADA-accessible. No sanitary dump station, but recently opened visitor's center with displays, bathrooms, and hot showers. We love this campground for its truly unique natural features, not its bare facilities. Bargain prices starting at just $10 off-season.
Las Cruces KOA Journey; Las Cruces, NM	814 Weinrich Rd.; **800-352-1627** or **575-526-6555;** https://koa.com/campgrounds/las-cruces/	$$–$$$	Total of 86 sites; 69 with full 30/50-amp hookups; 33 pull-throughs. CATV, laundry, grocery, pool, Wi-Fi. Wonderful views overlooking the Organ Mountains. At 4,000 feet, it's perfect for stargazing. Ask for one of the back-in sites on the edge of the bluff (spaces 10-29); the view is spectacular, especially at sunrise. They'll even loan you a saucer to go sledding at White Sands!
Silver City KOA Holiday; Silver City, NM	11824 Hwy 180 E; **800-562-7623** or **575-388-3351;** https://koa.com/campgrounds/silver-city/	$$$–$$$$$	Total of 56 sites with water and 30- or 50-amp electric; 49 full hookups; 33 pull-throughs. Laundry, pool, snack bar, Wi-Fi. Quiet location 5 miles east of town; cooler than other area campgrounds in summer. Offers copper mine tours, hiking trails, biking trail access, and an outdoor café in summer.
Town & Country RV Park; Roswell, NM	331 W. Brasher Rd.; **800-499-4364** or **575-624-1833** www.townandcountryrvpark.com	$$	Total of 119 spaces, all full hookups; 80 pull-throughs. Grills, CATV, laundry, Wi-Fi, pool. Top-rated Good Sam park; a favorite for holiday RVers and snowbirds during the winter. Close to downtown Roswell's shops and restaurants, it has embraced UFO kitsch.
Oliver Lee Memorial State Park; Alamogordo, NM	409 Dog Canyon Rd.; **575-437-8284;** https://www.emnrd.nm.gov/spd/find-a-park/oliver-lee-memorial-state-park/; must make reservations at https://tinyurl.com/mtws2mpf)	$	Total of 16 sites with water and 30- or 50-amp electric hookups; 3 ADA-compliant 50-amp sites. On-site dump station, grills, picnic tables, some shelters. Each campsite is slightly different in elevation, which helps with privacy. Closest state campground to White Sands National Park, with visitor's center, hiking trails, and history exhibits. Near historic Dog Canyon home of Alamogordo founder Oliver Lee.

Good Eatin' — New Mexico style

Restaurants and snack bars may be many miles apart in the wilds of southern New Mexico, so you'll be glad that you're carrying your own kitchen with a well-stocked pantry and refrigerator. At the same time, be aware that some of the smallest, scruffiest-looking country kitchens you encounter are treasured word-of-mouth secrets whispered from one chile-head to another.

Some like it hot (or not)

It can seem like almost every bite of food in this part of the world is made with one kind of chile or another, and while tons of folks love that zing in every meal, plenty of people don't. No restaurateur likes to see a depressed patron leave behind a plate of food with a single forkful missing. But chefs with the best of intentions can often ruin a perfectly good dinner by overdoing the hot stuff, and it's not just picky children who can't stand having their tongue melted to the roof of their mouth. There's no shame in asking questions about chiles and spice levels in a particular dish before you order; most restaurants are accommodating if you ask for a milder version of their food, or something that's entirely pepper-free, if possible. Just ask *before* you order, not after the food arrives.

HOW HOT IS THAT CHILE IN THE CHILI?

You spell it chili, and we spell it chile, but before we call the whole thing off, we should explain. In New Mexico, the name of the spicy *capsicum* seed pod is always spelled *chile*, and often the dishes made from it use that spelling, too. Texans prefer their spelling *chili*, and the local Native Americans often double the *L* and spell it *chilli*. New Mexico chile soup or stew is made primarily with fresh, frozen, roasted, or canned chiles, while Texas *chili con carne* is thicker, less soupy, mainly meat (without beans), and seasoned with dried chili peppers. Far be it from us to argue with anybody's favorite take on their chile/chili/chilli concoction (just don't mention adding pasta down here, 'cause them's fightin' words).

New Mexico leads the nation in total production of peppers, and the little town of Hatch is the center of the state's chile growing. Not surprisingly, the official state vegetables are chiles and *frijoles* (beans, usually the pinto variety). A dozen varieties of chiles are grown in the Hatch area and harvested in early September, when the air is heavy with the smell of roasting peppers. Local farmers freeze the roasted chiles, so they always have plenty for cooking.

Chiles come in two colors: red and green. The red chile is simply a riper version of the green chile. The most commonly grown variety here is the long green Hatch pepper (often served flattened out and roasted), and most New Mexico restaurants give you the choice of red or green chile stews, soups, and sauces. Always ask which is hotter, because it varies from pepper to pepper.

The Scoville scale measures pepper hotness by degrees called *Scoville heat units* (SHU), on a scale from 0 (sweet bell peppers), to 2,500–5,000 (jalapeños), to 30,000–50,000 (tabasco or cayenne peppers), to 2,500,000 (police pepper spray), all the way up to 16,000,000 (pure *capsaicin,* the chemical that makes hot peppers hot in the first place). ***Hint:*** Pure capsaicin has the same corrosive effect on your tongue that the monster's blood in the movie *Alien* had in melting through the floors of the *Nostromo* spaceship. Just sayin'.

The long Hatch chiles themselves can vary wildly between 1,000 and 8,000 SHU, making them quite mild.

Finding good local food

Following are some good local eating establishments in southern New Mexico and the area around El Paso, Texas:

» **Cattleman's Steakhouse,** 3450 S. Carlsbad Rd., Fabens, Texas (**915-544-3200;** www.cattlemansranch.com): This dude ranch and restaurant serves great steaks; a display case shows the raw steaks in each size, so you can gauge your appetite. Reservations are suggested. Open for dinner Tuesday through Sunday.

» **Chope's Town Bar & Café,** 16145 SR 28, La Mesa, New Mexico (**575-233-3420;** www.facebook.com/chopesbar): Located in an almost featureless 1880 adobe house (painted with an enormous graphic of grapes and several advertisements), Chope's is where the local chile growers have been going to eat chile rellenos, blue corn enchiladas, and green chile enchiladas since 1915. Be sure to wash it all down with Italian Swiss Colony wine, advertised on the front of the building. This is about as authentic as it gets when it comes to real New Mexico cooking. The Benavides family still owns and operates Chope's; it's so culturally important to the Mesilla Valley community, it's on the National Register of Historic Places. Open Thursday through Sunday.

BARGAIN ALERT

» **K-Bob's Steakhouse,** 1600 Mabry Drive, Clovis, New Mexico (**575-935-5262;** www.k-bobs.com): This very popular Southwest meat-and-potatoes steakhouse chain is famous for its hand-cut steaks, and especially its chicken-fried steak with a baked potato for a low, low price. If you've eaten chicken-fried steak before, you know it's a pounded cube steak dipped in industrial-strength batter and deep-fried. And if you *haven't* had it before, this is a good place to try it for the first time. K-Bob's has locations in both Texas and New Mexico, and it's a great economical choice if you're picking up the tab for a big group. The Clovis location is the original restaurant, opened in 1966. Open daily.

» **La Posta de Mesilla Restaurant and Chile Shop**, 2410 Calle de San Albino, Mesilla, New Mexico (**575-524-3524;** www.lapostademesilla.com/): At the chile shop, look for hot sauces, salsas, recipe books, canned chiles, and other cooking accessories. In the restaurant, feast on large portions of tacos, enchiladas, chile con queso, and tostadas. The historic building was first used in 1854 as a stage-coach stop and hotel. A family-owned restaurant since 1939, they claim to have many celebrity fans, and have packed up carryout meals for more than a couple U.S. presidents. Their reputation is so great, the nuclear submarine USS *New Mexico* named its galley La Posta in homage. Both the restaurant and the chile shop are open daily.

» **Little Diner and Tortilla Factory**, 7209 Seventh St., Canutillo, Texas (**915-877-2176;** https://littledinerep.com/): Technically, the Little Diner is in a northern neighborhood of El Paso, but it's just 2,000 or so feet from the New Mexico border, so we count it. Crowds are always standing in line at this popular place that sells tortillas to go and offers the gamut of other New Mexico treats to eat in or take out. (Don't be put off by the humble décor — former President George W. Bush likes to stop here when he's in El Paso.) We like the deep-fried *masa* (corn dough) patties called *gorditas* filled with spicy red chile sauce and chunks of pork, but the local children gobble them down stuffed with ground beef, chopped lettuce, and tomatoes, sort of a "McGordita." Open daily. Heck, there's even a laundromat next door, so stick your laundry in the wash while you're there, and go grab lunch.

» **Nellie's Café**, 1226 W. Hadley Ave., Las Cruces, New Mexico (**575-524-9982;** www.facebook.com/nelliescafelc): Servings are enormous at Nellie's, and the atmosphere is relaxed at breakfast, lunch, and dinner. Order anything with chiles, even the chile cheeseburger, and don't skip the refried beans, even at breakfast. Open Tuesday through Friday; closed from Thanksgiving through New Years.

Stocking the pantry

The first day of the drive from El Paso takes you past several notable tortilla factories and through the town of Hatch, famous for its chile products. We like the Little Diner and Tortilla Factory in Canutillo, Texas, north of El Paso, where you can take away both thick and thin homemade corn tortillas. Local and national supermarket chains in El Paso and throughout New Mexico usually stock both red and green versions of Hatch-brand enchilada sauces, which come in various strengths from mild to very hot.

In addition to chiles, this part of New Mexico grows an enormous variety of nuts, from pecans and pistachios, to piñons and Valencia peanuts. Keep an eye out for small roadside markets and stands selling local nuts.

Check out **McGinn's Pistachio Tree Ranch and Country Store,** 7320 U.S. 54/70, North Alamogordo (**800-368-3081;** www.pistachioland.com). They stock a big selection of locally made or grown specialties.

Supermarkets

You find **Albertsons** supermarkets in Alamogordo, Carlsbad, Mesilla, El Paso, and Roswell. **Walmart Supercenters** are in Alamogordo, Artesia, El Paso, Las Cruces, Roswell, and Ruidoso Downs.

You also find some excellent independent supermarkets worth checking out:

>> **Toucan Market,** 1701 E. University Avenue, Las Cruces (**575-521-3003;** https://toucanmarket.com/), stocks a large variety of local and specialty foods.

>> **Farmer's Country Market,** with 3 locations at 600 E. Second Street, 2800 N. Main Street, and 800 W. Hobbs Street, Roswell (www.farmerscoun trymarkets.com/), carries a wide selection of locally raised meats, fruits, and vegetables. Open daily year-round.

Farmers markets

If you're visiting in season, look for farmers markets that offer fresh local produce and specialty foods. Here are a couple of good ones:

>> **Carlsbad Downtown Farmers and Makers Market,** 102 Canal Street, Carlsbad, is open Saturday mornings, June through September.

>> **Silver City Farmers Market,** 901 N. Pope Street, Silver City, is open Saturday mornings. A midweek farmers market at 412 SR 211 in Gila is open Wednesday mornings.

Fast Facts for the New Mexico Route

Area Code
Area codes are **505** and **575** in New Mexico and **915** in El Paso, Texas.

Driving Laws
All RV occupants must wear seat belts in New Mexico. The maximum speed limit on interstates is 75 mph. Speed limits are lower in urban areas.

Emergency
Call **911.**

Hospitals
Along the route, major hospitals are in Alamogordo, Artesia, Carlsbad, El Paso, and Roswell.

Information
Resources include the New Mexico Tourism Department (**800-733-6396;** www.newmexico. org/), and El Paso Convention and Visitors Bureau (**800-351-6024;** www.visitelpaso. com/). For a New Mexico Vacation Guide, call **505-795-0343.**

For campground reservations, contact New Mexico State Parks through ReserveAmerica (**877-664-7787;** https://newmexicostate parks.reserveamerica.com).

Road and Weather Conditions
In New Mexico, call **800-432-4269.**

Taxes
New Mexico has a motel and campground tax of 10 percent. The average *combined* state and local sales tax is 7.84 percent. (The base state sales tax is 5.4 percent.) State gasoline and ethanol taxes are 19¢ per gallon; diesel fuel is 23¢ per gallon.

Time Zone
New Mexico and El Paso, Texas, are on Mountain time.

IN THIS CHAPTER

» **Planning to see the most spectacular coast on Earth**

» **Cruising up the PCH with the wind in your hair**

» **Flitting among a million monarch butterflies**

» **Reserving your California camping spot**

» **Sampling Santa Maria barbecue**

Chapter **15**

California's Central Coast: Malibu to Monterey

The dramatic California coastline winds for 1,200 miles between the Oregon border at Crescent City in the north and San Diego in the south, but the most scenic part is the Central Coast. This drive takes you along a famous stretch of two-lane seaside highway that begins just north of Los Angeles, moving through Ventura, Santa Barbara, San Luis Obispo, and Monterey, stopping just short of San Francisco, on Route 1, part of the old state highway system.

American highways once had colorful names that reflected their character, such as the Old Spanish Trail or the Dixie Highway — even the Ben-Hur Route. In 1925, it was decreed that all roads in the U.S. Highway System would have sensible numbers, not romantic names, but some were too famous to let go of. And none called to mind more stunning natural beauty than the Pacific Coast Highway. Originally spanning 1,687 miles, it was the longest stretch of paved road in the world, extending from San Diego near the Mexican border to Vancouver, British Columbia. Today, the Pacific Coast Highway is Scenic Route 1, running alongside the Pacific Ocean through the Central Coast of California.

The many faces of California make sense when you consider its size. In Southern California, the entertainment industry still reigns supreme because Los Angeles, in the end, is a company town. The collective image of the Southland includes the expensive boutiques of Beverly Hills, the amusement complex of Disneyland and Universal Studios, and the gated millionaire enclaves of Corona del Mar and Newport Beach. Northern California conjures up the hilly streets and cable cars of San Francisco, Yosemite and its massive redwoods, and the tech giants of Silicon Valley.

In this chapter, you discover the historical California, where you can still find lonely, windswept beaches as well as adobe walls sheltering the relics of 18th-century Spanish friars. Along the Central Coast and in the Central Valley, agriculture is the most important industry. This California turns green after winter rains, with wildflowers embellishing hillsides that grow golden under the summer sun. Here you see trail riders on horseback stirring up clouds of dust, some of them working the *ranchos*. Strawberries, lettuce, tomatoes, and peppers grow in long, neat rows, moistened by the coastal fog. *Enjoy the drive!*

Planning for the California Coast

The Central Coast is a splendid destination during any season, although summer coastal fogs and winter rains can make driving difficult. Rock and mudslides triggered by the winter rains may close the Pacific Coast Highway at intervals. Be prepared with sweaters and jackets if you visit in summer; cool, dense fog rolls in during the night, hangs on through the morning, but usually burns off before midday. (Mark Twain remarked that the coldest winter he ever spent was a summer in San Francisco.) Warm, sunny days often brighten up the route in February or March. September and October are frequently warm and clear, but most summer visitors are gone by then.

You need campground reservations throughout the year. In private RV parks, you can often slip into a space without a reservation, but the best ones are fully booked in summer and on holidays. And the state park campgrounds now require reservations. In "Sleeping along the California Coast," later in this chapter, we highlight our favorite campgrounds, as well as the rules for reserving a space in a state park.

When packing, take along warm clothes, even in summer. Packable down puffer jackets are great to have here; you wear them often at night when the sunny

California day turns chilly. Take sturdy hiking boots if you want to strike out along some of the coastal trails and beaches. Also, remember your binoculars and camera.

You can make the Central Coast drive in two or three days, but you need more time to visit the area's must-see attractions. To really enjoy the coast and its beaches, plan to spend several days camping in at least one serendipitous area that sings to you. You're going to hate to leave Morro Bay when your time there is up. Allow at least seven days for a perfect RV vacation.

Driving California's Central Coast

You set out from the famous beachside community of **Malibu,** only a few minutes north of **Santa Monica.** The drive follows SR 1, also called the **Pacific Coast Highway** (the *PCH*, as the locals say), for 340 miles north to the **Monterey Peninsula,** which juts out into the Pacific Ocean about 100 miles south of San Francisco. The PCH sometimes joins up with wider, faster **U.S. 101** (from the **Oxnard/Ventura** area to **Gaviota,** north of **Santa Barbara,** and then again from **Pismo Beach** to **San Luis Obispo**). And the path may sometimes take you onto east-west state roads between the two highways. But for much of the time, you and your RV are alone along the coastline, where you encounter surf pounding at the foot of the cliffs along the curving roadway. The Central Coast drive takes you through world-famous **Big Sur** and **Carmel-by-the-Sea,** to the Monterey Peninsula, a distance of some 340 miles. (See the route map in Figure 15-1.)

TIP

Our itinerary runs from *south to north*, which means milepost markers go down as you get farther north. It might sound like a silly consideration, but driving north favors the driver, not the passenger, when it comes to sea views. If you drive the coast from *north to south* instead, your passenger will get the best views outside of their window. It's dangerous for you to drive and try to take snapshots of the sunset over the beach at the same time. So, decide whether or not that's important to you and choose your direction and starting point early in your planning.

Note that you find more information on many of the attractions and eateries we highlight in this section later in the chapter. Also, be sure to check out the **Pacific Coast Highway Travel** website (www.pacific-coast-highway-travel.com) for all kinds of inspiration for more to see and do up and down the coast.

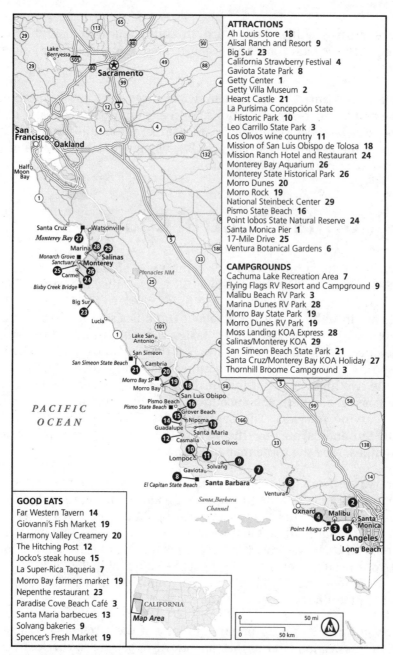

ATTRACTIONS
Ah Louis Store **18**
Alisal Ranch and Resort **9**
Big Sur **23**
California Strawberry Festival **4**
Gaviota State Park **8**
Getty Center **1**
Getty Villa Museum **2**
Hearst Castle **21**
La Purísima Concepción State
  Historic Park **10**
Leo Carrillo State Park **3**
Los Olivos wine country **11**
Mission of San Luis Obispo de Tolosa **18**
Mission Ranch Hotel and Restaurant **24**
Monterey Bay Aquarium **26**
Monterey State Historical Park **26**
Morro Dunes **20**
Morro Rock **19**
National Steinbeck Center **29**
Pismo State Beach **16**
Point lobos State Natural Reserve **24**
Santa Monica Pier **1**
17-Mile Drive **25**
Ventura Botanical Gardens **6**

CAMPGROUNDS
Cachuma Lake Recreation Area **7**
Flying Flags RV Resort and Campground **9**
Malibu Beach RV Park **3**
Marina Dunes RV Park **28**
Morro Bay State Park **19**
Morro Dunes RV Park **19**
Moss Landing KOA Express **28**
Salinas/Monterey KOA **29**
San Simeon Beach State Park **21**
Santa Cruz/Monterey Bay KOA Holiday **27**
Thornhill Broome Campground **3**

GOOD EATS
Far Western Tavern **14**
Giovanni's Fish Market **19**
Harmony Valley Creamery **20**
The Hitching Post **12**
Jocko's steak house **15**
La Super-Rica Taqueria **7**
Morro Bay farmers market **19**
Nepenthe restaurant **23**
Paradise Cove Beach Café **3**
Santa Maria barbecues **13**
Solvang bakeries **9**
Spencer's Fresh Market **19**

FIGURE 15-1: The Central California Coast map.

Startin' your surfin' safari

You start the Central Coast drive at Malibu, but before you depart, we recommend visiting two of our favorite attractions: the **Getty Center** near Brentwood and the **Santa Monica Pier.** You can take public transportation to these sights. When you're in Malibu — if you're a fan of all those old beach party movies with Frankie Avalon and Annette Funicello — have a drink as the sun sets at **Paradise Cove Beach Café,** on the beach where the movies were shot.

WARNING

Don't leave **Santa Monica** the next morning without topping off your fuel tank. The first leg of the drive encompasses almost 50 miles along the coast and through **Santa Monica Mountains National Recreation Area.** Along the way, you find no gas stations, truck stops, or convenience markets until you reach Oxnard.

You set out northward from scenic, exclusive Malibu, on a hilltop above SR 1. Looking at this first stretch of the PCH on a map or on Google, you may think it's a long, empty cliffside road next to the jagged shoreline. But in reality, it's lined with private, gated houses, condos and apartments that cling to the hills or open onto the beach itself. The path is interspersed with narrow access roads to an occasional patch of state or county beach.

REMEMBER

Most of these public beach areas are too small to bother negotiating an RV into, but **Leo Carrillo State Park** is a notable exception. The beach is named after Carrillo, an actor, conservationist, and politician who served on the California Beaches and Parks Commission for years. He was instrumental in acquiring William Randolph Hearst's castle at **San Simeon** as a tourist attraction for the state.

Other large beachfront parking spots between Malibu and Oxnard are at **Zuma Beach, Sycamore Cove Beach,** and **Mugu Beach** at **Point Mugu State Park.** And if you've got a Class A motorhome or van camper capable of boondocking, you can park it and camp on the beach at **Thornhill Broome Campground.** At Sycamore Cove, the PCH is finally surrounded by the unpopulated hills of the **Santa Monica Mountains** for a time, but we suggest waiting to do your beachcombing until you get out of the range of L.A.'s notorious overcrowding and development.

'Ventura Highway in the sunshine'

Crank up the old tune by the band America: At **Oxnard,** SR 1/PCH merges with U.S. 101 — Ventura Highway — for the first time on our trip, and traffic can be very heavy here. Bear with it, because you're already 60 miles away from downtown L.A., and you're getting farther by the mile. (But you've secretly snuck around some of the worst traffic jams in the country.)

When you see Oxnard's acres of strawberry fields, you're glimpsing part of California's vast agricultural industry. If you pass through in mid- to late-May, try to catch the annual **California Strawberry Festival** (just up the road at the Ventura County Fairgrounds), one of the largest of its kind in the U.S. Oxnard isn't just the strawberry capital of the world; it's also the lima bean capital. *That* honor doesn't come easily, you know.

For fans who grew up watching Raymond Burr as TV's **Perry Mason,** the coastal town of **Ventura** can claim to be the home of the famous lawyer/detective. This is where creator Erle Stanley Gardner lived and practiced law. The courtroom novels were monster hits; even lawyers read them, and in 2014, the American Bar Association began publishing reprints of the stories. They're still the third-best-selling book series of all time. Parts of the classic TV series were filmed at Ventura's city hall, formerly the courthouse. The **Ventura Botanical Gardens** in the hills just above the courthouse are a lovely place to stroll, with an incredible ocean view.

The drive from Malibu to **Santa Barbara** is 83 miles, so if you can time your arrival around midday, stop for lunch at the world's most written-about taco stand, the late Julia Child's favorite, **La Super-Rica Taqueria.** We don't recommend driving around in a large motorhome or towing a trailer in Santa Barbara itself, because you have to depend on street parking, and RV parking is banned on the city's streets. (In 2016, Santa Barbara became one of the first cities in the country to issue such a ban.) But sometimes you can find a space in the residential neighborhood around the taco stand. Santa Barbara offers a public transit service that visits many of the city's highlights.

Past Santa Barbara at **Gaviota,** the highway veers to the north, away from the ocean, and you climb through the narrow, windy Gaviota Pass up into the Santa Ynez Mountains. If you're inclined to explore a little, stay in the left lane as the highway turns, and take a hard left at the sign for **Gaviota State Park,** our favorite secret RV campground on the beach below a spectacular railroad trestle. (Unfortunately, at press time, the park is closed for repairs due to damage from storms in January of 2023; keep fingers crossed that repairs happen quickly.)

Finding Neverland, a bit of Denmark, and fields of flowers

Continuing north up through the pass, you go through a tunnel and stick with U.S. 101 instead of SR 1 when the road splits at **Las Cruces.** Then take Exit 140A at **Buellton** and visit the cute Danish town of **Solvang** (from SR 1 or U.S. 101, go east on SR 246) in the beautiful **Santa Ynez Valley.** The rolling valley is filled with ranches owned by actors, politicians, and other celebrities; past residents here include Ronald Reagan and Michael Jackson (with his Neverland compound).

Solvang is also home to the famed **Alisal Guest Ranch and Resort,** a 10,000-acre working cattle ranch, but also a classic dude ranch, where pasty Easterners can come to relax and play cowboy.

After taking in Buellton, Solvang, and the Santa Ynez Valley, pick up SR 246 and head west toward **Lompoc** and **La Purísima Mission**. The pretty country in Santa Ynez isn't just for wine; it's for horses too. Ranchers breed Arabians in this lush valley, and the ranches are home to some of the world's most famous horses. If you'd like to see some of the plants that make this valley so lush, you can stop at **Santa Ynez Valley Botanic Garden,** at the west end of **River View Park.** The garden is on the 246 just as you're leaving Buellton. This small, uniquely peaceful garden is open to the public free of charge, 365 days a year, until sunset.

Continue your encounter with nature's beauty by following SR 246 west to **Lompoc,** where the dazzling flower fields once produced 85 percent of the seeds for America's home gardeners. Although those glory days are gone — with fewer people growing flowers from seeds and more seeds being produced abroad — Lompoc is still a flower capital, concentrating on growing blossoms for bouquets. And summer is still a great time to look for the fields of blooms here.

TIP

Make sure to see at least some of Lompoc's 50 historical murals on public and private buildings all over the middle of town; we especially love the temperance-minded woman smashing a whiskey keg with an ax, at 137 South H Street. The murals depict events and influences in Lompoc's history, like the flower seed industry. They're fun, and really dress up the town.

Pick up SR 1, going north again, and you pass **Vandenberg Space Force Base** (previously Vandenberg Air Force Base), where the space shuttles once landed. It's now a space launch and missile testing area. We don't recommend stopping at Vandenberg, which has no museum of any sort. At one time it was possible to tour the base, at least the historic areas, but public tours ceased with COVID and are now canceled indefinitely.

Searching out mission bells and barbecue

In the 18th century, Spanish Franciscan friars created a string of 21 Catholic missions located a day's horseback ride apart. (The signs for **El Camino Real** you see by the highway marked with a mission bell denote the King's Highway, the old Spanish royal road built in the mid-1500s that once connected the missions along a 600-mile-long route.) Today, most of them sit in the middle of urban areas where parking is difficult for RVs and the ambience doesn't evoke the mission days. An exception is our favorite, **La Purísima Concepción,** five miles out of Lompoc, which remains in a rural setting. While this mission is owned by the state today and is no longer a religious community, it's still worth a special visit.

THE MATING GAME ON THE BUTTERFLY COAST

The **monarch butterfly** (Danaus plexippus) is one of the most exotic winter visitors to the Central Coast, arriving in late October by the hundreds of thousands at more than 300 nesting sites within 2 miles of the ocean. Although the migration territory ranges from a golf course in San Leandro in the San Francisco Bay area southward to the campus of the University of California at San Diego, the main sites are along the Central Coast.

Look for monarchs between mid-October and late February or early March. While you find monarchs all over the Central Coast, two of the best places to look are along your drive: **Pacific Grove** and **Pismo Beach.** Both are among only five sites that get an annual count of more than 100,000 monarch butterflies, and they go into high gear to greet them. The **Pacific Grove Monarch Sanctuary (805-773-4382;** www.pgmuseum.org/monarch-viewing), which is part of the **Pacific Grove Museum of Natural History,** is the most populous overwintering site on the coast. Pismo State Beach has a eucalyptus-filled **Monarch Butterfly Grove (805-773-7170;** www.experiencepismobeach.com/beach-and-outdoors/monarch-butterflies). If you're doing this itinerary in the winter, check out either of these spots. Remember that, on the Central Coast, you find an influx of monarchs anywhere near a eucalyptus tree, so keep a lookout.

TIP

Great barbecued steaks (the world's best, say the proprietors) are cooked at **The Hitching Post** in tiny **Casmalia,** a few miles south of Vandenberg's main gate. There's an offshoot of this eatery now in **Buellton,** just off U.S. 101. So, on either road you take north, you can lay hands on some great **Santa Maria barbecue.** Delicious food also abounds in **Guadalupe,** a farming community along the coast with a string of good Mexican restaurants.

Nipomo, home of towering sand dunes that have doubled for the Sahara Desert in many films, is now also an archaeological dig that is unearthing (are you ready?) the remains of a vast Egyptian movie set created by Cecil B. DeMille for his 1923 silent epic The Ten Commandments. You can see some of the artifacts at the **Dunes Center** at the north end of town.

REMEMBER

Pismo Beach has been a comic punch line since the 1930s, with a fictional reputation as a town full of sleepy rubes and retirees. When Jack Benny joked about playing the Pismo Beach Grunion Festival, he was *definitely* playing out of town. Even Bugs Bunny got in on the mockery. But Pismo Beach is a top-notch winter retreat for RV snowbirds, a great little town with a 17-mile stretch of public beachfront, mild weather, beautiful views — and don't forget the monarch butterflies.

Although the once-famous Pismo clams are more a memory than a reality today (none can be sold commercially, if you can even find one), you can get tasty chowders made from eastern and northwestern clams, or try dig your own local clams with a clamming license available from the state fish and game authorities. The problem with the big clams (the minimum legal size to keep is 4½ inches wide, and there's a catch limit of ten) is that most have already been eaten by California sea otters, those resourceful little critters that swim around in the Pacific carrying rocks for breaking shellfish against their chests.

At Pismo Beach, SR 1 rejoins U.S. 101 to take you as far as **San Luis Obispo,** home of **California Polytechnic State University** (Cal Poly for short), the **Mission San Luis Obispo de Tolosa,** and the 1884 **Ah Louis Store.** This historic building was the first general mercantile in the county and the first owned by a Chinese American shopkeeper. It's a pretty little town, and at times an oddball one. Look for **Bubblegum Alley**, a bizarre ongoing work of art in the 700 block of Higuera Street between Garden and Broad streets, with 15-foot-high walls plastered in used bubble gum; there's a machine selling gum at the entrance, if you're moved to participate. This easygoing town, nicknamed SLO, like the county, is also the scene of a famous **Thursday night farmers market,** when vendors cooking Santa Maria barbecue and farmers selling fresh produce line closed-off blocks of Higuera Street.

Rolling toward Big Sur

SLO is where SR 1 returns to the coast and the fishing town of **Morro Bay,** dominated by domed landmark **Morro Rock**, a 576-foot-tall volcanic plug that may be as much as 50 million years old. Peregrine falcons nest on the rock; great blue herons gather to lay eggs between January and June in a grove of eucalyptus trees by the estuary's wetlands. Brown pelicans and white gulls check out the fishing boats on the waterfront, and sandpipers leave their footprints on the wet sand of the beach as the tide washes in. RVers have two splendid hookup campground choices: **Morro Bay State Park** on the estuary, and **Morro Dunes** near the sea, sheltered by grass-topped sand dunes. Morro Bay marks the jumping-off point for the **Big Sur** section of the drive.

As you continue north on SR 1, you pass the pretty beach town of **Cayucos,** with a handful of antique shops and seafood restaurants on the pier. Next comes the eccentric and fascinating little town of **Harmony,** population 18, or so they claim. Back in 1979, a KABC radio show featured an unknown singer/songwriter named Jehry Miller, and his catchy song "Harmonizing in Harmony – Population 18." The welcome sign pays homage to the town's modest size as well as its quirkiness.

Newspaper publishing giant William Randolph Hearst used to stop in Harmony on his way to his castle-like home at San Simeon to get fresh buttermilk from the old **Harmony Valley Creamery** dairy cooperative that was once here. After the co-op closed, Harmony became a hippie mecca, with lots of arts and crafts, and that vibe remains. An episode of *Perry Mason* featuring beatnik painters, "The Case of the Absent Artist," was shot here for the local ambience. It's definitely worth stopping, particularly to shop at **Harmony Glassworks** and grab a scoop of ice cream from the revitalized Harmony Valley Creamery. Next comes the lovely seaside town of **Cambria,** with antique shops, art galleries, collectibles, and chic restaurants with lots of patio dining.

Coming up to the castle

Just up SR 1 from Cambria is **San Simeon,** or *the ranch,* as publishing tycoon William Randolph Hearst referred to the land where his family used to go camping and where he built his opulent 165-room hilltop castle. Allow most of a day if you want to visit the famous castle, because you must take one of several daily guided tours, the only option for getting through the gates. Film buffs immediately recognize Hearst Castle's connection with Orson Welles's masterpiece *Citizen Kane* and its fictional Xanadu; Rosebud is all that's missing.

From San Simeon, SR 1 winds nearly 100 miles to the **Monterey Peninsula,** passing through legendary **Big Sur** on a white-knuckle stretch. Be careful crossing traffic to get to the scenic turnouts that are on the north-to-south side. Don't miss stopping at a viewpoint to admire the delicate arches of **Bixby Creek Bridge,** spanning a 260-foot gorge against a backdrop of gently rounded treeless hills. After you cross over the bridge, the best views of this much-photographed 1932 concrete span are from the turnouts to the north. (You've seen it in dozens — if not hundreds — of movies, TV shows, and commercials, usually shot from a helicopter.)

WARNING

Take your time driving along the Big Sur stretch of the coast and pulling off into the turnouts (those that are big enough to handle your rig, that is). Be careful getting out to stretch and to photograph the spectacular scenery. However tempting some of the signs and driveways may be, before you enter, consider carefully whether you can turn your RV around and get back out. If possible, it may be safer to let your passenger get out and check while you remain behind the wheel. Use your flashers, and be wary of traffic on this curvy two-lane highway.

Nepenthe, the most famous eatery along the way, is noted for its ambrosia burgers; expect a crowd on a sunny afternoon. Sometimes there isn't enough room for a car to park in the restaurant's lot, let alone an RV. Opt for a space along the roadside instead.

Carmel, an artists' mecca in the early years of the 20th century, has turned into a traffic-clogged bed-and-breakfast town of restaurants and upscale shops. Once admired as the home of photographer Ansel Adams, the town is best known these days for resident and former mayor Clint Eastwood, whose **Hog's Breath Inn** was the focus of innumerable tourist cameras when he ran it; he still owns the building. Today, he runs **Mission Ranch,** a chic hotel filled with furniture he designed himself, south of town near the mission on Dolores Street. The hotel was converted from an 1850s ranch house that doubled as a New England estate in the 1959 three-hankie melodrama *A Summer Place.*

Entering Monterey and Steinbeck country

The **Monterey Peninsula** is John Steinbeck country. The author grew up in the area and wrote about it in such diverse books as *East of Eden* and *Cannery Row.* The **National Steinbeck Center** in **Salinas** joins must-see peninsula attractions like the **Monterey Bay Aquarium, Point Lobos State Natural Reserve, Cannery Row,** and **Old Fisherman's Wharf**.

When you get to the Monterey Peninsula — the end of the Central Coast route — the famed **17-Mile Drive** is something of an attraction in and of itself. You hear a lot about this expensive, much-touted toll road that swings past **Pebble Beach**, over a curving drive with some incredible ocean vistas, from Carmel gate to Pacific Grove gate, around a huge chunk of the peninsula. Chatter online claims RVs are prohibited, but according to authorities, the only restricted vehicles are motorcycles.

REMEMBER

The scenic 17-Mile Drive runs through a posh residential district, and you won't be permitted to park an RV anywhere near the gate, in case you thought of just hiking or biking it for free. You must pay a toll of $11.25, pass through the Carmel gate, and drive the beautiful, winding route. You can find several YouTube videos that give you a virtual idea of the drive, so you can assess whether you'd like to try it. You can even get a self-drive audio tour app from Tripadvisor, which you download to your phone for $10.

TIP

Although you can take your RV, it's the sort of drive we prefer to do in our SUV, leaving the Airstream in the RV park. We recommend you do the same. The drive has some narrow roads with no shoulder, and pull-offs for viewing have little room to maneuver. Also, you encounter some very low tree branches and full-grown cypress trees right up next to the white line. You have no margin for error, and you're dodging bicycles to boot. It's best to be in your *toad* (tow vehicle).

Making a weekend jaunt

You can make a quick weekend run from **Los Angeles** to **Monterey** comfortably in one direction if you're bound for other areas, but don't try to make it a round trip. If you have only a weekend, try driving from **Los Angeles** as far as **Morro Bay,** overnighting on the bay, and heading south again; or drive from **San Francisco** along the **Big Sur** coast as far as Morro Bay and return. You can catch the best scenery, enjoy some seafood or Santa Maria barbecue, and even do a couple hours of antiques shopping, but you won't have time for the major museums and the aquarium.

Must-See Attractions along the Central Coast

Getty Center and Getty Villa Museum
Los Angeles

Allow most or all of a day to see this complex of art galleries, gardens, gift stores, and restaurants. The gorgeously lit galleries display everything from Old Masters to Impressionists (Van Gogh's *Irises* is here), sculpture and decorative arts, to photography (including a major collection of Walker Evans's work), while the landscaped gardens invite strolling and contemplating a drop-dead view in all directions.

Travelers are told, "You can't miss it," but if you head north on I-405 from I-10 toward U.S. 101, you really *can't* miss the Getty Center. First, you see a huge stone complex crowning the top of a hill to the west of I-405 as the highway climbs toward the crest at Mulholland Drive. Next, you see signage labeled Getty Center and Getty Center Drive with arrows directing you to the garage. In a twist from the usual, the Getty charges for parking, but the museum is free. Open Tuesday through Sunday. Allow a half-day to a full day.

Just 13 miles from the Getty Center, off the PCH, is another Getty attraction — a one-of-a-kind re-creation of an ancient Roman country villa, appropriately called the **Getty Villa Museum.** This museum presents a large collection of ancient Greek and Roman art in idyllic surroundings. Open Wednesday through Monday.

Getty Center is at 1200 Getty Center Dr., Los Angeles; **310-440-7300;** *www.getty.edu/visit/center.* **RV parking:** *Cars are charged $20, but parking is by reservation and not suitable for most RVs; use a car or take public transportation. Metro bus 761 stops at the Getty; for more info, go to www.getty.*

edu/visit/center/parking-and-transportation. Food is available at the Getty; for all dining options, see www.getty.edu/visit/center/food-and-drink.

Getty Villa Museum is at 17985 E. Pacific Coast Hwy, Pacific Palisades; **310-440-7300;** *www.getty.edu/visit/villa. Admission is free for both.*

Hearst Castle

San Simeon

J. Paul Getty's museum was a long-planned gift to the people of California, while William Randolph Hearst's castle was his opulent hideaway until his death in 1951; the Hearst estate endowed the castle to the state, and it became a California state park in 1958.

Although construction lasted from 1919 to 1947, Hearst Castle, designed by Julia Morgan, was never finished. Hearst intended to eventually add a bowling alley, a clock tower, an aviary, a croquet lawn, and a polo field. The rich and famous of the 1930s who visited the castle dined at a long refectory table set with priceless china and silver, along with paper napkins and condiments like catsup still in their original bottles — they were, after all, "camping out at the ranch."

REMEMBER

It wasn't just cultural or political giants, from Winston Churchill to George Bernard Shaw, who made their way to Hearst's Enchanted Hill. The film *Citizen Kane* is a thinly veiled and somewhat cruel retelling of the 34-year love story between the married Hearst and actress Marion Davies. The added glitter (as if it needed more) attached to the castle came in the form of the famed actors, producers, and directors (friends of Davies) who charmed Hearst and earned a place in his glitzy orbit. Picturing one of the costume parties, or Douglas Fairbanks swimming with Johnny Weissmuller in the Roman pool, is one of the things that makes a trip to San Simeon such fun.

Visitors have a choice of numerous tours, including a wheelchair-accessible evening tour. First-time visitors are encouraged to take the Grand Rooms Tour. Allow time to visit the artifacts on view in the reception exhibit hall at the visitor's center and to see the 40-minute film *Building the Dream* at Hearst Castle Theater. Open daily, with tours from 9:00 a.m. to 3:20 p.m.; closed on major holidays. Allow at least a half day, but preferably a whole day.

750 Hearst Castle Rd.; **800-444-4445;** *https://hearstcastle.org.* **RV parking:** *Large lots at the visitor's center, where all tours begin. Admission varies by tour type and age.*

La Purísima Mission State Historic Park
Lompoc

Locals pronounce the town's name *lom*-poke, not *lom*-pock, as comedian W. C. Fields pronounced it in his film *The Bank Dick,* shot here in 1940. Comedians aside, little Lompoc, in the Santa Ynez Valley, is a charming town, with more than 20 wineries clustered together in what the locals call the Wine Ghetto.

But the jewel in Lompoc's crown for tourists is the mission that sits just outside town, founded by Franciscan friars in 1787 and restored to its 1820s period. Now a state park in a beautiful rural setting, it's the only example in California of a complete Spanish mission complex. The long, low adobe-and-wood buildings house chapels, a kitchen where candles are made by hand, a museum, Native American workshops, military barracks, and the simple, unadorned cells where the friars slept. A daily tour, about 90 minutes long, walks you through the complex and tells the story of what mission life was like.

Special events occur about once a month and feature costumed staff demonstrating the period crafts and daily routines; check the website for dates and times. You also find a visitor's center and gift shop. Open Tuesday through Sunday; closed on major holidays. Allow two hours for the visit, more if you want to hike or ride a horse on one of the trails around the mission.

2295 Purisima Rd.; **805-733-3713;** *www.lapurisimamission.org.* **RV parking:** *Large parking lot. Admission fee charged per vehicle.*

Monterey Bay Aquarium
Monterey

KID FRIENDLY

Design magic and some $50 million turned the last remaining sardine factory on Monterey's Cannery Row into one of the world's top aquariums. Inside, it's pure enchantment, from the three-story kelp tank to a two-level sea otter habitat. Hands-on exhibits let you touch anemones and bat rays, and you can even watch period films from the cannery days. Some 360,000 creatures — from jellyfish to sharks — are on-site, and giant whale models hang overhead. A massive window provides a look into the Open Sea exhibit, a million-gallon man-made ocean populated by tuna, sunfish, sea turtles, and other denizens of the deep. Open daily; closed on Christmas. Allow a half day (explore Monterey the rest of the day).

886 Cannery Row. **831-648-4800;** *www.montereybayaquarium.org.* **RV parking:** *In nearby lots; look for signage. Admission varies by age*

National Steinbeck Center

Salinas

Although the inland city of Salinas is a few miles off the coastal route, it's a beautiful little town, and the National Steinbeck Center, along with the surrounding pedestrian-friendly city center, makes this 16-mile detour more than worth the trip.

Nobel Prize–winning author John Steinbeck is one of the greatest voices America ever produced. He's got a lot of fans, but he holds a special place in the hearts of RVers, many of whom have read about his adventures on the road in his popular 1962 work *Travels with Charley*. It's the story of his ramblings around America — over 10,000 miles' worth — with his French poodle in a truck camper he named Rocinante, after Don Quixote's horse.

In the museum, you find Rocinante, along with walk-in galleries for each of his major works filled with interactive exhibits. Film clips from movies made from his books, including *Cannery Row* (1982), *East of Eden* (1955), *The Grapes of Wrath* (1940), *Tortilla Flat* (1942), *The Red Pony* (1949), and *Of Mice and Men* (1939), play in each area. The newest part of the museum documents the personal history of farmworkers in the Salinas Valley. Open Wednesday through Sunday. Allow two to three hours.

1 Main St. 831-796-3833 or **831-775-4721***; www.steinbeck.org.* **RV parking:** *Use the Amtrak and bus station lot across the street or park on the street. Admission varies by age.*

TIP

As long as you're in Salinas, if time allows, consider eating lunch at The Steinbeck House (132 Central Avenue; https://steinbeckhouse.com), a charming restaurant in the rambling Victorian where the author was born and raised. The walls are decorated with family memorabilia, and there's a gift shop.

It's about a 15-minute walk from Cannery Row south to **Old Fisherman's Wharf,** beyond the Presidio. (Parking can be a trial, especially in an RV, so plan on parking in the Cannery Row area and walking.) Old Fisherman's Wharf is lined with seafood places and fish markets, similar to Fisherman's Wharf in San Francisco; in fact, one local specialty is clam chowder served in hollowed-out loaves of sourdough bread. Forget the overpriced abalone — a former staple of coastal California, the delectable shellfish has been overfished and most of what's sold on the wharf today is frozen and imported. Instead, order the local calamari (squid), delicious when fried to a crunch and served with lemon wedges and tartar sauce.

MONTEREY'S CANNERY ROW AND OLD FISHERMAN'S WHARF

Cannery Row was, in the words of John Steinbeck, "a poem, a stink, a grating noise, a quality of light, a tone, a habit, a nostalgia, a dream." Today, it's mostly the nostalgia that remains, particularly for Steinbeck fans who come here to see the place he wrote about in several novels.

You may think of sardines as bait, but these oily little fish were popular at one time. Tins of ready-to-eat sardines were a nutritious convenience food in the 1930s and '40s, a great source of protein on a budget. America was a major sardine consumer, and Monterey was the center of the canning industry on the West Coast, packing over 10 million tins a year. By the 1950s the supply began to dwindle due to a natural population decline and overfishing. Other convenience foods appeared on grocery shelves, and the last cannery on the Row closed in 1973.

Only one building remains much as it was in Steinbeck's time. Pacific Biological Laboratories (Western Biological in the stories) at 800 Cannery Row was a small private marine lab. It belonged to Steinbeck's closest friend and beloved alter ego, Ed Ricketts, a marine biologist, pioneering environmentalist, and all-around philosopher. The character Doc is based on him.

As an aside, if you'd like to have an idea of what the Row looked like in its heyday, you should see the 1982 film *Cannery Row*. The art director, William F. O'Brien, designed a vast interior set that re-creates Cannery Row in the 1930's, in the funniest and most charming film ever made of any of Steinbeck's works.

Today's Cannery Row is an imaginative reuse of the closed canneries: With tons of shopping and seafood restaurants, it's a bustling tourist area. You won't lack for dining options. Try one of our favorite restaurants, Chart House, a popular waterfront chain with great steaks and seafood, and a somewhat upscale but comfortable ambiance. You also find several wineries that offer tastings.

Point Lobos State Natural Reserve
Carmel

KID
FRIENDLY

You see the same Monterey cypress trees and fog-misted headlands in Point Lobos as you do on the 17-Mile Drive (around the Monterey peninsula), but instead of driving through posh neighborhoods, you're traveling through natural coastal scenery. Go as early as possible in the morning so you won't be stuck in a long row of cars that brake upon sightings of sea otters, sea lions, harbor seals, and seabirds. You can explore 9 miles of hiking trails and 456 acres of reserve, and you find a whaling cabin with historical artifacts. Remember to carry binoculars to look for California gray whales during migration season in mid-January (southbound) and in April and early May (northbound).

No dogs are allowed, and vehicles longer than 21 feet are prohibited. However, you can park along the highway and walk in. This is a state park, but it's also a nature preserve, with a long list of rather strict rules, including no camping and no approaching or disturbing the animals. Picnicking is permitted. If you're a registered diver, you can explore an underwater marine reserve. Open daily. Allow anywhere from an hour to a half day, depending on your hiking plans.

SR 1 south of Carmel. **831-624-4909;** `www.pointlobos.org`. *Admission is charged per vehicle and age.*

More Cool Things to See and Do in Central California

Although the scenery is spectacular along every mile of this drive, you may want to check out these other cool activities:

» **Uncover "ancient" Egypt.** Movie fans and archaeology buffs love the **Dunes Center,** 8 miles northwest of Santa Maria, which combines hands-on educational exhibits about the Guadalupe-Nipomo Dunes ecosystem with the excavation of a long-buried movie set depicting Egypt in the biblical era.

In 1923, on the dunes south of Guadalupe, Cecil B. DeMille constructed a movie set only slightly less ambitious than the Great Pyramid of Giza for his original silent film *The Ten Commandments*. At the end of shooting, DeMille brought in a horse-drawn bulldozer and knocked down the whole set to keep some rival producer from coming in, shooting a cheap picture, and releasing it first. The moving sands soon buried the set. Some 60 years later, a storm uncovered part of it, and a pair of documentarians rushed in to preserve and catalog the artifacts.

The dig is not yet complete at this registered archeological site. The center offers docent-led hikes through the dunes that focus on the film, along with birdwatching, photography, and botanical and animal life. Open Monday through Friday. Allow two to three hours if you visit the dunes. Admission varies by age.

1055 Guadalupe St. (SR 1) in Guadalupe. **805-343-2455;** `http://dunescenter.org`. **RV parking** *is available on the street.*

>> **Partake of the mighty fine wine.** Off U.S. 101 in and around Los Olivos lie several Santa Barbara County wineries, including **Firestone, Fess Parker** (yes, it was owned by the late actor who played Davy Crockett and Daniel Boone), **Zaca Mesa, Foxen,** and **Gainey.** When you think of California wines, you may think of Napa Valley north of San Francisco, but the entire Central Coast — from Santa Barbara to San Francisco — is wine country, and Santa Maria Valley is a hotbed of Central Coast wine, particularly pinot noir.

Our first wine-tasting experience was an incredibly lucky one, a tour of the relatively new (at that time) Firestone Vineyard in Santa Ynez Valley. Young and dumb though we were, the gentlemanly Brooks Firestone and his wife, Kate, patiently gave us the tour and set off a lifelong love of wine and wine tasting. If you've never done it, you really should indulge at least once, particularly on this Central Coast drive, where you're surrounded by so many wineries that create a first-rate product.

Call Santa Barbara County Vintners Association at **805-688-0881** *or go to* https://sbcountywines.com. *For info on Santa Maria wines, go to* https://santamariavalley.com/blog/a-guide-to-wine-tasting-on-the-central-california-coast.

WINNING THE JUDGMENT OF PARIS

California has been making great wine since the 18th century. Wineries like Roma and Petri (both long gone) sponsored radio shows in the 1940s, aggressively marketing wine to Americans who didn't drink much of it. Some wineries, including Gallo and Paul Masson, moved their marketing into the TV age, but despite occasional successes, none of these efforts seemed to work in terms of making American wine respectable. For connoisseurs, the California wine industry was something of a joke, with punch lines about gallon bottles of Boones Farm Strawberry Hill and Gallo Hearty Burgundy. That is, until the Paris Wine Tasting of 1976, also known as the Judgment of Paris.

In an incredibly shrewd move, a group of winemakers in Northern California entered their wines alongside the French wines in a blind tasting organized by British wine expert Steven Spurrier. The panel of judges was made up exclusively of French wine experts. And to the snobby wine world's astonishment, the California wines ranked highest in both categories, Chardonnays and reds. In the next ten years, some California wines took the world by storm, and the industry changed overnight, no longer having any difficulty marketing their product. The last time we looked, a couple of our favorite California red wines were more expensive than their French counterparts, even considering import taxes.

>> **Pier into the past.** The **Santa Monica Pier,** at the intersection of Ocean and Colorado avenues, was originally earmarked to be the port of Los Angeles, but through political machinations, the area lost out to San Pedro at the turn of the 20th century. Undeterred, the town of Santa Monica created a broad, sandy beach and a pier with an amusement park between 1904 and 1921. A 1916 carousel (featured in the film *The Sting),* penny arcade, Ferris wheel, bumper cars, games of chance, fortune tellers — all lend a Coney Island or Jersey Shore feel to this sunny pocket of Southern California. After the 1983 storm that badly damaged the pier, many thought it was a goner. Today, the new pier is stronger and flashier than ever, with carnival rides, loads of vendors, and even an aquarium. Open daily. Allow two hours to half a day, depending on how many carousel rides you take.

*Contact the Santa Monica Visitor Information Center at **800-544-5319** or the Santa Monica Pier Corporation at **310-458-8900;** www.santamonicapier.org.* ***RV parking** is available in designated lots.*

Sleeping along the California Coast

Sometimes, finding an RV park in California can be tough. It can also be tough to find the RV park that suits you or fits your price range; private California RV campgrounds can be breathtakingly expensive, particularly near anything even remotely considered a resort. We spend Christmastime RVing near family in San Juan Capistrano, and the pickings are lean. However, this Central Coast drive offers more to choose from in areas that have been attracting campers for a long time, including the state park system.

The PCH is chockablock with state park campgrounds where you can overnight in your RV (usually without any water, electric or sewer hookups) if you've made advance reservations. *Note:* All California state park campgrounds now require reservations. At one time you could arrive early on a weekday when other campers were checking out and arrange for a space, but all state park campers today are told to use the **ReserveCalifornia** website (www.reservecalifornia.com) to reserve a spot. You can still make reservations by phone (**800-444-PARK [7275]**) from 8:00 a.m. to 6:00 p.m.

You must make reservations at least two days in advance, or you can schedule your stay as long as six months out. However, if you're in a situation where you had no time to plan ahead, 20 state parks do allow same-day reservations, and many of them are along this Central California drive. These parks include **El Capitán, Malibu Creek, Leo Carrillo, Morro Bay, San Simeon, Point Mugu,** and **Pismo Beach.** If you're trying to get into a particular campground and had no time to plan, always give same-day reservations a shot.

REMEMBER

Of course, with a private campground, you can make a phone call and reserve an open site for as long as you want to stay. But remember, private campgrounds will also fill up on weekends in summer.

Altogether, some three dozen RV parks, including state parks and national forest campgrounds, are located along this coastal route. **California's Best Camping** (http://www.californiasbestcamping.com/) is an excellent general info site about public campgrounds in Central California.

TIP

If you want to stay in the Malibu area and your pocketbook can't handle a commercial campground, you need to use the state park system. Try **Leo Carrillo State Beach** or **Malibu Creek State Park.** We've never stayed there, but we've seen some great reviews for **Point Mugu State Park's Sycamore Canyon Campground,** farther north on the PCH.

And if you have your heart set on camping near the beach and you're not made of money, your best option — again — is one of the state park campgrounds. We also recommend traveling in September or October, well after the high summer season, or perhaps in very early spring, when the weather is still nice but the campgrounds aren't as full. Campendium lists the "9 Best Campgrounds for Beach Camping in California" (https://go.campendium.com/best-beach-camping-california), and many of them are in the Central Coast area. Another helpful Campendium list, "RV Campgrounds Near Big Sur" (https://go.campendium.com/rv-campgrounds-near-big-sur), is loaded with information (about campgrounds and the Big Sur area in general).

WATER, WATER EVERYWHERE (JUST NOT IN STATE PARKS)

One thing to remember about California state park camping: Always arrive with a full freshwater holding tank, along with bottled water in your pantry — enough to see you through to your next stop, or at least to a store. Campground bathrooms tend to be low-functioning and not very clean. Paid showers are common; you keep pumping in coins (or buying tokens), usually a quarter for a minute or two, but they don't function well. Sometimes, you'll be told there's fresh water available in the park (or even a water hookup on your site), but you find a problem when you arrive — for example, the water isn't considered safe to drink. During a Southern California water emergency, all nonessential use of water is banned, and that may include access to water at your campground. Be prepared!

All campgrounds highlighted in Table 15-1 are open year-round in sunny California, and have flush toilets, showers, and sanitary dump stations unless otherwise noted. (Many dump stations in state parks now charge a use fee.) Toll-free numbers, where listed, are for reservations only.

TABLE 15-1 **Our Favorite California Coast Campgrounds**

Name and Location	Contact Info	Cost	What to Know
Malibu Beach RV Park; Malibu	25801 SR 1; **800-622-6052** or **310-456-6052;** www.maliburv.com	$$$–$$$$$	Total of 142 sites with water and 30/50-amp electric; 82 full hookups; nearly all sites are back-in; only 6 pull-throughs; tent sites. Laundry, no pool. With a knockout view of the Pacific, it's the only campground in Malibu. Even with a beach on the other side of the highway, you pay for the privilege of being oceanfront: Rates are seasonal, higher on weekends, and much higher in summer. Upcharges for pets (there are breed restrictions). The campground requires photos of your RV before you check in, and they can turn you down on arrival if they don't like the way it looks. 28-day maximum stay.
Morro Bay State Park; Morro Bay	State Park Road, off SR 1 at South Bay Boulevard; **805-772-7434** or **800-444-7275** for reservations; www.parks.ca.gov/?page_id=594	$$	Total of 120 sites with water and 20/30-amp electric; 28 pull-throughs. ADA accessible, pay showers, Wi-Fi. Spacious shaded and landscaped sites with picnic tables, wooden food lockers, and stone firepits/grills. Handy sightseeing location offers great bird-watching in Morro Bay estuary, scenic camping, and a pretty 1-mile walk into town. Wintering monarch butterflies sleep in eucalyptus trees from fall to spring. Adjacent to 18-hole golf course; kayak and canoe rentals nearby.
Morro Dunes RV Park; Morro Bay	1700 Embarcadero; **805-772-2722;** https://morrodunes.com	$$$	Total of 170 sites with water and 30/50-amp electric; 130 full hookups; 35 pull-throughs. CATV, ADA accessible, laundry, Wi-Fi, friendly staff. Small pet upcharge; charge for dump station if you don't have full hookups. On the dunes by the sea in Morro Bay. Most campsites have a view of Morro Rock and dramatic sunsets, and it's a short walk to the beach. Pull-throughs are at the back of the lot, still close to the beach but less noisy. Call ahead for reservations any time of year; this is one of the most popular campgrounds in California.

(continued)

TABLE 15-1 *(continued)*

Name and Location	Contact Info	Cost	What to Know
Cachuma Lake Recreation Area; Santa Barbara	1 Lakeview Dr.; **805-568-2460;** www.countyofsb. org/637/ Cachuma-Lake	$$–$$$	Total of 152 sites with water and 30-amp electric; 105 full hookups; 15 pull-throughs. Large campground worth the detour off the coastal route in the Santa Ynez Valley. Run by Santa Barbara County with many surprising amenities, including a camp store, laundry, and gas station. Park rangers offer (for a fee) a lake cruise to spot the local wildlife (like bald eagles, osprey, and wild turkeys). 14-day maximum stay.
Flying Flags RV Resort and Campground; Buellton	180 Avenue of Flags; **805-688-3716;** https:// flyingflags.com	$$$– $$$$$	Total of 274 sites with full hookups; 30/50-amp electric; back-ins and premium pull-throughs. CATV, laundry, pool, Wi-Fi. Resort campground right in town loaded with amenities, including an on-site brick-oven pizza restaurant and bar with a patio. Lively, social atmosphere; live music often. Playground, bocce court. Cabins, tents, and restored vintage trailers available.
San Simeon Beach State Park; Cambria	5 miles south of San Simeon on SR 1; **805-927-2035** or **800-444-7275** for reservations; https:// tinyurl.com/ bdfynju8	$$	No hookups; some ADA accessible sites; somewhat cramped with maximum 35-foot RV length. Should be potable water at dump station. Limited restroom facilities. Near the visitor center for Hearst Castle and a convenient place to overnight before or after your tour. Two campgrounds in the park: **San Simeon Creek** (shorter walk to the beach) and **Washburn** (primitive campground farther away). Moonstone Beach and Elephant Seal Beach are nearby. Reserve ahead for weekends.
Marina Dunes RV Park; Marina	3330 Dunes Dr.; **831-384-6914;** www.rvonthego. com/california/ marina-dunes- rv-park	$$$$	Total of 88 sites with full hookups; no pull-throughs. Showers, laundry, Wi-Fi. Loaded with amenities: clubhouse, fitness room, glamping tents, and easy access to the highway. All sites are back-ins, not particularly wide, but framed by foliage for privacy. Well-landscaped campground on the ocean near a wild stretch of beach and dunes. An Encore/Thousand Trails property.

TIP

If you're in need of an RV park in Monterey at the end of the itinerary, take note that there are no fewer than three KOA campgrounds in the area: Moss Landing KOA Express, Salinas/Monterey KOA, and Santa Cruz/Monterey Bay KOA Holiday.

Good Eats along the Central California Coast

Although chic and expensive restaurants line this route, some of them get uptight when they see an RV drive up. We prefer friendly, down–home takeout spots, and we like to focus on local and regional cooking.

THE REAL CATTLE KINGS ARE THE ELKS

Since 1935, the Santa Maria Elk's Lodge #1538 has been hosting a barbecue night, a local institution. Over the years, the pitmasters of the Elk's lodge are credited with developing and refining the Santa Maria-style of barbecue known today. Or, as one long-time lodge member put it, this is the *real* Santa Maria barbecue: "Everyone else is pretending."

The barbecue created in Santa Maria is unique, born in huge Spanish-style barbecues hosted by area ranchers in the 19th century. In the 1920s, the local Elks lodge began hosting similar barbecue events as fund raisers. Eventually, they could accommodate an astonishing 850 guests for the "Friday Night Cook-Your-Own" barbecue. It's still going strong.

The Elks originated in New York as a fraternal drinking club for theatrical people — their formal name is "Benevolent and Protective Order of Elks," (abbreviated as, B.P.O.E.) but members like to claim their group's initials *really* stand for "Best People On Earth." You gotta love any organization that provides free RV parking at their lodges for their members.

The Santa Maria rules are carved in stone: The wood has to be red oak, not white, and it has to burn down until the coals are perfect to grill over; use a huge hunk of rib eye or top-block sirloin, spitted and slow grilled. No gooey sauces, and a rub that's not over-whelming with spice — just salt and pepper and garlic salt. When the coals are ready, the steel skewers of meat are lowered to the fire, and sliced apart with killer-sharp knives when cooked to rare. Serve with fresh salsa, salad, local pinquito beans, mac and cheese and grilled baguette garlic bread; potatoes are apparently optional. Foodies have come from all over the United States to sample it.

You have to be an Elk yourself, or come as the guest of one to participate. One thing that's unique is that you can pick out your meat, fish, chicken or ribs, and cook it yourself

(continued)

(continued)

at the massive, 50-foot-long grill, with its industrial chains and pulleys, under the watchful eye of the volunteer pitmasters. Legendary pitmaster Ike Simas, who died in 2018 at the age of 91, passed on his vast knowledge to new generations, after having cooked for a fan no less than Ronald Reagan.

The Elks continue their long tradition of food and charity today; the lodge partners with Santa Barbara County in providing grocery bags of food to the needy. Hats off to them, of course, but hats off as well for keeping the Santa Maria barbecue, and the tradition of socializing and fun that goes with it, alive and healthy.

Santa Maria barbecue

After decades as a cherished secret Central Coast cuisine, **Santa Maria barbecue** reached national prominence in the 1980s when then President Ronald Reagan hosted a Santa Maria style barbecue on the White House lawn, and food magazines began featuring this unique barbecue variety. But it's still far better known on the Central Coast than in the rest of the country. There are many beloved styles of American barbecue, from Texas mesquite-smoked brisket to Kansas City slow-smoked ribs, but only Santa Maria Valley serves up side dishes of tiny, tasty *pinquito* (pink) beans, grown exclusively in Santa Barbara County, and piquant salsa inherited from the *Californios* (descents of Spanish and Mexican settlers).

The Santa Maria style began more than a century ago with the hospitable Californio ranch families who welcomed strangers with giant outdoor barbecues. Later, local ranchers celebrated the end of communal cattle roundups by throwing hunks of beef on live oak (also called red oak) logs in a hand-dug pit and having a party. Then, in the 1950s, Santa Maria butcher Bob Schutz perfected the *tri-tip*, a triangular cut of beef from the bottom sirloin usually designated for stew. Cooks seasoned it with salt, pepper, olive oil, garlic, and red wine vinegar, and tossed it on the grill.

Today you find Santa Maria barbecue in a few places — in sit-down restaurants along the Central Coast (a list follows) or in the little town of Santa Maria, about an hour north of Santa Barbara, in any parking lot along Broadway where you see the smoke rising from a portable barbecue between noon and 6:00 p.m. on Saturdays and Sundays. You can also hit the street market in San Luis Obispo on Thursday from 6:00 to 9:00 p.m., where vendors with portable cookers clog Higuera Street and sell sandwiches or cooked barbecue by the pound.

Or you can make the barbecue yourself by buying a tri-tip roast or other suitable cut of beef, sometimes already marinated, from any market in Santa Maria or another nearby market, such as **Spencer's Fresh Market** in Morro Bay. Local butchers will tell you with confidence that tri-tip (which used to end up, more often than not, ground up for hamburger) is the *only* roast for genuine Santa Maria barbecue.

Besides pinquito beans and salsa, side dishes in a restaurant meal of Santa Maria barbecue include a relish dish of pickles, olives, carrots, and celery sticks, shrimp cocktail, garlic bread, and a baked potato. When you buy barbecue from a roadside stand, take whatever they're offering on the side.

Since the 1950s, three legendary restaurants have been considered the best Central Coast purveyors of Santa Maria style barbecue:

>> **Far Western Tavern,** 300 East Clark Avenue, Orcutt (**805-937-2211;** https:// farwesterntavern.com/): This longtime resident of Guadalupe moved a decade ago to Orcutt, about 20 minutes away. The owners prefer to use *bull's-eye* (rib eye) steaks up to 20 ounces, and also offer cowboy-cut top sirloin cooked in the Santa Maria style with pinquito beans and salsa on the side. Appetizers include crisp *mountain oysters* or *calf fries* (testicles) with dipping sauce. (Be aware that on a menu out West, *Rocky Mountain oysters, prairie oysters, calf fries,* or *lamb fries* are all euphemisms for testicles. You're welcome.) Open Thursday through Sunday.

>> **The Hitching Post,** 3325 Point Sal Rd., Casmalia (**805-937-6151;** https:// hitchingpost1.com): The Hitching Post, north of Vandenberg Space Force Base, has been around since 1952. Their meat is cooked Santa Maria style and served with all the trimmings, except beans, on red tablecloths. Open daily.

A second location at 406 E. SR 246, Buellton (**805-688-0676**), is a slightly fancier version of its Casmalia parent, offering ostrich steaks, turkey, and quail, also cooked over live oak logs, along with the house appetizer, grilled artichokes with smoky, spicy chipotle mayonnaise. Open evenings daily.

>> **Jocko's Steakhouse,** 125 N. Thompson St., Nipomo (**805-929-3686;** https:// jockossteakhouse.com/): Standing on a corner in Nipomo like a pool hall or burger joint, Jocko's is notable for its Santa Maria barbecue. It's a busy place; consider making reservations. Open daily.

SOLVANG: A LITTLE BIT OF DENMARK

In 1911, a group of Danish immigrants came to the Santa Ynez Valley, where they founded the village of Solvang — the self-proclaimed "Danish capital of America." By the late 1930s, Danish-style buildings predominated, with four large wooden windmills, along with Little Mermaid and Hans Christian Andersen statues, giving the town a unique European village vibe.

In the 1920s, travelers between L.A. and San Francisco discovered that the little town of Buellton, filled with gas stations, diners and motels, was a natural stopping place — the newly-paved Pacific Coast Highway passed right through the center of town back then. They'd fill their tank, and have a bowl of Buellton's "world-famous" pea soup at **Pea Soup Andersen's** (www.peasoupandersens.com). When they discovered the little Danish village less than 4 miles away, a genuine tourist mecca was born. By the 1960s, they were coming from far and wide to buy Danish souvenirs and classic Danish food — especially pastries like *aebleskiver* (deliciously puffy pancake balls popular at Christmastime), almond custard *kringle*, and fresh apple danish.

Today, Solvang remains a busy tourist destination that draws more than 1.5 million people every year. It's still a lovely place to take a break from the road, grab a bite to eat, and stretch your legs with a little shopping. Shops sell Danish beer and chocolate, local wines, jewelry, and antiques, and there are loads of restaurants in every price range. Bakeries have always been Solvang's most popular businesses, and old family establishments here still sell true Danish pastries. For things to see and do, see the town website (www.solvangusa.com).

If you're staying overnight in the area, check out one of the top RV resorts in California, Buellton's **Flying Flags RV Resort Campground** (https://flyingflags.com). You can still get pea soup at Anderson's, almost a full century after it opened. Or, check out the very **fun A.J. Spurs Saloon & Dining Hall** (www.ajspurs.com), a big hit with families with its Wild West theme, taxidermied animals, gigantic portions, and decent prices.

Finding a supermarket

This part of California's coast has plenty of supermarkets, wineries, and just about every sort of specialty food supplier you can imagine. If you want to do some wine tasting and stock up on vintages from the area, see the information in "More Cool Things to See and Do in Central California" earlier in this chapter.

For your everyday grocery supplies in California, you have an embarrassment of choices. **Safeway** and **Albertsons** are longtime favorites here. **Ralphs,** owned by Kroger, will look very familiar to the typical Kroger shopper. They also have a slightly different type of store, **Ralphs Fresh Fare,** which carries more fresh and organic foods than their usual locations. Other large statewide chains include **Vons** and the oddly named **Smart & Final.**

Trader Joe's, notable for budget-priced wines and specialty foods, has a big market we like on a hilltop beside U.S. 101 in Arroyo Grande. They can also be found in Santa Barbara, Santa Maria, San Luis Obispo, and Carmel-by-the-Sea. Amazon-owned **Whole Foods** is in Oxnard, Santa Barbara, San Luis Obispo, and Monterey.

Outside the dense megalopolis of Los Angeles, **Walmart** has a strong presence statewide; with 278 locations in 191 California cities, they're easy to find on this route.

Specialty markets and meals

You may want to fill your fridge with fresh fish and produce from some of our other favorite spots. We also include options for when you want someone else to do the cooking. For information on picking up Danish treats, see the nearby sidebar "Solvang: A little bit of Denmark."

>> **Giovanni's Fish Market,** 1001 Front St., Morro Bay (**805-772-2123;** www. giosfish.com): This market has a live crab tank and cooker outside, a takeout window for fish and chips and other seafood goodies, and a full-fledged fish market inside, selling everything from cooked crab and shrimp to calamari salad and fresh-from-the-Pacific rock cod, halibut, and Petrale sole. The cooked and cleaned cracked crab comes in its own takeout box lined with a red-and-white-checked mini "tablecloth," and is ready to be devoured on the nearby picnic tables that overlook the fishing fleet. Open daily.

**BARGAIN
ALERT**

>> **La Super-Rica Taqueria,** 622 N. Milpas St., Santa Barbara (**805-963-4940;** www.facebook.com/lasuperricataqueria): This taco stand is America's most famous, thanks to a long-ago rave by food icon Julia Child. Instead of running with her plug to found a fast-food franchise, owner and chef Isidoro Gonzalez retained the same pleasant little restaurant he built in 1980, kept cooking what he and Child liked, and added new daily specials.

Diners still queue up to place an order, pay in advance, take a number, and sit in the casual eating area awaiting their cooked-to-order food. Beer and soft drinks are available, and the counter displays several varieties of homemade salsas. Recommended dishes include the Super-Rica, grilled tri-tip with a fresh cheese-stuffed poblano, pinto beans, vegetarian tamales, and a dynamite *posole* (hominy and pork stew), a special on weekends. Simple, hearty food, and no Santa Barbara prices. Open Thursday through Tuesday.

>> **Morro Bay Farmers' Market,** which is a **SLO County Farmers' Market,** 2650 Main St., Morro Bay (**805-503-9105;** www.slocountyfarmers.org): In the large parking lot of Spencer's Fresh Market on Thursday afternoon, you find just-picked fruits and vegetables plus local crafts and cut flowers. Inside Spencer's is a full selection of groceries, including homemade European-style sausages, local produce, eggs from Cal Poly farms in San Luis Obispo, dried pinquito beans, and marinated tri-tip roasts. A smaller farmers market on Saturday afternoon at Main Street and Morro Bay Blvd. (**805-824-7383;** https://www.morrobayfarmersmarket.com/) sells produce, specialty foods, local crafts, and everyone's favorite, kettle corn.

>> **Downtown SLO Farmers' Market,** Higuera Street, San Luis Obispo (**800-634-1414;** https://downtownslo.com/farmers-market): You can chow down on hot Santa Maria barbecue sandwiches while you shop. Along with the food, there's live music and a fresh, fun atmosphere. Traffic is banned in the market area, so look for parking on the streets nearby. It runs every Thursday evening year-round.

Fast Facts for Coastal California

Area Code
This chapter includes four area codes: **310** in the Los Angeles area, **805** south of San Luis Obispo, **831** north of San Luis Obispo, and **415** in San Francisco.

Driving Laws
California's maximum speed limit is 70 mph, but it has the toughest speed limits in the nation for RVs. All trucks and vehicles towing trailers have a limit of 55 mph. Class As are included in the speed limit for truckers.

All RV occupants must wear seat belts in California. Passengers are permitted to ride in towed trailers. No individual RVs longer than 45 feet and no combined RVs and towed vehicles longer than 65 feet are permitted in California.

Emergency
Call **911**. For roadside assistance, call **511** for Freeway Service Patrol, operated by the California Highway Patrol and California Department of Transportation (Caltrans).

Hospitals
Hospitals along the route are in San Luis Obispo, Arroyo Grande, Malibu, and Monterey.

Information
Helpful resources include the California Office of Tourism (**916-322-1266**; https://tourism.ca.gov), the California Department of Parks and Recreation, also known as California State Parks (**800-777-0369**; www.parks.ca.gov), Camp California (www.camp-california.com), and the California Department of Fish and Wildlife (**916-445-0411**; https://wildlife.ca.gov).

Road and Weather Conditions
For updated info on weather and road closures, call Caltrans at **800-427-7623**. Or dial **511** for directed info.

Taxes
Sales tax is 7.25 percent. Some city and county rates may raise sales tax to 10.25 percent. With per-gallon taxes and fees, including a 54.7¢ excise tax, 23¢ for the cap-and-trade program, and 18¢ for the low-carbon fuel program, gas prices in California are the highest in the nation.

Time Zone
California is on Pacific time.

IN THIS CHAPTER

» **Looking forward to those Route 66 kicks**

» **Driving the route through five states**

» **Romping through natural wonders and roadside attractions**

» **Scoping out spots to rest and relax**

» **Finding food and more fun**

Chapter **16**

Route 66: OK to L.A.

M ystique is an almost impossible thing to deliberately create — it happens organically. Route 66, the original federal highway from Chicago to Los Angeles, has earned its mythic status.

John Steinbeck called Route 66 "the mother road" (a nickname that has stuck) in his classic novel *The Grapes of Wrath*. The 2006 animated Pixar/Disney film *Cars* and its 2011 sequel introduced new generations to its kitschy charms. But whether it's being traversed by Steinbeck's dirt-poor Joad family in a broken-down truck, or by good-natured buddies Tod and Buz (of the 1960s TV series Route 66) in their hyper-cool Corvette, this famous highway has sung its siren song to anyone with a dream of hitting the road.

From the 1930s until the Arab oil embargo of the 1970s, Route 66 was the road of choice for Americans heading west to make a new life or just take a vacation. From East Coast urbanites to middle-class Midwesterners, Route 66 led people who'd never encountered a tumbleweed to discover wonders like the Grand Canyon and the Petrified Forest, Native American art and jewelry, and legendary places in the Old West they'd only seen in the movies. Not to mention goofy souvenirs and zany motels.

Lots of the oldest roadside attractions have been swallowed up by the sands that sweep across the desert. In this chapter, you find out about the next generation that's fighting to preserve the lure of the route that still survives. Pop on a Nat King Cole album, grab a tasty beverage, and read on, as we do our best to wrap you up in the mystique of the most famous stretch of highway in the world.

Planning Ahead for Your Route 66 Kicks

Overall, spring and fall are the best times to travel Route 66. In general, you can drive the stretch of the road we cover year-round, but businesses and campgrounds along the route can be seasonal, open only from April or May through September. After Labor Day, tourist traffic slows to a trickle, apart from snowbirds fleeing the cold on their way to Padre Island, Phoenix, or Tucson.

Allow at least 10 days, but preferably two weeks, to take a leisurely drive along Route 66.

ROUTE 66: THE ROAD WITH ITS OWN THEME MUSIC

No road has more glamour clinging to it than Route 66. It was the way West to the golden land of promise. It even had its own anthem — *Get Your Kicks on Route 66*. The song was written by jazz pianist and actor Bobby Troup in 1941; he composed it during ten days on the road when he and his wife moved to California. The song was first recorded by Nat King Cole and his trio in 1946, and became a jazz standard. It also became the unofficial anthem for people traveling this oh-so-American highway. During the bridge in the song, you hear most of the major cities 66 passes through, with one glaring exception: Troup couldn't come up with a word that rhymed with *Albuquerque*.

When the popular TV show *Route 66* came along in 1960, it seemed inexplicable that CBS didn't use Troup's song. But the instrumental theme Nelson Riddle wrote for the show turned out to be another hit on its own, proving there's always more room in the truck stop for another souvenir of Route 66.

So, put the top down, slide the seat back, and pop on your shades. Here are the lyrics, in case you want to sing along with Nat.

If you ever plan to motor west
Travel my way, take the highway that's the best
Get your kicks on Route 66
It winds from Chicago to L.A
More than two thousand miles all the way
Get your kicks on Route 66
Now it goes through Saint Looey
Joplin, Missouri
Oklahoma City looks mighty pretty
You'll see Amarillo
Gallup, New Mexico
Flagstaff, Arizona
Don't forget Winona
Kingman, Barstow, San Bernardino
Won't you get hip to this timely tip
When you make, make that California trip?
Get your kicks on Route 66
Get your kicks on Route 66

Checking out the seasonal elements

In winter, snow often falls in the upper elevations of New Mexico and especially in Arizona around Flagstaff. On a couple December drives to California, we've had to duck south on I-17 to Phoenix, picking up a more southern route to continue west, all because of a bad snow in Flagstaff.

Temperature-wise, the wintertime is mildest in the West (highs in the 70s, lows in the mid-30s), but the eastern parts of the route in Oklahoma, Texas, and New Mexico can be bitter cold and windy. The January winds of New Mexico are a legendary struggle for RVers. Nighttime temperatures in the 20s aren't uncommon, and your RV needs to be suitable for wintertime camping, with heated water tanks and a propane furnace to keep pipes from freezing. Campgrounds may have their water turned off entirely.

Conversely, summer can be dangerously hot along parts of the road in California, Arizona, and the Texas Panhandle. July temperatures in the Mojave Desert often hit 110 degrees F in the daytime, plunging into the 60s after sundown. Spring can bring gusty winds in these areas.

Reserving camping spots and packing

Campground reservations aren't usually necessary unless you have your heart set on a particular park. We often decide in early to midafternoon how much farther we want to travel, figure how far we'll get, and call ahead to a campground in that area to reserve a spot. We like the freedom to decide at the last minute. Just keep in mind that busy holiday weekends can put a kink in your plans.

When packing, take along hiking boots, rain gear, lightweight clothing for hot weather (even in winter), and warm clothing for cool days; we highly recommend a packable puffer jacket. The higher you climb, the colder it can get, particularly at night. Sunscreen and sunglasses are essential in the bright desert sunlight. Make sure to take your binoculars and your camera.

WHAT'S SO GREAT ABOUT 66?

For older generations, Route 66 is the highway that came to symbolize the golden age of the American automobile, painting the image of footloose Americans as car travelers, proving that the going can be as rewarding as the getting there. Cars became a symbol of American affluence and personal freedom, and into this auto age were born drive-in restaurants, drive-in movies, and even drive-in churches.

To service these new cross-country travelers, American entrepreneurs invented diners, tourist cabins, campgrounds, motels and motor courts, with their neon signs lighting up the desert darkness. All along Route 66, travelers were treated to motels shaped liked teepees and billboard teasers in comic-book colors hawking souvenir stands and roadside attractions, from rattlesnakes to *jackalopes* (the imaginary, fast-moving antlered offspring of jackrabbits and antelopes). Billboard advertising hit its heyday along Route 66, and the roadside was clogged with hundreds of them in every state, hawking gas stations, motels, eateries, tourist attractions, roadside souvenir stands and "trading posts."

Route 66 is so culturally important and so unique to the fabric of America that there are more than 250 buildings, bridges, road alignments and other related sites along 66 that are listed on the National Register of Historic Places. (Read all about them at www.nps. gov/subjects/travelroute66/index.htm.) There are hundreds more that didn't make the list, and that doesn't even count the incredible natural wonders along this famous ribbon of asphalt.

For the World War II generation, Route 66 was one of the auto trail highways, state roads cobbled together that became part of the U.S. Route system. These were roads built long before the massive Interstate Highway System project begun by President Eisenhower in 1956 and finally completed in 1981. The newer federal super-highways deliberately avoided going through town business areas that had traditionally been servicing travelers.

This was the difference between the new interstates and the old auto routes like Route 66 and old Route 40; the old highways went right through the smaller town centers, becoming, in effect, the nation's main streets. When the new interstates came through, far from the town centers, they helped create the suburbs and donut communities that abandoned so many downtowns, big and small. The new interstates deliberately went around them, and while large chain businesses that located out by the new exit ramps tended to do well, the small mom-and-pop businesses in the towns began, almost at once, to die. In the mid-1960s, big cities realized they'd made a terrible mistake by insisting interstates stay out of their downtowns — they hurriedly rushed to bulldoze through urban areas to bring the big multi-lane interstates through the hearts of their cities. But smaller communities didn't have the economic or political clout to reroute the big roads to their advantage.

Plotting Your Route 66 Itinerary

The original Route 66 measured 2,448 miles, snaking from downtown Chicago's Art Institute south and west to the last taco cart at the farthest end of the Santa Monica Pier in California. The itinerary we cover in this chapter (see Figure 16-1) is a 1,453-mile stretch that we believe is the best combination of kitsch, history, natural wonders, food, gift shops, and more.

Route 66, among its other nicknames, was officially dedicated in 1952 as the **Will Rogers Highway** to honor the famous actor, newspaper columnist, and cowboy humorist. And so we begin in his hometown of **Claremore, Oklahoma,** in eastern Oklahoma, inside the Cherokee Nation, and end five states later overlooking the Pacific Ocean in **Santa Monica, California,** where a plaque in Pacific Palisades commemorates Rogers and the highway.

REMEMBER

We admit up front, we love this drive. Even though our itinerary doesn't cover Route 66's *entire* length, it's still at least twice as long as the other itineraries in this book. Some of the detours onto old Route 66 add more miles to the journey.

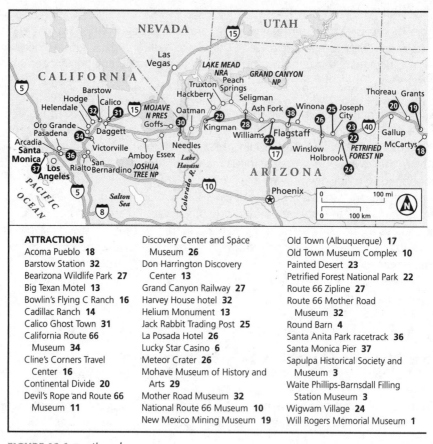

ATTRACTIONS

Acoma Pueblo **18**
Barstow Station **32**
Bearizona Wildlife Park **27**
Big Texan Motel **13**
Bowlin's Flying C Ranch **16**
Cadillac Ranch **14**
Calico Ghost Town **31**
California Route 66
  Museum **34**
Cline's Corners Travel
  Center **16**
Continental Divide **20**
Devil's Rope and Route 66
  Museum **11**

Discovery Center and Space
  Museum **26**
Don Harrington Discovery
  Center **13**
Grand Canyon Railway **27**
Harvey House hotel **32**
Helium Monument **13**
Jack Rabbit Trading Post **25**
La Posada Hotel **26**
Lucky Star Casino **6**
Meteor Crater **26**
Mohave Museum of History and
  Arts **29**
Mother Road Museum **32**
National Route 66 Museum **10**
New Mexico Mining Museum **19**

Old Town (Albuquerque) **17**
Old Town Museum Complex **10**
Painted Desert **23**
Petrified Forest National Park **22**
Route 66 Zipline **27**
Route 66 Mother Road
  Museum **32**
Round Barn **4**
Santa Anita Park racetrack **36**
Santa Monica Pier **37**
Sapulpa Historical Society and
  Museum **3**
Waite Phillips-Barnsdall Filling
  Station Museum **3**
Wigwam Village **24**
Will Rogers Memorial Museum **1**

FIGURE 16-1: *continued*

Driving Route 66 in Oklahoma

The must-see in **Claremore,** Oklahoma is the **Will Rogers Memorial Museum,** a large and well-displayed collection of his personal possessions, mementos, costumes, and many of his 70 films. Continue along Route 66, which parallels I-44, the **Will Rogers Turnpike,** through this part of Oklahoma.

WARNING

Be aware that you can get trapped on the **Oklahoma Turnpike.** Like most toll roads, it has few exits. Because the turnpike charges a toll and has limited on and off access, you need to stay on Route 66 instead, all the way to Oklahoma City, if you don't want to miss any of the classic landmarks along the way. At Tulsa, take I-44 or I-244 to the west side of town and rejoin Route 66 at Exit 220. This section of the old route is well maintained.

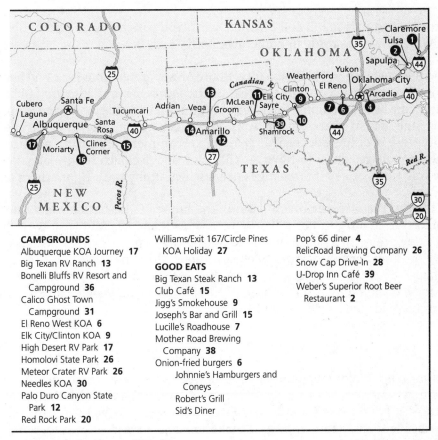

CAMPGROUNDS
Albuquerque KOA Journey **17**
Big Texan RV Ranch **13**
Bonelli Bluffs RV Resort and
   Campground **36**
Calico Ghost Town
   Campground **31**
El Reno West KOA **6**
Elk City/Clinton KOA **9**
High Desert RV Park **17**
Homolovi State Park **26**
Meteor Crater RV Park **26**
Needles KOA **30**
Palo Duro Canyon State
   Park **12**
Red Rock Park **20**

Williams/Exit 167/Circle Pines
   KOA Holiday **27**

GOOD EATS
Big Texan Steak Ranch **13**
Club Café **15**
Jigg's Smokehouse **9**
Joseph's Bar and Grill **15**
Lucille's Roadhouse **7**
Mother Road Brewing
   Company **38**
Onion-fried burgers **6**
   Johnnie's Hamburgers and
      Coneys
   Robert's Grill
   Sid's Diner

Pop's 66 diner **4**
RelicRoad Brewing Company **26**
Snow Cap Drive-In **28**
U-Drop Inn Café **39**
Weber's Superior Root Beer
   Restaurant **2**

FIGURE 16-1: Our Route 66 trek.

In Sapulpa, the "Heart of Historic Route 66," the **Waite Phillips-Barnsdall** Filling Station Museum, may be the first Route 66–specific museum you come across, and it's one of the better ones, with some nice 1920s autos on display, just across the street from the **Sapulpa Historical Society and Museum**.

Don't miss Arcadia's famous Round Barn. It's a beautiful restoration and a great stop — not just to admire the barn itself and its truly incredible roof but to wander the museum and gift shop to pick up some Route 66 souvenirs. Just a bit farther down the road (you can't miss it) is **Pops 66** diner and gas station, with its giant pop bottle; it's a corker when it's lit up at night.

Reaching Oklahoma City

Oklahoma City is home to the **National Cowboy and Western Heritage Museum**, worth a good half-day minimum for cowboy fans who like art or art aficionados who appreciate cowboys and Westerns. From the museum, follow I-44 West to

Route 66 at Exit 123-B and continue west. You pass through **Yukon,** displaying on a water tower its pride in hometown hero Garth Brooks.

On the west side of Oklahoma City, Route 66 separates from I-44 and becomes intertwined with I-40 for the rest of the journey into California. Oklahoma City can be challenging for RVers unfamiliar with its roads and confusing signage, and at press time in 2023, long stretches of interstates through the city were in desperate need of repair. We recommend studying a physical map before you get close to town — GPS and Google Maps both make a couple wrong turns at key interchanges because even they can't figure them out.

El Reno, the next town you pass, is the home of the **Lucky Star Casino** and the **onion-fried burger.** For folks from New York and the Midwest, we sniff a White Castle here, with a burger invented during the Depression that fleshes out expensive ground beef with reams of cheap onions. Other people call it a *smash burger* — shades of Steak 'n Shake, another Midwestern chain. In the end, these burgers survived the Depression because of their great taste. People come for them from far and wide, and fans are faithful.

Finding other Route 66 museums

Clinton is a major stop, not only for its well-preserved strip of old 66, which goes right through town past some of the most famous landmarks of the Mother Road, but also for its fine **Oklahoma Route 66 Museum.** If you want to pick up some barbecue to go, pause at **Jigg's Smokehouse** just west of town for some barbecue sandwiches or home-smoked meats.

Take Business Route/Route 66 through **Elk City,** which calls itself the Natural Gas Capital of the World. The skyline is dominated by a 181-foot-tall oil derrick towering over downtown to commemorate its biggest industry. Elk City also boasts a National Route 66 Museum as part of its **Old Town Museum Complex** on the city's west side. The lawns are decorated with painted metal *kachina dolls* (representing Native American ancestral spirits) and a metal buffalo, an opera house has cutout figures looking out of the upstairs windows, and a false-front Western town encourages even Nintendo kids to play cowboys. There's even a false-front Masonic Lodge door.

Clinton and Elk City are less than 30 minutes apart, leaving a confused newbie to ask, "Does every town in Oklahoma have a Route 66 museum?" Well, they don't, and both these are worth seeing; they can be done in a single day, though two may be more fun.

PHILLIPS 66: THE GASOLINE THAT WON THE WEST!

All along Route 66 you encounter restored service stations or museums displaying signs for Phillips 66, and plenty of the company's modern gas stations line the route today. From the 1920s on, Phillips Petroleum Company deliberately identified their gasoline with the most famous road in America. Their gas stations still feature signs shaped like the federal highway shield and the prominent number 66.

From the earliest years of automobile travel until the 1970s, nobody pumped their own gas — gas stations were full-service stops, and competition between brands was cut-throat. Since drivers really didn't care much about whose gas went into their tank, that meant stations had to find other ways to stand out in the crowd and earn customer loyalty. At Phillips 66 stations, a smartly uniformed attendant dressed in pristine white and wearing a hat and bow tie would run out to your car, ask what kind of fuel you wanted, and start filling the tank. They'd wash all your windows, check your oil level, top off the water to your radiator or battery, and add air to your tires. You got a heck of a lot of service for your 15-cents-a-gallon tank of leaded regular or high-test ethyl gas.

Stopping at Route 66 service stations usually meant potty breaks for the whole family, and gas station restrooms were notoriously filthy places. In the late '30s, Phillips hired a platoon of registered nurses they called Highway Hostesses and dressed them up in full nurse regalia; the hostesses regularly inspected their gas station bathrooms as *guardians of public health*. They'd make sure Phillips managers were keeping their restrooms clean and sanitized and recommend better housekeeping habits. They also acted as tourist advisors, giving tips to travelers, passing out brochures, suggesting side trips, and even offering first aid services.

Phillips 66 stations along the Mother Road benefited tremendously from the road's legendary popularity among tourists — so much so that they added the slogan "The gasoline that won the West!" in the 1960s.

Traipsing through Texas

In Texas, Route 66 zips you across the Panhandle. Stop at **Shamrock** to visit the 1930s-era **Conoco Tower Station** (the real-life model for Ramone's body shop in the animated Pixar/Disney film *Cars*). The station now contains a museum, a visitor's center and gift shop, and the charming **U-Drop Inn Café.** (No gasoline here anymore, but they keep up with the modern-day traveler — there's a lineup of Tesla charging stations out back.)

You'll also want to pause in tiny McLean for a look at the beautifully restored 1930s Phillips 66 service station on the west end of town. The **Devil's Rope Museum** on Route 66 at the corner of **Kingsley** chronicles the history of barbed wire and offers a small Route 66 Museum in the same building.

Steering clear of falling water towers

As you pass Exit 114 for the town of **Groom,** the **Leaning Tower of Texas** will make you momentarily panic. It's an aged water tower that startlingly lists at an 80-degree angle, looking as though it may fall down in a stiff breeze. Most people think it was damaged by a tornado, but it was deliberately installed that way in 1980 by local entrepreneur Ralph Britten to call attention to his roadside truck stop, Britten USA. Until the fuel stop burned down in the early 1990s, the gimmick worked for years as motorists frantically pulled off to warn customers, "Hey! That tower's falling over!"

Ordering the biggest steak ever

The city of Amarillo is the one Texas metropolis along Route 66, and its best-known landmark greets the I-40 traveler for many miles with billboards advertising a free 72-ounce steak at the **Big Texan Steak Ranch**. There's also a **Big Texan Motel,** but best of all, you find the **Big Texan RV Ranch** nearby, with shuttle service to the steak ranch. If you've got a budding chemist or lover of party balloons on board, visit the **Helium Monument** and the adjacent **Don Harrington Discovery Center,** which celebrate the discovery of helium here in the 1860s.

Just west of Amarillo, in plain sight from I-40 and accessible by a designated turnoff road, is the renowned Cadillac Ranch, erected in 1974. The ranch displays ten vintage Cadillacs dating from 1948 to 1964 buried grill-end first in the dirt with tail fins erect, all planted at the same angle as the Great Pyramid of Egypt (so they say).

Taking on the New Mexico stretch

You're ushered into New Mexico at the town of **Glenrio.** At milepost 369, stop at **Russell's Travel Center.** Part museum, part refueling stop, it's got a Route 66 diner, a terrific classic car museum, and even a chapel. You also find a small grocery store, a great place to stop and restock.

Once upon a time, **Tucumcari** was the unofficial capital of Route 66, after its long battle with the federal government to keep the interstate from being routed around it. Although Tucumcari isn't as vibrant as it was in the 1960s, you still see lots of historic properties along the main drag, which is called Historic Route

66, or Tucumcari Boulevard. Take advantage of the full grocery store at 105 West Tucumcari, **Lowe's Market** — it's the last you see for some time on this route. Numerous motels, motor courts, and other businesses have restored their 1950s-era neon signs, and a nighttime drive through is always a fun time.

Stopping for sourdough biscuits, fireworks, and pinto beans

The town of **Santa Rosa** contains a number of Route 66 landmarks, including the notable **Club Café,** founded in 1935 and sadly torn down in 2015. But **Joseph's Bar and Grill,** dating back to 1956, still flourishes, resurrecting some signature dishes from Club Café, including sourdough biscuits. There's also a gift shop.

Between Santa Rosa and **Moriarty** are two fun stops of long standing:

>> At I-40/Route 66 Exit 234 is **Bowlin's Flying C Ranch.** It's not a ranch, and not exactly a truck stop, though there's gas and diesel fuel, and plenty of truck parking. It's a nice travel center on a lonely stretch (with a Dairy Queen), and it sells more than the usual trinkets and T-shirts. You find a big selection of fireworks to separate teenagers from their cash, as well as a surprisingly good selection of quality Native American jewelry.

>> At Exit 218 is **Clines Corners Travel Center,** something of an institution. Clines Corners calls itself an *unincorporated community,* meaning a town without a town council, and it was built here at the junction of I-40 and U.S. 285 in 1934 by Roy E. Cline. The center has grown to include a convenience store, small RV park, and over 30,000 feet of truly goofy retail. (Its whimsical address, incidentally, is 1 Yacht Club Drive.)

Neighboring Moriarty, another 22 miles on, claims it's the Pinto Bean Capital of the World, offering a favorite local cookie made with mashed pinto beans and chocolate chips.

From Albuquerque to Arizona

In **Albuquerque,** I-40 zips right through the middle of town, but if you want to take the time, Central Avenue (which is Historic Route 66) crosses I-40, passing through scenic **Old Town,** filled with historic colonial buildings erected around a plaza, and restaurants and shops featuring New Mexican food, art, and crafts.

After Albuquerque, the road skirts several Native American communities, including the Isleta lands; Laguna Pueblo and **Mission San José de Laguna;** and the wonderful Acoma Pueblo. If gambling appeals to your sense of fun (we're too cheap for it), stop at **Route 66 Casino,** probably the gaudiest, glitziest of all the

Native American–owned casinos along the Mother Road. It's also got places to eat and an adjacent inexpensive RV park.

About 78 miles beyond Albuquerque, you reach **Grants,** where a Navajo rancher named Paddy Martinez found uranium ore in 1950, triggering a latter-day mini gold rush. Today, Grants is home to the **New Mexico Mining Museum,** with a rec-reated uranium mine in the basement.

About halfway between Grants and **Gallup** is the **Continental Divide,** the high-est elevation along Route 66 at 7,200 feet above sea level. The Great Divide is the symbolic point in America where water runs to the west on one side and to the east on the other. There's a fun couple of souvenir and gift shops here (and occa-sionally a small stand selling Chris's favorite snack, fry bread). Some 25 miles to the west, Gallup treasures its status as a Route 66 landmark city, showcasing the 1937 **El Rancho** at 1000 E. Route 66. It was a hangout for Hollywood stars in the 1930s and '40s.

Arriving and thriving in Arizona

Arizona is where Route 66 reached the epitome of its 1930s image, lining its right-of-way with attractions. At Exit 311 from I-40, you're near **Petrified Forest National Park** and **Painted Desert. Holbrook** is home to several older motor-court motels from the 1930s and '40s, along with **Wigwam Village,** one of only three remaining motels in a former national chain offering cement teepees as sleeping quarters. (Another is in Rialto, California, on Foothill Boulevard, which is also part of old Route 66; a third survives in Cave City, Kentucky.) Holbrook has a good-sized business district along the Route, so it makes a great place to stop, eat, and snap pictures.

Nearby **Joseph City** still treasures the roadside **Jack Rabbit Trading Post,** the sub-ject of innumerable yellow billboards along Route 66 that originally started show-ing up as far east as Missouri in the 1950s. Its sign proclaiming "HERE IT IS!" is a long-standing photo op. (In the movie *Cars*, the yellow "HERE IT IS!" billboard for Lizzie's Curio Shop features the silhouette of a Model T roadster instead of a rabbit.) Jack Rabbit survives, but between **Winslow** and Flagstaff, you see the crumbling and graffiti-covered ruins of what were once some of the best-known roadside attractions on Route 66, including **Two Guns, Twin Arrows,** and the **Meteor City Trading Post.**

Taking it easy and looking ahead

At Winslow, you can "take it easy" while "standing on a corner," just as the Eagles song says, and then drop by and see the beautiful **La Posada Hotel,** designed in the 1920s by architect Mary Elizabeth Jane Colter. About 28 miles west is **Meteor Crater,** the largest meteorite impact crater in the world.

By now, you can spot **Flagstaff** in the distance, rising out of the desert floor on its pine tree–covered mountain on the horizon. Take advantage of the high altitude and clear skies to visit the 1894 *Lowell Observatory,* where the dwarf planet Pluto was discovered in 1930. Then tour the historic **Weatherford Hotel** and stop in at the taproom of the **Mother Road Brewing Company.**

Going for the grand view and Route 66 guardians

KID
FRIENDLY

Williams, 28 miles west of Flagstaff, is the gateway to the Grand Canyon. If you want to see the canyon without taking your RV — you won't be permitted to drive it along the scenic Rim Road — consider hopping the **Grand Canyon Railway** in Williams for a one-day round trip by train. Williams may be a small town, but you find a great deal to see and do there, and the attractions are overwhelmingly kid-friendly, from **Route 66 Zipline** to **Bearizona Wildlife Park,** making it an excellent base for a longer stop. You also find the **Williams and Forest Service Visitor Center,** with a replica of an old roadside diner that's a memory bank for travelers along Route 66. Lots of websites have the skinny on Williams; our favorite is https://experiencewilliams.com. Also try the Williams page of the Visit Arizona website (www.visitarizona.com/places/cities/williams).

From Ash Fork to Kingman, you want to drive the old route, which parallels I-40, making a point to pause at **Seligman** (pronounced *slig*-man), where the **Snow Cap Drive-In** still brightens up the historic district with its singular retro charm. It's more than a hamburger stand. Snow Cap's founder, Juan Delgadillo, and his brother Angel were the driving force behind the Historic Route 66 Association of Arizona; Juan Delgadillo died in 2004, but Angel, a barber in Seligman, is still the guardian angel of Route 66, while Juan's son and daughter are carrying on with his restaurant. The entire area is evocative: The nearby towns of **Truxton** and **Hackberry** house landmark diners and gas stations, and **Peach Springs** has resurrected some of the old Burma-Shave signs that lined roadways across the U.S.

Kingman remembers native son Andy Devine, a comic sidekick for cowboy movie stars between the 1930s and 50s, in the **Mohave Museum of History and Arts.** Near the museum is the turnoff on **Historic Route 66 National Back Country Byway** to **Oatman** (often just called the Oatman Highway or the Oatman Cutoff) where wild burros walk the streets expecting handouts, and a few colorful gift shops and cafés survive on mostly weekend tourist business. Just be aware that the drive from Kingman to Oatman in a big RV can be a white-knuckle experience.

Camping near London Bridge

Just before leaving Arizona on I-40, consider a side trip from Exit 9 south on SR 95 for 20 miles to **Lake Havasu City,** on the Colorado River. There are loads of boondocking opportunities around the lake, along with the unusual attraction of **London Bridge.** The bridge was originally built in 1831 across the Thames River in London, but investor Robert McCulloch (of the McCulloch chainsaw company fame) bought it in 1968, dismantled the whole thing, shipped it to Arizona, and had it reassembled across Lake Havasu to attract real estate buyers.

WARNING

Gas up in Arizona before leaving the state; California fuel prices are among the highest in the nation. Also take note that California has a maximum speed limit of just 55 mph for all trucks and vehicles towing trailers, including motorhomes towing cars behind them.

Ending the trek in California

We cross into California's side of the **Mojave Desert** after passing over the Colorado River. **Needles** may be familiar to comic-strip fans as the hometown of Snoopy's brother Spike in Peanuts. The strip's late creator, Charles Schulz, lived in Needles as a child.

At **Daggett,** 12 miles west, you can take a short connecting side road to Calico Ghost Town, an abandoned mining town. A few miles farther, movie buffs might want to pull off at **Newberry Springs** to see the location of the 1987 film *Bagdad Café*. Unfortunately, the café itself is closed.

And yes, another Route 66 museum

Barstow is endearing for its **Route 66 Mother Road Museum** in **Casa del Desierto,** the original **Harvey House** hotel, a historic building that's also the Amtrak/Santa Fe Railroad train depot. For years we passed through Barstow, like so many people on their way to Los Angeles, and we never knew this grand building was here, nor the relatively recent work being done on the several museums in it.

REMEMBER

Incidentally, don't confuse the real **Barstow Amtrak/Santa Fe** station and Harvey House, which sits in town well north of Main Street, with the similar-sounding Barstow Station, just off I-40/Route 66 at the East Main Street Exit. This second station is a large "entertainment architecture" building with a railroad theme, housing a Subway, a McDonald's, a Panda Express, some old railroad passenger cars and a caboose for decoration, as well as a truck stop, convenience store, and vendors selling Route 66 souvenirs. A fun stop for the kids, or if you're searching out fast food. It's also open 24 hours, a convenience increasingly hard to find in California.

Dropping down to Los Angeles

From Barstow, you can drive the original Route 66 roadway south to **Victorville** through **Helendale**.

WARNING

The long, slow descent into the eastern edges of the vast **Los Angeles** metropolitan area starts after Victorville and threads down through the wide curves of the Cajon Pass. This stretch of road may be your introduction to L.A.'s notorious traffic jams, which often happen in both directions. Before you get here, we strongly recommend that you pull off and carefully study a decent physical map of L.A. to get your bearings before the traffic gets heavier. If possible, try to stay in the middle lanes of the interstates because exit ramps and interchanges can be on either side of the highway. Also be aware that L.A.'s highway lanes are slightly narrower than most interstates, and larger RVs often have only a few inches of clearance on either side.

The final stretch of Route 66 into **Los Angeles,** also called Foothill Boulevard, flies through **San Bernardino; Rialto,** where another **Wigwam Motel** offers teepee-shaped units; **Arcadia,** home of the Art Deco racetrack Santa **Anita Park;** and **Pasadena**'s Colorado Boulevard, where **Old Pasadena** has been turned into a row of shops and restaurants.

And on to Santa Monica

After you pass Pasadena, don't attempt to follow the twists and turns of old Route 66 in downtown Los Angeles; little, if any, remains of the color and ambience. Instead, take the Pasadena Freeway (CA 110) to I-10 and follow that west to **Santa Monica.** Here, you reach the end of the journey, with the plaque commemorating the Will Rogers Highway; it's small, angled on a low stone base in **Palisades Park,** at the corner of Ocean Avenue and Santa Monica Boulevard. But this isn't *quite* the end of Route 66 itself; officially, that's the **Santa Monica Pier,** our favorite hangout when we were college kids. In 1983, we watched as a major storm carried off half the pier, damaging it badly, but great changes have happened since that sorry day. Now, a small amusement park stands on the rebuilt pier, along with an aquarium. It's a fun place to spend the afternoon.

Must-See Mother Road Attractions

Acoma Pueblo
Acoma, New Mexico

Called Sky City, this hilltop pueblo is said to be the oldest continuously inhabited community in the U.S., dating back to 1250. Constructed atop a 367-foot sandstone mesa near Grants, the village is open to visitors by guided tour only. A dozen families are still in residence, although most tribal members have settled in the valley below. Visitors can purchase Acoma pottery and bread baked in the outdoor adobe ovens. Visitors are not permitted to enter the *kiva* (sacred chamber) and should expect other restrictions, including paying a fee for using cameras or sketch pads. Allow one or two hours. Open daily; check online for hours of operation.

66 miles west of Albuquerque; **505-552-7861;** *www.acomaskycity.org.* ***RV parking:*** *In the designated lot in the village below Sky City.* ***Note:*** *No one is allowed beyond the parking lot in the village below the mesa without joining a tour.*

Calico Ghost Town
Calico, California

KID FRIENDLY

Extremely popular with European and Japanese Old West aficionados, Calico isn't the built-for-tourists ghost town that some people expect; it's a real silver-mining town that thrived from 1881 to 1907 with a population of 3,500. Walter Knott of Knott's Berry Farm fame, who worked in the mines as a youth, restored and preserved the town, which is operated today by the San Bernardino County park system. Calico Ghost Town Campground is nearby, virtually on-site; RVers camping there get free admission to the ghost town. Original and reconstructed buildings, including a house made of glass bottles, sometimes serve as a backdrop for staged gunfights and other Western shenanigans on weekends and in summer. There are also ghost tours every Saturday night after the park closes. Allow a half-day or more. Open daily. ***Note:*** Visitors not staying at the campground must pay to enter the town; attractions charge additional admission fees.

Calico Exit from I-15 or I-40 east of Barstow; **760-254-1123;** *https://parks. sbcounty.gov/park/calico-ghost-town-regional-park. For additional info on attractions, check out www.calicoattractions.com; for ghost tours, call* **760-985-5347.** ***RV parking:*** *Large parking lots at entrance.*

Grand Canyon Railway
Williams, Arizona

A steam train to the Grand Canyon leaves daily at 9:30 a.m. year-round from the restored 1908 train station in the town of Williams. Passengers ride the refurbished 1928 railcars 65 miles north to the canyon, have a few hours for sightseeing, and then return in late afternoon. At the canyon, the train stops near El Tovar Hotel, where shuttles frequently depart for tours of the South Rim. Allow a full day. Reservations are recommended; check online for days, hours, and Christmastime Polar Express. Prices include Grand Canyon entrance fee.

TIP

To plan a trip within **Grand Canyon National Park**, start by seeing the "plan your visit" website at https://tinyurl.com/5jcw2nsj. Taking the train into Grand Canyon National Park is a good idea during the busy season because you may get stuck for hours in a long line of cars at the south entrance if you don't arrive before 9:00 a.m.

Also, in summer, adequate parking space isn't always available in the lots at the entrance or in the visitor's centers, especially for RVs. Williams has several nice campgrounds if you want to stay the night. You also find Grand Canyon Railway RV Park adjacent to the historic train depot; it's clean and well-run with surprisingly reasonable rates for such a high-profile location.

233 N. Grand Canyon Blvd.; **800-843-8724;** *https://www.thetrain.com.* **RV parking:** *Lot by the station is big enough for any size RV.*

National Cowboy and Western Heritage Museum
Oklahoma City, Oklahoma

Framed against the windows at the end of the massive entry hall where your tour begins, James Earle Fraser's famed marble sculpture, End of the Trail, depicts a Native American warrior astride his horse, his body slumped in exhaustion and defeat, his lance drooping at the same angle as his horse's head. For Fraser, his subject represents the end of an era, the passing of the Old West. This excellent museum displays outstanding art and artifacts from the Old and New West. Recently added or expanded galleries include the American Rodeo Gallery, Western Performers Gallery with movie posters and film and video clips, and Prosperity Junction, a life-size replica of an Old West town. Allow two hours or more. Open daily; closed Thanksgiving, Christmas, and New Year's days.

1700 NE 63rd St.; **405-478-2250;** *https://nationalcowboymuseum.org.* **RV parking:** *Designated area in front of the museum. Admission varies by age.*

Petrified Forest National Park and Painted Desert
I-40 in northeastern Arizona

These two Route 66 landmarks lie across the highway from each other about 25 miles east of Holbrook. A loop road goes through both areas. Stop first at the visitor's center near the entrance to Petrified Forest to get a map and some idea of how this landscape was formed. In the time of the dinosaurs, 225 million years ago, a forest of trees fell into the water and gradually began to petrify, a process in which quartz replaces the organic cells of the trees. Allow a half day. Open daily; closed Christmas Day.

WARNING

Tempting as it may be, picking up any pieces of petrified wood is against the law and bad luck, as letters on display in the Rainbow Forest Museum attest; people who picked up rocks returned them after having unsettling experiences with the park's constabulary. For those who want to acquire the wood legitimately, samples are for sale at the **Crystal Forest Museum** in the southern end of the area.

TIP

Painted Desert is best seen early or late in the day, when the sunlight hits at an angle that makes the colors brighter. If you wear polarized sunglasses and photograph the desert using a polarizing filter, you get more dramatic colors. Petrified Forest doesn't have campgrounds; however, you're near gas stations, convenience markets, and even a bookstore. Go to the website and link to Goods and Services on the Eating and Sleeping page if you're in need.

From Exit 311 on 1-40, Petrified Forest is to the south and Painted Desert is to the north; **928-524-6228;** *www.nps.gov/pefo/planyourvisit.* **RV parking:** *At the visitor's center and at turnouts along the loop road. Admission for a 7-day pass charged per vehicle.*

Will Rogers Memorial Museum
Claremore, Oklahoma

KID FRIENDLY

This rather majestic memorial on a crest of hill with a view across the landscape is a museum devoted to the life and times of the famous humorist and film star as well as his final resting place. A theater shows clips from some of his 70 films, radios play excerpts from his popular radio show, and a children's interactive center makes finding out about him fun. A gift shop also is on the premises. The museum recently received $7 million from the state of Oklahoma to do major renovations; their goal is to complete them by the 100th anniversary of Route 66 in 2026. Allow two hours or more. Open Wednesday through Sunday; closed on Thanksgiving and Christmas.

1720 W. Will Rogers Blvd.; **918-341-0719;** *www.willrogers.com.* **RV parking:** *Large open parking lot. Admission varies by age.*

ROUTE 66 MUSEUMS

Several museums along the tour display artifacts, signs, and photographs of old Route 66 with varying degrees of sophistication. Barbed wire is the main focus of the **Devil's Rope Museum** in McLean, Texas, which is housed in a former bra factory with the **Route 66 Museum.** We like the **Oklahoma Route 66 Museum** in Clinton, Oklahoma, for its multi-gallery re-creation of the highway decade by decade, from a battered 1920s truck loaded down with family possessions, to a painted hippie van of the 1960s. It seems strange to have two great Route 66 museums within 30 minutes of each other, but we also love the **National Route 66 Museum** in nearby Elk City, Oklahoma, with its fun re-creation of an entire town of the period. If you start early and don't dawdle, you can do them both in a day. The new **Route 66 Mother Road Museum,** housed in part of the old train station in Barstow, California, displays license plates, road signs, and a 1926 Dodge touring sedan that drove the highway when the trip was a real adventure.

We list the major ones here, but you find more places along the route calling themselves Route 66 museums than you can shake a stick at. If you're stopping for gas and groceries anyway, check out the Route 66 and vintage car museum inside **Russell's Travel Center,** just west of the Texas/New Mexico border at Exit 369. And the **Williams and Forest Service Visitor Center** in Williams, Arizona, has a replica of an old diner with a diary for road pilgrims to record their Route 66 experiences, along with a video showing the highway's past.

- **California Route 66 Museum,** 16825 D St., between Fifth and Sixth streets, Victorville, CA; **760-951-0436;** www.route66ca.org/california-route-66-museum. Allow one hour. Admission is by donation. The museum is open Friday, Saturday, and Sunday. **RV parking** is available in the designated lot or on the street.

- **Devil's Rope Museum** and **Route 66 Museum,** Old Route 66 at 100 Kingsley St., McLean, TX; **806-779-2225;** www.barbwiremuseum.com. Admission is by donation. Open Monday through Saturday, March through November. **RV parking** is available on the street.

- **Route 66 Mother Road Museum,** 681 N. First Ave., Barstow, CA; **760-255-1890;** http://www.route66museum.org/. This museum shares its building with the Western America Railroad Museum and a NASA Deep Space Network exhibit on the second floor. Originally called Casa del Desierto, this beautifully restored building was a Harvey House hotel, and is still an active train station. Allow one hour. Admission is free. Open Friday through Sunday. **RV parking** is available in the designated lot or on the street.

(continued)

(continued)

- **National Route 66 Museum** in the Old Town Museum Complex, 2717 W. 3rd St., Elk City, OK; **580-225-6266**; https://tinyurl.com/2p9bhha2. You can't miss this place with its huge Route 66 sign next to a giant Native American kachina doll. The museum complex also includes the Old Town Museum, Blacksmith Museum, and Farm & Ranch Museum. This first-rate Route 66 museum tells the history of the entire road, not just the parts in Oklahoma. Allow two hours. Admission varies by age. Open daily. **RV parking** is available in a large lot at the complex or in the grocery store lot across the street.

- **Oklahoma Route 66 Museum**, 2229 W, Gary Blvd., Clinton, OK; **580-323-7866**; www.okhistory.org/sites/route66. Smaller than Elk City's, it's a clean, well-run museum. Allow one hour. Admission varies by age. Open Monday through Saturday; closed on state holidays. **RV parking** is available in a small lot at the museum or on the street.

More Cool Things to See and Do on Route 66

Some of our favorite zany attractions line Route 66, the classic road to America's imagination. Where else can you see a line of vintage Cadillacs half buried in the ground, or hunt for ghosts in a former mining town with its own campground?

BARGAIN ALERT

» **Bury the gas guzzlers.** At **Cadillac Ranch,** ten vintage tail-fin Cadillacs are buried nose-first in an open field on a ranch just west of Amarillo, Texas, always causing the I-40 traffic to slow down and gape. Allow 30 minutes. Always open, always free, and almost always full of folks taking selfies.

*Take the Hope Road Exit. **RV parking:** Permitted on the shoulder, from where you can walk across some 1,500 feet of often-muddy field to get a closer look.*

» **Wake Andy Devine. At the Mohave Museum of History and Arts,** a casual, homespun museum, Kingman's favorite son is the main exhibit. The late actor Andy Devine, with his unforgettable raspy falsetto voice, appeared in numerous Westerns, including *Stagecoach* and *The Man Who Shot Liberty Valance,* and was the comedy relief sidekick for stars like Roy Rogers. Movie posters, a replica of his dressing room, and his costumes fill his part of the museum. Elsewhere, you find everything from World War II airplane nose art, to displays of local turquoise jewelry. Route 66 souvenirs are for sale in the gift shop. Allow one hour or more. Open Tuesday through Saturday.

*400 W. Beale St., Kingman, AZ; **928-753-3195;** www.mohavemuseum.org. **RV parking** is available in the designated lot or on the street. Admission varies by age.*

» **Dig for uranium.** Go into a simulated uranium mine, check out local tribal regalia, and eyeball geology exhibits in the **New Mexico Mining Museum,** one of a only a handful of museums in the world dedicated to uranium mining (minus the pesky radiation). Allow two hours. Open Monday through Saturday.

100 Iron St., Grants, NM; 505-287-4802; www.newmexicominingmuseum.org. RV parking is available in a medium-size off-street lot or on the street. Admission varies by age.

» **Stand on a corner in Winslow, Arizona.** Just like the old Eagles song says, you can take it easy and pose for a selfie at the corner of Route 66 and Kinsley Avenue. The song became a hit in 1972, and enough Route 66 trippers and music fans came to town over the years hunting for "the corner" that the city decided to give them one in 1999. **Standin' on the Corner Park** (www.standinonthecorner.org) sits smack in the middle of town and features a bronze statue of a musician with his guitar (named Easy) and a red flatbed Ford truck parked on the street. An adjacent brick wall has a mural depicting the "reflection" of the truck with "a girl (*My Lord!*) in a flatbed Ford" slowing down to take a look at you.

After lead singer Glenn Frey passed away in 2016, a statue of him was added halfway down the block. You can't miss it — a Route 66 sign painted in the intersection is just about big enough to spot from low Earth orbit, and the corner's lit up all night long in case you arrive after sundown.

Sure, laugh if you like, but almost 100,000 people stop here every year. (Think of it as America's answer to the Beatles' famed Abbey Road zebra crossing in London.) In September, there's even an annual Standin' on the Corner live music festival. After you take your pictures, cross the street for a beer and a meal at **Relic Road Brewing Company,** one of our favorites. And while you're in Winslow, swing by and have a look at the historic **La Posada Hotel,** the last Harvey House railroad hotel, designed in the 1920s by architect Mary Elizabeth Jane Colter.

» **Gape at a meteor crater.** Apart from the Grand Canyon, Arizona has another gigantic hole in the ground that's worth a stop along Route 66. About 50,000 years ago (give or take a year), a 160-foot-wide lump of iron meteorite made its way through the atmosphere intact and crashed into Earth at almost 30,000 miles per hour. The impact blasted a huge crater nearly three-quarters of a mile wide and 560 feet deep into the countryside. That happens on the moon all the time, but rarely on our own planet. The Arizona climate has kept this one from eroding away, making it the biggest and best-preserved meteor impact crater in the world. In the 1960s, NASA used the crater to train astronauts for moon exploration missions, and that's starting up again for the space agency's upcoming 21st century lunar missions.

TIP

The Discovery Center and Space Museum on the north rim of the crater has observation sites, a café, and a wonderful book and gift shop with loads of items for stargazers, space exploration fans, and rock collectors. A short animated film explains when and how the crater was formed, and you can take a walking tour of the rim. There's even a Pet Ramada — a shaded, fenced-in kennel area to get your dog out of the blazing Arizona sun. Allow one to two hours. The Discovery Center is open daily.

Up at the exit you also find **Meteor Crater RV Park,** in case you want to overnight here. (Look for the office inside the geodesic dome.) A clean, well-run, gated campground that's ideal for dark-sky stargazing, with shade trees at most campsites.

Located about halfway between Winslow and Flagstaff off I-40 at Exit 233; **928-289-5898;** *https://meteorcrater.com.* **RV parking:** *Large area on-site.*

Sleeping along the Mother Road

The original Route 66 establishments pioneered roadside sleeping and eating, but many of the businesses that sheltered early *tin-can campers,* as RVs were called, are boarded up, for sale, or long gone. Much of this journey parallels I-40 and I-44, which are lined with RV parks and fast-food options all the way to the coast.

Most of the campgrounds listed in Table 16-1 are open year-round; all have public flush toilets, showers, and sanitary dump stations unless designated otherwise.

TABLE 16-1 ## Our Favorite Route 66 Campgrounds

Name and Location	Contact Info	Cost	What to Know
Oklahoma			
El Reno West KOA Journey; El Reno, OK	301 S. Walbaum Rd.; **800-562-5736** or **405-884-2595;** https://koa.com/campgrounds/el-reno/	$$–$$$	Total of 77 sites with water and 30/50-amp electric; 31 full hookups; 31 pull-throughs. Laundry, pool, showers, and restrooms. Sites are narrow; some hookups side by side. But we love this campground! Cherokee Trading Post, with bargain-price moccasins, and Cherokee Restaurant are within walking distance. It's close to 4 restaurants that make onion-fried burgers, and there's a live buffalo compound, freshwater fishing, and a snack bar on the premises.
Elk City/Clinton KOA Journey; Foss, OK	21167 Route 66 N; **800-562-4149** or **580-592-4409;** https://koa.com/campgrounds/elk-city/	$$	Total of 102 sites with water and 30/50-amp electric; 52 full hookups; 43 pull-throughs. Laundry, pool, Wi-Fi. Moderately wide sites with mature shade trees. Conveniently halfway between Route 66 museums in Clinton and Elk City. Hot home-cooked breakfasts and dinners available in season.
Texas			
Palo Duro Canyon State Park; Canyon, TX	11450 State Hwy Park Road 5; **806-488-2227;** https://palodurocanyon.com	$$	Total of 79 sites with water and 30/50-amp electric; no full hookups; 7 pull-throughs. Comfortable 40-foot-wide sites, each with an individual look. Some offer access for campers with disabilities. Biking and hiking. Don't miss spectacular Palo Duro Canyon, carved out of the red rock by the Red River. Reach the campground in the canyon via a downhill road that crosses dry washes; take dips slowly and carefully.
New Mexico			
Albuquerque KOA Journey; Albuquerque, NM	12400 Skyline Rd. NE; **800-562-7781** or **505-296-2729;** https://koa.com/campgrounds/albuquerque/	$$$$–$$$$$	Total of 170 sites with water and 30/50-amp electric; 101 full hookups; 122 pull-throughs. Propane available, CATV, bike rentals, hot tub, laundry, mini golf, pool, sauna, Wi-Fi. Convenient, well-run, gated campground with wide sites; some extra-large for big rigs, some with patios and pull-throughs. Pricey but convenient to explore Albuquerque.

(continued)

TABLE 16-1 *(continued)*

Name and Location	Contact Info	Cost	What to Know
High Desert RV Park; Albuquerque, NM	13000 Frontage Road SW; **505-839-9035**; www.high desertrv park.net/	$$	Total 75 full hookup 30/50-amp sites, 45 pull-throughs; picnic tables, laundry, Wi-Fi. Gated park, clean and well-run, decorated with Wild West metal sculptures of horses, cowboys, and even a full-size stagecoach by the gate. Close to Love's truck stop, Camping World, and several RV dealers. Downtown about 15 minutes away.
Red Rock Park; Church Rock, NM (near Gallup)	825 Outlaw Rd; **505-722-3839**; www.co.mckinley.nm.us/437/Red–Rock–Campground	$	Total of 245 sites with water and 30/50-amp electric; no full hookups; 150 pull-throughs. 103 extra-wide (50–55 ft.) pull-throughs; narrower back-ins (30–40 ft.). Park is administered by McKinley County; reservations are required. Home to Inter-Tribal Ceremonial (ITC) Celebration, a gathering of Native American tribes every August; call ITC at 575-863-3896 for info. In summer, traditional tribal dances on premises; nearby museum displays kachina dolls, rugs, pottery, silver and turquoise jewelry.
Arizona			
Williams/ Exit167/ Circle Pines KOA Holiday; Williams, AZ	1000 Circle Pines Rd.; **800-562-9379** or **928-635-2626**; https://koa.com/campgrounds/williams/	$$	Total of 120 sites with water and 30/50-amp electric; 81 full hookups; all pull-throughs. Bike rentals, laundry, Wi-Fi. Kid-friendly with extras: outdoor café for breakfast and dinner, nightly movies in season, horse stables and trail rides, indoor pool and two spas, go-cart track, gem mining, 18-hole mini golf, and jumping pillow. Staff helps book attractions nearby, including Grand Canyon Railroad and rafting tours.
Homolovi State Park; Winslow, AZ	I-40, Exit 257 onto SR 87; **928-289-4106** or **877-697-2757**; https://azstateparks.com/homolovi/camping	$	Total of 53 campsites with water, or water and 30/50-amp electric; 11 pull-throughs. Water at campsites April through October; showers and restrooms open year-round. Nearby Homolovi Ruins are an archaeological dig where ancestors of today's Hopi people lived around 1200 CE. Archaeological workshops available; visitor's center and museum. Hopi elders offer storytelling and traditional farming demonstrations; park rangers lead bird-watching and wildlife-viewing trips. Park no longer accepts self-pay registrations; make same-day reservations at the visitor's center and call ahead for dig activity info.

Name and Location	Contact Info	Cost	What to Know
California			
Calico Ghost Town Campground; Yermo, CA (near Barstow)	36600 Ghost Town Road; **877-387-2757;** `https://parks.sbcounty.gov/park/calico-ghost-town-regional-park`	$$	Total of 104 sites with 30/50-amp electric; 64 with water; 46 full hookups; 23 pull-throughs. Free access for 4 people to Calico Ghost Town. Lovely sunsets; can be windy; kid-friendly reenactments of gunfights and other live shows; shops and cafés line main street. Some weekends busy with special events; call ahead for reservations whenever possible.
Bonelli Bluffs RV Resort and Campground; San Dimas, CA	1440 Camper View Rd.; **909-599-8355;** `www.bonellibluffsrv.com`	$$$–$$$$	Total of 518 sites; 329 with 30/50-amp electric and full hookups; 15 pull-throughs. CATV, laundry, pool. A Good Sam campground with breezy hilltop and less-breezy lakeside sites. Mature shade trees surround paved sites; freshwater lake fishing.
Needles KOA Journey; Needles, CA	5400 National Old Trails Rd.; **800-562-3407** or **760-326-4207;** `https://koa.com/campgrounds/needles/`	$$	Total of 85 sites with water and 30-amp electric; 67 full hookups; 85 large and shady pull-throughs. Laundry, pool, camp store, snack bar. Especially nice weather in winter; good bird-watching. Close to Oatman ghost town, Lake Havasu City, AZ, and casinos in Laughlin, NV. Seasonal café November through April.

Good Eats on Route 66

When you're in the towns along Route 66, especially near the highway or I-40, you're going to be surrounded by diners and cafés calling themselves *Route 66-something-or-other*. Many are only open for breakfast and lunch — some have little more to offer than a cool neon sign and retro turquoise stools at the counter. Others are really worth the stop, with food good enough to shout about.

If they didn't actually invent the hamburger, Route 66 restaurants can take credit for making it popular. You find some debatable historical claims on the Mother Road. For example, Rick Bilby, whose family runs **Weber's Superior Root Beer Restaurant** (3817 S. Peoria Ave., Tulsa, OK. **918-742-1082;** www.webersoftulsa.com), says his great-grandfather served hamburgers in Indian Territory as early as 1891. With its great root beer and 1950s hamburger-stand ambiance, it's an Oklahoma institution. The restaurant is open Tuesday through Saturday.

The following list includes a few of the best spots along old Route 66 that still make old-fashioned burgers by hand:

>> **El Reno's onion-fried burgers:** In El Reno, Oklahoma, three local eateries cook beef patties on a grill with thinly sliced onions, pressing them together as they cook so the onion caramelizes, and then turning the burger and sizzling it. They pop the whole business on a bun and garnish it with trimmings that may include tomatoes, lettuce, mustard, mayonnaise, and sliced dill pickles. We confess we're partial to Robert's because the diner is so tiny and colorful. Here's the skinny on the three restaurants:

- *Johnnie's Hamburgers and Coneys,* 301 S. Rock Island Ave. **405-262-4721;** www. johnnieselreno.com. Open Monday through Saturday.

- *Robert's Grill,* 300 S. Bickford Ave. **405-262-1262;** www.facebook.com/ robertsgrill1926. Open daily.

- *Sid's Diner,* 300 S. Choctaw Ave. **405-262-7757;** http://sidsdinerok.com/. Open Monday through Saturday.

>> **Emma Jean's Holland Burger Café,** 17143 D St., Victorville, California (**760-243-9938;** www.hollandburger.com/home): This old-time diner, right on old Route 66 in Victorville, serves up classic burgers from the short-order grill. Open Monday through Saturday.

Looking for something other than a hamburger? You're in luck — several options await.

>> **Big Texan Steak Ranch,** 7701 I-40 East, Exit 75, Amarillo, Texas (**806-372-6000;** www.bigtexan.com): The billboards promise a free 72-ounce steak, but you have to eat it *all,* including the side dishes — shrimp cocktail, baked potato, roll, and green salad — in less than an hour or you pay $72 for it. This challenge is now the stuff of legend; it was exactly the same when we first ate here in 1978. Many are called, but few can finish. Open daily.

The big news here is an RV park — called, of course, **Big Texan RV Ranch** — that's now part of this mini empire of beef. We stayed at the park recently, and found it clean, level, and well-run, with large, Texas-sized gravel spaces. You get complimentary shuttle service back and forth to the Big Texan restaurant in a fleet of Cadillacs with a set of steer horns mounted on the hood. How can you beat it?

» **Lucille's Roadhouse,** 1301 N. Airport Rd., Weatherford, Oklahoma (**580-772-8808;** http://lucillesroadhouse.com/): This restaurant looks deceptively, from the outside, like one more charming Route 66 neon café. But Lucille's is a relatively new, modern place — it's not a long-standing veteran of the classic days. Once you're inside, an on-the-ball waitstaff helps you choose from an extensive menu: hearty sandwiches, good steaks, great ribs, and an array of sides, from loaded baked potatoes to fried okra. The dining room side has pretty booths, while the more relaxed café side is classic Route 66 turquoise and stainless steel. There's a second location in Clinton. Open daily.

» **RelicRoad Brewing Company,** 107 W. 2nd Street, Winslow, Arizona (**928-224-0045**; www.facebook.com/brewery2017/): If you're standing on a corner in Winslow, Arizona (sorry — like we said, they've got that tagline all over town), then take time, after the selfies, to cross the street and eat at this old-style Route 66 joint, with some of the best bar food we've ever tasted. You find an imaginative menu with something for everyone, from deep-fried pickles and fish tacos, to classics like the Relic Rueben and Philly cheesesteak, all of them generously sized. The appetizers are particularly good: homemade onion rings and mozzarella sticks, and to-die-for potato croquettes. It's rounded out by a good selection of some excellent local craft beers. (No, they don't overwhelm you with 83 flavors, like peanut butter chili lager.) Excellent service helps make this a great place to relax and recharge your batteries. Open daily.

Fast Facts for the Route 66 Drive

Area Codes
The following area codes are in effect along Route 66: **928, 602, 520,** and **623** in Arizona; **213, 310, 323, 626, 760, 818, 747, 657, 909,** and **949** in California; **405, 580, 539,** and **918** in Oklahoma; **505** and **575** in New Mexico; and **806** in the Texas Panhandle.

Driving Laws
Seat belts must be worn by those riding in the front seat in Arizona, Oklahoma, and Texas, and those riding anywhere in the vehicle in California and New Mexico. Children riding anywhere in a vehicle in Texas also must wear seat belts. The maximum speed limit on interstate highways in Arizona, New Mexico, Texas, and Oklahoma is 75 mph, and in California it's 70 mph. (Portions of I-10 and I-20 in Texas are 80 mph, but not through the Panhandle or on Route 66.) In all states, speed limits are lower in urban areas. California has a 55 mph limit for all trucks and vehicles towing trailers or toads.

Emergency
Dial **911** in all states. In Texas, **800-525-5555** is a nonemergency road assistance number.

Hospitals
Major hospitals along the route are in Oklahoma City, Tulsa, Albuquerque, Gallup, Flagstaff, Barstow, San Bernardino, and Los Angeles.

Information
Resources include the Arizona Office of Tourism (**866-275-5816;** www.visitarizona.com), California Office of Tourism (**916-322-1266;** https://tourism.ca.gov), New Mexico Tourism Department (505-795-0343; www.newmexico.org), Oklahoma Tourism and Recreation Department (**800-652-6552;** www.travelok.com), and Texas Department of Tourism (**512-463-2000;** www.traveltexas.com).

Road Conditions
In Arizona, call **888-411-ROAD (7623)** or go to www.az511.com. In California, call **800-427-7623** or go to https://roads.dot.ca.gov for Caltrans. In New Mexico, call **800-432-4269** or go to www.nmroads.com. In Oklahoma, the road info hotline is **844-465-4997** or check online at https://oklahoma.gov/odot.html. And in Texas, call **800-452-9292** or go to https://drivetexas.org. Also, in California, Arizona, and New Mexico, the **511** system is available; calls will be routed to road info on the state they're coming from.

Taxes
Arizona sales tax is 5.6 percent; local taxes can raise it to 11.2 percent; gas tax is 18¢ per gallon.

California sales tax is 7.25 percent; it can go as high as 10.25 percent with local taxes added. Gas tax is 54¢ per gallon; with local taxes and fees, tax on a gallon of gas in California is running on average $1.40 in total.

New Mexico sales tax is 5.125 percent; local taxes can raise this to 9.0625 percent; gas tax is 18.9¢ per gallon.

Oklahoma sales tax is 4.5 percent; local taxes can raise it to 11.5 percent; gas tax is 19¢ per gallon.

Texas sales tax is 6.25 percent; local taxes can raise it to 8.5 percent; gas tax is 20¢ per gallon.

Time Zone
Oklahoma and Texas are on Central time. New Mexico and Arizona are on Mountain time, but Arizona doesn't observe daylight saving time, so their clocks never "spring forward or fall back." California is on Pacific time.

IN THIS CHAPTER

» **Preparing for the weather and fabulous sights**

» **Taking a weeklong or weekend coastal drive**

» **Discovering aquariums, history, and recreation on the coast**

» **Digging for clams and meeting elks**

» **Camping in the RV-friendly Northwest**

» **Partaking of Oregon Coast specialties**

Chapter **17**

The Oregon Coast: California to Washington

This itinerary is probably the most scenery-centric trip in this book. It's also a very laid-back tour, but Oregon is a pretty laid-back state, with a strong hippie heritage that shapes it to the present day. The hiking, swimming, and beachcombing here are first class. Above the Pacific shoreline, you find rugged hills thick with forests, and beyond them, the majestic Cascade Mountains. So much of Oregon is covered with pines and redwoods that the government owns and preserves more than a quarter of the state's land as national forests.

But Oregon has more than natural beauty. Astoria, on the Columbia River, is the oldest city in Oregon, founded by fur trader John Jacob Astor, America's first multimillionaire. The town grew into a busy port with a lively San Francisco-style waterfront that included drinking, gambling, prostitution, and the ever-present danger of being *shanghaied* (drugged or knocked in the head and forced to crew the vessels of the lucrative China trade).

In this chapter, you find out more about the unique history of the Oregon Coast and the adventures awaiting you there. Alert beach strollers may discover Japanese glass fishing floats, bits of agate, and driftwood twisted into fantastic shapes. Kite flyers love the nearly constant sea breezes, and sandcastle builders compete for the most grandiose constructions. As you move farther away from the main beach access roads, you find dramatic volcanic coastlines, untrampled dunes, lonely beaches, and the wild surf of your dreams.

Planning Ahead for Your Oregon Trip

You can drive along the Oregon Coast year-round, but summer is still the best time for this trip. Temperatures are warmer, and there's less rain. Fall offers dry, sunny days interspersed with days of drizzle. Between December and February, the gray whales migrate south along the Oregon Coast from Alaska to their calving grounds in Baja, Mexico. They head north again from March through May, passing closer to the coast with their babies nearby, so winter and spring are best for whale watching.

Adapting with the weather

The winter weather in Oregon is a mixed bag. The Oregon Tourism Commission itself warns:

You've heard the old joke that people in Oregon don't tan. They rust. But lest you assume that it rains every day here in winter, let's set the record straight: Some days it snows.

WARNING

Whenever you go to the Oregon Coast, be prepared for some rainy days. Always carry an umbrella when you venture out. On the worst days, you can hunker down in your RV, reading, working puzzles, or baking cookies to munch on down the road.

Obviously, you want to pack rain gear. Those two-piece yellow slicker suits can come in handy if you enjoy walking along the beach in light rain when no danger of lightning is present. Although coastal temperatures range from comfortable to cool, a short drive inland takes you into warmer weather, so bring along lightweight cotton clothing. Sweaters, sweatshirts, and sweatpants make good Oregon travel clothes for RVers.

When the sun comes out, drop everything and head for the beach. Expect crowds on summer weekends at the beaches, but during the rest of the week, long stretches of coastline can be amazingly empty. State parks are popular with Oregonians in the summer, so make campground reservations early whenever possible during that season. The rest of the year, you may well have a campground to yourself.

Bringing the extras you need

Even in the best restaurants in Oregon, folks don't dress up much; we can't imagine a place where you'd need a tie or dress shoes unless you're combining your RV vacation with a business trip. Take sturdy walking shoes — preferably hiking boots — with a spare pair in case one pair gets wet, and a pair of knee-high "wellies" (waterproof rubber boots) if you want to explore tidal pools.

TIP

Possibly more than for any other trip in this book, we urge you to bring the very best camera you can, not just a smartphone. A long telephoto lens can reward you with beautiful photos of the endlessly dramatic rock formations scattered along the rugged coast and the river valleys that cut through the mountains and forests on their way to the sea.

Wintertime RVing in snow and subfreezing temperatures shouldn't be taken lightly. If you're going to try it here, be sure your RV is an all-season rig capable of functioning in low temperatures. That means a propane furnace, not just an electric heat pump, and heated water and sewer holding tanks that stay warm, even when you're driving. Don't let the interior temperature of your trailer drop below 40 degrees F or so.

REMEMBER

For retirees or the just plain lucky, this trip combines beautifully with our California Central Coast route in Chapter 15. The traditional Pacific Coast Highway trip on California's SR 1 runs between San Diego in the south and a point north of San Francisco in Mendocino County. But U.S. 101 continues onward through Oregon and Washington, up to Puget Sound, near the Canadian border. One of the things that makes the drive so pleasant is that most commercial truck traffic uses nearby I-5 to the east, limiting the traffic on the entire scenic coastal route.

Driving Coastal Oregon

Keep in mind, throughout this drive, that Oregonians are wedded to their coast. If you look at a road map of Oregon, you can see that its major cities are lined up in a vertical row parallel to I-5, an hour or two inland. But each of them — Portland, Salem, and Eugene — has a corridor road leading west to the closest beach. The heaviest tourist developments — restaurants, shops, motels, dune-buggy rentals — are clustered for a mile or two on either side of the place where these corridors reach the sea.

U.S. 101 follows the Oregon coastline for almost all of its 365 miles, dipping inland occasionally, but always returning to the sea. In California, it's called the Pacific Coast Highway, but once you cross the state line, the 101 is marked on maps as the **Oregon Coast Highway.** It's also been designated the **Persian Gulf, Afghanistan and Iraq Veterans Memorial Highway,** and you find those signs along the drive as well. When the main route swings away from the water, minor side roads still cling to the coast. Figure 17-1 shows the Oregon coast route.

Choosing the route direction

Our drive begins in the south, at the Oregon/California border, and continues north to end at Astoria, the spot where the Lewis and Clark Expedition spent the winter of 1805–06 before turning back east. Or you can make the drive the opposite way simply by reversing the route directions. Just remember that official mileposts along U.S. 101 begin at the *north* end with 0 up at the Oregon/Washington border (in the middle of the Columbia River) and continue through mile 363 at the Oregon/California border.

TIP

From a practicality standpoint, the northbound route gives the driver the best view of the ocean, while the southbound drive favors the passenger's view. (Nobody thinks of this until the tenth time you hear, "Move your *head!* I can't *see* anything!") Also, when you stop to snag a photo of the sunset, southbound drivers won't have to dodge the traffic to run for the ocean.

We've cheated slightly and included the Long Beach Peninsula in Washington, just across the Columbia River from Astoria, because many Oregon Coast visitors consider that beach an extension of the coastal drive. Visiting the Long Beach Peninsula adds 40 or so miles to the trip. Our entire route covers approximately 400 miles, or more if you take some of our detours.

TIP

Keep an eye out for the free *Original Highway 101 Mile-by-Mile Guide,* published by *Oregon Coast Magazine.* It's available at rest areas, welcome centers, truck stops, and other places frequented by tourists. You can see the guide online at www.oregoncoastmagazine.com, or you can order the dead-tree version. Also, note that later sections of this chapter contain additional information about many of the attractions and eateries mentioned in this section.

Give yourself at least a week for a leisurely tour up the Oregon Coast, although you can drive the route straight through in a couple of days (something we don't recommend, because you'd miss some truly wonderful experiences).

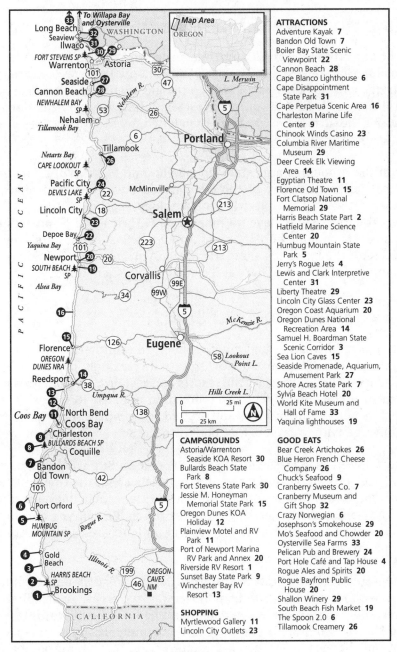

ATTRACTIONS

Adventure Kayak **7**
Bandon Old Town **7**
Boiler Bay State Scenic
    Viewpoint **22**
Cannon Beach **28**
Cape Blanco Lighthouse **6**
Cape Disappointment
    State Park **31**
Cape Perpetua Scenic Area **16**
Charleston Marine Life
    Center **9**
Chinook Winds Casino **23**
Columbia River Maritime
    Museum **29**
Deer Creek Elk Viewing
    Area **14**
Egyptian Theatre **11**
Florence Old Town **15**
Fort Clatsop National
    Memorial **29**
Harris Beach State Part **2**
Hatfield Marine Science
    Center **20**
Humbug Mountain State
    Park **5**
Jerry's Rogue Jets **4**
Lewis and Clark Interpretive
    Center **31**
Liberty Theatre **29**
Lincoln City Glass Center **23**
Oregon Coast Aquarium **20**
Oregon Dunes National
    Recreation Area **14**
Samuel H. Boardman State
    Scenic Corridor **3**
Sea Lion Caves **15**
Seaside Promenade, Aquarium,
    Amusement Park **27**
Shore Acres State Park **7**
Sylvia Beach Hotel **20**
World Kite Museum and
    Hall of Fame **33**
Yaquina lighthouses **19**

CAMPGROUNDS

Astoria/Warrenton
    Seaside KOA Resort **30**
Bullards Beach State
    Park **8**
Fort Stevens State Park **30**
Jessie M. Honeyman
    Memorial State Park **15**
Oregon Dunes KOA
    Holiday **12**
Plainview Motel and RV
    Park **11**
Port of Newport Marina
    RV Park and Annex **20**
Riverside RV Resort **1**
Sunset Bay State Park **9**
Winchester Bay RV
    Resort **13**

SHOPPING

Myrtlewood Gallery **11**
Lincoln City Outlets **23**

GOOD EATS

Bear Creek Artichokes **26**
Blue Heron French Cheese
    Company **26**
Chuck's Seafood **9**
Cranberry Sweets Co. **7**
Cranberry Museum and
    Gift Shop **32**
Crazy Norwegian **6**
Josephson's Smokehouse **29**
Mo's Seafood and Chowder **20**
Oysterville Sea Farms **33**
Pelican Pub and Brewery **24**
Port Hole Café and Tap House **4**
Rogue Ales and Spirits **20**
Rogue Bayfront Public
    House **20**
Shallon Winery **29**
South Beach Fish Market **19**
The Spoon 2.0 **6**
Tillamook Creamery **26**

FIGURE 17-1: Mapping the Oregon coast journey.

Heading northward from California

Our trip begins on the **Oregon/California border** on U.S. 101, just south of **Brookings.** Brookings is a fair-size town with plenty of opportunities to stock your pantry and fridge with necessities and fill up the gas tank before heading north — a good idea because the first leg of this trip doesn't have any services along the way. We like to hit the farmers market and grab lunch here to fortify ourselves for the drive.

Weather in the Brookings area stays unusually mild because of a unique climate pattern that keeps this part of the Oregon Coast warmer than anywhere else in the state. (It's what people with meteorology degrees call Oregon's *banana belt,* even though bananas have nothing to do with it.) The commercial flower-growing business is huge here: Most of America's Easter lilies are grown in this area, so look for the lily fields along the road as you approach Brookings. You also find an annual azalea festival here at the end of May, over Memorial Day weekend.

From Brookings to Gold Beach

Thanks to the mild weather and great scenery, the southern coastal towns from **Brookings** and **Gold Beach** to **Port Orford** are increasingly popular with retirees and vacationers. They appreciate the resorts and restaurants along this part of the boulder-strewn coastline (including more than a dozen RV resorts), especially those clustered along the beaches and around areas where the pine and redwood forests converge with the rivers that pour into the sea.

At milepost 362 in the **Crissey Field State Recreation Site** is an **Oregon Welcome Center,** where you can pick up maps and materials about the Oregon Coast. What will amaze you is how dramatically the coastline scenery changes just 8 or 9 miles north of the California border. Beginning at **Harris Beach,** you encounter loads of small oceanfront parks, scenic drives, and pull-off areas, and every view is a beautiful photo op.

The **Samuel H. Boardman State Scenic Corridor** is spread along a 12-mile stretch of U.S. 101, with numerous turnoffs, pullovers, picnic areas, and trailheads. These spots offer some of the most heavily photographed, calendar-worthy views in the American Northwest, and the highway is deliberately designed so you can easily and safely pull off the road at the most interesting or photogenic points. Watch for **Lone Ranch Beach, House Rock Viewpoint, Whaleshead Beach,** the spectacular **Thomas Creek Bridge, Natural Bridges, Secret Beach, Spruce Island Viewpoint,** and **Arch Rock.**

TIP

Wear your hiking boots in case you want to climb to better vantage points. Also, slow down and keep a sharp eye out for pedestrians randomly scampering across the road. Some beaches on the corridor aren't easily accessible from a parking turnout.

China Beach is one of the loveliest beaches on the Boardman corridor, but perhaps the least visited, due to its inaccessibility; you get there by hiking down from the 101, and the climb down is rated for the relatively fit. Find information about making the China Beach hike at www.oregonhikers.org/field_guide/China_Beach.

At **Gold Beach,** Oregon's famous **Rogue River** surges into the Pacific Ocean. Miners discovered gold on the beach in the mid-1800s, giving the town its name. Jet boat tours leave daily between May 1 and October 30, traveling various distances up the river.

Humbug! But not bah

Humbug Mountain State Park at milepost 305.5 stands 1,730 feet above the beach, waiting for hikers to accept the challenge of its 3-mile loop trail. **Port Orford,** the oldest town site along the Oregon Coast, is free of so-called tourist attractions, but you can stroll around the boats at the marina. At low tide, you can walk over to the **Battle Rock** landmark at milepost 301; it's a really good place for whale watching. North of town, **Cape Blanco Lighthouse** and **Hughes House** at milepost 296.6 are open for tours in summer, and **Cape Blanco State Park** has a campground with water and electrical hookups.

Something you *won't* find along this stretch of highway are fast-food chain restaurants, so don't be afraid to stop and savor the local favorites: Fish and chips at Port Orford's **The Crazy Norwegian's** is a popular stop; **The Spoon 2.0** in **Langlois** was known for decades as one of the only eateries in America that really was named *Greasy Spoon Café*. New owners have rechristened it, and the food's a big hit with area residents.

From Bandon and berry bogs to Coos Bay

Bandon (or as they've begun calling it, **Bandon-by-the-Sea**) is one of our favorite coastal towns because, if you come in the off-season or early in the day, you can drive in, park in one of the designated RV parking lots or along the street, and explore. At Bandon's Old Town, you find art galleries, an old fish-processing plant that now houses retail outlets, a candy company with free samples, and a fish-and-chips takeout joint. You can rent a sea kayak here and explore the **Coquille River.**

Just north of Bandon are Oregon's cranberry bogs, a surprise to New Englanders who thought Massachusetts had the corner on the Thanksgiving berry market. From Bandon, U.S. 101 turns inland for 17 miles to the **Coos Bay** area. Take some time to drive the back road that passes a string of state parks on its way into Charleston; to get to the back road, take a left turn on West Beaver Hill Road about 8 miles north of Bandon. **Shore Acres State Park** has some of the most spectacular wave action along the entire coast; you can watch winter storms from a shelter in the park. It's also got 5 acres of beautiful formal gardens and a Japanese lily pond that were once part of the fabulous estate of a wealthy Coos County timber baron named Louis J. Simpson.

A mile north, **Sunset Bay State Park** has a sheltered year-round RV campground with water and electric hookups. A half mile farther up is the inaccessible decommissioned 1934 Cape Arago Lighthouse, located where the first lighthouse in the state was built in 1859. You can still find several places along the highway marked for a scenic view of the lighthouse, including one very near the RV campground at Sunset Bay.

Charleston is an off-the-beaten-path fishing community with a good fish market and oyster company, **Chuck's Seafood,** on the west end of the bridge. Oregon State University's Institute of Marine Biology operates the Charleston Marine Life Center, a small aquarium and museum open to the public.

Coos Bay is a 12-mile-long region along the coast where the **Coos River** flows from the forested mountains into the sea. Sir Francis Drake tucked his ship in here to get away from bad weather way back in 1579. The towns of **Coos Bay** and **North Bend** snug up against each other, and you find loads of services and retail stores here, if you need supplies.

REMEMBER

Coos Bay is the largest city on the coast, and it's a fun place to spend a day or more. If you're here on Wednesday, stop by the farmers market. Try to catch a movie at the **Egyptian Theatre** on Broadway, one of the most beautifully restored movie palaces we've ever stumbled across. The Oregon Film Festival happens here in January.

You have plenty of camping options in this area — nearly 20 RV campgrounds dot the route between Coos Bay and Florence. **The Mill Casino** has an RV park in North Bend with a view of the bay, a Sun Outdoors resort is on **Yoakam Point,** and KOA is across from **Oregon Dunes National Recreation Area.** If locally-made myrtlewood art is your thing, there's an RV campground adjoining **Myrtlewood Factory.** The quirky **Plainview Motel & RV Park** combines a vintage roadside motel covered in murals painted by a local artist with a campground to make a truly unique place. There's even an RV park right on the shore of **Charleston Marina.**

Onward — North Bend to Cape Perpetua

North of North Bend, the beautiful **McCullough Memorial Bridge** (named for the man who designed many of Oregon's coastal bridges) and **Coos Bay Causeway** cross over the bay. Halfway over is a turnoff to the west for **Oregon Dunes National Recreation Area,** but keep going straight, because the highway will run right through it. Oregon Dunes comprises a 40-mile stretch of oceanfront between Coos Bay and Florence that's the largest expanse of coastal sand dunes in the U.S. and one of the largest in the world — more than 31,000 acres. Some of the dunes reach up to 500 feet high. If you've brought along an ATV, about half the area has been authorized for off-road vehicle use — in fact, ATVers come here from all over to experience this unique convergence of ocean beach, sandy dunes, and dense forest. It's a great place for horseback riding too. Oregon Dunes continues through **Reedsport,** where the visitor's center is located, and on north to **Florence.** U.S. 101 marks the protected area's eastern boundary, and there are multiple entrances along the way.

But the dunes area is just part of the even bigger **Siuslaw National Forest** you're driving through. This stretch of road between Coos Bay and Florence is one of the most popular outdoor recreation areas in Oregon, and it can be crowded in summer. You find campgrounds in and outside Oregon Dunes itself, horseback riding stables, ATV/off-highway vehicle (OHV) rental companies, and more.

From Reedsport, SR 38 turns inland for 3½ miles to the **Dean Creek Elk Viewing Area,** where you stand a pretty good chance of getting a look at some of the 100 or so resident Roosevelt elk at almost any time. On one autumn day, near sunset, we saw a dozen or more grazing and hanging out quietly close to the roadway and viewing platform.

The sand dunes don't just end at the U.S. Forest Service's property line; they continue farther north outside the officially protected area. At Florence you find trailheads with parking areas large enough for RVs, so you can stop and play in the sand. **Florence's Old Town** is a pleasant place to wander, shop, and grab a bite.

KID FRIENDLY

Florence is near **Sea Lion Caves,** one of the most interesting Oregon Coast attractions (and probably the stinkiest). Instead of scrambling down the rocks or peering over the edge to see the wild Steller sea lions, you ride an elevator 208 feet down to sea lion level and get a great view into the gigantic cliffside cave itself. The creatures spend most of the fall and winter months inside the caves, where they're safe from sharks and killer whales, and then move outside in spring and summer to breed and bear their pups.

Cape Perpetua is what's left of a massive volcano, and it's the highest point accessible by car along the Oregon Coast. At **Cape Perpetua Scenic Area,** visit the interpretive center, with a **Discovery Loop Trail Quest** for kids. If you're so inclined, allow time to hike at least some of the 26 miles of trails: The Giant Spruce Trail is 2 miles round trip along a creek through tall trees; the Captain Cook Trail is a 1-mile trek down to the sea; and the Cape Perpetua Trail climbs the south face of the 803-foot cape itself.

Making it from Yaquina Bay to Depoe Bay

Yaquina Bay divides the next metro area into **Newport** on the north side and **South Beach** on the south side. The towering **Yaquina Bay Bridge** connecting the two sides is high enough for fishing boats to sail under. Newport/South Beach has a unique waterfront area around Yaquina Bay, with restaurants, shops, and inns sharing spaces with Oregon's largest fishing fleet and the U.S. Coast Guard. On the South Beach side, you can visit the **Oregon Coast Aquarium** and **Hatfield Marine Science Center.** There are also two photogenic lighthouses in the area: the 1872 **Yaquina Head Light Station** (Oregon's tallest), and the 1871 **Yaquina Bay Lighthouse.**

Consider lunch at **South Beach Fish Market** for some of the best fish and chips on the Oregon Coast. Native Yaquina Bay oysters farmed in the beds of the bay were popular with miners who struck it rich during the California Gold Rush in 1849. You can even do a little clam digging on your own.

While you're near the aquarium on the South Beach side, stop in at the world headquarters of **Rogue Ales & Spirits** (makers of Dead Guy beers and whiskey).

We know you're probably not going to stay here, but **Sylvia Beach Hotel** is named for the expatriate American publisher and bookseller who opened the legendary Shakespeare and Company bookstore in Paris in 1919 and befriended countless authors of the 1920s. Each of the hotel's 21 literary-themed rooms is decorated in the spirit of a noted author, from John Steinbeck to Agatha Christie, Dr. Seuss to Ernest Hemingway. The rooms don't have TVs, radios, phones, or Wi-Fi, but books and games are everywhere, and the ocean *is* right outside your window. If you want a chance to explore this historic building, it has a nice restaurant called Tables of Content.

Skip the hotel if you like, but for sheer convenience, you can't beat **Port of Newport RV Park & Marina,** smack-dab on the tip of the South Beach side of the bay. The aquarium is a short walk away, and guests get to ride the City Loop bus to the Newport side for free.

Drive across the bridge (it's way too long, too tall, too windy, and too harrowing to walk) to the Newport side and check out the **Historic Bayfront.** The clam chowder champion in these parts is **Mo's Seafood & Chowder** — so popular, there's Mo's Original on one side of Bay Boulevard, and Mo's Annex on the other side.

While you're near Mo's, stroll along **Bay Boulevard,** and you find **The Wax Works** celebrity wax museum and a **Ripley's Believe It or Not!** museum of unusual artifacts. **Rogue Bayfront Public House** is also here, in case you missed Rogue's other drinkeries across the bay.

Depoe Bay is considered a prime area for whale watching and for spotting seals and sea lions. The harbor, one of the smallest in the world, is fascinating to watch as vessels maneuver the narrow channels between rocks. *Spouting horns* — rock formations that turn waves into plumes of water — line the town's seawall. Gray whales come in close, locals say, because they like to scratch their backs on the rocks. **Boiler Bay State Scenic Viewpoint,** north of town, is one of the best bird- and whale-watching spots in the area.

Halfway to the North Pole and on to Tillamook

Lincoln City is one of the more commercial beach towns along the Oregon Coast, with the area's first factory outlet center (**Lincoln City Outlets**) at milepost 115.6. RVs are welcome. You also discover some decent antique stores here, along with **Lincoln City Glass Center,** where you can design custom glass objects, watch them being made, and pick them up the next morning when they've cooled. **Chinook Winds Casino,** belonging to the Siletz tribe, sometimes promises coupons for cheap gas to winners. Heck, that's even more valuable than cash these days.

Stop at milepost 111.8 north of Lincoln City and snap a selfie at the **45th parallel,** the midway point between the North Pole and the equator. You may have to pull aside the blueberry bushes so you can stand next to the modest sign.

Detour off 101 and head east to **Pacific City,** have some fish and chips and a Pelican beer at **Pelican Pub & Brewery,** and drive the curvy but beautiful **Three Capes Scenic Route** into Tillamook.

Tillamook is one of our favorite stops along the Oregon Coast because of its delicious cheeses, but **Tillamook Creamery,** right on U.S. 101, also makes rich ice cream and sells other made-in-Oregon items. **Blue Heron French Cheese Company,** off U.S. 101 on a marked driveway, offers wine tasting along with cheese tasting. Both spots have plenty of RV parking.

From Cannon Beach to Columbia's banks

Cannon Beach (named for a big cannon that washed ashore back in 1842) is a popular resort community with a sandcastle competition and a kite-flying festival that touts itself as Oregon's answer to California's Carmel-by-the-Sea (see Chapter 15 for that trip). You find lots of galleries, restaurants, and resorts to explore in this picture-postcard town. But RVers beware: The town is almost entirely made up of *very* narrow streets with *very* limited parking. Between April and October, you may see tufted puffins around **Haystack Rock** at milepost 30.5.

KID FRIENDLY

Seaside, only 10 miles up the coast from Cannon Beach, was the Oregon Coast's first resort; its original amusement park and **Seaside Promenade** (nicknamed the Prom) dates from 1873. A reproduction of a period carousel operates today, along with bumper cars, paddleboats, an arcade, and the **Seaside Aquarium** (one of the oldest on the West Coast). The area has lots of shops and eateries to explore. Younger kids may enjoy the tame carnival-like rides at **Captain Kid Amusement Park** on the south end of town, unrelated to the historic amusement area.

Members of the Lewis and Clark Expedition ventured to Seaside from their quarters at **Fort Clatsop** during the winter of 1805–06 to boil seawater for salt to preserve meat for the long journey home. A statue marking the end of the **Lewis and Clark Trail,** featuring the two explorers and their dog Seaman staring out at the wide Pacific Ocean, stands at the Turnaround on the Prom.

On up the road, **Astoria** can claim to be the oldest American city west of the Missouri River, because John Jacob Astor founded it in 1811 as a fur-trading port. (Astor was a German immigrant who became America's first multimillionaire, in part by cornering the fur trade.) The **Columbia River Maritime Museum,** one of the best of its kind, has an interesting gift shop. Even though feisty residents like to display grumpy bumper stickers proclaiming "We Ain't Quaint," Astoria retains much of its historic charm. If you doubt us, ride the restored 1913 trolley along the riverbank; hike **Cathedral Tree Trail** to climb up the **Astoria Column;** and visit the beautiful and opulent **Liberty Theatre,** built at the end of the vaudeville era.

The 4,300-acre **Fort Stevens State Park** is the site of a large military fort built during the Civil War to guard the mouth of the Columbia River from possible attacks by Confederate and British gunboats. A concrete gun emplacement called **Battery Russell,** at **Point Adams** inside the fort's coastal defenses, has the distinction of being one of the only spots in the continental U.S. that was shelled by the Japanese Navy during World War II.

Crossing the Columbia into Washington

From Astoria, we suggest driving north across the Columbia River over the incredible 4-mile-long **Astoria–Megler Bridge** into Washington to explore the **Long Beach Peninsula,** which has a stretch of sandy beach on the ocean side and some of the best oysters on the West Coast on the **Willapa Bay** side. Take U.S. 101 across the bridge (although you may want to avoid driving a big RV rig across it on an exceptionally windy day; also, it often closes in winter due to icy conditions), follow it west to **Ilwaco** and **Seaview,** and then take SR 103 to **Oysterville** at the northern tip of the peninsula. Along the peninsula, you find the **World Kite Museum and Hall of Fame** and the **Lewis & Clark Interpretive Center** near **Cape Disappointment.** You also pass **Oysterville Sea Farms,** which sells fresher-than-fresh oysters and homemade condiments. This visit to the peninsula adds 40 miles to the journey.

Taking a weekend coastal drive

TIP

Although driving the 400 or so miles of U.S. 101 described in this itinerary in one very long day is *possible*, no one wants to do that much at a time. You miss so much if you roar through at that pace, so let us suggest these nice weekend RV jaunts:

>> **Along the northern coast,** start from **Portland's** main access route of U.S. 26, then drive over to **Seaside** and **Cannon Beach,** go south through **Tillamook** to **Lincoln City,** and return to the Portland area by SR 18 through **McMinnville** and Oregon wine country.

>> **To highlight the central coast,** start from **Eugene,** drive across SR 126 to **Florence,** head north to **Newport,** and return to I-5 via U.S. 20 to **Corvallis.** A short 45-mile drive down I-5 returns you to Eugene.

>> **On the southern coast,** start from **Brookings** at the California border, drive north to Florence, and cross SR 126 to Eugene.

Must-See Oregon Coast Attractions

Bandon's Old Town

Bandon-by-the-Sea, Oregon

The Old Town of Bandon isn't *that* old. In 1936, a fire destroyed the original town, which was later rebuilt along the mouth of the Coquille River. Known as the Storm Watching Capital of the World and the Cranberry Capital of

Oregon, this town is a great place to look for agates on the beach, dig clams at Coquille Point, browse local art galleries, order fish and chips to go, and munch on a superlarge cone of Umpqua Dairy ice cream. (The Umpqua ice cream alone makes the visit worthwhile.) Old Town is ten square blocks of shops and eateries. The fun here is making your own special discoveries while you stroll around. We suggest that you explore the area between First and Second streets along Alabama, Baltimore, Chicago, Delaware, Elmira, and Fillmore streets. The Bandon Visitor's Center and shops are typically open daily. Give yourself at least a half day.

Bandon Visitor's Center at 300 2nd Street; **541-347-9616;** `https://bandon.com/old-town/`. **RV parking:** *Designated lots; plenty of street parking.*

Columbia River Maritime Museum
Astoria, Oregon

The museum (renovated and expanded recently) has an indoor and outdoor collection that includes the conning tower of a submarine, the bridge of a U.S. Navy destroyer, and displays of fishing boats, lighthouses, and fishing, navigation, and naval history. A full-size Coast Guard rescue boat blasts up through the floor, frozen in mid-wave. You can tour the lightship *Columbia* (a floating lighthouse), ponder the personal effects of passengers who went down in ships hitting the reefs at the mouth of the Columbia River, and browse the museum store. Open daily; closed Thanksgiving and Christmas days. Allow three hours.

1792 Marine Dr.; **503-325-2323;** `www.crmm.org`. **RV parking:** *Two large parking lots adjacent to the museum and street parking. Admission varies by age; 3-D movie is extra.*

Fort Clatsop at Lewis and Clark National Historical Park
Astoria, Oregon

This replica of the old fort where the members of the Lewis and Clark Expedition spent the winter of 1805–06 turned out to be more accurate than expected: In 1999, an anthropologist turned up a 148-year-old map showing that the site of the original was very close to where the copy was built. During the summer, buckskin-clad, fur-hatted expeditioners show visitors what day-to-day life was like for the Corps of Discovery. A gift shop has expedition books and videos. Open daily; closed Christmas Day. Allow three hours.

92343 Fort Clatsop Rd.; **503-861-2471;** `https://www.nps.gov/lewi.` **RV parking:** *Large parking lot capable of handling tour buses. Admission varies by age.*

Oregon Coast Aquarium
Newport, Oregon

This is one of the top-rated aquariums in the U.S. You can see tufted puffins in a walk-through aviary with windows that let you watch them dive for fish underwater. A glass tunnel envelops you in the ocean with sharks, sea lions, seals, sea otters, and a giant Pacific octopus. Oregon Coast Aquarium is where Keiko, star of the film *Free Willy,* was rehabilitated before returning to the wild. Open daily; closed Christmas Day. Allow three to four hours.

2820 SE Ferry Slip Rd.; **541-867-3474;** `https://aquarium.org.` **RV parking:** *Designated north lot. Admission varies by age.*

The aquarium is adjacent to the **Hatfield Marine Science Center,** operated by Oregon State University. Its extensive visitor's center has exhibits on marine life and research. Open Thursday through Monday. Pay admission online in advance.

2030 SE Marine Science Dr.; **541-867-0100;** `https://hmsc.oregonstate.edu/about.`

Oregon Dunes National Recreation Area
Reedsport, Oregon

Stretching more than 40 miles along the coast between North Bend and Florence, with headquarters and the visitor's center at the middle in Reedsport, Oregon Dunes has access areas with off-road parking at multiple locations off U.S. 101, some large enough for RVs and some not quite. The dunes are actually the western boundary of the much larger **Siuslaw National Forest.** For areas that require fees, you can buy a digital day pass online; America the Beautiful Passes are also accepted.

If you brought along an ATV, dirt bike, or dune buggy, the dunes are fantastic for off-highway vehicle (OHV) riding and pretending you're conquering the Sahara — almost half the national recreation area is set aside for off-roading use. Avid ATVers come from all over the country to roar up and down these unique sandy hills. Permits, good for two years, are required for all OHV use. If you didn't bring your own, you find more than a dozen rental places along the length of Oregon Dunes.

REMEMBER

If you're dreading the notion of nonstop dune buggy noise completely destroying the natural tranquility, know that OHV areas are kept substantially separate from the rest of this massive stretch of ocean beach, wind-sculpted sand, and dense forest. More than 31,000 acres usually supply room enough for everybody, but just be aware that summer weekends can be a madhouse.

Open daily, the recreation area includes

» The **South Jetty** area, which provides day use access to the beach and dunes, with separate areas for OHV and nonmotorized use.

» The **Siltcoos** area, a quiet region with campgrounds and hiking trails along the river and leading out to the beach.

» The **Oregon Dunes Day Use** area, miles away from all the noisy OHV areas, where you can explore the dunes on foot.

» The **Tahkenitch** area, which provides two campgrounds, lake access for boaters, and dune access for hikers only (no OHV users).

You also find several RV camping areas within the larger recreation area. Research them at https://www.fs.usda.gov/activity/siuslaw/recreation/camping-cabins/?recid=42257&actid=31.

Visitor's center at 855 Highway 101; **541-271-6000;** www.fs.usda.gov/recarea/siuslaw/recreation/recarea/?recid=42465.

Other nearby attractions include

» **Many opportunities to go horseback riding** throughout the area and miles of horse trails at the dunes, which provide a rare chance to go riding on a beach. Numerous stables along U.S. 101 cater to all levels of riders.

C&M Stables, U.S. 101, Florence, is highly rated; **541-997-7540;** https://oregonhorsebackriding.com.

TIP

» **Spinreel Dune Buggy and ATV Rental** in North Bend is the only dune rental company on the Oregon Coast that will lead you on a 2-hour, drive-it-yourself guided tour with 2- or 4-seat RZR dune buggies across sand, beach, dunes, and woods. Many other non-tour 1-, 2-, and 4-passenger models are available if you want to go it alone without a guide.

67045 Spinreel Road, North Bend; **541-759-3313;** *www.ridetheoregondunes. com. Guided tours for a fee and fuel charge; helmets and goggles provided. Drivers must be 18 or older with a valid driver's license, or 25 if any passengers are under 18. All riders must be at least 52 inches tall.*

Sea Lion Caves
Florence, Oregon

Wild Steller sea lions, the largest of the sea lions, inhabit these caves and the rocks outside them year-round, spending fall and winter inside and spring and summer outside. Formed more than 25 million years ago, this is supposedly the world's largest sea cave. Open since 1932, this attraction is fascinating for anyone who hasn't been to a sea lion or seal rookery. An elevator descends 208 feet into a cave that's 12 stories high and as wide as a football field; you do have to negotiate some stairs and ramps. Take a sweater or jacket, camera, and binoculars, and be prepared for plenty of noise and some very strong smells. Most kids get a kick out of the elevator ride, the seals, and the novelty of being in a cave — although they may complain about the aroma. Open daily. Allow one hour. Call ahead, as bad weather may close the caves.

91560 U.S. 101; **541-547-3111;** *www.sealioncaves.com.* ***RV parking:*** *Designated RV lot. Admission varies by age*

Tillamook Creamery
Tillamook, Oregon

This creamery tour, with its free samples, is one of Oregon's most popular tourist attractions. It draws many people who have no idea how milk from black-and-white cows turns into mild or sharp cheddar cheese. The Tillamook County Creamery Association was founded in 1918, and today's modern factory turns out 40 million pounds of cheese a year, plus excellent ice cream and other dairy products. Self-guided tours of the exhibits and galleries are free; premium tours are offered for a fee. Tours are conducted through a viewing gallery, not on the factory floor itself. Open daily; closed on major holidays. Allow two hours.

4165 U.S. 101; **503-815-1300;** *www.tillamook.com/visit-us.* ***RV parking:*** *Designated lots.*

More Cool Things to See and Do in Coastal Oregon

Oregon seems as big as all outdoors, with so much to do along its beaches and in its parks that you can never get bored. The best place to start looking for outdoor recreation locations and ideas online is the **Oregon State Parks** website (`https://stateparks.oregon.gov`).

KID FRIENDLY

>> **Dig in.** Clam digging and crabbing in the tidal bays doesn't require a license in Yaquina, Alsea, Coos Bay, Tillamook, Newport, Cannon Beach, or Netarts — just some basic skills and equipment. You can rent the equipment, and the vendor can clue you in to the technique. Get information booklets and locations from the **Oregon Department of Fish and Wildlife (503-947-6000;** `www.dfw.state.or.us`**).**

>> **Meet the elks.** At **Dean Creek Elk Viewing Area** near Reedsport, you can often get a good look at a Roosevelt elk, or maybe a whole herd; between 60 and 100 of them hang out here at any given time. The best viewing times are early morning and late afternoon until sunset. Bring a camera with a zoom lens. Just remember, these guys can weigh 1,000 pounds or more, and they're fast, strong, and unpredictable. Please don't try to feed them to coax them closer.

Pasture and a viewing platform maintained by the U.S. Bureau of Land Management is 3 miles east of Reedsport on SR 38; **541-756-0100;** `www.blm.gov/visit/dean-creek-elk-viewing-area`. **RV parking** *is available. Admission is free, and the viewing platform is always open. No overnight camping is allowed.*

KID FRIENDLY

>> **Follow the trail.** The **Lewis & Clark Interpretive Center** overlooks the often-foggy mouth of the **Columbia River,** where a lighthouse towers above **Cape Disappointment.** The Center has activities for kids like trying to pack a canoe without capsizing it, checking out the food the explorers ate, and even a treasure hunt. Walk along a series of ramps that traces the expedition, and then have a look at the lighthouse from the grounds. If you climb quietly up the path from the parking lot, you may see the deer that hang around the picnic area. A campground with hookups is located in the park. Open daily. Allow two hours.

SR 100 loop from Ilwaco to Cape Disappointment State Park (formerly Fort Canby State Park), Ilwaco, WA; **360-642-3078;** `www.parks.wa.gov/187/Cape-Disappointment`. **RV parking** *is limited to roadside parking at the foot of the stairs leading up to the interpretive center and lighthouse. Admission to the park is free; inexpensive Interpretive Center admission fee varies by age*

FINDING A FLOAT

Mark Twain once referred to golf as being a "good walk spoiled." He probably wouldn't have embraced one of the older traditions of Oregon beachcombers, namely, wandering the beach looking for Japanese fishing floats. For loads of sharp-eyed sand walkers, these glittery glass baseball-sized orbs are very real bits of treasure given up by the sea.

Thousands of them used to get washed up all over the Pacific shore, though a promising area for the find is a seven-mile stretch of beach between Road's End Recreation Site and Siletz Bay, in the area of Lincoln City. The floats are hollow glass balls, like thick Christmas tree ornaments, often green in color, and usually the size of a baseball, though they come in many sizes. They were used to keep large areas of drifting fishing nets afloat, and each was originally encased in a protective woven cover to help prevent accidental cracking. The **North Lincoln County Historical Museum** has many of these on display, and many are as big as a basketball. (You'll probably see reproductions of them draped over mirrors in pubs or tucked in the rafters of local restaurants as part of the seafaring décor.)

Nowadays, fishermen use a much cheaper substitute, made of Styrofoam, to buoy their nets, but Asian fishing fleets still used the glass ones on into the 1970s. The original glass floats may be a rare find nowadays, but people do still find them. So, *happy hunting!*

» **Make your own fishing float.** Beachcombing for Japanese glass fishing net floats was once a huge pastime around Lincoln City, but as the number of authentic baubles washing ashore dwindled over the decades, local glass artists calling themselves Float Fairies decided to salt the beaches with their own glass ball creations to keep up tourists' interest in finding these bits of buried treasure. At **Lincoln City Glass Center,** you can design your own custom glass float, have it made and cooled overnight, and pick it up the next morning. Reservations are required to book a session with an artist to make a custom object, from glass floats and votive candle shades, to hearts and paperweights. Open daily; closed Thanksgiving, Christmas, and New Year's days.

4821 SW Highway 101, Lincoln City; **541-996-2569;** *www.lincolncityglasscenter.com.* **RV parking** *is limited.*

» **Lighten up.** Discovered in 1603 by a Spanish explorer, **Cape Blanco** is the westernmost point of Oregon. **Cape Blanco Lighthouse,** built in 1870, is one of the oldest surviving lighthouses along the Oregon Coast. Climb to the top of the lighthouse, take a selfie with the giant Fresnel lens, and watch for whales from this great vantage point. **Historic Hughes House,** an adjacent restored Victorian ranch home built in 1898, is open for free tours. The lighthouse and Hughes

House are open Wednesday through Monday, May through October. Allow one hour. ***Note:*** Cape Blanco State Park's campground has 52 back-in RV campsites with water and electric hookups, and a horse camp with corrals, in case you're traveling with your pony.

> *Located in Cape Blanco State Park, 91814 Cape Blanco Rd., Port Orford;* ***800-551-6949;*** *https://oregonstateparks.org/park_62.php.* ***RV parking*** *is available a quarter mile from the building. Lighthouse admission varies by age and family group.*

» **Hike the coast.** The scenery is dramatic, the waves thundering, and the trails exciting. RV roadside parking can be limited at some lookouts and trailheads. Follow the trails; information is at each trailhead. Some great hiking areas include **Oregon Dunes National Recreation Area, Cape Perpetua Scenic Area, Samuel H. Boardman State Scenic Corridor, Humbug Mountain State Park**, and **Shore Acres State Park.** Allow at least a half day at any of these sites, depending on how far you hike.

> *The U.S. Forest Service's* ***Oregon Dunes National Recreation Area Office*** *is in Reedsport at 855 Hwy 101;* ***541-271-6000;*** *https://tinyurl.com/ordunes. The website has information about the Oregon Dunes.*

> *The* ***Siuslaw National Forest*** *website www.fs.usda.gov/recmain/siuslaw/recreation has links to information about trails throughout the area.*

> *You can contact the Cape Perpetua Visitor Center at* ***541-547-3289.***

> *State parks information is available at* ***800-551-6949*** *or https://stateparks.oregon.gov.*

KID FRIENDLY

» **Cruise the bay.** Board the 49-passenger *Discovery* from Newport for tours of Yaquina Bay that may include a visit to Oregon Oyster Farms, an introduction to crabbing by onboard naturalists, whale watching, and a close-up look at sea lions. Cruises depart from the Bayfront, about halfway between Mo's restaurants and Ripley's. Operates March through October. Allow a half day. Call for tour types, times, rates, and reservations.

> ***Marine Discovery Tours,*** *345 SW Bay Boulevard, Newport;* ***541-265-6200;*** *https://www.marinediscoverytours.com.*

» **Float up a roguish river.** Rogue River jet boat excursions start from Gold Beach and go upriver, making stops to watch and photograph wildlife. Trips vary from 64 to 108 miles, and reservations are strongly suggested. Allow at least one day. Daily cruises depart May 1 through October 30. Call for times, rates, and reservations.

*Jerry's Rogue Jets, 29985 Harbor Way, Gold Beach; **800-451-3645;** www. roguejets.com.*

» **Knock on wood.** Consider a visit to the **Myrtlewood Gallery** for something truly unique from Oregon. The gallery offers products made from myrtlewood, a distinctive-looking hardwood that grows along the southern coast, especially around the Coos Bay area. The unique, honey-colored wood features beautiful whorls in the grain, and often natural fissures that give each piece a one-of-a-kind character. It's often made into bowls, utensils, jewelry, and various knick-knacks, but it's also widely used in making acoustic guitars. There are several small artisan shops and factories in the area, and the Myrtlewood Gallery is one of just several shops making and selling these often one-of-a-kind objects. Open Tuesday through Saturday.

1125 U.S. 101, Reedsport; **541-271-4222;** https://myrtlewoodgallery.com.

KID FRIENDLY

» **String yourself along.** The stretch of sandy beach in Long Beach has the greatest conditions for kite flying anywhere in the country. And the **World Kite Museum and Hall of Fame** is likely the only American museum dedicated exclusively to kites. Open year-round, but check the website because days and hours vary.

303 Sid Snyder Dr., Long Beach, WA; **360-642-4020;** www.worldkitemuseum. com/. ***RV parking*** *is available on the street. Admission varies by age.*

CHARTER YOUR OWN FISHING BOAT

If you're an adventuresome angler or a would-be Captain Ahab in search of your first big catch, consider chartering a fishing boat and guide to head out to sea and catch halibut, sea bass, salmon, lingcod, cabezon, and more. Newport is the perfect spot for it, and area boat captains offer seasonal charters, depending on what's biting and when. Most charters will provide all the gear and bait; you just have to bring the beer, the food, and a valid fishing license. While you're out, you may even see a gray whale or two in December–January or March–April. Check out **Newport Oregon Fishing Charters** at https://newportoregonfishingcharter.com.

People much smarter than us in these matters say that if you're trying to catch Chinook, coho, sockeye salmon, flounder, and lingcod around here, stick to June through September. Go for chum salmon between October and December, and in early summer, try for rockfish. Of course, they tell this to everybody else too, so book a charter early in your trip planning. Truly optimistic and prepared fishermen secretly bring tarter sauce, you know, just in case.

Camping along the Oregon Drive

Oregon is a very RV-friendly state; the coast is dotted with campgrounds at both state parks (19 of them with RV camping) and commercial parks (one or more in 26 coastal communities). Making reservations is still a good idea, particularly for beachfront state parks on summer weekends; you should be able to find a spot during the rest of the year. Contact **Oregon State Parks** (**800-551-6949;** https://oregonstateparks.org) for a brochure, or pick one up at any state welcome center. For reservations, call **800-452-5687** or go online (https://oregonstateparks.reserveamerica.com).

The majority of state park campgrounds accept advance reservations (from one day to six months out), but some parks hold a number of spots on a first-come, first-served basis. The prices are reasonable — even sites with full hookups in oceanfront state parks run $26 to $47 a night. As in many states, residents pay less than out-of-state campers.

In Oregon, the developed state park campgrounds are generally open from mid-May to early October. But some are open all year, particularly on the coast; all the state park campgrounds we list in this chapter are open year-round. Check out this website for a complete list of state park campgrounds open all year: www.outdoorproject.com/travel/best-year-round-camping-oregon.

State parks once had a "discovery" program with lower rates for campgrounds in winter. It was only $4 off per night, but the point is well-taken, to encourage winter camping. Private campgrounds that are open year-round generally offer substantially lower rates off-season. No, we wouldn't want to be camping up in the Cascades in February, although others have done so, of course. But much of the weather in coastal areas is controlled by the sea; summers are cooler, and winters are warmer. A winter trip to coastal Oregon — perhaps in the shoulder months, November or April — offers dramatic, windswept beaches that you feel belong to you alone. In November, daily temps are around 55 degrees F, rarely falling below 45, and can go as high as 65 degrees. (On the coldest day of the year, December 23, oceanside temps average a doable 39 to 48 degrees.) If your rig is a four-season, winter can be a beautiful time to go camping, especially in coastal Oregon.

REMEMBER

Making a reservation for Oregon camping on the **ReserveAmerica** website (www.reserveamerica.com) is pretty straightforward, but know your nomenclature: A *Standard* site is water and electric only. Sometimes, full hookups are called *Standard Full.*

All the campgrounds in Table 17-1 are open year-round and have flush toilets, showers, and sanitary dump stations unless stated otherwise. Toll-free numbers are for reservations only unless noted. If you have non-RVing friends who'd like to meet you, be aware that most of these campgrounds offer tent camping, cabins, and the newly fashionable *yurts* (circular domed tents).

TABLE 17-1 **Our Favorite Oregon Coast Campgrounds**

Name and Location	Contact Info	Cost	What to Know
Astoria/ Warrenton/ Seaside KOA Resort; Hammond, OR	1100 NW Ridge Rd.; **800-562-8506** or **503-861-2606**; https://koa. com/campgrounds/ astoria	$$–$$$	Total of 231 mostly shaded sites with water and 30/50-amp electric; 142 full hookups; 96 pull-throughs. Bike rentals, CATV, grocery and camp store, wheelchair accessible, laundry, Wi-Fi. Many amenities: indoor and outdoor pools, hot tub, mini golf, playground, ping-pong, pool table, arcade, and summer movie nights. Across from Fort Stevens State Park and convenient to Astoria and Fort Clatsop National Memorial. At the mouth of the Columbia River a mile from the beach; offers free shuttle service in summer. Fishing and clamming nearby. Free pancake breakfasts served on weekdays; programs and activities on weekends.
Bullards Beach State Park; Bandon, OR	Off MP-249; **541-347-2209** or **800-452-5687**; https:// stateparks. oregon. gov/index. cfm?do=park. profile& parkId=50	$$	Total of 103 full hookup sites; 82 with water and electric; no pull-throughs; 3 ADA-compliant sites. RV dump station. At the mouth of the Coquille River, freshwater fishing and boating available; 1,266-acre Bullards Beach offers access for RVers, horse campers, hikers, and bicycle campers, with full hookup sites available. Varied terrain includes beach, forest, dunes, and a jetty with a lighthouse. Whiskey Run mountain bike trail and Old Town Bandon, with shopping and restaurants, are nearby. 10-day maximum stay at bargain prices.

(continued)

TABLE 17-1 *(continued)*

Name and Location	Contact Info	Cost	What to Know
Fort Stevens State Park; Hammond, OR	1675 Peter Iredale Rd.; **503-861-3170;** https:// stateparks. oregon. gov/index. cfm?do=park. profile& parkId=129	$$	Total of 477 sites; 174 full hookups; 30 pull-throughs; 302 with electric and water. Wheelchair access. Sites are wide, paved, and well-spaced; upgrades made in 2023. The 4,300 acres of park include a freshwater lake, golf course, kayaking, and 15 miles of biking and hiking trails. For history buffs, the Friends of Fort Stevens Museum is within walking distance, surrounded by extensive batteries from the Civil War and both world wars. A 1906 shipwreck is an iconic part of the beach. The Columbia River Maritime Museum is in nearby Astoria.
Jessie M. Honeyman Memorial State Park; Florence, OR	U.S. 101, 3 miles south of Florence; **800-452-5687** or **541-997-3641;** https:// oregonstate parks.org/ park_134.php	$$–$$$	Total of 121 sites with water and 30/50-amp electric; 47 full hookups; no pull-throughs. Wheelchair access. Magnificent sand dunes in Oregon Dunes National Recreation Area offer hiking trails, freshwater swimming in two lakes, fishing, boating, and ATVing (seasonal ATV access with some restrictions and frequent noise). Nearby ATV rentals.
Oregon Dunes KOA Holiday; North Bend, OR	68632 U.S. 101; **800-562-4236** or **541-756-4851;** https://koa.com/ campgrounds/ oregon-dunes/	$$$–$$$$	Total of 53 full-hookup sites; 41 pull-throughs; "big boy" sites available for RV rigs over 90 feet. Camp store, laundry, CATV, Wi-Fi, wheelchair access. Best area full-service private park for ATVers with full ATV and OHV access to Oregon Dunes National Recreation Area. ATV rentals nearby. Kid-friendly rec room, axe throwing, ping-pong, indoor basketball, and many special events in summer. Hayrides, paddleboats, jump pads, and ice cream socials on Friday and Saturday night. Beach, lighthouse, casino, and fishing are also nearby.
Port of Newport Marina RV Park and Annex; Newport, OR	2301 SE Marine Science Drive; **541-867-3321;** www. portofnewport. com/rv-parks	$$	Total of 144 full-hookup sites; 30/50-amp electric; 45 pull-throughs; maximum 60-ft. length. Laundry, CATV, Wi-Fi. The Annex has legacy gravel or grass pads; the Marina RV Park's 92 sites are all paved. Convenient, highly rated Good Sam campground on the South Beach point of Yaquina Bay. Ideal spot for boat watching and taking in the sunset. A free (for campground guests) City Loop bus runs daily over the bridge and back to take in Newport's Historic Bayfront, with its shops and restaurants, both area lighthouses, Nye Beach, and more.

Name and Location	Contact Info	Cost	What to Know
Riverside RV Resort; Brookings, OR	97666 Chetco River Road; **541-469-4799**, http://riverside-rv.com	$$–$$$	Total of 36 sites, 25 with full-hookups; no pull-throughs; 20/30/50-amp electric; riverfront sites available. Laundry, firepit by the Chetco River, CATV, Wi-Fi. Advertises itself as a seniors resort. With an embarrassment of campgrounds in this area just north of the California border, we like this one for being green, serene, and well-run. Deer and quail wander through the peaceful spot. A great place to start your trip along the Oregon Coast, or to finish it.
Sunset Bay State Park; Coos Bay, OR	10965 Cape Arago Hwy; **800-452-5687**; https://oregonstateparks.org/park_100.php	$$	Total of 63 wide paved sites with water and 30-amp electric; 30 full hookups; no pull-throughs. Wheelchair access. A short walk from stunning beaches and towering cliffs, with great views from the hiking trails. Sunset Bay connects to Shore Acres and Cape Arago state parks by a 4-mile trail as part of the Oregon Coast Trail. Fishing, swimming, boating, horseback riding, and nearby public golf course. Also nearby is the fishing village of Charleston. 10-day maximum stay.
Winchester Bay RV Resort; Winchester Bay, OR	120 Marina Way; **541-271-0287**; www.winchesterbayresort.com	$$– $$$	Total of 138 full-hookup sites with 30/50-amp electric; 60 pull-throughs; special double-rig sites available. CATV, Wi-Fi, wheelchair access, laundry. Large, level sites and great views of the bay or the Umpqua River. Bike path, hiking trail, clamming, and saltwater fishing are available. Located near Oregon Dunes National Recreation Area (though ATVs are not allowed here) and Umpqua River Lighthouse. Restaurants and shops in easy walking distance.

Good Eatin' on the Oregon Coast

Coastal Oregon towns have small diners and cafés, cheese and candy shops, chowder houses, and bakeries. For fresh seafood, you find everything from mom-and-pop diners and crab shacks, to full-blown fish markets with real fishing boats tied up out back. While the chowder hounds dig for Oregon razor clams and giant geoducks (pronounced *gooey*-ducks), the area along the coast in large part revolves around the various runs and seasons for fishing. Some homes along the coast are occupied only during the fishing seasons, and the many rivers emptying into the ocean are an angler's delight. If you're not up to catching your own, the local eateries offer terrific fish and chips and fish sandwiches.

Finding a fun local haunt

One thing you won't see a lot of on this whole trip are the big chain restaurants you find everywhere else. It's not like being in the safe surroundings of suburban shopping mall sameness here.

» **South Beach Fish Market,** 3640 U.S. 101, South Beach (**541-867-6800;** www. southbeachfishmarket.com): Grab some halibut and chips, oysters and chips, shrimp and chips, or the day's special, and then pick up some fresh local seafood — wild salmon filets, oysters, razor clams, albacore tuna — to cook on the road or take home. This isn't a full-service restaurant; it's a fish market with a couple tables inside and some outdoor seating. But the food is as fresh as it gets, straight off the boats, and you'll appreciate the difference. Open daily.

» **Mo's Seafood & Chowder,** 622 SW Bay Blvd., Newport (**541-265-2979;** https:// www.moschowder.com): **Mo's** serves clam chowder (of course) and many other seafood dishes in their original Newport diner and others along the coast. If the line is long, visit **Mo's Annex,** just across the street from the Newport

» **Port Hole Café and Tap House,** 29975 Harbor Way, Gold Beach (**541-247-7411;** https://portholecafe.com): This café offers clam chowder, fresh seafood, chicken, steaks, and homemade pies. Open daily.

Regional specialties

Northwest treats include artichokes, lemon meringue pie candy and wine, oysters, and more. In the following list, discover what to look for and where to find it:

» **Artichokes:** Head to **Bear Creek Artichokes,** 1604 Fifth St., Tillamook (**503-398-5411;** www.facebook.com/bearcreekartichokes/menu/), for a nice selection of sandwiches and pizza. Eleven miles south of Tillamook on U.S. 101. Open daily.

» **Boutique beer:** Newport is the world headquarters of **Rogue Ales & Spirits** (www.rogue.com), makers of Dead Guy beers and whiskey. Their two-story brewpub overlooking the bay from the point on South Beach proffers their 40 beers and ales on tap, while **Rogue Spirits Sunset Bar** across the parking lot serves up cocktails made with their locally distilled liquor and has a beautiful view of the bay and the bridge as the sun sinks slowly in the west. Over on the Newport Bayfront, **Rogue Bayfront Public House** serves brews from ales to porters, along with fish and chips. Open daily.

Another option for local beer is **Pelican Pub & Brewery,** on the beach at 33180 Cape Kiwanda Dr., Pacific City (**503-965-7007;** https://pelicanbrewery.com). Order a Doryman's Dark Ale or Tsunami Stout to wash down their good, hearty pub food. Open daily.

KID FRIENDLY

» **Cranberry candy:** Try **Cranberry Sweets & More Co.,** at the corner of 1st Street and Chicago, Bandon (**541-347-9475**; https://cranberrysweets.com). Besides nibbling their cranberry jelly candy, sample dozens of other sweets, from lemon meringue pie candy and wine jelly, to chocolate puddles and cheddar cheese fudge. Open daily.

Or stop at **The Cranberry Museum and Gift Shop,** 2907 Pioneer Road, Long Beach, Washington (**360-642-5553**; https://cranberrymuseum.com), to try local cranberry products and tour the farm. Open Friday through Monday.

» **Eccentric wines:** Head to **Shallon Winery,** 1598 Duane St., Astoria (**503-325-5978**; www.shallon.com). A truly unique winemaker named Paul van der Veldt makes chocolate orange wine, cranberry wine (he calls it *cran au lait*), and lemon meringue pie wine, among other flavors — there's even one made from whey (as in Little Miss Muffet sitting on a tuffet, eating her curds and whey). It's a one-man operation, "the smallest winery in America," so he's only able to turn out about 500 gallons a year. But he's been open every afternoon for more than 30 years. Call and make sure he's there before you go — one-man shops sometimes run on their own clocks.

» **Smoked salmon:** Try **Josephson's Smokehouse,** 106 Marine Dr., Astoria (**503-325-2190**; www.josephsons.com), an old-fashioned store with fine smoked salmon. Open daily.

» **Willapa Bay oysters:** Stop at **Oysterville Sea Farms,** 34300 1st St., across the Columbia River in Oysterville, Washington (**360-665-6585**; http://willabay.com/), to get fresh oysters in the shell or in a jar from this humble, unassuming, shingled cottage. Also on sale are clam chowder fixings, crab, smoked oysters, and razor clams. Pick up some Oysterville Victorian cake mix or cranberry condiments and preserves. While you're there, sit out on the deck and snack on oyster shooters, shrimp cocktail, and cranberry specialties like crannie salsa or crannie pecan cookies. Open daily in summer, Friday through Sunday in winter.

Oregon cheese, please!

Although Oregon seafood, hazelnuts, wines, pears, and cranberries may be famous, few think of cheese as a major food product here. But Oregon is one cheesy state, as the following cheese producers in the Tillamook area prove:

» **Blue Heron French Cheese Company,** 1 mile north of Tillamook at 2001 Blue Heron Road (**800-275-0639** or **503-842-8281**; www.blueheronoregon.com): French-style brie and Camembert cheeses are specialties, but they also feature a tasting room for regional Oregon wines, deli, espresso bar, and gift shop. There's even a petting zoo with sheep, goats, llamas, and a donkey to occupy the kids. Great place to stop for lunch, too. Open daily.

» **Tillamook Creamery Visitors Center,** 4165 U.S. 101 North, Tillamook (**503-815-1300;** www.tillamook.com/visit-us/creamery): You can take a self-guided tour through this huge cheese factory where they also make Tillamook ice cream, among other products. Enticements include free samples of cheese and recipes; a deli; an ice cream bar selling Tillamook ice cream on waffle cones; the Creamery café, serving up cheese curds, cheeseburgers, and mac and cheese; plus a gift shop carrying Oregon food products and plenty of cow-related kitsch. Open daily.

Supermarkets

You find Kroger-owned **Fred Meyer,** plus **Albertsons** and **Safeway** supermarkets in the bigger towns along the Oregon Coast. There are **Ray's Food Place** supermarkets in Bandon, Gold Beach, Port Orford, and Waldport. You can find a **Walmart Supercenter** in Astoria, Newport, and North Bend.

Farmers markets

If you're in the area during farmers market season, here are a few good ones to check out:

» **Astoria Sunday Market,** at 12th and Commercial streets, Astoria (**503-440-7168;** www.astoriasundaymarket.com), features more than 200 vendors with locally grown produce, arts and crafts, a popular food court, and even live entertainment. Lots of downtown stores are open for even more shopping chances. Open Sundays, mid-May to mid-October.

» **Brookings Harbor Farmers Market,** 15786 U.S. 101, Harbor (**541-661-3860;** http://brookingsharborfarmersmarket.com), features local farmers, artisans, baked goods, eggs, meat, services, music, and hot food on Wednesdays and Saturdays year-round. Also open on Fridays in the summer.

» **Cannon Beach Farmers Market,** Corner of S. Hemlock and E. Gower streets, Cannon Beach (**503-436- 8044;** www.facebook.com/cannonbeach-farmersmarket), has flowers, produce, organic cheeses, pasture-raised meat, and lots of hand-crafted artisan products. Open Tuesdays from mid-June to the end of September.

>> **Coos Bay Farmers Market,** Central Avenue at U.S. 101, Coos Bay (**541-266-9706;** https://coosbaydowntown.org/farmers-market), showcases more than 80 vendors who sell fresh food from local farmers and businesses, including fresh fruits and vegetables, homemade jams, jellies, and candy, and handmade artisan products. Open Wednesdays, May through October.

For more markets, consult the website of the Oregon Farmers Markets Association (www.oregonfarmersmarkets.org).

Fast Facts for the Oregon Route

Area Code
The area codes for Oregon are **503** and **541.** Washington's area code is **360.**

Driving Laws
All RV occupants must wear seat belts in Oregon. The maximum speed limit on interstates is 65 mph. Speed limits are lower in urban areas. You find conflicting information on the internet, but according to the Oregon State Police, your speed limit in an RV is the posted speed limit; RVs do not have to abide by the lower speed limit set for commercial trucks.

Emergency
Call **911.**

Hospitals
Along the route, major hospitals are in Astoria, Coos Bay, Florence, Newport, Reedsport, and Seaside.

Information
Resources include the **Oregon Tourism Commission (800-547-7842;** https://industry.traveloregon.com/about/oregon-tourism-commission/, **Oregon State Parks (800-551-6940** for information or **800-452-5687** for reservations; https://stateparks.

oregon.gov), and **Oregon Department of Fish and Wildlife (503-947-6000;** www.dfw.state.or.us).

Road and Weather Conditions
Call **511,** or contact the Oregon Department of Transportation at **800-977-6368** (available only in Oregon) or online at https://www.oregon.gov/ODOT.

Taxes
Oregon is one of five states that adds no state sales tax to purchases. However, local governments are permitted to add their own local sales taxes "with discretion" (whatever that means). You may encounter a local tax on restaurant food and lodging (like hotel rooms and RV camp sites), and Oregon does have excise taxes on alcohol, tobacco products, and fossil fuels. The gasoline, diesel, and propane tax is 38¢ per gallon in Oregon. Be aware that it's illegal to pump your own gas at many Oregon gas stations; however, the anti-self-serve law was eased in 2018, and rural counties with fewer than 40,000 people now have self-service stations.

Time Zone
Oregon is on Pacific standard time.

6

The Part of Tens

IN THIS PART . . .

Tour ten factories cranking out cool stuff across America.

Wander through ten of the zaniest museums you'll find anywhere.

Chapter **18**

Ten Cool Factory Tours

E verybody has a built-in curiosity to find out how something gets made, especially if they own one. For instance, there are always RVs in the parking lot for RV manufacturers' tours. This chapter highlights nine of the coolest factory tours in the United States, plus one website you can visit virtually.

WARNING

Just be aware that many factory tours aren't accessible for people with disabilities and may require a fair amount of walking. Some may not have much in the way of climate control, and many may be quite noisy. Also, many truly industrial factories that take you onto their factory floor instead of allowing you to view their operations through a visitor's gallery won't permit children or pets for obvious safety reasons.

Ben & Jerry's Ice Cream (Waterbury, Vermont)

KID FRIENDLY

In 1978, longtime buddies Ben Cohen and Jerry Greenfield took a correspondence course in how to make ice cream. Armed with $12,000, they renovated an old gas station in downtown Burlington, Vermont and opened their first ice cream shop, where they became famous for their offbeat names for flavors (Phish Food, Chubby Hubby, Schweddy Balls, Cherry Garcia), celebrity tie-ins (Steven Colbert, Jimmy Fallon, Chance the Rapper), and unique ingredients (cookie dough, giant chocolate chunks, peanut butter cups). The rest, as they say (whoever it is who says these things), is ice cream history. The two partners sold the company to Unilever back in 2000, but it's still going strong.

Tours of **Ben & Jerry's Ice Cream Factory** start every 10 to 30 minutes, depending on the season, and sign-up is on a first-come, first-served basis. The tour consists of a seven-minute "MOO-vie," a guided overview of the manufacturing process, free samples of the day's flavor, and finally a stop in the Scoop Shop and gift shop. Don't forget to visit the graveyard of discontinued flavors to mourn and pay your respects to old, forgotten favorites. Open Tuesday through Sunday; closed Thanksgiving, Christmas, and New Year's days. Allow at least one hour for the tour.

> *1281 Waterbury-Stowe Rd Route 100, Waterbury, VT (take Exit 10 off I-89 and drive north on SR 100 for 1 mile to the entrance on the left);* **802-846-1500;** *www.benjerry.com.* **RV parking** *is in a designated lot. Admission for the Factory Experience varies by age; the Scoop Shop, gift shop, and outdoor playground are free.*

Original American Kazoos (Eden, New York)

KID FRIENDLY

The **Original American Kazoo Company** claims the distinction of being the only remaining factory in the world still producing the prized metal kazoo. The humble American kazoo is arguably the most democratic instrument on the face of the Earth, because anyone can play one. If you can hum a tune, you can master the kazoo in seconds.

The first known kazoo was made of wood in Georgia in the 1840s, but in 1912, a New York salesman concocted the idea of mass-producing metal ones. He teamed up with a pair of metalworkers to form the Original American Kazoo Company in Eden, near Buffalo, in 1916. The company received a patent for the instrument in 1923, and they've been making kazoos ever since.

Visitors get a free look around the 1916 facility (or a free guided tour Tuesday through Thursday, if you call ahead for an appointment). The boutique and museum are open Monday through Saturday. Closed on holidays. At the boutique, you can even make your own kazoo!

> *8703 S Main St, Eden, NY (about halfway between Fredonia and Buffalo off I-90's Exit 57A);* **716-992-3960;** *http://www.edenkazoo.com. Free admission.*

Crayola Crayons (Easton, Pennsylvania)

KID FRIENDLY

We'd like to say that you're watching the real crayon assembly line at the **Crayola Experience,** but this handsome, visitor-friendly facility is more of a demonstration of how Crayola manufactures the world's favorite crayons. Built several years ago when the factory itself got swamped with visitors, this facility is designed for families, and so are the hands-on coloring and crafts areas for kids. The presentations usually keep adults just as spellbound as their offspring. You can purchase souvenirs at the General Store gift shop and the big Crayola Store next door. Open daily. Allow at least two hours.

30 Centre Square, Easton, PA; **610-515-8000;** *www.crayolaexperience.com.* **RV parking** *is available on the street. General admission is the same for all ages over 3; discount for online ticket purchase.*

TIP

Not passing through Pennsylvania? Crayola has other locations, offering similar activities, in Chandler, Arizona; Minneapolis, Minnesota (at the Mall of America); Orlando, Florida; and Plano, Texas.

While in Easton, you're close to the **National Canal Museum,** which offers 45-minute canal boat rides on the Lehigh Canal beginning at noon. Admission to the museum includes the boat ride. The complex is closed in winter; the museum reopens in late April; boat rides resume in early summer.

FAST Fiberglass Molds (Sparta, Wisconsin)

True connoisseurs of wackiness instinctively know that kitsch is always better when it's *BIGGER*. Face it: Dairies everywhere need giant fiberglass cows in their driveways; tack shops need rearing horses out front; kiddie pools need frog-shaped waterslides. Ever wonder just where that life-size pink fiberglass elephant in front of the liquor store came from?

Welcome to the mold graveyard of **Fiberglass Animals, Shapes, and Trademarks (FAST).** Since the 1970s, FAST has specialized in creating bigger-than-real-life sculptures of animals, people, cartoon characters, mascots, and other props. Cities and towns all over the country have bought FAST sculptures (cows, pigs, horses, and college mascot characters) for their local artists to individually decorate.

The FAST sculptors create a big master mold into which they spray fiberglass until it hardens into a masterpiece of the advertising arts. The good news for fanatical fans of fiberglass frippery is, FAST never throws anything away. Even better, the molds are huge and time-consuming to make, so they put them in a field out back in case they're ever needed again. Trains, sharks, a 5-foot-tall Mount Rushmore, Paul Bunyan, giant pumpkins, an army of Santas, Big Boy delivering a stack of pancakes, a banana as big as a Buick — you name it, they've made it.

There's no actual factory tour to speak of here; it's the enormous mold storage yard that's open to the public. Signs do warn you to come in and wander around at your own risk, and keep a wary eye out for hornets, which sometimes like to build nests inside grinning bunny molds. Just remember that an outdoor field scattered with hundreds of molds, sculptures, and fiberglass shards is not a pristine place. So wear heavy shoes and long pants, and don't let little kids wander off by themselves. And no climbing on the molds! Allow one hour.

> *14177 County Highway Q, in Sparta, WI;* **608-269-7110;** *www.fastfiberglass. com.* **RV parking** *is plentiful in surrounding parking lots and driveways. There's no admission fee, but you can get a brochure for $4.*

TIP

Since you're already in the area, it should come as no surprise that FAST is just an hour away from the **Wisconsin Dells,** one of the kookiest, kitschiest vacation destinations in the country. The Dells is known for its natural wonders, as well as for some of the most peculiar and over-the-top roadside attractions anywhere, a place where fiberglass forms flourish. If giant fiberglass elephants appeal to your sense of fun, wait'll you see the upside-down White House replica and the Mount Olympus-themed hotel/amusement park complex.

And finally, to see some of FAST's finest work, check out the massive 145-foot fiberglass muskie at the **Freshwater Fishing Hall of Fame** in Hayward, Wisconsin, complete with an observation deck built into its mouth so you can experience the last few seconds in the life of a worm on a hook.

Jelly Belly Jellybeans (Fairfield, California)

**KID
FRIENDLY**

Jelly Belly jellybeans are the favorite treat of discerning candy lovers like the late former President Ronald Reagan. These gourmet jellybeans have strongly flavored fillings in addition to the candy coating on the outside.

No surprise that the **Jelly Belly Candy Company** offers our hands-down favorite of all the factory tours in the United States. Watch the candies being made on the assembly line and taste them at different stages, get free samples at the end of the tour, and pick up low-priced factory rejects called *Belly Flops,* which are usually two jellybeans that fused together during the process, like a mutation. The tour also includes a collection of portraits of famous people, including Reagan, made from jellybeans. No production line runs on weekends, holidays, the last week of June, or the first week of July — a video shows the production line instead. Open daily for factory tours (or video) and museum access. Allow one hour.

*2400 N. Watney Way, Fairfield, CA; **707-399-2390;** www.jellybelly.com. **RV parking** is available in a huge lot. Admission varies by age.*

Louisville Sluggers (Louisville, Kentucky)

Fans of America's favorite pastime enjoy the **Louisville Slugger Museum**. Walk through the museum, which salutes famous baseball sluggers, and then see the actual bat making process.

The typical pro baseball player orders 120 or more bats every season, and while they may all look the same from up in the cheap seats, Slugger has made more than 8,000 variations in every combination of length, weight, and shape. Some 95 percent of their bats are machine made, but a few special orders are still hand-turned. A hot brand sizzles the Louisville Slugger logo, model number, and player's autograph into the wood. You even get a souvenir mini bat as a memento. Tours run daily, with the last tour beginning one hour before closing. Allow two hours.

*800 W. Main St., Louisville, KY; **877-775-8443;** www.sluggermuseum.com. **RV parking** is available in a designated lot. Admission varies by age.*

PEZ® Candy (Orange, Connecticut)

KID
FRIENDLY

When PEZ candy first appeared in Austria in 1927, inventor Eduard Haas III marketed his peppermint-flavored tablets as an aid to stop smoking. The mints came in a tin box and didn't yet have the bobbly head on top of the package that we all know and love today. (The name PEZ is a contraction of the German word for peppermint, *pfefferminz*.) In 1935, the company changed the round candy drops to a small brick shape and in 1948 introduced a unique pocket-sized plastic mechanical dispenser made to look like a stylish gold cigarette lighter.

When the company expanded into the United States in the mid-1950s, a clever marketer stuck a 3-dimensional witch's head on top of the package as a Halloween novelty, creating the first iconic head-topped PEZ dispenser. They've been collector's items ever since. The world's biggest and most comprehensive collection of PEZ dispensers is right here at the **PEZ Candy Factory and Visitor's Center**. The center is 4,000 square feet packed with all things PEZ, and you can see the factory packaging assembly line through a visitor's gallery. Don't miss the PEZ motorcycle built by Orange County Choppers and the world's biggest PEZ dispenser. Open daily; self-guided tours.

35 Prindle Hill Road, Orange, CT; **203-298-0201;** https://us.pez.com. **RV parking** *is available in the factory lot. Admission varies by age.*

TABASCO® Sauce (Avery Island, Louisiana)

As a couple, we've been together since high school, over four decades. So long, in fact, that we just opened our third bottle of Tabasco sauce. It was a solemn moment.

The world's most famous hot sauce was invented on the Avery Island plantation just after the Civil War and has been made here ever since. Although the peppers come from all over the world, the sauce is made only at the McIlhenny Company's **Tabasco Factory and Museum** on Avery Island. You can watch the sauce being bottled, labeled, and packed into shipping boxes, and you get a miniature bottle of Tabasco with some recipes at the end of the tour. The gift shop is full of cool souvenirs with the Tabasco logo. Self-guided tours run daily; usually no production on Saturday; closed on holidays and long weekends. Allow at least one hour.

32 Wisteria Rd, Avery Island, LA; **337-365-8173;** www.tabasco.com/visit-avery-island/tabasco-tour. **RV parking** *is in a designated lot. Admission varies by age and cash is not accepted.*

Winnebago RVs (Forest City, Iowa)

The **Winnebago Industries, Inc., Visitor's Center** offers tours of the world's largest RV production plant. You follow a catwalk around the plant for a bird's-eye view of the manufacturing process, watching RVs move down assembly lines at 21 inches a minute. The dramatic finish is when each unit is tested for leaks inside a water bay that simulates a rainstorm. You can buy Winnebago merchandise in the gift shop. Open for tours Monday through Friday, April through October. Allow two hours.

1316 S. Fourth St., Forest City, IA; **641-585-3535;** *www.winnebago.com/about-us/ factory-tours.* **RV parking** *is available in designated areas. Admission is free.*

TIP

Most RV makers are proud to show off their factories to existing or potential customers. Since the COVID closures, most have restarted their tours. Winnebago-owned **Grand Design** and **Newmar** also have tours at their factories in Indiana. In fact, Elkhart is home to an unbelievable cluster of RV manufacturers; more than 80 percent of the RVs made in America are made in northern Indiana. If you own or are interested in a particular manufacturer's RVs, be sure to check their official website or email the company and ask about tours. Elkhart is also home to the **RV/Mobile Home Museum (574-293-2344** or **800-378-8694**; www.rvmhhalloffame.org).

If you're already hanging around Indiana doing RV tours, consider jumping the border into nearby Ohio. In 2021, **Airstream** opened a huge new factory complex in Jackson Center (north of Dayton), where their motorhomes and signature aluminum trailers are made. Airstream owners fondly refer to Jackson Center as the Mother Ship, and it has an impressive new museum, shop, and visitor's center. In fact, if you order a brand new unit from Airstream, ask your dealer for its factory build number. The company can notify you when your trailer will be put together so you can tour the factory and see yours as it's still being built. Reserve a spot at www.airstream.com/company/factory-tours.

WARNING

Because these are all working factories with major construction and assembly going on, they frequently have age restrictions — usually no children under 16 and no pets for obvious reasons. Most won't permit photography in the factory itself (corporate and media spies are everywhere).

Virtual Factory Tours with Mr. Rogers

KID FRIENDLY

Parents, keep this one in your back pocket, because it's perfect for one of those miserable, rain-soaked days when the kids are restless and no one feels like going anywhere.

We're not big on encouraging couch-potato lethargy, especially on an RV vacation, but here's a **group of factory tours** that you can take without leaving your campsite — if you have a computer or other portable internet device. Visit `www.misterrogers.org/articles/factory_visits` to join the late Fred Rogers from *Mister Rogers' Neighborhood* as he narrates several featured factory tours. See how they make sneakers, wagons, plates, construction paper, crayons, and even fortune cookies. Sure, the shows are designed for kids, but even grown-ups can discover a thing or two.

You can explore the factories via video, slides, or just narration, depending on what kind of software you have and the speed of your internet connection. Open year-round 24/7.

Chapter 19

Ten Zany Museums

We've been visiting wacky museums for years, and these are our favorites — so far. We're still looking. Of course, one person's wacky obsession may be another's cherished interest. But there's always the giggle and snort factor whenever you run across museums dedicated to saltshakers (Gatlinburg, TN), mustard varieties (Middleton, WI), or barbarous bevies of barbed wire (McLean, TX). Make more than two kinds of anything and somebody will collect it.

Fans of these zany spots may also want to take note of the Moxie collection at the Matthews Museum of Maine Heritage (Chapter 6), the Lucy-Desi Museum and the Jell-O Gallery (both in Chapter 7), or the Key Underwood Coon Dog Memorial Graveyard (Chapter 10).

Harland Sanders Café/Museum (Corbin, Kentucky)

The original **Harland Sanders Café** is at the junction of U.S. 25E and U.S. 25W in Corbin, Kentucky. Colonel Sanders came up with his pressure-cooker fried chicken in 1940, and the world beat a path to his door until the highway system rerouted the main road away from his café. So, he took to the road himself to sell his cooking method to Kentucky Fried Chicken franchisees, and today, KFC, as it's now known, has grown to more than 25,000 stores in 145 countries.

The Colonel's 1940 Sanders Court café building has been turned into a museum, with restorations of the original dining room, kitchen, and Colonel Sanders's private office and a re-creation of one of the original motel rooms. There's also an operating KFC restaurant on the premises. The Colonel's house next door was recently purchased by KFC's owners. It's being renovated, and the café's current indoor dining area is also being enlarged. Give yourself an hour and don't leave without a bucket of chicken. Open daily.

> 688 US 25W; **606-528-2163;** www.sanderscafe.com. To get there, take the Corbin/Barbourville Exit 29 from I-75. **RV parking** is available in a large lot. Admission is free.

International Circus Hall of Fame (Peru, Indiana)

In 1892, Peru, Indiana, became the wintertime quarters for the **Hagenbeck-Wallace Circus** and other circus performers when the traveling big tent circuit shut down every fall. Legendary lion tamer Clyde Beatty, famous sad clown Emmett Kelly, and other top members of the American circus community also favored the Indiana town during the winter. In the 1920s, Peru sometimes appeared on road maps as Circus City.

By 1920, owner Benjamin Wallace had acquired other circuses, and his operation was on par with Ringling Brothers. After he died, Hagenbeck-Wallace Circus became the American Circus Corporation, operating nine different traveling circuses out of Peru. The company would eventually build gigantic barns with stables, construction and repair shops, bunkhouses, dining halls, a hospital, and more to accommodate the performers, trainers, and crews, as well as store all the tents, wagons, and other equipment. There were also facilities to care for hundreds of horses and mules, along with a huge number of exotic animals like giraffes, camels, big cats, elephants, and more. The complex was enormous. There was even a small rail yard in town for storing the circus train cars.

Today, many of Peru's citizens are proudly descended from some of the most legendary circus performers of all time and the hundreds of crew members who made the town their home for a half century. A local amateur circus of young children and teens performs for the **Circus City Festival** every July, winding up with a huge parade, and highly acclaimed local programs train the next generation of circus performers.

The **International Circus Hall of Fame** at is located in the American Circus Corp's original buildings from the 1920s. There, you'll find mementos of those heady days, with posters, costumes, trapezes, calliopes, and a huge collection of elaborately carved and painted show wagons. Allow at least an hour, unless you have a secret desire to be a clown and run off to join the circus. Open June 1 through Labor Day, Wednesday through Saturday, or by appointment.

> *Peru (Hoosiers often say "PEE-roo," lest you mistake it for South America) is in north-central Indiana on U.S. 31. 3076 E Circus Ln;* **765-472-7553;** `https://` `circushalloffame.com/`. **RV parking** *is available. Admission varies by age.*

REMEMBER

As an alternate suggestion, Ringling Brothers' original wintertime headquarters were in Baraboo, Wisconsin, and are preserved today as part of **Circus World,** 25 minutes south of the Wisconsin Dells (`https://circusworld.` `wisconsinhistory.org/`).

International Cryptozoology Museum (Portland, Maine)

If you can't go real live monster hunting yourself, the next best thing is a visit to the **International Cryptozoology Museum,** or ICM. You'll discover a collection of more than 10,000 artifacts dedicated to documenting the existence of *cryptids* — what science generally regards as mythological or folkloric creatures. Bigfoot is certainly the most popularly known of these mysterious critters, but you'll find out about Sasquatch, Feejee mermaids, the Yeti (the creature, not the cooler), the Loch Ness Monster, chupacabra, fur-bearing trout, the fearsome but elusive jackalope, and a lot more.

The museum is the creation of famed author Loren L. Coleman, who has written more than 40 books on animal mysteries, cryptids, and other *Fortean* (unexplained) phenomena. An expert on the topics of folklore and pop culture, he's a fascinating gentleman. The museum has a vast assortment of fossil remains, unexplainable skulls, modern reproductions, including a mysterious pterodactyl from the Civil War era, numerous plaster casts of footprints from Bigfoot and his large-footed abominable cousins all over the world, and even a purported lump of Yeti poop. There's also a large research library on-site and a gift shop. Open daily; closed Easter, Thanksgiving, Christmas Eve, and Christmas days. Depending on your interest in the subject, you may give it two hours or more (especially if Coleman is there that day), just for the sheer number of unusual objects on display.

*32 Resurgam Pl. **RV parking** and a big rig turnaround area are available in a gravel lot on the right just as you cross the railroad tracks on Thompson's Point Road, about a 4-minute walk from the museum. All parking on Thompson's Point is paid via smartphone 24/7. Admission varies by age.*

REMEMBER

Kids should love this place, but if it just creeps them out, take them across the parking lot to the very interactive **Children's Museum and Theatre of Maine** (www.kitetails.org/). If you're in Bangor instead, the ICM also has a smaller museum and bookstore there at 585 Hammond Street.

International UFO Museum and Research Center (Roswell, New Mexico)

On July 4, 1947, a Nevada sheep rancher was riding through his property surveying storm damage from the night before when he came across a pile of odd-looking debris. Later that week, he took some of it to the town of Roswell, New Mexico, about 46 miles away, where the closest Air Force base was located, to see if anyone could identify it. And so began the story of the most famous UFO incident in the world.

"The truth is out there," they used to say on *The X-Files*, and "out there" begins in Roswell. Since the 1970s, Roswell has been synonymous with space aliens, flying saucers, and all things connected with intergalactic visitors. (If you want to know more about the Roswell event and the growth of UFO sightings after it, check out our book *Conspiracy Theories and Secret Societies For Dummies*, 2008 Wiley.)

The **International UFO Museum and Research Center** features exhibits and dioramas of the more famous incidents connected with the Roswell event, such as the collection of debris, an alleged autopsy of an alien, the several explanations from the military, along with paintings and sculptures related to UFO sightings. There are UFO movie prop replicas like Gort from *The Day the Earth Stood Still* and an enormous research library with one of the world's largest repositories of alien encounter reports. Open daily; closed Thanksgiving, Christmas, and New Year's days.

Not surprisingly, the biggest industry in Roswell is UFO tourism, and nearby are several UFO-related businesses and shops, like the **Roswell Space Center** and the **Roswell UFO Spacewalk**, as well as the **Robert Goddard Planetarium** at the non-UFO-related Roswell Museum. Roswell is in southeastern New Mexico, approximately three hours from Albuquerque or four hours from Amarillo, Texas.

It's a good-sized town of 50,000 people with plenty of services and things to see and do. It's also on the way to the spectacular Carlsbad Caverns.

*114 N. Main Street, **575-625-9495**; www.roswellufomuseum.com. **RV parking** is available across the street. Admission varies by age. If you need to camp overnight, the highly rated Trailer Village RV Park is on the eastern edge of town on East 2nd Street.*

Miss Laura's Social Club (Fort Smith, Arkansas)

Claiming to be the only one-time bordello listed on the National Register of Historic Places, **Miss Laura's Social Club** doubles as a museum and the visitor center for Fort Smith, Arkansas. You could say that when this old Victorian hotel was converted into a house of ill repute in 1898, it was a visitor's center even back then.

It's odd that Fort Smith was considered to be a Wild West frontier town right up into the 20th century. But it sat on the eastern edge of Indian Territory, which became the state of Oklahoma in 1907. Miss Laura Ziegler's establishment was part of Bordello Row, the town's notorious red-light district. Hers was considered a higher-class bawdy house, with the finest reputation in the Southwest, and her ladies were said to be the most cultured, sophisticated, and — always very important — healthiest in all of Fort Smith.

By the 1940s, the area had become a major slum, and the building was abandoned. After it sat empty for several decades, a local investor began restoring it, and in 1980 it was refurbished to look the way it did at the turn of the 20th century, at the height of its bordello grandeur, complete with overstuffed Victorian furniture, gaudy wallpaper, and sumptuous guest rooms (each named for one of the finer ladies of the house). In 1992, it was officially made Fort Smith's visitor center. Open daily. Allow one hour.

*2 N. B St.; **800-637-1477** or **479-783-8888**; www.fortsmith.org/miss-laura-s-visitor-center. **RV parking** is available in an adjacent lot and on the street. Admission is free.*

Musical Instrument Museum (Phoenix, Arizona)

The **Musical Instrument Museum** is the creation of the former CEO of Target stores. Here you'll find a collection of 8,000 exotic musical instruments from 200 countries, including a giant Japanese Taiko drum, a pink Selmer tenor saxophone like the one used by jazz artist John Coltrane, and other instruments created especially for the museum. There's even an entire gallery of mechanical music-making machines and automatons, like player pianos, a self-playing trumpet (called an *organette*), and the enormous Decap "Appollonia" orchestrion. If there's an obscure, kooky instrument they *don't* have, it would be astonishing. Open daily; closed Thanksgiving and Christmas days. Expect to spend two or three hours, especially if you have children — there are loads of kid-friendly activities and noise-making opportunities.

> *4725 E. Mayo Blvd.;* **480-478-6000;** *https://mim.org. Admission varies by age. Special exhibits may have an extra charge. A series of evening concerts features performers from around the world.*

National Museum of Funeral History (Houston, Texas)

C'mon, who *wouldn't* want to see an exhibit on the history of embalming? Look no further than the **National Museum of Funeral History**. Opened in 1992, this massive (30,000 square feet!) modern facility covers everything from ancient Egyptian burial ceremonies and global mourning customs to the lavish funerals of modern celebrities. There are 17 permanent exhibits about presidential funerals. Jazz funeral customs in New Orleans, hearses, historical coffins, and lots more are presented — and none of it in a ghoulish manner. You even find out why houses today have "living rooms" and not "parlors." (*Spoiler alert:* The "parlor" in centuries past is where the body was laid out — hence the name *funeral parlor*.) Open daily.

Don't think this is some cheesy roadside tourist trap. You won't find grisly horror movie exhibits here — it's a serious funeral museum, but it may not be great for kids, especially if they've never dealt with death.

> *415 Barren Springs Dr.;* **281-876-3063;** *www.nmfh.org.* **RV parking** *available on-site. Admission varies by age.*

Rancho Obi-Wan (Petaluma, California)

WARNING

Unlike most other museums in this chapter, **Rancho Obi-Wan** has some major requirements to get in. You'll see why when you get there. This is the most expensive (but quite unique) museum on our list, and it has the tightest restrictions for visitors.

Star Wars creator George Lucas is hard at work building his own multimillion-dollar Star Wars museum in Los Angeles, but while he's got plenty of actual props and relics from the movies themselves, he's got a long way to go to catch up with Steve Sansweet's humongous private collection of Star Wars props, models, toys, figures, fan art, and every other imaginable bit of ephemera. Sansweet was in a prime position to begin building his staggering collection: In 1998, he was made director of content management and head of fan relations at Lucasfilm, and he spent 13 years organizing *Star Wars* Celebration conventions. He opened up Rancho Obi-Wan as a limited-access museum in 2011, and the artifacts fill two former chicken ranch barns. The *Guinness Book of World Records* has named it the largest collection of *Star Wars*–related objects in the world.

Now, about those restrictions. Because Rancho Obi-Wan is part of a private gated home, they do not give out their address unless you arrange for a private, docent-led tour first. Drop-ins are definitely NOT permitted. Moreover, someone in your party must pay $55 to join as a supporting member in order to purchase the tickets. Paid members also have a year's access to a "virtual museum" online, in case you want to scope it out before dragging your partner and the teenagers there.

> *Located in Northern California about an hour north of San Francisco on U.S. 101, in the West Hills area of Petaluma; https://ranchoobiwan.org/. Admission varies by age; children under 10 are not permitted. Membership and tickets must be purchased online. Check with the museum's folks ahead of time when you schedule your tour. No* **RV parking** *is available. If you're staying overnight, you find the KOA San Francisco North/Petaluma nearby at 20 Rainsville Road, just off U.S. 101 at Petaluma Blvd. (open all year).*

SPAM® Museum (Austin, Minnesota)

If you only know the word *spam* to describe the hundreds of junk e-mail messages that clog your inbox every day, then you've somehow missed the origin of the world-altering meat product in the little blue can. SPAM stands for "spiced ham," a canned luncheon meat created in 1937 by Hormel Foods that would become an American icon and make history in Army mess kitchens during World War II. In the 1970s, SPAM was famously praised in a sing-along anthem by the Monty Python comedy troupe; the ditty has become a good-natured earworm the world over. And because of its 3- to 5-year shelf life, SPAM's a fave in the pantries of hard-core *preppers* (people who stockpile supplies in preparation for a major disaster). Heck, you may have a couple cans in your own RV pantry. Not bad for a lowly potted meat product of slightly mysterious content and disturbing color.

Hormel Foods spared no expense in creating a 14,000-square-foot museum in 2016 dedicated to this marvel of meatpacking art and its cultural significance. At the **SPAM Museum,** interactive exhibits include a simulated production line that visitors can play in by donning rubber gloves and a hard hat, a game show about meat trivia, a survey of SPAM around the world, and more. Open Monday through Saturday; closed on holidays. Give yourself an hour or longer to see everything. Yes, really.

> *101 3rd Avenue NE;* **800-588-7726** *or* **507-437-5100;** *www. spam. com/museum.* **RV parking** *is available nearby in a designated lot. Admission is free. Stay at nearby Adventure Bound Beaver Trails RV Resort, 7 miles east on I-90.*

The Super Museum (Metropolis, Illinois)

The town of Metropolis in Illinois has the distinction of being the only place in America with that name, and so, in 1972, DC Comics authorized the city to call itself the "adopted Home of Superman." Metropolis put up a 15-foot statue of the Man of Steel in the middle of Superman Square in front of the courthouse, hired an actor to appear in costume, erected giant billboards, and painted the all-American hero on the water tower. Lois Lane has her own bronze statue in the likeness of Noel Neill, who played the intrepid reporter in the 1950s TV show *Adventures of Superman.* And they set up a phone booth where you can pick up the receiver and hear a message from Superman. You can even grab a copy of the local newspaper — the *Daily Planet,* of course. (One thing missing from Metropolis are any deposits of kryptonite, although the largest U.S. provider of processed uranium for nuclear reactors is located nearby.)

The Super Museum and gift shop, with its $2.5 billion (!) collection, is on Superman Square's Market Street. Inside, you find every conceivable drawing, tie-in, figurine, poster, prop, or tchotchke related to the Man of Steel. Every comic book variation from the character's different eras is presented, along with every TV and movie portrayal. Open daily.

If you're in Metropolis the second week in June, join 30,000 fellow fans at the annual Superman Celebration festival (www.supermancelebration.net). You knew there had to be one. **Harrah's Metropolis riverboat casino** is docked on the Ohio River on the south edge of town, for those in your group who aren't superhero fans.

*517 Market St.; **618-524-5518;** https://supermuseum.com. For more information, contact the Metropolis Chamber of Commerce (**800-949-5740;** https://metropolischamber.com/). Admission varies by age. Stay at the RV campground in nearby Fort Massac State Park.*

Index

About the Authors

Christopher Hodapp is the author of *Freemasons for Dummies*, the world's best-selling guide to the Masonic fraternity. Before becoming an author, Chris spent more than 20 years as a commercial filmmaker. He is the founding Editor Emeritus of the *Journal of the Masonic Society* and is presently the Director of the Masonic Library & Museum of Indiana. His other books about the Freemasons include *Solomon's Builders* and *Heritage Endures*.

Alice Von Kannon has been RVing since the age of sixteen. Before becoming an author, she worked for many years in advertising as a writer and broadcast producer. Alice has written several historical novels under various names, and released her most recent historical romance, *Heart's Blood*, in 2020. Its sequel, *Night's Bloom*, is next up.

Between them, Alice and Chris have grown up around, worked with, or owned motorhomes and trailers for much of their lives, and this is their second volume about RVing. Together, the couple has co-written *RV Vacations For Dummies*, *The Templar Code For Dummies*, and *Conspiracy Theories and Secret Societies for Dummies* for Wiley. They have both appeared many times on programs for the History, Discovery, NatGeo, TruTV, and American Heroes channels, most recently *America's Book of Secrets*, *The Curse of Oak Island*, and *America, Facts vs. Fiction*.

While they call Indianapolis their home, Chris and Alice spend as much time as possible crisscrossing the country in their 30-foot Airstream Flying Cloud with their traveling companion, Sophie the flying poodle. Together ever since the first *Star Wars* movie appeared in theaters, they have visited and camped in 44 of the 50 states, in literally hundreds of campgrounds and parks. So far.

Dedication

To Bob and Vera Funcannon, who thought to buy that second-hand Lance trailer all those decades ago, thinking the whole family might find it fun to have an RV. Yes it was. Yes it is. And it always will be.

Authors' Acknowledgments

The original edition of this book first appeared two decades ago, and has been an ongoing, collaborative effort by several authors since then. We'd like to gratefully acknowledge the original work done by authors Harry Basch, Shirley Slater, and Dennis C. Brewer, who created and revised the six prior editions over the years.

Without their labors, we wouldn't have known exactly where to start tackling this project. But because this is our second volume about RVing for the *For Dummies* series, we've tried to do more than just update listings and repair broken website addresses. In many ways, this is an entirely new and different book. We hope our predecessors will approve.

We deeply admire and salute all the shops, restaurants, museums, campgrounds, and other tourism-related organizations that managed to survive everything thrown at them since the spring of 2020. The economic carnage that COVID shutdowns wreaked on so many of the businesses and campgrounds we contacted has been breathtaking; almost a third of the listings from the previous editions of this book have closed, changed ownership, or simply vanished without a trace. So, we wish to acknowledge all who have persevered, as well as all who have started over. We hope you'll visit the places we mention in the book and thank them for their part in keeping the United States the very best RV tourist destination in the world.

At Wiley, our deepest appreciation goes to Steven Hayes for inviting us back to craft another *For Dummies* volume about our passion for RVing, for putting up with the unpredictable nature of our extended road trips, and for understanding our delays as deadlines went whizzing by. Thanks to our fearless Project Editor Leah Michael for being a steady, good-natured hand all the way, and for beating our windy submissions into a more manageable guide for RV trips. Thanks also to Senior Editor Kristie Pyles and Wiley's template guru Steve Arany for putting up with our ongoing demands to break every single formatting rule Wiley's spent 30 years perfecting. The entire team patiently resisted the urge to swat us with a rolled-up iPad.

And finally, thanks to the thousands of internet RVers who share their knowledge, experience, surprises, and disasters every day with the camping community on countless websites, Facebook pages, blogs, and more. Cruising these online resources can often feel like all of us are gathered around the world's biggest communal campfire, swapping stories, comparing experiences, and trading tips (just without the mosquitoes and stink bugs). Like an enormous fraternity, we support each other, share in each other's joys and sorrows, and make this lifestyle better than any other way to travel. Just remember our rolling fraternity's tradition to never say good-bye.

We simply say, "We'll see you down the road."

Publisher's Acknowledgments

Acquisitions Editor: Steve Hayes

Development Editor: Leah P. Michael

Copy Editor: Kelly Brillhart

Fact Checker: Kristi Bennett

Production Editor: Mohammed Zafar Ali

Cover Image: © Joshua Woroniecki/ Shutterstock